Veterans Benefits
FOR
DUMMIES®

by Rod Powers

WILEY

Wiley Publishing, Inc.

Veterans Benefits For Dummies®

Published by
Wiley Publishing, Inc.
111 River St.
Hoboken, NJ 07030-5774
www.wiley.com

For general information on our other products and services, please contact our Customer Care
Department within the U.S. at 877-762-2974, outside the U.S. at 317-572-3993, or fax 317-572-4002.

For technical support, please visit www.wiley.com/techsupport.

Wiley also publishes its books in a variety of electronic formats. Some content that appears in print may
not be available in electronic books.

Library of Congress Control Number: 2008943502

ISBN: 978-0-470-39865-4

Manufactured in the United States of America

10 9 8 7 6 5 4 3 2 1

WILEY

About the Author

Rod Powers joined the U.S. Air Force in 1975 intending to become a spy. He was devastated to learn that he should've joined the CIA instead because the military doesn't have that particular enlisted job. Regardless, he fell in love with the military and made it both a passion and a career, retiring with 23 years of service. Rod spent 11 of those years as a first sergeant, helping to solve the problems of the enlisted corps.

During Rod's military career, he traveled the world — twice. He's been assigned or deployed to so many countries that he doesn't even remember them all. He's a veteran of the Korea "Tree War," Grenada, Desert Shield, and Desert Storm. He's a distinguished graduate of the Air Force Leadership School, the Noncommissioned Officer Academy, the Senior Noncommissioned Officer Academy, and the Air Force First Sergeant Academy.

Since his retirement from the military in 1998, Rod has become a world-renowned military careers expert. Through hundreds of articles on his highly popular U.S. Military Information Web site at About.com (usmilitary.about.com), Rod has advised thousands of troops about all aspects of U.S. armed forces careers. *Veteran Benefits For Dummies* is his third military-related book. One of his other books, *ASVAB For Dummies*, was published by Wiley.

Rod is the proud single-parent father of twin girls, both of whom enjoy successful careers in the U.S. Air Force. Rod currently lives in Daytona Beach, Florida, where he gratefully enjoys the devoted attentions of his girlfriend, Jackie, and his pet tomato plant, Oscar. Even today, Rod tries to run his life according to long-lived military ideals and standards, but he gets a bit confused about why nobody will obey his orders anymore. Not even Oscar.

Dedication

To Charisa Raine Lindsy, an angel with Angelman Syndrome, who has won a special place in my heart. To get more facts about this devastating genetic condition and find out how you can help, visit the Angelman Syndrome Foundation at www.angelman.org.

Author's Acknowledgments

First and foremost, I offer my most sincere gratitude, appreciation, and respect to our nation's veterans. Without your sacrifices, dedication, and loyalty to our country, this book, nor any freedom of expression, would not be possible.

Many thanks to the Department of Veterans Affairs and the Department of Defense for their invaluable information and assistance. Special thanks to Scott Langhoff for reviewing the manuscript for technical accuracy and keeping me informed on the latest changes to veterans benefits.

I am grateful to Barb Doyan, my literary agent, for her encouragement, support, and hard work in getting this project off the ground. Thanks to Mike Baker, acquisition editor at Wiley, and likewise to my project and copy editors, Natalie Harris and Vicki Adang, both editors *par excellence*. Their contributions to this book cannot be overstated.

Finally, to my girlfriend, Jackie Gatton, who stuck with me and had faith in me, even when I sometimes had to break a date to meet a deadline.

Publisher's Acknowledgments

We're proud of this book; please send us your comments through our Dummies online registration form located at `http://dummies.custhelp.com`. For other comments, please contact our Customer Care Department within the U.S. at 877-762-2974, outside the U.S. at 317-572-3993, or fax 317-572-4002.

Some of the people who helped bring this book to market include the following:

Acquisitions, Editorial, and Media Development

Project Editor: Natalie Faye Harris

Acquisitions Editor: Mike Baker

Senior Copy Editor: Victoria M. Adang

Assistant Editor: Erin Calligan Mooney

Editorial Program Coordinator: Joe Niesen

General Reviewer:
Scott H. Langhoff, CPO USN (Retired)

Editorial Manager: Christine Meloy Beck

Editorial Assistants: Jennette ElNaggar, David Lutton

Cover Photos: Thinkstock Images

Cartoons: Rich Tennant
(`www.the5thwave.com`)

Composition Services

Project Coordinator: Erin Smith

Layout and Graphics: Reuben W. Davis, Melissa K. Jester, Christin Swinford, Christine Williams

Proofreaders: Laura Bowman, Caitie Kelly

Indexer: Broccoli Information Management

Publishing and Editorial for Consumer Dummies

Diane Graves Steele, Vice President and Publisher, Consumer Dummies

Kristin Ferguson-Wagstaffe, Product Development Director, Consumer Dummies

Ensley Eikenburg, Associate Publisher, Travel

Kelly Regan, Editorial Director, Travel

Publishing for Technology Dummies

Andy Cummings, Vice President and Publisher, Dummies Technology/General User

Composition Services

Gerry Fahey, Vice President of Production Services

Debbie Stailey, Director of Composition Services

Contents at a Glance

Table of Contents

Introduction

*1*f you're reading this book, there's a very good chance that you're a military veteran or you have a close friend or family member who is. Perhaps you've always wondered what our nation offers in the way of thanks to those who have defended our country, or perhaps you want the lowdown on a specific benefit you may have heard about.

Numerous benefits are available to those who have served our country. There are also many benefits available for family members of such veterans. However, it can be frustrating to look for information about specific benefits, including what the benefit is all about and who qualifies for it, when you have to decipher paragraphs and paragraphs full of government gobbledygook. You shouldn't have to hire a lawyer to have a veterans benefit explained to you in order to figure out whether you qualify. If only there were a single resource that explained veterans benefits in clear, simple, everyday language.

That's why I decided to write this book. I've spoken to hundreds of veterans across the country. Although most knew about veterans benefits, many didn't believe they qualified for one reason or another, and many others had heard the horror stories of how the government and the Department of Veterans Affairs (VA) have screwed up the system so badly that it's nearly impossible to apply for benefits.

I won't lie to you. The VA's record of benefits administration, in many cases, has been dismal. At the time of publication of this book, more than 512,000 benefit claims are waiting to be processed, and more than 90,000 benefit appeals have not yet been decided. Gather together a group of veterans and ask them to talk about the problems they've had when dealing with the VA, and you may as well get comfortable. They'll still be talking when the beer and chips run out.

But there's good news. Most benefit claims are delayed or denied because the veteran didn't fully understand the qualification criteria or failed to provide the correct documents and supporting evidence. That's not the veteran's fault. Wading through the pages and pages of legal language to find out how to submit a simple benefit claim can be a daunting task. That's where *Veterans Benefits For Dummies* comes in. I explain each benefit in everyday terms, list the eligibility requirements, and let you know exactly what forms and supporting documents you need to gather to support your claim for benefits.

About This Book

The full-disclosure doctrine requires that I inform you that you probably won't find any new or secret information in this book. The information I present here is readily available on both the VA and Department of Defense's (DOD) massive Web sites, as well as in various federal laws, regulations, and other publications that are also available on the Internet.

So why should you spend some of your hard-earned money on this book? Because here you find all this information laid out in one place in a logical manner, with the details explained in a way that won't give you a headache. *Veterans Benefits For Dummies* will save you loads of time, and think of all the money you'll save on aspirin.

I'm not going to waste your time by pointing out what's wrong with the system and what I think the government should do to fix it. I leave that to other authors. My goal is to help you understand the benefits, determine whether you qualify, and work within the current system so you can get the benefits you want and deserve.

Although you won't read anything new here, I can absolutely, 100 percent fully guarantee that *Veterans Benefits For Dummies* contains enough valuable information to hold the covers apart.

Conventions Used in This Book

I include a lot of Web addresses where you can find the necessary forms to apply for benefits. (You can identify a Web address by its appearance in `monofont`.) When this book was printed, some Web addresses may have needed to break across two lines of text. If that happened, rest assured that I haven't put in any extra characters (such as hyphens) to indicate the break. So when using one of these Web addresses, just type in exactly what you see in this book, pretending as though the line break doesn't exist.

As you move through this book, you may encounter new terms. Wherever necessary, I define *italicized* terms for you.

What You're Not to Read

This book has a number of sidebars (the shaded gray boxes) sprinkled throughout. They're full of interesting information about benefit(s) described in that chapter, but you don't have to read them if you don't want to. They don't contain anything you simply *must* know about the benefit(s).

You also run across special icons, titled *Technical Stuff,* from time to time. These paragraphs include concise, detailed information, which is usually interesting, but is a little more technical or in-depth about the topic at hand. You can skip these tidbits if you wish.

Foolish Assumptions

While writing this book, I made a few assumptions about you — namely, who you are and why you picked up this book. I assume the following:

- ✔ You aren't a dummy. You just want information about veterans benefits.
- ✔ You're a veteran or the friend or family member of a veteran, and you're interested in applying for a specific benefit or group of benefits.
- ✔ You're tired of government bureaucratese and prefer your information in easy-to-take doses.

How This Book Is Organized

There's a method to my madness, the reason why this book is organized the way you see it today. I've arranged this book according to subject matter. Benefits relating to pensions and finances are grouped together, benefits relating to education and employment are grouped together, and so on.

Part 1: Benefiting From Benefits

If you're not sure what a veteran is or whether you meet the basic qualifications for veterans, turn to this part. This part also tells you how to work with the VA and military service departments, how to gather your supporting documentation, and what to do if your claim for benefits is denied.

Part II: A Healthy Look at Medical Care and Compensation Programs

In Part II you find out how the DOD and the VA can take care of your medical needs and your pocketbook after your discharge or retirement from the U.S. military. You can read about the VA healthcare program, available to most veterans, and the DOD healthcare system, known as Tricare, for military retirees and their family members. You also get the lowdown on pensions for low-income veterans, compensation for disabilities, and military retired pay. There's also information for families of deceased veterans, regarding survivor compensation, education, insurance, and medical programs, and how they can lay their loved ones to rest with the dignity and respect they deserve.

Part III: Understanding Education and Employment Programs

A free education is a terrible thing to waste. Part III explains how you can take full advantage of education programs available to veterans. Not only can you get a free college degree, but you may qualify for special vocational training programs available to certain disabled veterans.

After you've earned a degree or completed a training program, it's time to enter the real world and earn a living. Many veterans qualify for special preference when applying for federal government jobs, so Part III also explains what you need to do to qualify for one of these positions. If you'd rather work for yourself, you can obtain a small business loan guarantee from the Small Business Administration.

Part IV: Home Is Where the Heart Is — Except When You're Traveling!

This part tells you how the VA can help you get a low-interest loan to finance your dream house. It also informs you about services available to homeless veterans, and I outline how you can spend your golden years in a garden-spot military retirement home.

Also included in Part IV is valuable information about shopping on military bases and how you can spend your next vacation in a luxury condo or vacation resort available only to military members, certain veterans, and their family members. Part IV even tells you whether you qualify to fly around the world for free on military aircraft.

Part V: The Part of Tens

It wouldn't be a *For Dummies* book if I didn't include a Part of Tens. If you want to get right down to it and find out where you can get help with veteran benefits, turn to Part V. I give you a list of organizations that can assist you on your benefits crusade. This part also has tips about improving your chances of getting your claim approved and some pointers for traveling on the military's dime.

Part VI: Appendixes

Here you find contact information for state veterans offices, VA medical centers, cemeteries, vet centers, and regional offices.

Icons Used in This Book

Throughout this book I've added icons to help you use the material to your best advantage. Here's a rundown on what they mean:

This icon alerts you to helpful hints regarding the subject at hand. Tips can help you save time and avoid frustration.

This icon reminds you of important information you should read carefully.

This icon flags information that may prove hazardous to your plan of applying for a specific benefit. Often this icon accompanies common mistakes people make when applying for a veterans benefit. Pay special attention to the Warning icon so you don't fall into one of these pitfalls.

This icon points out information that is interesting, enlightening, or in-depth but isn't necessary for you to read. You don't need this information to understand or apply for a benefit, but knowing these facts may make you a better informed applicant.

Where to Go from Here

You don't have to read this book from cover to cover to understand and apply for veterans benefits. You may be interested in a specific benefit, or only a few of the benefits. If so, feel free to read only those chapters that apply to the benefit(s) you're interested in.

If you decide to skip around, look over the table of contents and choose your favorite benefit. You'll find all the information you need to know about that benefit in the chapter indicated.

Before applying for a benefit, however, I do recommend that you read Chapters 2 and 3. These chapters provide invaluable information about ensuring your eligibility status and getting your supporting documentation in order.

No matter where you start, I wish you all the best in getting the benefits you've earned. Thank you, from a fellow veteran, for your sacrifice and dedication to our country.

Part I
Benefiting From Benefits

The 5th Wave — By Rich Tennant

"You did a good job of converting your military experience into civilian terms on your resume. But you need to fix the typo that says you were a '...tanked operator.'"

In this part . . .

*I*f you're like most veterans, you're proud of your military service and proud to call yourself a veteran. But the title of "veteran" and 35 cents will buy you much more than a cup of coffee. You may be eligible for a world of benefits — more than you probably thought possible — available only to those who have served in the military. But to get your hands on them, you need to know what they are and what you need to do to get them. The chapters in Part I are here to help you get started. They give you the basics on the type of coverage available for you and your loved ones, how to qualify, how to work with the Department of Veterans Affairs (VA), and more. Read on!

Chapter 1

The Wonderful World of Veterans Benefits

In This Chapter

▶ Preparing to receive benefits

▶ Taking a joyride through the benefits playground

*E*xactly what is a *benefit?* My handy-dandy pocket dictionary says it's "a theatrical performance or other public entertainment to raise money for a charitable organization or cause." Wait a minute, that's not right. Sorry, wrong definition. It's also defined as "something that is advantageous or good, or a payment or gift."

Okay, I can live with that. That means a veterans benefit is something good, and this book is chock-full of good things available only to veterans (and sometimes their spouses and dependents too).

If you thought this book was going to be about how the government takes advantage of veterans, or how hard it is to get veterans benefits, or how the system is all messed up, I'm afraid you're going to be disappointed. Plenty of that negative attitude is already available between the covers of other books and on the pages of magazines, newspapers, and Web sites. I'm not going to add to that. This book is all about what benefits are available and how you — the veteran or veteran's family member — can get your hands on them.

In my extensive travels throughout the United States in recent years, I've spoken to hundreds of veterans. After the obligatory war stories about how we each individually saved the world a time or two, the topic often turned to veterans benefits. I was surprised to find out how many veterans have no clue about the benefits they're entitled to in exchange for the services they gave and the sacrifices they made in defense of their country.

That's my goal in writing this book. It's not to lambaste the powers-that-be for not doing enough. I'm not going to criticize the Department of Veterans Affairs or the Department of Defense. I'm not going to tell you horror stories of veterans who have been tangled up in the system for years. If that's what you're looking for, you can pick up one of the other books out there in book land that address those topics.

I have a brand-new approach, one that's never been tried before. In this book, I tell you in simple, plain language what veterans benefits are available to you and what you need to do to apply for them. Sounds fun, right? I knew you'd agree.

Getting Familiar with the Benefits You Deserve

I think you're going to be surprised at the number and types of benefits that are available to you. Of course, nobody is going to walk up to your door and hand them to you. That would be too easy. Instead, you have to know what benefits there are, you must find out what the eligibility criteria is to receive a particular benefit, you need to know which government agency is in charge of that benefit, and then you have to ask for the benefit.

You would think, by now, that our government would agree on who is entitled to call themselves a veteran. You'd think so, but you'd be wrong. As you read Chapter 2, you discover that there's no single legal definition for the term *veteran* when it comes to veterans benefits. Because different benefits were enacted into law at different times by different Congresses, each benefit has varying qualification criteria. You can qualify for some benefits with just one day of military service. Other benefits require you to serve a minimum amount of time. Still others require that you meet certain conditions, such as having a disability resulting from military service.

You'd also think that the government would have some kind of massive computer system that would have all the details about your service in the United States military. You would think Uncle Sam would know when you served, where you served, how long you served, what medals you may have earned, and what kind of discharge you received. Once again, you'd be wrong. Maybe in the future, but right now if you want a particular benefit, it's up to you to prove your status as a veteran. You do this by providing copies of your military discharge paperwork. Chapter 2 tells you what paperwork you need and — if you don't have it — how you can get it.

You may be one of those who think that you need an honorable discharge to qualify for a veterans benefit. Many veterans believe that. If you're in this camp and you don't have an honorable discharge, you'll be very glad you bought this book. The information in Chapter 2 dispels that myth. Some benefits require an honorable discharge, but there are many benefits you can receive with a general or other than honorable discharge as well.

Breaking Down Your Benefits

You may be surprised to find out how many goodies are available to veterans and their family members. Some of these benefits are well-known, such as medical care and disability compensation. You may have never heard of other benefits, ranging from loans to open a small business to free headstones when you finally move on to that big battlefield in the sky.

Other goodies include free or low-cost medical care, cash payments directly from Uncle Sam, plans designed to help you get a college degree or vocational training, programs that assist you in finding and getting your dream job, programs that help you buy a house or find a place to live in your golden years, shopping and travel perks, memorial and burial benefits, and services and programs available to surviving family members.

In the beginning, there were veterans benefits

I was planning to title this sidebar "In the beginning, there were no veteran benefits" because I thought it would be a catchy title. Turns out, however, that statement's not true. We Americans began offering benefits to our soldiers even before our founding fathers got together and told the British to take a hike. In 1636, the folks in Plymouth Colony, when they weren't busy wearing funny hats and shooting at turkeys, declared that any soldier who received a disabling injury while defending the colony would be taken care of by the colony for life.

In 1780, during the Revolutionary War, the Continental Congress attempted to boost recruitment by promising officers half pay for seven years and enlisted soldiers a mustering-out bonus of $80 if they served to the conclusion of the war. The Congress also provided pensions for those disabled in the conflict. Other soldiers and sailors were promised land deeds in exchange for their military service. We Americans have a proud tradition of taking care of our veterans.

"No" doesn't always mean *no*

You may ask for a benefit and be told no. You may be told that you're not eligible for the benefit because of this or that, even though you read this book from cover to cover and believe that you meet the eligibility criteria. Maybe you asked for a benefit years ago, only to be told you don't qualify, so you gave up.

Maybe you were told no, and you don't even know why. The Department of Veterans Affairs (VA) has developed a bad habit over the years of phrasing its rejection letters in such a way that even legal eagles couldn't understand them. Fortunately, the agency isn't allowed to do that anymore. A brand-new law (passed in September 2008 by your friendly neighborhood Congress critters) now requires the VA to use plain, simple, everyday language when it rejects a benefit claim. Wow! What a great idea! I wonder why nobody ever thought of this before?

Even if the VA says no in simple, plain, everyday language, it doesn't mean that it's right. Most of the time when the VA rejects a claim, it's because you didn't provide the correct paperwork — what the VA calls *supporting evidence.* Chapter 3 not only helps you avoid that mistakes by getting your ducks in a row before you apply in the first place, but it also tells you what you can do if the VA says no and you think it's wrong (you'd be surprised to know how often the VA is wrong).

You can ask the VA to take another look at your case, and if it still says no (stubborn little rascal, isn't it?), you can appeal the decision. There's even a federal court that does nothing else but hears appeals for veterans benefit claims.

Meeting your healthcare needs

Most veterans are eligible for healthcare, either through the Department of Veterans Affairs (VA) or through the Department of Defense (DOD). It may or may not be cost free, depending on your particular status and annual income. In today's world of rising healthcare costs, this is a very valuable benefit.

The VA's healthcare program is designed to meet the basic medical needs of all veterans, whether they have an injury or illness related to their service in the military or not. As with most modern healthcare programs, the VA's system emphasizes preventive care, including examinations, vaccinations, primary care, emergency care, hospitalizations, surgeries, mental health care, counseling services, and more. Some veterans may even be eligible for free eyeglasses, hearing aids, and dental services.

Under the VA system, the government will even pay your travel expenses to receive healthcare in certain circumstances. When's the last time you heard of a healthcare program that paid you to go see the doctor? That's pretty cool, if you ask me. You can read all about it in Chapter 4.

A special group of veterans, known as military retirees, has access to a separate healthcare system managed by the DOD, called Tricare. Of course, most of these retirees are eligible for the VA system as well, but Tricare gives you more options when selecting medical providers, and — unlike the VA program — it's available to immediate family members as well. The bad news is that it's not available to all veterans, just those who served for 20 or more years in the military. Chapter 5 tells you everything you ever wanted to know about Tricare.

Pocketing a monthly check

Millions upon millions of military veterans qualify to receive a monthly check from the government. Well, it's not really a check . . . these days everything is done by direct deposit. Oh, well, think of the trees we're saving.

Veterans who can show that they have a disability or medical condition that was caused or made worse by their service in the military may qualify for a special monthly payment, called *disability compensation*. The VA rates such disabilities on a rating scale of 10 percent to 100 percent, in 10 percent increments, depending on how severe the condition is.

The amount of disability compensation depends on the severity of the rated disability and other factors, such as number of dependents who live with the veteran. The minimum monthly payment is currently $117 per month (veteran with no dependents and a 10 percent service-connected disability), but some veterans may receive more than $7,000 per month. Does that sound interesting? If so, take a look at Chapter 6.

Even if you don't have a service-connected disability, you may still qualify for monthly payments from the VA. Veterans with even one day of wartime service who are 100 percent disabled or over the age of 65 and have a low income may be eligible for a VA pension. Chapter 6 has information on this program as well.

Anyone who's ever stepped foot in a military recruiter's office knows that if you serve for 20 or more years in the military, you receive monthly military retirement pay for life. But did you know that, in some cases, it's possible to retire from the military before 20 years of service? Or did you know that ex-spouses may be entitled to a portion of your military retirement pay? You can read all about it in Chapter 7.

Sometimes old soldiers do die: Memorial benefits and taking care of survivors

With all due respect to General MacArthur, he was wrong. Dying is a part of life and a part that nobody can avoid. Veterans may die, but that doesn't mean they're forgotten or that benefits stop.

We not only owe our nation's veterans a debt of gratitude, but their family members deserve our thanks as well. Chapter 8 includes programs available to surviving family members of military veterans. Various life insurance programs are available only to veterans, and survivors may also be eligible for medical care, pensions, and education benefits.

A host of burial and memorial benefits are available for most deceased veterans, including free burial services, no-cost markers and headstones, reimbursement for funeral and burial expenses, free national and state veterans cemeteries, and military funeral honors performed by a precision military honor guard. You can read all about these benefits in Chapter 9.

Getting educated about education benefits

You've probably heard of the GI Bill. It's been around in one form or another since World War II. But the GI Bill education program you know of may not bear any resemblance to the GI Bill today. My, oh my, has this program changed over the years. There's even a brand-new GI Bill, created in 2008, called the *GI Bill of the 21st Century*. It's applicable to most veterans who have active-duty service after September 11, 2001. If you served in the military after 9/11, you most certainly want to read all about this valuable education program in Chapter 10.

Even if you got out of the military before 9/11, there may be a GI Bill program applicable to your situation. However, you'll want to hurry to check out the information in Chapter 10. The GI Bill isn't forever — there's a time limit on how long you have to use it.

If you're not eligible for education benefits under the GI Bill, you may still be eligible to go to college or receive vocational training on the government's dime if you have a service-connected disability that affects your ability to get and hold a job. Details about this program are in Chapter 11.

Take this job and . . . well, just take this job

Want to know who's the largest employer in the United States? I'll give you a hint: It's not Walmart (although it's the largest *private* employer in the U.S.). The single largest employer in the United States is the federal government. The U.S. government has more than 1.8 million employees, and that doesn't even count the 785,989 folks who work for the U.S. Postal Service. Walmart only has a measly 1.1 million employees.

Did you know that some veterans may qualify for special hiring preference for federal government jobs? It's true. Most veterans are eligible for additional points when competing for federal jobs. If you served during certain periods, you can get even more hiring points.

You say that you don't want a government job? Well, I can't say that I blame you. The only government job I'm personally interested in is becoming the president, and that's probably not going to happen (plus, veterans preference points don't apply for that particular job).

Perhaps you'd like to own your own business, instead? Ah, that would be the life. You could take expensive business trips and lord over the peons you hire to do your bidding. The Small Business Administration has a program that may help you fulfill your dreams. Veterans can receive preferential treatment and reduced interest rates for small business loans guaranteed by the federal government.

Chapter 12 has more information about these two valuable benefits.

There's no place like home

Everyone wants to own their own home one day. I know I do. I can't live with my children for the rest of my life. I'm just kidding. I don't live with my kids — there's no way that they'd put up with me. Writers are no fun to live with. We're often cranky; we're lazy; and sometimes we forget to shower.

When I'm ready to buy my own home, I'm certainly going to take advantage of the VA Home Loan Program. Every eligible veteran should, in my opinion. Under this program, the government doesn't actually lend you any money, but it guarantees the loan. In other words, if you default, the government pays off the loan (up to a certain amount). That makes you a very attractive candidate to certain mortgage lenders. It's kind of like having Big Brother as a co-signer. If you're eligible for this program, you may find it easier and cheaper to finance your next dream house. But you'll certainly want to read Chapter 13 first.

When I reach my golden years, I may consider giving my dream home to my kids (if they continue to be nice to me and remember my birthday, and they stop asking me for an allowance) and move into a military retirement home. You say you've never heard of such a place? The federal government operates two retirement homes for certain veteran enlisted members; several private, nonprofit organizations offer retirement communities for officers. If the thought of golf and shuffleboard and trips and home-cooked meals when you're old and gray tickles your fancy, check out Chapter 14.

Shopping and sight-seeing

My personal copy of *Writing Dummies Books For Dummies* says I should avoid sexism. I'm sorry, but I can't help engaging in a little sexism here. Many women love to shop. The only thing they seem to love more than shopping is finding huge discounts when they shop. I know my own girlfriend is certainly hard-wired for shopping. Fortunately for her (and my wallet), tons of shopping and discount opportunities are available to military retirees and certain other veterans.

Want to buy a diamond bracelet for 50 bucks or a new TV for $10? I'm sorry, but that's not going to happen on a military base — this is a benefit, not a pipedream. However, you can save up to 30 or 40 percent by shopping on military bases or through the military exchange system's Internet sites. Ready to snag a bargain? Take a look at the information in Chapter 15.

My girlfriend may love to shop, but I love to travel. I'd spend every waking moment traveling if I could. I love to see things I've never seen before and meet people I've never met before. It's lucky for me that many veterans qualify for military travel benefits, including free aircraft flights, discount luxury condominium rentals in exotic locations, Armed Forces Recreation Centers, and cheap overnight stays in military hotels. Chapter 16 has the 411 on these benefits.

Chapter 2

Determining Veteran Status and Qualifying for Benefits

*W*hen I was a kid, I thought I knew what a military veteran was. They were all those old people hanging out at the American Legion or the local VFW, right? Then my dad told me that he was a veteran, having served during the Korean War. I was confuced because my dad never hung out at these two clubs. Confusion being the natural state of my life at that age, I didn't let it hinder me. I wrote an article about veterans for my high school newspaper during the week of Veterans Day. Not only did I learn a lot about military veterans, but that article got me a date with Lori Geller, who thought the article was "far out."

The truth is, millions upon millions of veterans are living in the United States. Some veterans are very vocal about their status, active in veterans affairs, and belong to various veteran organizations, while others go quietly through their lives, never even mentioning their status as an American veteran of the armed forces.

You probably know several veterans, whether you know them to be veterans or not. Perhaps your neighbor, teacher, doctor, lawyer, dog catcher, or best friend is a veteran. As I said, I didn't even know my own dad was a veteran until the year of that glorious date with Lori Geller.

Many veterans never take advantage of benefits available to them. My dad certainly didn't. It's possible that Dad didn't even know about most of them. To my dad, veterans benefits were just for those who were "shot up during the war." Not true, Father. Not true.

This chapter explains who can be called a veteran and how that status relates to benefits, and tells you what proof you need to show to get the benefits you're entitled to.

What Is a Veteran? The Legal Definition

What exactly is a veteran? Are you a veteran if you spend one week in the military and are then discharged because you're injured in basic training? Are you a veteran if you spend four years in the National Guard or Reserves, but never spend any time on active duty? Are you a veteran if you spend 15 years on active duty, but are then given a dishonorable discharge?

My handy-dandy pocket dictionary defines the term *veteran* as "(1) a person who has served in the armed forces; (2) an old soldier who has seen long service." That can't be true. The first definition would mean that everyone who has ever seen a day of military service would qualify, even if they receive a dishonorable discharge. The latter would imply that only "old soldiers" could qualify as veterans.

Title 38 of the Code of Federal Regulations defines a veteran as "a person who served in the active military, naval, or air service and who was discharged or released under conditions other than dishonorable."

That makes sense to me. In other words, a veteran is someone who, at one point in his or her life, wrote a blank check made payable to the United States of America for an amount "up to and including my life."

This probably all seems very simple, right? Well, when it comes to benefits, the legal definition of *veteran* sometimes isn't enough. You need to consider other things, such as the type of service involved, or even where you served. More on those issues in the following sections.

Understanding the Difference between Types of Military Service

You'd be surprised how many people I meet who don't know the difference between active-duty service, service in the Reserves, and National Guard service. If I had a dime for every time I've had to explain the differences, well, I'd have a lot of dimes. But because you've given up quite a few dimes for this book, I happily review the distinctions between these types of services in the following sections.

Full-time warriors

Active-duty service is full-time service. This is generally what most people think of when someone says he was in the military. Except when on *leave* (vacation) or *pass* (authorized time off), active-duty members are subject to duty 24 hours per day, 7 days per week. Think of it as a full-time job.

These folks serve in the Army, Air Force, Navy, Marine Corps, and Coast Guard. These military branches fall under the direction of the U.S. Department of Defense.

Active-duty service counts toward length-of-service requirements when qualifying for veterans benefits.

Weekend warriors

Members of the Reserves and National Guard normally perform duty one weekend per month, plus two weeks of training per year. It's actually not fair to refer to them as weekend warriors anymore. Ever since the United States jumped onto the sand with both feet during the first Gulf War in 1990, these warriors have been spending more and more time called to full-time active duty in support of contingency operations.

The average National Guard or Reserve enlistment contract is for six years. These days, a Guard or Reserve member can expect to spend about two years of that six-year enlistment period performing full-time active duty.

Reserves

Each of the military services has a Reserve branch. There's an Army Reserve, Air Force Reserve, Navy Reserve, Marine Corps Reserve, and Coast Guard Reserve. Like the active-duty forces, the Reserves fall under the auspices of the Department of Defense, so they are federal agencies. The primary purpose of the Reserves is to provide additional support and manpower to the active-duty forces in times of need.

When you join the Reserves, you first attend basic training and military job school full time. This is called *active duty for training,* or *ADT,* and doesn't count as active-duty time for most veterans benefits.

Upon completion of basic training and military job school, reservists return to their home, resume their lives and normal civilian jobs, but train *(drill)* with their unit one weekend per month. Once per year, they receive 14 days of full-time training. The weekend drills are called *inactive duty training (IDT),* and the annual training falls into the category of ADT. Neither IDT nor ADT counts toward service requirements for veterans benefits.

The president and the secretary of defense can recall reservists to active duty at any time to support military missions. In fact, at any given time, about 65,000 reservists are performing active duty in support of military contingency operations. Active duty of this type *does* count toward veterans benefit service requirements.

National Guard

There are only two National Guard services: the Army National Guard and the Air National Guard. The Navy, Marine Corps, and Coast Guard don't have National Guard branches.

The main difference between the National Guard and the Reserves is that the Reserves belong to the federal government, while the National Guard units belong (primarily) to the individual states.

Like reservists, National Guard members attend basic training and military job school full time under ADT (active duty for training). They then return to their homes, where they drill with their units one weekend per month (inactive duty training [IDT]), plus 15 full-time training days per year. As with Reserve duty, this ADT/IDT time doesn't count toward veterans benefit service requirements.

State governors can call National Guard members to active duty in response to state emergencies, such as disaster relief or protection of property and people, when it's beyond the scope of local law enforcement agencies. This is officially known as a "Title 38 Call-up," and is commonly referred to as *state duty*. State duty doesn't count toward veterans benefit service requirements.

National Guard members can also be called to active duty by the president or secretary of defense in support of military contingency operations. This is called "Title 10 Call-up," or *federal duty*. This type of duty *does* count toward service requirements for veterans benefits. During any given month, about 40,000 members of the Air and Army National Guard are performing federal duty in such garden spots as Afghanistan and Iraq.

Active Guard/Reserves

Some members of the Reserves and National Guard perform full-time active duty, just like active-duty members. This program is called the *Active Guard/ Reserves,* or *AGR*. AGR members provide day-to-day operational support needed to ensure that National Guard and Reserve units are ready to mobilize when needed. For veterans benefit service requirements, AGR duty is the same as full-time active-duty service (see the "Full-time warriors" section).

Individual Ready Reserve

It may surprise you to find out that everyone who joins the U.S. military for the first time incurs a minimum eight-year military service obligation. Yep. When you sign that enlistment contract, you're obligating yourself to the military for a total of eight years. Whatever time isn't spent on active duty or in the Guard/Reserves must be spent in the inactive reserves, officially known as the *Individual Ready Reserves (IRR)*.

Say you enlist in the Navy for four years. You serve your four years and get out. You're really not "out." You're transferred to the IRR for the next four years. Members of the IRR don't perform weekend drills or annual training, and they don't get paid. However, IRR members can be recalled to active duty at any time in support of military operations. Time in the IRR doesn't count toward veterans benefit service requirements, but if you're recalled to active duty, that time does count.

An average of about 15,000 IRR members have been recalled to active duty each and every year since 2004, the vast majority by the Army and Marine Corps.

Digging Into the Details: Other Considerations for Benefits

Each time Congress passes a new veterans benefit law, the lawmakers establish specific eligibility criteria for that particular benefit. It can be confusing, to say the least. Luckily, you made the wise decision to buy this book.

For the purpose of benefits, being a veteran is not enough. Whether you qualify for benefits, or certain types of benefits, depends on several factors:

- Your length of service
- Where and when you served
- Your discharge characterization

More on these in the following sections. I cover the individual benefit issues in the other chapters.

Length of service

Eligibility for most veterans benefits requires a minimum length of military service. Take a gander at Table 2-1. As you can see, to qualify for full Montgomery GI Bill education benefits, you have to serve for a minimum of 36 months.

On the other hand, you could qualify for VA disability compensation or VA medical care with only one day of active duty. Don't get too excited, because for disability or medical care, you have to meet a slew of other qualification requirements. Chapters 4 and 6 give you the complete lowdown on these two programs. (And if you're wondering about the "Discharge Characterization" column, I cover that topic later in this chapter.)

Table 2-1	Veterans Benefits Basic Eligibility Criteria			
Benefit	**Minimum Service Requirement**	**Period of Service**	**Discharge Characterization**	**Complete Information**
VA healthcare	Any	Any	Honorable, general, or VA determination	Chapter 4
Military health insurance	20 years	Any	Honorable	Chapter 5

Benefit	Minimum Service Requirement	Period of Service	Discharge Characterization	Complete Information
VA pension	90 days active duty	Before Sept. 7, 1980	Honorable, general, or VA determination	Chapter 6
VA pension	2 years active duty	On or after Sept. 7, 1980	Honorable, general, or VA determination	Chapter 6
VA disability compensation	Any	Any	Honorable, general, or VA determination	Chapter 6
Military retirement	20 years	Any	Honorable	Chapter 7
Military life insurance programs	Any	Any	Honorable, general, or VA determination	Chapter 8
Burial and memorial benefits	Any	*Enlisted:* Service on or before Sept. 7, 1980 *Officers:* Service on or before Oct. 16, 1981	Honorable, general, or VA determination	Chapter 9
Burial and memorial benefits	24 months continuous active duty	*Enlisted:* Service after Sep. 7, 1980 *Officers:* Service after Oct. 16, 1981	Honorable, general, or VA determination	Chapter 9
Active-Duty GI Bill	36 months active duty	Any	Honorable	Chapter 10
Reserve GI Bill	After initial training	Any	N/A	Chapter 10
21st Century GI Bill	90 days continuous active duty or 6 months total active duty	After Sept. 11, 2001	Honorable	Chapter 10

(continued)

Table 2-1 *(continued)*

Benefit	Minimum Service Requirement	Period of Service	Discharge Characterization	Complete Information
Vocational training for disabled veterans	Any	Any	Honorable, general, or VA determination	Chapter 11
Veterans job preference	1 day	Any	Honorable, general, or VA determination	Chapter 12
Veterans small-business loans	Any	Any	Honorable general, or VA determination	Chapter 12
VA Home Loan Program	90 days active duty	Sept. 16, 1940, to July 25, 1947; or June 27, 1950, to Jan. 31, 1955; or Aug. 5, 1964, to May 7, 1975	Honorable, general, or VA determination	Chapter 13
VA Home Loan Program	181 days continuous active duty	*Enlisted:* July 26, 1947, to June 26, 1950; or Feb. 1, 1955, to Aug. 4, 1964; or May 8, 1955, to Sept. 7, 1980 *Officers:* May 8, 1975 to Oct. 16, 1981	Honorable, general, or VA determination	Chapter 13
VA Home Loan Program	24 months continuous active duty	*Enlisted:* Sept. 7, 1980, to present *Officers:* Oct. 16, 1981, to present	Honorable, general, or VA determination	Chapter 13
VA Home Loan Program	6 years Guard/ Reserve service	Any	Honorable	Chapter 13
Homeless veterans programs	Any	Any	Honorable, general, or VA determination	Chapter 14

Benefit	Minimum Service Requirement	Period of Service	Discharge Characterization	Complete Information
Military retirement homes	20 years	Any	Honorable	Chapter 14
Military retirement homes (100% disabled)	1 day	Any	Honorable, general, or VA determination	Chapter 14
Military shopping benefits	20 years or 100% disabled	Any	Honorable	Chapter 15
Military travel benefits	20 years or 100% disabled	Any	Honorable	Chapter 16

Note: *The table shows basic eligibility criteria only. As with most things in life, there are exceptions. For complete information, see the referenced chapter.*

Where and when you served

I don't know why Congress can't make things simple. Just to complicate things, where and when you served in the military can have an impact on your eligibility for certain veterans benefits.

Take another look at Table 2-1. To qualify for the VA Home Loan Program, you need at least 90 days of active-duty service if you served during the Vietnam War. However, if your military service was during the Gulf War, you must have at least 24 months of *continuous* active-duty service to qualify. A member of the National Guard or Reserves must have at least six years of Guard/Reserve service to qualify (unless they otherwise qualify due to active-duty service).

Service discharges

I'm always amazed at how many people, including military people, think that there are only two types of military discharges (sometimes called *characterizations*): honorable and dishonorable. I mean, really . . . didn't anyone ever watch *JAG* on TV? I've lost track of the times that veterans, many with several years of military service, have said to me, "I want to apply for benefits, but I think I got a dishonorable discharge."

Trust me. If you received a dishonorable discharge, you'd know it. This is the worst kind of military discharge possible, and it can only be imposed by a general court-martial (the most serious kind of military court-martial). It's only given for serious crimes and is almost always accompanied by a lengthy stay in a military prison.

Military discharges come in two basic flavors:

- ✔ **Administrative:** Administrative discharges are granted by the discharge authority, who is usually a high-ranking commanding officer.

- ✔ **Punitive:** Punitive discharges can be imposed only by a military court-martial.

More on each in the next two sections.

Administrative discharges

The vast majority of those who serve in the military receive an administrative discharge, of which there are four types:

- ✔ **Honorable discharge:** Most people receive an honorable discharge (HD) following their service in the military. An HD means your command feels that you generally met the standards of conduct and performance of duty during your time in the military. It's also granted if your service was otherwise so meritorious that any other characterization would be clearly inappropriate. For example, if you received a military medal for valor or bravery on the battlefield, you would usually be given an HD, even if you were a bit of a troublemaker otherwise.

- ✔ **General (under honorable conditions) discharge:** Usually simply referred to as a "general discharge," or GD, this type of discharge is granted if your commander determines that your service has been honest and faithful, even if you got into a bit of trouble here and there. If you were discharged for reasons such as failure to progress in training; failure to maintain military standards, such as dress, appearance, weight, or fitness; or minor disciplinary infractions, you may have received this discharge characterization.

- ✔ **Other than honorable discharge:** This is the worst type of administrative discharge you can receive. Other than honorable (OTH) discharges are warranted when the reason for discharge is based upon a pattern of behavior that constitutes a significant departure from the conduct expected of members of the military services. Examples of factors that may be considered include an act of serious misconduct, abuse of authority, fraternization, or a pattern of continued misconduct. Individuals who receive court-martial convictions that don't include punitive discharges are often given this discharge characterization.

✔ **Entry-level separation:** This type of discharge isn't actually a characterization. In fact, an entry-level separation (ELS) has no characterization at all. It's not honorable, it's not general, and it's not other than honorable. Commanders may grant an ELS only for members who have been in the military for less than 180 days. It's the commander's way of saying, "Look, we tried you out, and you didn't make it. However, I don't know you well enough to fairly judge you."

If you were discharged with less than 180 days of service, don't assume you received an ELS. Commanders may elect this option only if they feel it's the most appropriate. If you punched out your drill instructor after only five days in basic training, it's doubtful you received an ELS.

Punitive discharges

Only special and general courts-martial have the authority to impose a punitive discharge. Summary courts can't impose discharges. However, if you're convicted of an offense by any court-martial, and the court doesn't (or can't) impose a punitive discharge, your commanding officer can elect to initiate administrative discharge proceedings as a separate matter (see the preceding section for more on these).

There are three kinds of punitive discharges:

✔ **Bad conduct discharge:** A bad conduct discharge, or BCD, can be imposed by both special and general courts. However, it can only be given, as part of the court punishment, to enlisted members. Officers can't receive a BCD. This discharge is usually given for convictions of such crimes as absent without leave, drunk on duty, driving while under the influence, adultery, bad checks, disorderly conduct, and so on.

✔ **Dismissal:** Dismissal from military service can only be imposed on officers. Special and general courts may impose this on officers when the maximum punishment listed in the Manual for Courts-Martial (MCM) includes a BCD (bad conduct discharge). Dismissal is the officer version of a BCD.

✔ **Dishonorable discharge:** A dishonorable discharge (DD) is the worst type of military discharge you can receive. It can be imposed only by a general courts-martial, and then only if the MCM (Manual for Courts-Martial) authorizes a DD for the offense you've been convicted of. In most cases, a DD is accompanied by a very long vacation in a military prison.

How discharges affect eligibility

If you received an honorable or general discharge, you're eligible for most veterans benefits, assuming you meet the other qualifying factors for that benefit. A few benefits, such as GI Bill education benefits (see Chapter 10), require an honorable discharge.

If you received a dishonorable discharge, a bad conduct discharge, or a dismissal from a *general* court-martial, you're not entitled to veterans benefits.

If you received an OTH administrative discharge, or a BCD or dismissal imposed by a *special* court-martial, you may or may not be eligible for veterans benefits. In these cases, the Department of Veterans Affairs (VA) makes a determination as to whether your service was "other than honorable." In making this determination, the VA is required by law to apply the standards set forth by Congress in Title 38, Section 3.12, of the Code of Federal Regulations (CFR).

You can view the CFR online at `edocket.access.gpo.gov/cfr_2007/ julqtr/pdf/38cfr3.12.pdf`.

Generally, the VA evaluates your military service as "other than honorable" if

- ✔ You were discharged as a conscientious objector who refused to perform military duty, wear the uniform, or comply with lawful order of competent military authorities.

- ✔ You resigned as an officer for the "good of the service."

- ✔ You accepted an OTH discharge rather than face a trial by general court-martial.

- ✔ You were discharged for desertion. The crime of desertion is defined as *absent without leave (AWOL)* with the intent to remain away permanently.

- ✔ You were discharged for AWOL in excess of 180 continuous days.

- ✔ You were discharged for the offense of mutiny or spying.

- ✔ You were discharged for an offense involving moral turpitude (or depravity). This includes, generally, conviction of a felony.

- ✔ You were discharged for willful and persistent misconduct.

- ✔ You were discharged for homosexual acts involving aggravating circumstances or other factors affecting the performance of duty. Examples include child molestation, homosexual prostitution, homosexual acts or conduct accompanied by assault or coercion, and homosexual acts or conduct taking place between service members of different ranks, or when a service member has taken advantage of his or her superior rank.

You can have your military discharge characterization upgraded, or even have your reason for discharge changed. For details, see Chapter 3.

You may be eligible for VA medical care (see Chapter 4) even if the VA determines that your discharge doesn't qualify for benefits. To qualify, the VA must find that you have a medical condition that was caused or aggravated by your military service.

Changing your discharge

If you have a disqualifying discharge characterization, does it mean you're out of luck for receiving benefits? Not necessarily. If you believe your discharge characterization or your reason for discharge to be inequitable or improper, you can apply to the appropriate Discharge Review Board (DRB) for a discharge upgrade or to change your reason for discharge.

- *Inequitable* means the reason for or characterization of the discharge isn't consistent with the policies and traditions of the service. An example would be, "My discharge was inequitable because it was based on one minor, isolated incident in 28 months of service with no other problems."

- *Improper* means that the reason for or characterization of the discharge is in error (that is, it's false or violates a regulation or a law). An example is, "I was discharged because I failed the physical fitness test one time, and the regulation requires that I be given three chances before being discharged."

There are separate DRBs, depending on which branch issued your military discharge. The Army, Air Force, and Coast Guard have separate boards. The Navy operates the board for Navy personnel and members of the U.S. Marine Corps. Members of the board are civilians, not military members. They are appointed to the board by the secretary of the corresponding service branch.

To apply for a discharge upgrade or a change of reason for discharge, you use DD Form 293, Application for Review of Discharge from the Armed Forces of the United States. You can download this form online at www.dtic.mil/whs/directives/infomgt/forms/eforms/dd0293.pdf. The form is also available at VA regional offices (see Appendix B) or by sending a written request to Army Review Boards Agency (ARBA), ATTN: Client Information and Quality Assurance, Arlington, VA 22202-4508.

You should complete the form by typing or clearly printing the requested information. Attach copies of statements or records that are relevant to your case. The board will upgrade your discharge only if you can prove that your discharge is inequitable or improper. You do this by providing evidence, such as signed statements from you and other witnesses or copies of records that support your case. (Chapter 3 has more information about submitting reliable documents and evidence.) It's not enough to provide witnesses' names because the board won't contact them to obtain statements. You should contact your witnesses to get their signed statements, and then submit them with your request.

Requesting a review of your discharge isn't a means of clemency or "time off for good behavior." The board isn't interested in your behavior after you left the military. Restrict your statements to the periods that were directly related to your military service.

Sign the completed form and mail it to the appropriate board address located on the back of the form.

If the board denies your request, there is no further appeal, except through the federal court system (you'd have to file a lawsuit against the Department of Defense). However, you can request that the board reconsider your case, but only if you provide newly discovered relevant evidence that wasn't available when you filed your original application. Re-argument of the same evidence won't get your case reconsidered.

If your discharge is more than 15 years old, you can only change it by using the procedures for fixing errors in military records, as described in Chapter 3.

Service Records: Proving Your Eligibility

You can't just walk into a VA office and say, "Here I am. Give me my benefits." You first have to prove that you're entitled to them. This is accomplished by presenting an official copy of your DD Form 214/215, or NGB 22/22A.

These forms are among the most important documents the military will ever give you. They are your key to participation in all VA programs as well as several state and federal veterans benefits programs.

DD Forms 214 and 215

DD Forms 214 and 215 are used for certification of military service for active-duty members and members of the Reserves. DD Form 214, Certificate of Release or Discharge, displays reserve and active-duty time, military job, awards, education, dates and places you entered and left the military, military assignments, and, at the bottom of the form, why you left the service and what your discharge characterization was. DD Form 215 is used to correct errors or make additions to a DD Form 214 after the original has been delivered.

There are two versions of these forms:

- ✔ **The deleted version:** You can show this version to future civilian employers when you apply for a job. It excludes your discharge characterization and the reason for your discharge (on the assumption you may not want your future employer to know this information).

- ✔ **The undeleted version:** The undeleted version must be used when applying for VA benefits. It includes your discharge characterization and the reason for your discharge.

You should receive a copy of both the deleted and undeleted versions of DD Form 214 when you process for separation from the military. However, the military being the military, this doesn't always happen. If you didn't receive a copy, or you lost it, you can request a replacement from the National Personnel Records Center in St. Louis, Missouri (see the next section).

Getting replacement copies

The National Personnel Records Center maintains copies of all active-duty and reserve military records. You can request a copy of any portion of your military records, including your DD Form 214/215, by submitting a signed copy of SF Form 180, Request Pertaining to Military Records. You can download this form at `www.archives.gov/research/order/standard-form-180.pdf`. Mail the completed form to

National Personnel Records Center
Military Personnel Records
9700 Page Ave.
St. Louis, MO 63132-5100

You can now complete a records request online at `www.archives.gov/veterans/evetrecs/index.html`. You must still print and sign a signature verification form (and mail or fax it), because federal law requires a signature on all records request. However, completing the application online can be easier and faster than completing SF Form 180.

How long does it take?

Not all that long ago, turnaround time for military records was miserable. It wasn't unusual for a simple DD Form 214/215 request to take up to 180 days.

However, in the past couple of years, the National Personnel Records Center has received some extra money from Congress to upgrade its computers. As a test, I requested a copy of my DD Form 214 in June 2008, using the online system. I was pleasantly surprised to receive my DD Form 214 copy in just seven days.

However, the folks at the center are still busy bees. They process nearly 20,000 requests per week. Turnaround times for records requested from the National Personnel Records Center can vary greatly depending on the nature of the request, so please have a little patience.

NGB Forms 22 and 22A

What DD Forms 214 and 215 are for active-duty and reserve service, NGB Forms 22 and 22A are for service in the Army and Air National Guard. Like its active-duty/reserve counterpart, NGB Form 22, Report of Separation and Military Service, includes information about your National Guard service time, military job, decorations, reason for discharge, and discharge characterization. NGB Form 22A is used to document changes to your military records after the fact.

Because the National Guard belongs to the individual state, not to the federal government, there's not a central repository for National Guard records.

To obtain a copy of your NGB Form 22/22A, you have to contact the National Guard Adjutant General's Office for the particular state in which you performed National Guard service. For contact information, visit www.ngb. army.mil/resources/states.aspx.

Military medical records

Anyone who has ever spent even one day in the military has a military medical record. The first entry in your medical record is the details of the physical examination you underwent as part of the process of joining the military. After that, every single time you received medical care from a military medical facility, the details were entered into your military medical record.

The VA relies heavily on military medical records when making determinations as to whether you have a medical condition that was caused or aggravated by military service.

You can request a copy of your military medical record by sending a written request to

National Personnel Records Center
Military Personnel Records
9700 Page Ave.
St. Louis, MO 63132-5100

If you plan to file a claim for medical benefits (see Chapter 4) or disability compensation (see Chapter 6) with the VA, you don't need to request a copy of your military medical record. When you file a claim, the VA will request the record automatically as part of the claims process. Likewise, if you've ever filed a claim for disability benefits from the VA, it already has a copy of your medical records. You can request a copy from the VA regional office having jurisdiction over your claim. See Appendix B for VA regional office locations.

Protecting Your Paperwork

You should take steps to protect your DD Form 214/215 or NGB Form 22/22A as you would any other sensitive document (wills, marriage and birth certificates, insurance policies, and so on). You may want to store it in a fireproof lock box at your home, a safe-deposit box at your bank, or at some other secure location where it will be protected.

In most states, you can register or record your separation documents just like a land deed or other significant document. So as soon as you separate from the military, consider registering these documents with your county recorder or town hall. If you register your documents, you can quickly retrieve them later for a nominal fee.

To ensure documents will be safeguarded from viewing by unauthorized individuals, ask the registering agency whether state or local law permits the public to access the recorded document. If public access is authorized and you register your separation documents, a member of the public could obtain a copy for an unlawful purpose (for example, to obtain a credit card in your name). If public access is permitted, you may choose not to register your separation document.

Chapter 3

Navigating Your Way through the Red Tape of Claims and Appeals

f I've heard it once, I've heard it a hundred times: "You can't fight city hall." It's a good thing that the Department of Veterans Affairs (VA) and the Department of Defense (DOD) military service offices aren't city hall. You actually can fight them. Well, you can consider several avenues of appeals if your claim for veterans benefits is denied.

Actually, you may be pleasantly surprised when working with the VA and DOD. The old days of "baffle them with bureaucracy" is fast fading away. The new days of "let's see if we can help you with this" seems to be taking hold. Perhaps this reflects the fact that the American people seem to have become proud and supportive of our veterans again.

However, it's still not all a bed of roses. The VA is seriously overworked, and this can be frustrating when you're trying to make a benefits claim. As of September 2008, the VA had a backlog of 512,700-plus claims pending and 90,800-plus appeals pending. The average new-claim processing time for disability compensation and pensions is a little over six months, while appeals may take several years. This backlog is frustrating and unacceptable to everyone concerned, especially veterans and their families. The reasons for this backlog are numerous, complex, and in all fairness to the VA, beyond its immediate control.

Only Congress can fix this. The VA needs loads of additional funds to hire and train more claims processors and to bulk up its appeal divisions. So get out your No. 2 pencils and crayons, boys and girls, and let your representatives know that you want the VA to receive more funding (Congress has this annoying habit of adding new veterans benefits, but then not providing any money to the VA to provide those benefits). In the meantime, in this chapter I give you some pointers on how to navigate your way through the morass and get what you need.

Meeting the Two Main Benefits Agencies

Two government agencies have pretty much cornered the market when it comes to veterans benefits. Virtually all benefits are managed by either the Department of Veterans Affairs (VA) or the Department of Defense (DOD).

Okay, there are two exceptions: the veterans' preference program for government jobs is managed by the Office of Personnel Management (OPM), and the veterans small business loan program belongs to the Small Business Administration. Chapter 12 has complete information about those two programs. For now, here's an introduction to the VA and DOD, starting with the VA.

The Department of Veterans Affairs

The VA has been around in one form or another since it was created as the Veterans Administration by President Herbert Hoover on July 21, 1930. Today the VA is huge. It has an annual budget of about $86 billion and employs about 230,000 people. It operates 1,357 facilities, including regional offices, vet centers, medical centers, and outpatient clinics, throughout the United States and its territories.

The VA has staked its claim for most veterans benefits. This includes, but is not limited to

- VA healthcare, as explained in Chapter 4

- Disability compensation, as explained in Chapter 6

- The GI Bill education program, detailed in Chapter 10

- VA pensions, as explained in Chapter 6

- Veteran survivor benefits, as outlined in Chapter 8

About 5.3 million veterans are enrolled in the VA's healthcare program, and more than 3.7 million veterans receive disability compensation and pensions through the agency. The VA processes an average of 805,000 new claims for disability compensation or pensions each year (and the number keeps rising). Millions of other veterans are served through the VA's other benefit programs.

With the exception of medical care, when you apply for a VA benefit, you usually work with the VA regional office closest to where you live. Counselors are also available at VA veterans centers, scattered throughout most cities. These counselors can assist you in filling out paperwork and getting your documents in order. Appendix B shows a complete list of VA regional offices and vet centers.

For VA medical care, you generally apply through a VA medical center. Appendix C shows where you can find your closest VA medical center.

The Department of Defense and military services

If you're retired from the military (that is, you have more than 20 years of military service, as explained in Chapter 7), you receive many of your benefits through the Department of Defense (DOD) or your individual military service branch. The DOD covers all five military branches:

- ✔ Army
- ✔ Air Force
- ✔ Navy
- ✔ Marine Corps
- ✔ Coast Guard

Each of these branches has an active-duty component (full-time service) and a reserve component (part-time service). The Army and the Air Force also have a National Guard, which is organized under the parent branch and under the individual state.

What the DOD covers

Benefits covered by the DOD include

- ✔ Military retirement pay, as explained in Chapter 7
- ✔ Shopping and travel benefits, as explained in Chapters 14 and 15
- ✔ Military healthcare (Tricare), as explained in Chapter 5
- ✔ Combat-related special compensation, as explained in Chapter 6

The key to many military retiree benefits is the military retired identification card (see Chapter 15). Retirees and their family members receive this card at the Pass & ID section of any military base. You don't need to go to your parent service base to do this. In other words, if you retired from the Air Force and you happen to live close to an Army base, you can go to the Army base to renew or replace your military ID card.

Getting help from the Defense Finance and Accounting Service

Retiree pay matters can't be resolved by visiting a military base. Retirees have to contact the appropriate branch of the Defense Finance and Accounting Service (DFAS). Its Web site is www.dfas.mil. You also can ask questions, get answers, and resolve problems with your military retired pay by contacting DFAS at 800-321-1080.

DFAS also has a nifty online system, called myPay, that retirees can use to access their pay information and make changes to their retiree pay account. The system is available on the DFAS Web site at www.dfas.mil.

Double-Checking Your Documentation and Eligibility

One reason the veterans benefit claims system is so backlogged is that many veterans apply for benefits that they aren't eligible for. The VA has to take extra time to make sure the person is ineligible for the benefit and then write a rejection letter.

Each and every VA benefit has different eligibility rules. Why? Each and every veterans benefit represents a different law, passed by Congress, at a different time. Eligibility for a particular benefit depends on what the lawmakers' whims were when they wrote the specific law to authorize that benefit.

For example, to qualify for the Montgomery GI Bill education program (Chapter 10), you need an honorable discharge. If you have a general (under honorable conditions) discharge, you're not eligible. However, for many other veterans benefits, a general discharge is qualifying. See Chapter 2 for more information about discharge characterizations and how they affect VA benefits.

It's a good thing you've shown the forethought, intelligence, and good ol' common sense to buy this book. You're well on your way to understanding the rules for each benefit.

Collecting your documents

Another factor that affects the VA's backlog of veterans benefit claims is insufficient documentation or incorrect documentation. For most claims, you must prove two things:

- ✔ That you meet the qualifications of military service and discharge characterization for that benefit. You prove your status as a veteran by providing a copy of your military discharge form, such as your DD Form 214. The form includes information about when you served in the military, where you served, medals and awards you earned, and your discharge characterization. If you don't have a copy of this form, you can get a replacement. Chapter 2 explains how to request a copy of your discharge form.

  For almost any benefit, you'll need to provide a copy of DD Form 214, or its equivalent, to prove you meet the active-duty service and discharge requirements to be eligible for the benefit.

- ✔ That you meet any other criteria required for that benefit (for example, a service-connected disability). This is where many veterans run into trouble. There's no all-inclusive list of necessary supporting documentation because it differs for each situation, but common sense plays a large part. Remember that, for the most part, the burden of proof to show eligibility for a particular benefit lies with you.

Supplying examples of proof

There is no all-inclusive list of possible documents you can use to support your benefit claim. It depends on your particular situation and the benefit you're applying for.

Citations from military medals and decorations may help. For example, if you submit a citation for the award of the Purple Heart, which is a decoration awarded only to those who are wounded in combat, that makes a pretty clear case that you received an injury in the line of duty.

Sworn witness statements may also help your case, but be careful with those. If they're not worded correctly and are vague, they may actually hurt your case (see the next section).

It's quality, not quantity, that counts

It's not the amount of supporting documentation that's important, but whether that documentation supports your claim. The best supporting evidence is

✔ **Specific:** Your documentation and witness statements should relate directly to the benefit you're claiming and contain as much specific information as possible. Exact dates and times are more persuasive than "sometime around March of 1976." A doctor's report that says, "The patient is suffering from a wound that was caused by shrapnel injury, consistent with wounds often received in combat zones," is a whole lot better than, "The patient hurt his knee."

✔ **Verifiable:** Anyone can write something on a piece of paper and sign it. That doesn't necessarily mean it's true. The evidence you provide should be verifiable. That means you should be able to support it from other sources. If you claim you were injured during a combat operation in Afghanistan, you should be able to provide evidence that you were actually deployed to Afghanistan (deployment orders, unit rosters, and so forth).

✔ **Authoritative:** Witness statements signed by your mom, best friend, or postal carrier aren't going to help you much. A witness statement signed by your commanding officer or platoon leader is going to carry more weight than a witness statement signed by your best combat buddy. Statements signed by medical corpsmen or doctors about treatment received in the combat zone are similarly effective.

For example, if you submit a sworn statement from your former commanding officer that says, "On July 17, 2003, my unit was undergoing simulated combat training at Dicklehead Army Post. I personally witnessed a tank run over Private Hurtsalot's foot. I immediately summoned medical care, and he was transported to the medical facility with a crushed foot," that would be acceptable documentation.

On the other hand, if you submit 20 sworn witness statements, which all state something along the lines of, "We were practicing war games a few years ago, and tanks were running around everywhere. I didn't actually see his foot get run over, but I remember hearing him scream, and the next day I noticed a bandage on his foot," that probably wouldn't be very helpful to your case.

Using the VA's "duty to assist"

Under the law, the burden of proof for benefit eligibility falls directly on your shoulders. However, you don't have to do it all alone. In the year 2000, the thoughtful folks who roam the halls of Capitol Hill got together and passed a new law, obligating the VA to assist you in gathering supporting documentation. This is referred to as the VA's *duty to assist*.

First and foremost, the law requires the VA to tell you, in simple words, exactly what evidence is required to support your claim. That's a big help in itself. You don't have to guess what evidence you should and shouldn't submit. The VA will tell you exactly what you need.

The law also requires the VA to make a "reasonable effort" to obtain the evidence for you. The standard by which the VA must apply this is slightly different depending on the sources of the records.

- ✔ **Federal records:** The VA must make a continued reasonable effort to try to obtain those records. The VA can stop pursuing the records only after it is reasonably sure the records don't exist or that a continued effort to get the records would be futile. If the VA comes to this determination, the law requires the agency to notify you and inform you of possible alternatives.

- ✔ **Nonfederal records:** The VA must make a reasonable effort to get records such as private doctor records or sworn witness statements. The law requires the VA to send a request for such documents, and if it doesn't receive them within two months, it must make another request. If there is still no response, the VA must continue to request the records, unless it has reason to believe that the records are unobtainable.

For nonfederal records, you should make every attempt to obtain them yourself, especially medical records. It's not uncommon for medical facilities to ignore such requests unless they come from the patient. Additionally, some of these facilities charge a fee to copy the records, and the VA isn't allowed to pay such fees.

Submitting Your VA Claim

It would be nice if the VA had just one claim form that said, "Gimme all the benefits I'm entitled to." Unfortunately, it doesn't work that way. For each and every veterans benefit, there is a different claim form requiring different information. And most forms are submitted to different locations.

Luckily, I've hooked you up. As I explain each benefit in this book, I include information about what form you should fill out, where you can get the form, the minimum supporting documentation required, and where you submit the completed claim.

Most VA claims are delayed or denied because of lack of supporting evidence. I can't emphasize this point enough. Before you officially submit your claim for a benefit, you should be 100 percent positive that you've included all the paperwork you need.

You need to be very careful when submitting a claim. The VA makes its decision based on your claim's individual merits. If you submit an application and the VA denies it based on the merits of the evidence, it may be very difficult to reopen the claim in the future. You may have to submit new and material evidence, which can be difficult. Additionally, even if your claim isn't denied right off the bat, your claim may be delayed for months if the VA has to stop processing it to request additional records.

Take full, and I mean *full,* advantage of the VA's duty to assist before you submit your claim. Take another look at the "Using the VA's 'duty to assist'" section earlier in this chapter. This advice alone is worth the price of the book.

You can visit any VA regional office or VA veterans center (see Appendixes B and D), and counselors there are required by law to do everything possible to help you get your supporting evidence in shape. Make sure you take them up on this offer. It's the most important thing you can do to speed up your claim and give it the best possible chance of approval.

When taking advantage of the VA's duty to assist, always try to work with the same office and the same counselor so your representative knows what's being submitted. Being inconsistent can cause problems with your claim.

Playing the Waiting Game: The Big Decision

After you submit your claim, get ready to wait. In many cases, get ready to wait a long, long time. Exactly how long depends on which benefit you're applying for.

For example, the VA averages about 23 days to make decisions on claims concerning Montgomery GI Bill benefits (see Chapter 10). Claims for VA medical benefits (enrolling in the VA healthcare program, as detailed in Chapter 4) are generally processed within 30 days. On the other hand, claims for disability compensation and pensions, which are often the most difficult claims to decide, average 183 days.

The good news is that the VA has a goal to process all claims within 73 days. The bad news is that that goal was established in 2001, and the VA's not even close yet.

So be prepared to wait. Decisions for most claims aren't made at the main headquarters in Washington, D.C. Instead, decisions are made at the VA regional office that serves the area where you live.

An advantage of this setup is that claims can be processed faster, but the system has undergone substantial criticism because it often results in disparities from one state to another. A veteran in California may have a claim approved, while a veteran with the exact same condition and supporting documentation in Wyoming may have his claim denied. However, that's what the appeals process is for, because appeals decisions are made by HQ in Washington (see the later "Deciding to Appeal" section).

Ultimately, the VA regional office sends you a decision, either approving your claim or denying it. You can either accept the decision or appeal it.

Fixing Errors in Your Military Record

What if an error in your military record, such as on your DD Form 214, makes you ineligible for a certain benefit? Perhaps DD Form 214 doesn't include all of your active-duty service or maybe it's missing a critical medal, such as the Purple Heart.

When you're getting ready to leave the military, one of the final out-processing actions you accomplish is to sit down with a military personnel clerk and go over your DD Form 214 in detail. You're supposed to make sure everything is correct before you sign it. However, we all know how that goes. You've got a thousand things on your mind, and you're in the middle of going to about 2 million out-processing appointments. It's easy to miss something, especially if you're not thinking about possible veterans benefits in the future.

Each service has its own Board for Correction of Military Records (BCMR) that handles the correction of records. The Navy establishes the board for sailors and Marines. Board members are high-ranking civilian employees of the service and are assigned to the board by the secretary of the service. Board members are assigned to three-person panels that decide the cases.

Knowing the grounds for requesting a change

To apply for a change of your military record, you must convince the board that the information in your record is in error or that it has resulted in an injustice.

- ✔ *In error* is pretty obvious. It simply means the information in your record isn't correct. For example, you performed 26 months of active duty, but your record shows you performed only 20 months.

- ✔ An example of an *injustice* would be if there were a letter of reprimand or a negative performance report in your record that was written by a military supervisor who clearly was out to get you.

You should submit your request within three years of discovering, or reasonably could have discovered, the error or injustice. The boards review the merits of untimely applications. If the board finds your case to be meritorious, it can waive the timeliness in the interest of justice. You shouldn't assume, however, that a waiver will be granted.

Submitting the proper paperwork

You submit your request by using DD Form 149, Application for Correction of Military Record. This form is available from VA regional offices (see Appendix B) and online at www.dtic.mil/whs/directives/infomgt/forms/eforms/dd0149.pdf. Mail the completed application to the appropriate board address listed on the second page of the form.

You should be very careful when you complete this form. Attach copies of statements or records that are relevant to your case. For example, if your DD Form 214 includes an error concerning your active-duty service time, you'd want to submit copies of your military orders placing you on active duty.

Your own statement is important. Begin with item 9 of DD Form 149 and continue to item 17, if necessary. You may also put your statement on plain paper and attach it to the form. Limit your statement to no more than 25 pages. Explain what happened and why it is an error or injustice in simple, direct terms.

Providing evidence is important!

Normally, the best evidence is statements from people who have direct knowledge of or involvement with the situation. For example, you can submit statements from people in your rating chain if you're contesting a performance report. Another example would be a statement from the person who counseled you if you are alleging improper counseling.

The board will correct your military record only if you can prove that you're the victim of error or injustice. This decision is made solely on the evidence you provide. You can't simply include witnesses' names. The board won't contact them. You need to obtain and provide the statements yourself.

Understanding the advisory opinion

After your application is received, one or more offices within your military service (Judge Advocate General's office, military hospital, personnel center, and so on) will prepare an advisory opinion on your case. The advisory opinion is sent to the board with your case file. If the advisory opinion recommends denial of your request, the board will send it to you for comment.

The advisory opinion is only a recommendation. The board actually makes the decision in your case.

You have 30 days to submit your comments on the advisory opinion. You may request an additional 30 days if you need it. The board usually grants reasonable requests for additional time.

It may be unnecessary for you to comment on the advisory opinion. If you have nothing further to say, don't bother to respond. Failure to comment on an advisory opinion doesn't mean you agree, nor does it prevent a full and fair consideration of your application.

If the board denies your request, there is no appeal, except if you decide to sue the Department of Defense in federal court. However, if you provide newly discovered relevant evidence that you didn't know about when you filed your original application, the board may agree to reconsider your case.

Do You Need a Lawyer or Additional Help?

If you can afford a lawyer, you may as well hire one to help you. A knowledgeable attorney can be very beneficial to your case, especially if your claim is denied and you have to enter the appeals process (see the "Deciding to Appeal" section). Many attorneys out there in lawyer land specialize in VA claims and in submitting requests for discharge upgrades or changes in military records. However, they don't work for free (well, I don't know of any who do), and I don't know very many rich veterans.

If you decide to go the lawyer route, check with your state's bar association and ask for a list of local attorneys who specialize in veterans legal issues. You can usually find your state bar in the white pages of the phone book. Or go to www.romingerlegal.com/natbar.htm on the Web for a listing of all state bar associations.

If you want some help but not as much as an attorney would provide, or you don't want to pay for advice, you can turn to a veterans service organization (VSO). Many VSOs, such as the Veterans of Foreign Wars (VFW), American Legion, and Disabled Veterans of America (DVA), have veterans representatives who are experienced in the confusing world of veterans benefit claims. These representatives can represent you for free. So what's the downside? VSOs receive thousands of requests for representation each year. They're swamped. That means their representation is often limited to looking over your package and giving you advice. Usually, you've still got to do all the running around and getting your paperwork together yourself.

I include a list of VSOs that can provide representation service, as well as their contact information, in Chapter 17.

Many state veterans offices also have representatives who can assist veterans from that state with VA claims and appeals. A list of state veterans offices can be found in Appendix A.

If you decide to go with a VSO or state veterans office, make sure your representative is accredited with the VA General Counsel's Office. These representatives have received special training and have been certified by the VA that they know what they're doing. Such representatives carry a photo identification card issued by the VA regional office, as well as a card signed by the VA general counsel, attesting to their accreditation.

Additionally, counselors at VA regional offices and vet centers (see Appendixes B and D) can be a big help in putting your claim together. See the "Using the VA's 'duty to assist'" section earlier in this chapter.

Deciding to Appeal

An *appeal* is a request for the Board of Veterans Appeals (BVA) to review the VA regional office's decision made on your claim. The BVA is part of the Department of Veterans Affairs and is located in Washington, D.C. You may appeal any decision that you aren't satisfied with.

The vast majority of appeals (more than 90 percent) are made by veterans who are dissatisfied with their VA regional office's decision concerning eligibility for disability compensation, disability ratings, or pension. The two most common reasons for appeal are

✔ The VA denied you benefits for a disability that you believe is service connected (see Chapter 6 for more information about service-connected disabilities).

✔ You believe that your disability is more severe than the VA rated it (Chapter 6 has information about the VA disability rating system).

However, you can appeal for any reason.

Well, not quite any reason. Under the law, decisions concerning the need for medical care or the type of medical treatment needed, such as a physician's decision to prescribe (or not to prescribe) a particular drug or whether to order a specific type of treatment, can't be appealed through the VA appeals process. You need to address such matters to the director of the

VA medical center concerned. However, decisions concerning eligibility to enroll in the VA healthcare program (see Chapter 4) can be appealed.

Getting the appeals process rolling

You start the appeals process by submitting a *Notice of Disagreement,* often called an *NOD,* to the VA regional office that denied your claim. There's no specific form used for an NOD. It's simply a written statement from you to the VA regional office stating in simple, clear terms why you disagree with the decision.

The NOD must be submitted within one year of the date the VA regional office mailed you its original decision denying your claim.

Receiving a thumbs up or thumbs down

After the VA regional office receives your NOD, it will take another look at your case. It's possible that it will agree with your argument in the NOD and approve your claim. If the folks at the regional office disagree, they'll prepare a *Statement of the Case (SOC).*

The SOC is the VA regional office's way of telling you that the board isn't reversing the original decision and why. The SOC will summarize the evidence and applicable laws and regulations, and include a detailed discussion of the reasons for the decision.

The SOC will also explain that to continue with your appeal, you must submit a VA Form 9, Appeal to Board of Veterans' Appeals. This form will be included in the mailing from the regional office with the SOC.

Preparing to send your appeal up the chain

Up to this point, all decisions have been made by the VA regional office that serves your area. If you still disagree with them, it's time to jack it up a notch and take your case to Washington, D.C., or more specifically, the Board of Veterans Appeals (BVA).

At this point in the process, about 90 percent of all veterans decide to seek representation to help them through the appeals process and represent their case (see the "Do You Need a Lawyer or Additional Help?" section). About 85 percent of all veterans select a representative from a veterans service organization (VSO) or state veterans office, probably because they work for free.

If you want someone to represent you on your appeal, you need to submit VA Form 21–22, Appointment of Veterans Service Organization as Claimant's Representative, to authorize a VSO to represent you, or VA Form 21-22a, Appointment of Individual as Claimant's Representative, to authorize an attorney to represent you. Your VA regional office can provide these forms, or you can download them from www.vba.va.gov/pubs/forms/VBA_21-22-ARE.pdf and www.vba.va.gov/pubs/forms/21-22a.pdf, respectively.

You begin your appeal to the BVA by completing VA Form 9, Appeal to Board of Veterans' Appeals. You should have received a copy of this form with the Statement of the Case (SOC; see the "Receiving a thumbs up or thumbs down" section). You can also get a copy of this form at your nearest VA regional center (see Appendix B) or online at www.va.gov/vaforms/va/pdf/VA9.pdf.

When you fill out VA Form 9, you should state the benefit you want, any mistakes you find in the SOC, and whether you want a personal hearing. You send the completed Form 9 to the VA regional office that denied your claim.

You must submit VA Form 9 within 60 days of when the VA regional office mailed the SOC or within one year of when the regional office notified you of the original denial of your claim, whichever date is later. If you fail to meet these deadlines, you may lose your right to appeal.

If you submit new information or evidence with your VA Form 9, the VA regional office will again reconsider your case. It's possible that the new evidence or information will cause it to reverse its decision and grant your claim. If not, it will prepare a *Supplemental Statement of the Case,* or *SSOC.* An SSOC is similar to the Statement of the Case, but it addresses the new information or evidence you submitted. If you aren't satisfied with the SSOC, you have 60 days from the date when the SSOC is mailed to you to submit, in writing, what you disagree with.

At any time during this process, you (or your representative, if you have one) can request a local office hearing. As its name implies, a *local office hearing* is a meeting held at the VA regional office between you and a hearing officer from the local office's staff. To arrange a local office hearing, contact your local VA regional office or your appeal representative as early in the appeals process as possible.

A face-to-face meeting probably won't add weight to your claim, nor will it speed up the claims process, but it gives you the opportunity to ask questions. It's often helpful in determining the strength of your claim and whether you need additional supporting documentation.

Getting on with the appeal

After you (or your representative) get finished passing SOCs, SSOCs, and responses back and forth, everything (your VA Form 9, all the evidence, SOCs, SSOCs, your responses, and a check for $10,000 — no, I'm kidding about that last item!) is gathered together by the VA regional office and placed into your claims folder. All of this paperwork is the basis for your official appeal to the BVA.

When the VA regional office sends your appeal to Washington, it sends you a letter letting you know that you have 90 days from the date of the letter during which you can add more evidence to your file, request a hearing with the VBA, or select (or change) your representative. This is known as the 90-Day Rule.

Each time you submit new information or evidence, the VA regional office will take a fresh look at your case. If it still disagrees, it'll write an SSOC, to which you have 60 days to respond. All of this delays the time your appeal is sent to the BVA. This is why it's very important to submit all relevant information when you first make your claim. See the "Submitting Your VA Claim" section.

When your appeal finally reaches the Washington center, it's placed on the BVA's docket. The *docket* is the record of all appeals awaiting the BVA's review, listed in the order of receipt. When your appeal is placed on the docket, it's assigned the next higher docket number than the one received before it. This is important because the BVA reviews appeals in the order in which they were placed on the docket. The lower the docket number, the sooner the appeal will be reviewed. It's kind of like when you visit the Department of Motor Vehicles and the sign says to take a number.

Your claims folder actually remains at the VA regional office until three to four months before your docket number is expected to come up, after which it is transferred to the board's office in Washington. The VA regional office will notify you in writing when your paperwork is ready to be transferred. Then the BVA will notify you in writing when it receives your file.

Until your file is transferred to the board, your local VA regional office is the best place to get information about your appeal. If your file is at the board, you can call 202-565-5436 to check on its status.

When your docket number finally comes up, your case is assigned to a board member who decides on your appeal. Think of him as a judge. These board members, who are attorneys experienced in veterans law and in reviewing benefit claims, are the only ones who can issue board decisions. Staff attorneys, also trained in veterans law, review the facts of each appeal and assist the board members.

Trying to speed up the waiting game

Get ready for a very, very long wait. There is a huge backlog of appeals on the docket, waiting for their turn to come up. In 2008, the average length of time it took to get an appeal decision after it had been placed on the docket was 1,608 days, or nearly 4½ years. Yikes!

If you believe your case should be decided sooner than others that were filed before yours, you can request to have your case advanced on the docket. To submit a motion to advance on the docket, write directly to the board (not the VA regional office) and explain why your appeal should be moved ahead of other appeals.

Because most appeals involve some type of hardship, you need to show convincing proof of exceptional circumstances before your case can be advanced. Some examples of exceptional circumstances are terminal illness, danger of bankruptcy or foreclosure, or a VA error that caused a significant delay in the docketing of an appeal. To file a motion to advance on the docket, send your request to Board of Veterans Appeals (014), Department of Veterans Affairs, 810 Vermont Ave., NW, Washington, DC 20420.

Don't get your hopes up. Over the years, the BVA has granted fewer than 3 out of every 20 requests for advancement on the docket.

Making your case at a board hearing

In addition to a local office hearing (see the earlier "Preparing to send your appeal up the chain" section), you also have the right to present your case in person to a BVA member. In most areas, you can choose whether you want to have the BVA hearing at the local VA regional office, called a *Travel Board hearing,* or at the BVA office in Washington. Most VA regional offices are also equipped to hold BVA hearings by videoconference. Check with your regional office to see if a videoconference hearing is a possibility in your area.

Experts disagree about whether a personal hearing is advantageous to your claim. On one hand, it gives you the chance to verbally clarify and add to the supporting documentation submitted with your claim, and the transcript of the hearing is reviewed before a claims decision is made. On the other hand, the supporting evidence is the prime factor when making an appeal, not the hearing, and requesting a hearing can add several months to the appeals process.

When deciding whether you want your hearing held at the BVA office in Washington or locally, keep in mind that the VA can't pay for any of your expenses — such as lodging or travel — in connection with a hearing.

VA Form 9 has a section for requesting a BVA hearing, and this is the usual way to request a hearing. However, if you didn't ask for a BVA hearing on VA Form 9, you can still request one by writing directly to the board. This is subject to the 90-Day Rule, as explained in the "Getting on with the appeal" section. Make your request to Board of Veterans Appeals (014), Department of Veterans Affairs, 810 Vermont Ave., NW, Washington, DC 20420.

If you want a BVA hearing, be sure you state whether you want it held at the regional office or at the board's office in Washington, D.C. You can't have a BVA hearing in both places.

When a hearing will be held depends on what type of hearing you request and where you request that it be held.

The scheduling of Travel Board hearings is more complicated because board members must travel from Washington to regional offices to conduct the hearings. Factors that affect when Travel Board hearings can be scheduled include the docket number, the total number of requests for hearings at a particular regional office, how soon the board will be able to review the cases associated with the hearings, and the resources, such as travel funds, available to the board.

Because videoconference hearings don't involve travel by board members, they are less complicated to arrange and can be scheduled more frequently than Travel Board hearings.

Hearings held at the board's offices in Washington, will be scheduled for a time close to when BVA will consider the case — ideally about three months before the case is reviewed.

Bracing yourself for the ultimate decision

When your appeal's docket number is reached, your file is examined by a board member and a staff attorney who check for completeness and review all of your evidence and arguments, as well as the regional office's Statement of the Case (and Supplemental Statement of the Case, if there is one), the transcript of your hearing (if you had one), the statement of your representative (if you have one), and any other information included in the claims folder. The staff attorney, at the board member's direction, may also conduct additional research and prepare recommendations for the board member's review.

The board member then decides whether to approve your appeal, deny your appeal, or remand it. A *remand* is an appeal that is returned to the VA regional office, usually to perform additional work on the case. After performing the additional work, the regional office may issue a new decision. If a claim is still denied, the case is returned to the board for a final decision. Your case keeps its original place on BVA's docket, so it's reviewed soon after it's returned to the board.

If your claim is approved, the board notifies the VA regional office that has jurisdiction over your case, and it will start your benefits automatically. You won't have to reapply to receive them.

If your appeal is denied, the board will send you a *Notice of Appellate Rights* letter that describes additional actions you can take.

 Your decision will be mailed to the home address that the board has on file for you, so it's extremely important that you keep the VA informed of your correct address. If you move or get a new home or work phone number, you should notify the regional office handling your appeal.

When All Else Fails: Appealing the Appeal

If the Board of Veterans Appeals denies your appeal, you're not dead in the water yet. If you still believe that you're entitled to the benefit(s) you claimed, you have three options: Ask the board to reconsider, ask the local VA regional office to reopen your appeal, or appeal the board's decision to the U.S. Court of Appeals for Veterans Claims. I explain each of these options in the following sections.

Motion to reconsider

If you can demonstrate that the board made an obvious error of fact or law in its decision, you can file a written *motion to reconsider* your appeal. If you were represented at the time of the decision, you may want to consult with your representative for advice about whether you should file a motion (and for assistance in preparing one). There's no specific VA form for this action.

If you do file a motion to reconsider, it should be sent directly to the board, not to your local VA regional office. Send the motion to Board of Veterans Appeals (014), Department of Veterans Affairs, 810 Vermont Ave., NW, Washington, DC 20420.

You should not submit a motion to reconsider simply because you disagree with the BVA's decision. You need to show that the board made a mistake in fact or law and that the board's decision would have been different if the mistake had not been made.

Reopening an appeal

You can request that your VA regional office reopen your appeal, but only if you can submit *new and material evidence.* Because the VA is the king, and the king makes the rules, the VA decides whether your evidence is new and material. To be considered new and material, the evidence you submit must be information related to your case that wasn't included in the claims folder when your case was decided.

For example, if your appeal was denied because the VA considers your discharge characterization to be under dishonorable conditions (see Chapter 2), and you then persuade the Discharge Review Board to change your discharge characterization or discharge reason, this would be an example of new and material evidence.

If the VA regional office agrees to reopen your case, this starts the whole appeals process all over again.

U.S. Court of Appeals for Veterans Claims

Taking your appeal to the U.S. Court of Appeals for Veterans Claims is your final option. The court is an independent federal court that's not part of the Department of Veterans Affairs. You may appeal to the court only if the BVA has denied some or all of your benefits. You may not appeal a BVA decision to remand your claim back to the VA regional office.

Normally, to appeal a BVA decision, you must file the Notice of Appeal with the court within 120 days from the date the board's decision is mailed.

If you filed a motion to reconsider with the BVA (see the "Motion to reconsider" section) within the 120-day time frame and that motion was denied, you have an additional 120 days to file the Notice of Appeal with the court. This 120-day period begins on the date the BVA mails you a letter notifying you that it has denied your motion to reconsider.

Filing your court appeal

You must file your appeal by mail or by fax. The court doesn't accept electronic submissions. Send your Notice of Appeal, including your name, address, phone number, and the date of the BVA decision, to Clerk of the Court, U.S. Court of Appeals for Veterans Claims, 625 Indiana Ave., NW, Washington, DC 20004, or fax it to 202-501-5848.

To be or not to be a lawyer: That is the question

Although you don't have to have a lawyer to file an appeal, remember that this is a full-blown federal court, and it requires certain forms and has certain legal ways of doing things, just like any other court. I can guarantee that the VA is going to have its lawyer there to argue its side of the case. If you decide to represent yourself, you'll be at a distinct disadvantage.

There is an old lawyers' saying that a man who represents himself has a fool for a client.

If you do decide to represent yourself, at the very least, take a thorough look at the court's Web site at www.vetapp.uscourts.gov.

Finding representation

The Court of Appeals for Veterans Claims isn't a criminal court, so the court can't appoint an attorney to represent you. However, the clerk of the court maintains a list of attorneys who have been admitted to practice before the court and have expressed an interest in representing veterans who want to appeal denied claims. Although most of these lawyers charge a fee to represent clients, some of them will collect a fee only if you win your case or will accept the case without charging a fee. To view this list of attorneys, visit www.vetapp.uscourts.gov/practitioners.

In addition to the court's list of attorneys, Congress, recognizing the difficulties veterans and their dependents face in proceeding in a court case without a lawyer, has funded the Veterans Consortium Pro Bono Program. This program is a private, nonprofit organization that helps find lawyers who will represent veterans before the court free of charge. You can contact the organization through its Web site at www.vetsprobono.org or by calling 888-838-7727.

Part II
A Healthy Look at Medical Care and Compensation Programs

The 5th Wave   By Rich Tennant

"You put in your height, weight, and marital status here. At the end of your workout, it shows your heart rate, blood pressure, and the type of insurance you should be carrying."

In this part . . .

1 know of very few people who don't worry about their healthcare needs and how they're going to pay for medical care in the future. I also know of very few people who don't care how much money they make each month. The two topics seem to go hand in hand. You need money (or a very good healthcare plan) to pay for your medical care, and you need to be in good health to earn the money to pay for your medical needs.

Many veterans are eligible for free or reduced-cost healthcare from the government for life. Have you checked into the cost of a doctor's visit lately? These healthcare plans are valuable benefits that aren't available to just anyone.

Additionally, depending on your situation, you may be eligible to receive monthly payments from good old Uncle Sam. Through programs such as disability compensation, veterans pensions, and military retirement, the U.S. government puts millions of bucks into veterans' pockets every single month. The chapters in this part tell you whether you qualify for these benefits. It also gives you information on the unpleasant-but-necessary topics of coverage for your survivors and burial and memorial benefits.

Chapter 4

Veterans Affairs Healthcare

- -

- -

*T*he Department of Veterans Affairs (VA) healthcare system has gotten a bad rap through the years. For several years after Vietnam, Americans didn't think very much of the military or veterans. This negative attitude was reflected in the amount of money that Congress made available to provide healthcare benefits for those who had served in the military. In short, the VA medical system was in an underfunded, understaffed shambles.

Oh, what a difference three decades (and a few extra billion bucks) make. Today, the VA operates one of the largest, most respected healthcare systems in the country. It treats about 5.3 million patients per year. About two-thirds of physicians practicing in the U.S. received part or all of their medical training at VA medical centers. The VA trained more than 90,000 healthcare professionals in 2007 alone. The medical system is, by far, the largest benefit program the VA administers. Eighty-eight percent of VA employees work at VA medical centers.

Many veterans mistakenly believe that they can receive medical care from the VA only if they suffer from a medical condition that was caused by military service. That's incorrect. All veterans who meet the eligibility criteria I outline in this chapter are eligible for VA medical care. Have I gotten your attention yet? Now, aren't you glad you made the wise decision to buy this book?

Medical Benefits Package: The Backbone of the System

The VA medical system has changed over the years. It used to be reactive. In other words, the philosophy was, "Wait until it breaks, and then see if you can fix it."

In October 1996, Congress passed the Veterans' Health Care Eligibility Reform Act of 1996. This legislation paved the way for the creation of a *Medical Benefits Package,* a standard enhanced health benefits plan available to all veterans enrolled in it. The new philosophy is, "Let's see if we can keep it from breaking."

Once enrolled, veterans receive their healthcare at 155 VA medical centers (hospitals) and 881 outpatient clinics located throughout the United States and its territories. Appendix B has a complete list of VA medical centers.

VA medical centers and their associated outpatient clinics employ more than 16,000 physicians and 62,000 nurses, who are willing and able to meet your healthcare needs.

When you first enroll (see the "Making your case for VA medical care" section), you're assigned to the VA medical center closest to where you live. The fine folks who work there become your primary provider, and you receive most of your medical care from that VA medical facility or one of its outpatient clinics. That doesn't mean you get all your care there. If your chosen facility can't provide the care you need in a reasonable period of time, it can refer you to another facility that can meet your needs.

You can also use your VA healthcare benefits when you travel. That's right, they're portable! Enrolled veterans who are traveling or who spend time away from their primary treatment facility may obtain care at any VA healthcare facility across the country without having to reapply (see the "VA Medical Care Eligibility and Enrollment" section).

What's covered

Like other standard healthcare plans, the Medical Benefits Package emphasizes preventive and primary care, offering a full range of outpatient and inpatient services. I cover some of these in more detail in later sections, but for now here's the main list:

  ✔ Outpatient and inpatient medical, surgical, and mental healthcare, including care for substance abuse.

✔ Prescription drugs, including over-the-counter drugs and medical and surgical supplies, when prescribed by a VA physician.

✔ Immunizations.

✔ Physical examinations, healthcare assessments, and screening tests.

✔ Health education programs.

✔ Emergency care in VA facilities.

✔ Dental care for eligible veterans.

✔ Bereavement counseling.

✔ Comprehensive rehabilitative services other than the vocational services explained in Chapter 11.

✔ Consultation, professional counseling, training, and mental health services for the veteran's immediate family members or legal guardian.

✔ Durable medical equipment and prosthetic and orthotic devices. This includes eyeglasses and hearing aids for some veterans.

✔ Reconstructive (plastic) surgery required as a result of a disease or trauma, but not including cosmetic surgery that's not medically necessary.

✔ Respite, hospice, and palliative care.

✔ Pregnancy and delivery service, to the extent authorized by law. This means the VA can provide services to the pregnant veteran, up to and including delivery, but can't provide free services for the child. The veteran must reimburse the VA for any services associated with the child after birth.

What's not covered

The preceding list of covered services probably seems to include everything but the kitchen sink, right? It really doesn't. Under current laws, the VA isn't allowed to provide the following services:

✔ Abortions and abortion counseling

✔ Cosmetic surgery except where determined by the VA to be medically necessary for reconstructive or psychiatric care

✔ Drugs, biologicals, and medical devices not approved by the FDA unless the treating medical facility is conducting formal clinical trials

✔ Gender alteration

✔ Health club or spa membership

✔ In vitro fertilization

✔ Services not ordered and provided by licensed or accredited professionals

✔ Special private-duty nursing

✔ Hospital and outpatient care for a veteran who is a patient or inmate in an institution of another government agency if that agency is required to provide care or services

✔ Emergency care in non-VA facilities, except as explained in the section "Emergency care in non-VA facilities" later in this chapter

Military sexual trauma counseling

The VA provides counseling and treatment to help male and female veterans overcome psychological trauma resulting from sexual trauma while serving on active duty. This counseling is usually conducted at VA vet centers. In addition to counseling, related services are available at VA medical facilities. You can find listings of VA medical facilities and vet centers in Appendix C and Appendix D, respectively.

You don't have to enroll in the VA healthcare program to receive these services. Veterans can receive care at no charge for conditions related to military sexual trauma.

Bereavement counseling

VA healthcare facilities offer bereavement counseling to veterans who are enrolled in the VA healthcare program. This counseling is also available to their family members.

Bereavement counseling is also provided to parents, spouses, and children of armed forces personnel who died in the service of their country. Also eligible are family members of Reservists and National Guardsmen who die while on duty. Counseling is provided at VA vet centers located throughout the United States. Check out Appendix D to find the nearest vet center location.

Assistance for blind veterans

In addition to other healthcare benefits listed in this chapter, blind veterans may be eligible for additional services or for admission to a VA blind rehabilitation center or clinic. Services are available at all VA medical facilities (see Appendix C). Aids and services for blind veterans include:

✔ A total health and benefits review by a VA visual impairment services team

✔ Adjustment-to-blindness training

✔ Home improvements and structural alterations to homes

✔ Specially adapted housing and adaptations

✔ Low-vision aids and training in their use

✔ Electronic and mechanical aids for the blind, including adaptive computers and computer-assisted devices such as reading machines and electronic travel aids

✔ Guide dogs, including the expense of training the veteran to use the dog and the cost of the dog's medical care

✔ Talking books, tapes, and Braille literature

Prosthetics and adaptive automobiles

Enrolled veterans receiving VA care for any condition may receive medically necessary VA prosthetic appliances, equipment, and devices, such as artificial limbs, orthopedic braces and shoes, wheelchairs, crutches and canes, and other durable medical equipment and supplies. If you need the prosthetic items for a service-connected disability or you have been rated as being 50 percent disabled by the VA (as explained in Chapter 6), you may receive prosthetic items from the VA, even if you're not enrolled in the healthcare program.

You may qualify for adaptive automobile assistance from the VA if you have any of the following:

✔ A service-connected loss or permanent loss of use of one or both hands or feet

✔ A permanent impairment of vision of both eyes to a certain degree

✔ Entitlement to VA disability compensation (see Chapter 6) for ankylosis (immobility) of one or both knees or one or both hips

The VA provides a one-time payment of not more than $11,000 toward the purchase of an automobile or other vehicle. The VA also pays for adaptive equipment and for repair, replacement, or reinstallation required because of your disability.

Taking care of your smile: VA dental care

VA dental care may or may not be something you want to smile about, depending on your situation. It's not available to all veterans enrolled in the VA healthcare system. To receive partial or full dental care from the VA, you must meet one of the conditions shown in Table 4-1.

Table 4-1	Eligibility for VA Dental Care
If You	*You Are Eligible For*
Have a service-connected dental condition or disability that the VA has rated as 10% or more (see Chapter 6)	Any needed dental care
Are a former prisoner of war	Any needed dental care
Have service-connected disabilities rated 100% disabling or the VA determines you're unemployable due to service-connected conditions (see Chapter 6)	Any needed dental care
Are participating in a VA vocational rehabilitation program (see Chapter 11)	Dental care needed to complete the program
Served on active duty for 90 days or more after August 2, 1990, and you have a dental condition or disability that existed at the time of discharge from the military	One-time dental care if you apply for dental care within 180 days of separation from active duty and your certificate of discharge doesn't indicate that all appropriate dental treatment was rendered before discharge
Have a service-connected but noncompensable dental condition or disability resulting from combat wounds or service trauma	Needed care for the service-connected condition(s)
Have a dental condition that the VA determines to be currently aggravating a service-connected medical condition	Dental care to resolve the problem
Are receiving outpatient care or are scheduled for inpatient care and require dental care for a condition complicating a medical condition currently under treatment	Dental care to resolve the problem
A veteran enrolled in a VA homeless program (see Chapter 11) for 60 consecutive days or more	Medically necessary outpatient dental services

All the better to see and hear you with: Eyes and ears

Although you can get vision and hearing exams while enrolled in the VA healthcare program, you can't get free eyeglasses or hearing aids for normal vision and hearing loss unless you

- ✔ Receive an increased pension for regular aid and attendance or being permanently housebound, as explained in Chapter 6
- ✔ Receive disability compensation for a service-connected disability (see Chapter 6)
- ✔ Are a former prisoner of war
- ✔ Received a Purple Heart medal

Getting your meds from VA pharmacies

The VA will provide you with medications that are prescribed by VA providers in conjunction with VA medical care. Medications are prescribed from an approved list of medications called a *formulary*. When your VA physician writes a prescription, you get it filled at the pharmacy located within the VA medical facility. Appendix C has a listing of such facilities.

Getting your fill of refills

The VA doesn't provide routine refills at its pharmacy windows unless there are special circumstances. You can get refills of your VA-prescribed medications in two ways:

- ✔ **Through the routine refill program:** You can request medication refills by mailing the refill notice provided to you at the time of your original fill. Your order will be processed through the VA's pharmacy mail-out program. To ensure you receive your medication promptly, you'll want to order refills at least 20 days before you run out of medication.

  Some VA pharmacies have toll-free automated telephone refill systems. Check with the VA pharmacy that filled your original prescription to see if it has this capability.

- ✔ **Online through the VA's "MyHealtheVet" Web site:** This is probably the easiest way to manage your prescription refills. The prescription service on the site is designed exclusively for VA patients to manage medications prescribed by VA doctors. To access Prescription Refill, you need to be a registered user of My HealtheVet. The service is available at www.myhealth.va.gov.

What about filling non-VA prescriptions?

The VA won't fill or rewrite prescriptions prescribed by your private physician. If you see a non-VA provider and want to have prescriptions filled by the VA, you must meet all the following conditions:

- ✔ You must be enrolled in VA healthcare. See the "Making your case for VA medical care" section.
- ✔ You need to have a primary-care provider assigned by the VA.
- ✔ You must provide your VA healthcare provider with your medical records from your non-VA provider.
- ✔ Your VA healthcare provider has to agree with the medication prescribed by your non-VA provider.

Your VA healthcare provider is under no obligation to prescribe a medication recommended by a non-VA provider.

Emergency care in non-VA facilities

Certain conditions must be met in order for the VA to pay for emergency care you may receive in non-VA facilities. You're eligible for emergency care in a non-VA medical facility if the care is provided in connection with a disability or medical condition that the VA has determined to be connected with your service in the military, according to the procedures explained in Chapter 6.

To reimburse for such care, the VA must determine that VA healthcare facilities weren't readily available; that a delay in medical attention would have endangered your life or health; and that you're personally liable for the cost of the services.

For example, if you have a service-connected injury to your leg and a car hits you and aggravates the injury, the VA wouldn't pay for the care if the driver of the car was liable for your injury. On the other hand, if you slipped and fell in the bathtub and aggravated the injury, the VA would pay, assuming you had no other healthcare plan that would pay.

Congress has also given the VA authority to pay for emergency care in non-VA facilities for veterans enrolled in the VA healthcare system under certain circumstances. This benefit pays for emergency care rendered for non-service-connected conditions for enrolled veterans who have no other source of payment for the care. To qualify you must meet *all* the following criteria:

- ✔ You received emergency care in a non-VA medical facility, such as a hospital emergency room.
- ✔ You're enrolled in the VA healthcare system. See the "Making your case for VA medical care" section.

✔ You have been provided care by a VA healthcare provider within the last 24 months.

✔ You're financially liable to the provider of the emergency treatment for that treatment.

✔ You have no other form of healthcare insurance, including Medicare, Medicaid, state programs, or Tricare (which is explained in Chapter 5).

✔ You have no other contractual or legal recourse against a third party that will pay all or part of the bill.

✔ VA or other federal facilities (such as military hospitals) weren't readily available at time of the emergency.

✔ The medical condition required immediate care. If delaying treatment in order to use a VA facility would have been hazardous to your life or health, the VA will pay for emergency room care in a non-VA facility. The VA isn't going to pay for your treatment if you go to the emergency room for a hangnail.

You shouldn't cancel any current healthcare insurance just to be eligible for non-VA emergency treatment. Remember that your spouse and children don't qualify for the VA healthcare program. If you cancel your current insurance, your family may not retain health insurance coverage. If you're covered by Medicare Part B and you decide to cancel it, it can't be reinstated until January of the next year.

If you are hospitalized after emergency care, the VA will be in regular contact with your physician at the private hospital. As soon as your condition stabilizes, the VA will arrange to move you to a VA or VA-designated facility.

The VA will pay for your emergency care services only until your condition is stabilized. If you voluntarily stay beyond that point, you will assume responsibility for the payment of costs associated with treatment.

VA Medical Care Eligibility and Enrollment

Like most veterans benefits, in order to be eligible for VA medical care, you must first have a military discharge that the VA determines is other than dishonorable. (I explain how the VA makes this determination in Chapter 2.) If you're good to go on your discharge characterization, you must meet the minimum military service requirements. After you've established your eligibility, you need to know what priority group you fit into, how and where to enroll, and when you can begin to use the VA's healthcare service. These topics are covered in the upcoming sections.

Minimum service requirements

If you have even one day of active-duty service before September 8, 1980, as an enlisted member, or before October 17, 1981, as an officer, you're eligible for benefits.

Otherwise, you must have 24 months of continuous active-duty military service to be eligible for VA medical benefits, unless you meet one of the following exceptions:

- ✔ You were a Reservist or member of the National Guard who was called to federal active duty, and you completed the entire term for which you were called.
- ✔ You were discharged from active duty for reasons of a hardship.
- ✔ You were discharged with an *early out* (that is, during a time when the military was undergoing a downsizing).
- ✔ You were discharged or released from active duty for a disability that began in the service or got worse because of the service.
- ✔ You have been determined by the VA to have a service-connected disability, entitling you to compensation as I explain in Chapter 6.
- ✔ You were discharged for a reason other than disability, but you had a medical condition at the time that was disabling and, in the opinion of a doctor, would have justified a discharge for disability. In this case, the disability must have been documented in your military medical records. (See Chapter 2 for more information about military medical records.)

You also don't have to meet the minimum service requirements if you are only seeking medical benefits for or in connection with

- ✔ A service-connected condition or disability (see Chapter 6)
- ✔ Treatment and/or counseling of sexual trauma that occurred while on active military service (see the earlier section in this chapter)
- ✔ Treatment of conditions related to ionizing radiation
- ✔ Head or neck cancer related to nose or throat radium treatment while in the military

Make sure you join the right group!

Just because you're eligible for VA healthcare doesn't necessarily mean you're going to get it. The number of veterans who can be enrolled in the healthcare program is determined by the amount of money Congress gives the VA each year. Because Congress never gives the VA as much money as it needs, the VA has established priority groups to make sure that certain groups of veterans can be enrolled before others. There are eight categories, with Group 1 as the highest priority for enrollment in the VA healthcare system.

If you're eligible for more than one category, the VA places you in the highest category for which you are eligible.

Some of the groups contain requirements that are a bit complicated, but most are pretty straightforward. Here's an overview of each group:

- **Group 1, 50 percent disabled:** Veterans whom the VA has rated as 50 percent or more disabled with a service-connected disability, as described in Chapter 6, receive this highest category rating. Also included are veterans whom the VA has determined to be unemployable, as explained in Chapters 6 and 11.

- **Group 2, 30 percent disabled:** Veterans with VA-rated service-connected disabilities of 30 or 40 percent disabling (see Chapter 6) are placed in Group 2.

- **Group 3, 10 percent disabled:** Veterans whom the VA has determined have a 10 or 20 percent service-connected disability, as described in Chapter 6, are placed into this category. Also included in this category are

    - Veterans who are former prisoners of war (POWs)

    - Veterans awarded a Purple Heart

    - Veterans whose discharge was for a disability that happened or was aggravated in the line of duty

    - Veterans who became disabled because of treatment or vocational rehabilitation from a VA facility

- **Group 4, Veterans receiving aid:** Veterans who receive a VA pension, along with additional monthly compensation from the VA because they require in-home aid and assistance or are housebound, make up the majority of Group 4 participants. (I explain these programs in Chapter 6.)

    Also included in this category are veterans whom the VA considers to be catastrophically disabled, even if the disability is not service-connected.

    Catastrophically disabled means a severe, permanent disability that requires personal or mechanical assistance to leave the bed or house, or requires constant supervision to avoid harm.

- **Group 5, Veterans receiving pensions:** This group includes veterans who receive a VA pension or those eligible to receive a VA pension, as explained in Chapter 6.

Also included are veterans who have income and assets below the VA's national income limit, as detailed in the "Addressing Financial Concerns" section.

Veterans who are eligible for state Medicaid programs are also eligible for Group 5.

✔ **Group 6, Special periods of service:** This category is for World War I veterans and veterans who served in a combat zone after November 11, 1998, as follows:

- Veterans discharged from active duty on or after January 28, 2003, who were enrolled in the VA healthcare system as of January 28, 2008.

- Veterans who apply for enrollment after January 28, 2008. Such veterans may enroll and be placed automatically in Group 6 for five years post-discharge.

- Veterans discharged from active duty before January 28, 2003, who apply for enrollment after January 28, 2008, until January 27, 2011.

To be automatically qualified for Group 6 placement for service after November 11, 1998, you must have served at least one day in a designated combat zone.

Veterans who have a service-connected medical condition or disability that is rated as zero percent disabling by the VA, as explained in Chapter 6, are also eligible for this category.

Veterans who were exposed to ionizing radiation as a result of testing, development, or employment of the atom bomb in World War II are also qualified for Group 6. Atomic veterans may have been exposed to ionizing radiation in a variety of ways at various locations. Veterans exposed at a nuclear device testing site (the Pacific Islands, Bikini, New Mexico, Nevada, and so on) or during the occupation of Hiroshima and Nagasaki, Japan, are included.

Group 6 also includes Vietnam veterans who were exposed to Agent Orange while serving in Vietnam. To be eligible, you must have served on active duty in Vietnam between January 9, 1962, and May 7, 1975, and suffer from one of the following conditions that the National Academy of Sciences found evidence of a possible association with herbicide exposure:

- Acute and subacute peripheral neuropathy

- Adult-onset (Type 2) diabetes

- Chloracne

- Chronic lymphocytic leukemia (CLL)

- Hodgkin's disease

- Multiple myeloma

- Non-Hodgkin's lymphoma

- Porphyria cutanea tarda

- Primary amyloidosis

- Prostate cancer

- Respiratory cancers (cancer of the lung, bronchus, larynx, or trachea)

- Soft-tissue sarcoma (other than osteosarcoma, chondrosarcoma, Kaposi's sarcoma, or mesothelioma)

Gulf War veterans, including those who served in Operations Desert Shield, Desert Storm, and Iraqi Freedom, who suffer from any of the several medical conditions grouped together into what is called "Gulf War Illness," are placed in Group 6.

For more information than you'll ever want to know concerning Gulf War Illness, visit the VA's Web site at www1.va.gov/gulfwar.

Also included in Group 6 are veterans who were participants in Project 112/SHAD (you know who you are).

For those of you who don't know about Project 112/SHAD, I can tell you, but if you read further, I'll have to kill you. I'm just kidding. This project was declassified years ago. Project SHAD, an acronym for *Shipboard Hazard and Defense,* was part of a larger effort called Project 112, which was conducted during the 1960s. Project SHAD consisted of tests designed to identify U.S. warships' vulnerabilities to attacks with chemical or biological warfare agents and to develop procedures to respond to such attacks while maintaining a war-fighting capability. Participants on Navy ships were exposed to various chemical and biological "simulates." Unfortunately, it was later found that many of these "simulates" weren't as medically harmless as was thought at the time.

✔ **Group 7, Veterans with low incomes:** This category is for veterans who don't qualify for Groups 1 through 6 and have an annual income or net worth above the VA's national income limit, but their income is below the Department of Housing and Urban Development's (HUD) income threshold for the area in which they live. More details about the VA's national income limits and the geographical income threshold are in the "Addressing Financial Concerns" section.

Veterans with income limits below both the national income limits and HUD's geographic income threshold are placed in Group 5.

Veterans placed in Group 7 must agree to pay co-pays, as explained in the "Addressing Financial Concerns" section.

✔ **Group 8, All others:** This includes veterans who don't fit into one of the first seven categories. It mostly includes veterans who have an annual income or net worth above both the VA's national income limit and HUD's geographic income threshold. See the "Addressing Financial

Concerns" section for more information about these two income measurements.

As with Group 7, veterans in Group 8 must agree to pay for a portion of their medical care, as described in the "Addressing Financial Concerns" section.

Effective January 16, 2003, the VA no longer accepts new enrollments in Group 8. Veterans who enrolled in the VA healthcare system before this date, and remain enrolled, are still eligible for this category. For example, if you were enrolled in Group 7, but your income level increases beyond the limits required for that category, you can still be moved to Category 8. This policy only affects new enrollments.

Making your case for VA medical care

You can apply for VA healthcare by completing VA Form 10-10EZ, Application for Health Benefits. You can obtain this form from any of the VA medical centers listed in Appendix C. You can also request that a copy of this form be mailed to you by calling the VA's Health Benefits Service Center toll free at 877-222-VETS (877-222-8387) Monday through Friday between 7 a.m. and 8 p.m. (eastern time). The VA Form 10-10EZ is also available for download at https://www.1010ez.med.va.gov/sec/vha/1010ez/Form/vha-10-10ez.pdf.

Mail the completed form to the VA medical center of your choice.

You can also apply in person at the VA medical center of your choice. This may be a good idea because VA staff members can assist you in completing the form.

If you're not already enrolled in the VA system (that is, you've not applied for other VA benefits), you should also include proof of your military service and discharge characterization. Chapter 2 has information about these important documents.

The VA will notify you by mail when you're enrolled and inform you which priority group you've been placed in (see the "Make sure you join the right group!" section).

Not everyone is required to enroll

Most veterans must enroll in the VA healthcare program to receive medical benefits. However, every rule has its exceptions, as I sometimes tell the police officer who stops me for speeding. You don't have to be enrolled if you

> ✔ Have been determined by the VA to be 50 percent or more disabled from
> service-connected conditions (see Chapter 6).
>
> ✔ Are seeking care for a VA-rated, service-connected disability only.
>
> ✔ Were discharged less than one year ago for a disability that the military
> determined was a result of or aggravated by your service, but that the
> VA has not yet rated (see Chapter 6).

If any of these situations applies to you, you can contact any VA medical
center (see Appendix C) and make an appointment for medical care, even if
you're not enrolled in the VA healthcare program.

Making your first appointment

You don't have to wait until your enrollment is approved to make your first
appointment for medical care. If you're applying in person, you can make an
appointment when you apply. If you're not applying in person, the application
form has an area where you can request that an appointment be scheduled.

Not all veterans are created equal. When scheduling appointments, the VA
uses a priority system. Those with service-connected disabilities of 50 percent or more and those seeking care for a service-connected medical condition get first crack. The VA guarantees to make them an appointment within
30 days (although it's usually much sooner). All other veterans are scheduled
for a primary-care appointment as soon as one becomes available.

Seeking Extended Care

Extended care is care outside of the traditional hospital environment. The VA
extended care program includes such services as nursing homes, domicili-
aries, and other programs.

Depending on your financial situation, VA extended care may cost you. For
more information about possible co-pays, see the "Addressing Financial
Concerns" section.

The VA's nursing home programs include

> ✔ **Community living centers:** These centers are designed for veterans with
> chronic stable conditions including dementia, those requiring rehabilita-
> tion or short-term specialized services such as respite or intravenous
> therapy, or those who need comfort and care at the end of life. The

centers' primary purpose is to restore residents to maximum function, prevent further decline, maximize independence, or provide comfort when dying. Generally, they are designed to provide short-term, restorative, and rehabilitative care up to 100 days.

✔ **Contract community nursing homes:** Intended for longer-term care than community living centers, community nursing homes are commercial operations that are under contract to a VA medical center to provide nursing home services to enrolled veterans who reside in the community. They provide compassionate care and an entire range of medical services to veterans who can no longer care for themselves.

✔ **State veterans homes:** A state home is owned and operated by a state. The home may provide nursing home care, domiciliary care, and/or adult day care. The VA pays a percentage of the cost of construction or renovation and/or per diem costs to the state. In addition, the VA checks up on state homes through annual inspections, audits, and reconciliation of records to make sure the state veterans homes are meeting VA standards for quality of care.

To receive extended care under the VA nursing home program, you must be

✔ A veteran who has a service-connected disability rating of 70 percent or more. See Chapter 6 for information about service-connection and disability ratings.

✔ A veteran who has a 60 percent service-connected disability rating and is unemployable, or has an official rating of "permanent and totally disabled." Again, Chapter 6 has more details.

✔ A veteran with a combined disability rating of 70 percent or more. Chapter 6 includes a table that shows how the VA computes combined disability ratings.

✔ A veteran whose service-connected disability is clinically determined to require nursing home care.

✔ A veteran with a service-connected or non-service-connected disability with income and assets below the VA's national income limits and HUD's geographical income threshold, explained in the "Addressing Financial Concerns" section.

✔ If space and resources are available, other veterans on a case-by-case basis with priority given to veterans with service-connected disabilities and those who need care for rehabilitation, respite, hospice, geriatric evaluation and management, or spinal cord injury.

Domiciliary care is a residential rehabilitation program that provides short-term rehabilitation and long-term health maintenance to veterans who require minimal medical care while they recover from medical, psychiatric, or psychosocial problems. Most domiciliary patients return to the community after a period of rehabilitation. An example would be a residential drug or alcohol treatment program.

Other services under the VA's extended care program include

- **Hospice/palliative care,** which provides comfort and support in the advanced stages of a terminal disease.

- **Respite care,** which temporarily relieves the spouse or other caregiver from the burden of caring for a chronically ill or disabled veteran at home.

- **Geriatric evaluation and management (GEM),** which evaluates and manages older veterans with multiple medical, functional, or psychological problems and those with particular geriatric problems. Veterans enrolled in this program receive assessment and treatment from an interdisciplinary team of VA health professionals.

- **Community residential care,** which provides room, board, limited personal care, and supervision to veterans who don't require hospital or nursing home care but can't live independently because of medical or psychiatric conditions, and who have no family to provide care.

- **Home healthcare,** which provides long-term primary medical care to chronically ill veterans in their own homes under the coordinated care of an interdisciplinary treatment team.

- **Adult day care,** which provides health maintenance and rehabilitative services to veterans in a group setting during daytime hours.

- **Homemaker/home health aide services,** which provides health-related services for veterans needing nursing home care. These services are provided by public and private agencies under a case management system provided by VA medical staff.

Addressing Financial Concerns

I know you're probably concerned about your finances. I know I always am. You're probably wondering how much all these health goodies will cost? That depends on several factors. In some cases, there may be no cost at all. In other cases, you may have to share a portion of the costs for your VA healthcare. In still other cases, the VA may even pay you to come see them. When's the last time you were in a healthcare plan that paid you to go see the doctor?

Travel reimbursement

In some cases, the VA pays you to travel to the VA medical facility to receive care. You're eligible for travel reimbursement of 28.5 cents per mile if you meet one of the following conditions:

- ✔ You have a service-connected disability rating of 30 percent or more, as detailed in Chapter 6.

- ✔ You're traveling for treatment of a service-related condition.

- ✔ You receive a VA pension, described in Chapter 6.

- ✔ Your income doesn't exceed the maximum annual VA pension rate (see Chapter 6).

- ✔ You're traveling for a scheduled examination to determine your eligibility for VA disability compensation or pension (Chapter 6).

You are eligible to receive reimbursement for special transportation (ambulance, wheelchair van, and so on) if you meet one of the first four criteria listed here and the travel is preauthorized by the VA (preauthorization isn't necessary for emergencies if a delay would be hazardous to your life or health).

If you are traveling for medical care under one of the first two conditions, your travel is subject to a deductible of $7.77 per one-way trip ($15.54 for a round trip). However, the maximum deductible you'd have to pay in one month is $46.62. After that amount is reached, the rest of your trips during that month aren't subject to the deductible.

 If, through no fault of your own, you must return to the VA medical facility, to repeat a lab test, X-ray, or other exam to obtain VA disability compensation or VA pension (see Chapter 6), the VA will pay you 17 cents per mile in travel reimbursement. This payment isn't subject to the travel deductible.

Co-pays for medical care

If you're in priority Groups 1 through 5 (see the "Make sure you join the right group!" section), you're not required to share in the costs of your inpatient or outpatient medical care obtained through the VA.

If you've been placed in Group 6, you don't have to pay any cost-share for VA medical treatment you receive for a service-connected medical condition or disability. However, if you receive medical care from the VA for conditions that aren't connected to your military service, you're required to pay the full co-pay amounts shown in Table 4-2.

Table 4-2	Basic Co-Pays for VA Medical Care
Length of Care	*Co-Pay*
First 90 days of inpatient care during any 365-day period	$1,024
Additional 90 days of inpatient care	$512
Inpatient per diem rate	$10 per day
Co-pay for outpatient services (care provided by a primary physician)	$15 per visit

Veterans in Group 7 must pay 80 percent of the co-pay rates listed in Table 4-2 for inpatient care and the full rate for outpatient care. Those in Group 8 pay the full co-pay.

For specialty care, which includes services provided by a clinical specialist such as a surgeon, radiologist, audiologist, optometrist, and cardiologist, as well as specialty tests such as magnetic resonance imagery (MRI), computerized axial tomography (CAT) scan, and nuclear medicine studies, the co-pay is $50 per visit.

Co-pays don't apply to publicly announced VA health fairs or outpatient visits solely for preventive screening, health education classes, smoking secession programs, and/or immunizations. Laboratory, flat film radiology, and electrocardiograms are also exempt from co-pays.

Co-pays for extended care

If you're enrolled in Groups 1 through 4 (see the "Make sure you join the right group!" section), you don't have to pay anything to receive extended care (see the "Seeking Extended Care" section).

Those in Group 5 must pay a co-pay, unless they receive a VA pension or have assets and income levels that would qualify them for a VA pension (see Chapter 6). Veterans placed in Group 6 must pay the co-pay, unless they are receiving extended care for a service-connected disability or condition that resulted in their placement in Group 6. If you've been placed in Group 7 or 8, you must pay the applicable co-pay for extended care.

Unlike co-pays for medical treatment and prescriptions, there are no set fees for extended care co-pays. Instead, the VA determines your co-pay (up to the maximum amount allowed) based on your particular income level and assets.

The VA makes this determination based on financial information you provide on VA Form 10-10EC, Application for Extended Care Services. This form is available at any VA medical facility (see Appendix C) or online at www.va.gov/vaforms/medical/pdf/vha-10-10EC-fill.pdf.

The maximum co-pay for inpatient extended care facilities, which includes nursing homes, respite centers, geriatric evaluation centers, community residential care, home healthcare, and homemaker/home health aid services, is $97 per day. Outpatient extended care can include geriatric evaluation, respite, adult day care, and hospice/palliative services. The maximum co-pay for these services is $15 per day. The maximum amount you can be required to pay for domiciliary care is $5 per day.

Co-pays for extended care services start on the 22nd day of care. The first 21 days are free.

Co-pay for VA medications

You may also be required to pay a share of the costs for prescription medications and refills you receive from the VA.

Those in Group 1 or 4 aren't required to pay a co-pay for their VA medications. (See the section, "Make sure you join the right group!" earlier in this chapter.) If you're in Group 2, 3, or 5, you don't have to share in the costs of your medication if you are an ex-prisoner of war, require medication for treatment of a service-connected medical condition, or have an income below the VA pension level, as described in Chapter 6. Veterans who are placed in Group 6 may receive free medication if it's required to treat a medical condition associated with their placement in Group 6. Individuals in Group 7 or 8 must pay the medication co-pay amount of $8 per 30-day supply.

There is a medication co-pay *cap* (the most you will have to pay) of $960 per calendar year for all enrolled veterans except those in Group 7 or 8.

All co-pays are subject to change at the whims of Congress. For current co-pay amounts, visit the VA's Web site at www.va.gov/healtheligibility/Library/pubs/CopayGlance/CopayGlance.pdf.

Using private health insurance

If you have other healthcare insurance, the VA is required to bill your private health insurance provider for medical care, supplies, and prescriptions provided for treatment of non-service-connected conditions. This includes your spouse's healthcare insurance, if you are covered under it. Generally, however, the VA can't bill Medicare, but it can bill Medicare supplemental health insurance for covered services.

When you apply for VA medical care (see the "Making your case for VA medical care" section), you're required to provide information on other health insurance coverage, including coverage provided under your spouse's policy.

This doesn't mean you should dump your private medical insurance to make sure the VA will pay for all your care. Remember, you may have a spouse or family member covered under a private plan. Also, there's no guarantee that in subsequent years Congress will appropriate sufficient funds for the VA to provide care for all enrollment priority groups (see the "Making sure you join the right group!" section). If this happens and you're enrolled in one of the lower priority groups, you'd be without healthcare coverage.

Dealing with VA income limits

The VA uses two financial means to determine veteran placement into Groups 7 and 8 (see the "Making sure you join the right group!" section earlier in the chapter). You're eligible for placement in Group 7 if your income is above the VA's national income limit but below the geographical income threshold; you can be placed in Group 8 if it's above both standards.

National income limits

The *national income limits* measure your household income and total assets against the national mean. The maximum household income limits also affect whether you receive free VA medical care or are subject to co-pays.

Income includes all gross household income (money earned by you, your spouse, and any kids who live at home), including Social Security, retirement pay, unemployment insurance, interest and dividends, workers' compensation, black lung benefits, and any other gross household income. The 2008 national income limits are shown in Table 4-3.

Table 4-3	National Income Limits		
Veteran With	*Free VA Prescriptions and Travel Benefits If You Have an Income Of*	*Free VA Healthcare If You Have an Income Of*	*Allowable Medical Expense Deduction*
0 dependents	$11,181 or less	$28,429 or less	$546
1 dependent	$14,643 or less	$34,117 or less	$716
2 dependents	$16,552 or less	$36,026 or less	$809

(continued)

Table 4-3 *(continued)*

Veteran With	Free VA Prescriptions and Travel Benefits If You Have an Income Of	Free VA Healthcare If You Have an Income Of	Allowable Medical Expense Deduction
3 dependents	$18,461 or less	$37,935 or less	$902
4 dependents	$20,370 or less	$39,844 or less	$996
Each additional dependent	$1,909	$1,909	5% of the maximum allowable pension rate as described in Chapter 6

In addition to the income levels shown in Table 4-3, you must have a net worth of $80,000 or less. *Net worth* includes assets such as the market value of property (excluding your primary residence), stocks, bonds, notes, individual retirement accounts, bank deposits, savings accounts, and cash.

These rates can change. For the latest rates, see www.va.gov/ healtheligibility/Library/pubs/VAIncomeThresholds/ VAIncomeThresholds.pdf.

Geographical income threshold

The VA also compares your financial assessments with *geographically based income thresholds.* If your income is above the VA national means test (Table 4-3) but below the geographic income threshold, you qualify to be placed in Group 7, which means you get a 20 percent reduction in inpatient co-pay rates (see the "Co-pays for medical care" section).

The geographic rates depend on where you live, right down to the individual county. Because there are a few thousand counties and parishes in the United States, reproducing the list here would make this book massive, thereby significantly increasing its cost. See how I look out for your welfare? You're very welcome. You can look up the latest limits online at www. va.gov/healtheligibility/Library/pubs/GMTIncomeThresholds.

Chapter 5

Tricare: The Military's Health Insurance

. . . .

In This Chapter

▶ Pursuing a positive medical plan

▶ Identifying the eligible

▶ Taking a dose of medicine

▶ Preparing yourself for what you'll pay

▶ Details about dental and vision care

. . . .

I'm probably not the best person in the world to write this chapter. I hate going to the doctor. I absolutely despise going to the dentist. To me, doctors and dentists are evil. They spend most of your allotted appointment time telling you that you're no longer allowed to do the things you love to do, instructing you to start doing things that you hate to do, and commanding that you not eat the foods you love to eat. They do things to you that are uncomfortable and sometimes downright painful. Then they have the gall to charge you for all of this.

However, as age continues to creep up on me, I'm discovering that doctors and dentists are often necessary. My girlfriend is a nurse and informs me that such medical professionals can be extremely beneficial at times. Who am I to argue with her? I never win arguments with her, in any case.

At least I don't have to pay an arm and a leg for the services of these medical professionals. I belong to that special group of veterans who are authorized to participate in Tricare, the military's version of health insurance. So I have some personal knowledge of the program as I give you details about the different plans and their costs in this chapter.

Tricare: Pick a Plan, Any Plan

Tricare is the military's health insurance program that covers everyone — active-duty members, retirees, and their families. However, retirees and their dependents have to chip in for the cost of coverage (see "How Much Does All of This Cost?" for more details); medical care is free for those who are still serving and their families. Because this is a book about veterans benefits, and because I have to keep this guide from becoming a novel (even though I've always wanted to write a novel), I'm limiting the information in this chapter to that which affects the veteran and the veteran's family members — in other words, those no longer in the military.

For veterans and their authorized family members, Tricare comes in four flavors, depending on your needs:

✔ Tricare Prime

✔ Tricare Extra

✔ Tricare Standard

✔ Tricare for Life

Tricare Prime: An HMO by another name

The Tricare Prime option is very much like an HMO, or health maintenance organization. Like an HMO, you're assigned to a primary care provider (PCP). This is usually, although not always, a military medical facility (on-base hospital or medical clinic). You receive most of your healthcare needs through the PCP. Like most HMOs, in order to receive care from a specialist you must first receive a referral from your PCP.

Tricare Prime requires you to enroll and pay an annual enrollment fee; plus you pay a small fee (called a *cost-share* in the military) each time you receive medical care (see the "How Much Does All of This Cost?" section in this chapter). When you receive medical care under Tricare Prime, you don't have to file a reimbursement claim. The provider automatically does this for you.

Tricare Prime is the most cost-effective Tricare option, but you generally have to live close to a military base to take advantage of it. However, many military retirees choose to live near a military base because of the on-base shopping discounts they receive (see Chapter 15).

To enroll in Tricare Prime, you must fill out some paperwork. Enrollment forms are available online at www.tricare.mil/mybenefit/Forms.do or at any military medical facility.

Tricare Extra: When an HMO just won't do

The Tricare Extra program gives you more flexibility than Tricare Prime, but it can result in additional costs. If you're eligible for Tricare benefits, you don't need to enroll in advance to use Tricare Extra. You're enrolled automatically the first time you use any benefits and present your military or dependent ID card as an insurance card to the provider.

Under this program, you can go to any Tricare network provider (TNP), present your military or dependent ID card, and receive medical care. There are thousands of TNPs across the country. You can find a TNP close to you by visiting www.tricare.mil/mybenefit/home/Medical/FindingAProvider. The TNPs have a contract with the military to limit costs to designated amounts.

Under Tricare Extra, you pay an annual deductible. After the deductible is paid, Tricare pays 80 percent of the medical expenses, and you pay 20 percent of the authorized costs (see the "How Much Does All of This Cost?" section for details). TNPs have also agreed to do all the paperwork for you. Under Tricare Extra, you don't have to file claims to be reimbursed.

Tricare Standard: A little more cost equals much more freedom

The Tricare Standard program gives you the greatest flexibility, but it costs the most. Under this program, you can see just about any medical provider you want. As with Tricare Extra, you pay an annual deductible. In addition to the deductible, you have to pay 25 percent of what Tricare says the medical service should cost (see the "How Much Does All of This Cost" section).

If you want to find out what the Tricare allowable cost is for a particular medical procedure, use the nifty search tool at www.tricare.mil/allowablecharges.

Medical providers under Tricare Standard can be broken into two groups:

- **Participating providers:** Participating providers, although they're not under contract as a TNP (Tricare network provider), have agreed to file claims for you, accept payment directly from Tricare, and accept the Tricare allowable charge, less any applicable cost-shares paid by you, as payment in full for their services.

There's no national list of participating providers. You need to ask your provider if she participates in the Tricare program. The general rule is, if the provider fills out the claims paperwork for you, she's a participating provider. If you have to fill out the claim form yourself, she's a nonparticipating provider.

✔ **Nonparticipating providers:** Nonparticipating providers have not agreed to accept the Tricare allowable charge for services or file your claims. Under the law, nonparticipating providers may charge up to 15 percent above the Tricare allowable charge for services (in addition to your regular cost-shares). This amount is your responsibility and isn't shared by Tricare.

If you see a nonparticipating provider, you may have to pay the provider first and file a claim with Tricare for reimbursement. To file a claim, you need DD Form 2642, Patient's Request for Medical Payment. The form is available online at `www.tricare.mil/mybenefit/Download/Forms/dd2642.pdf`, or you can call 303-676-3400 and ask to have a copy mailed to you.

You don't have to enroll in Tricare Standard. You're enrolled automatically the first time you use any benefits and present your military or dependent ID card as an insurance card to the provider.

Be sure to check with the provider to see if she is a participating or nonparticipating provider. The doctor may decide to participate on a claim-by-claim basis. This means that for one type of service, the provider will participate (agree to accept the Tricare allowable charge and file claims on your behalf), but for another she won't. Using a participating provider is your best option if you use Tricare Standard.

Tricare for Life: Medicare plus Tricare equals free care

Until a few years ago, when a retiree or retiree family member reached the age of 65, they were no longer eligible for Tricare. Instead, they were expected to receive medical care under the provisions of Medicare. This changed in 2001 with the introduction of Tricare for Life.

To remain eligible for Tricare benefits, you must enroll in Medicare Part B. This is the Medicare program where you pay monthly premiums ($96.40 in 2009) in exchange for receiving medical care from authorized Medicare providers.

Under Tricare for Life, you receive your medical care from Medicare providers, but Tricare becomes a secondary insurer and picks up any costs that Medicare doesn't cover. You pay no annual deductible or cost-share under this program.

Checking Your Tricare Eligibility

More than 9.3 million people are eligible for Tricare. For brevity's sake, I'm limiting the lists here to veterans who are no longer in the military and their family members.

As a veteran, you're eligible for Tricare benefits if you

- ✔ Are a retired active-duty member. See Chapter 7 for information about military retirement.

- ✔ Are retired from the reserves or National Guard and are age 60 or older. Again, Chapter 7 has more information.

- ✔ Served in the military (for any length of time) and were awarded the Medal of Honor, our nation's highest military award.

If you're a spouse or dependent of a veteran, you're entitled to Tricare benefits if you are

- ✔ A spouse or child of an eligible veteran (see the preceding list). Children include

  - Unmarried children under the age of 21

  - Those under the age of 23 if attending college and the parent(s) provide at least 50 percent of their support

  A child may be covered beyond these limits if he is severely disabled and the condition existed prior to his 21st birthday, or if the condition occurred between the ages of 21 and 23 while the child was enrolled in college.

- ✔ A surviving spouse of a military member who died on active duty. In this case, your Tricare benefits expire three years after the death of the active-duty member.

- ✔ An ex-spouse of a military member or retiree, if — as of the date of the divorce — you were married to the member or veteran for at least 20 years, and your ex was in the military for at least 20 years of the marriage.

- ✔ An ex-spouse of a military member or retiree, if — as of the date of the divorce — you were married to the member or veteran for at least 20 years, and your ex was in the military for at least 15 years, but less than 20 years, of the marriage. In this case, your Tricare benefits expire one year after the date of the divorce.

If you are a surviving spouse or a former spouse and you remarry, you lose your Tricare benefits. Unlike many veterans benefits, you *do not* regain Tricare if that subsequent marriage later ends.

Enrolling in DEERS

No, I don't mean Bambi. In addition to meeting the eligibility criteria outlined in the previous section, veterans and family members need to ensure they are enrolled in the *Defense Enrollment Eligibility Reporting System (DEERS)*. This is the massive computer system that tracks military members, veterans, and family members who are eligible for military benefits.

If you're eligible for Tricare, you're probably already enrolled in DEERS, but it doesn't hurt to make sure the information is up to date. Mistakes or outdated information in the DEERS database can cause problems with Tricare claims.

You can verify and update your DEERS information in several ways:

- ✔ **In person:** To add or remove family members, or to change your mailing address, phone number, or e-mail address, visit a local ID card office. ID card offices are located on all military bases.

- ✔ **By phone:** Call the Defense Manpower Data Center Support Office at 800-538-9552 to update your mailing address, e-mail address, and phone number. You can't add or remove family members over the phone.

- ✔ **By fax:** Fax any mailing address, e-mail address, or phone number changes to the Defense Manpower Data Center Support Office at 831-655-8317. To add or remove family members, you have to fax supporting documentation (marriage certificate, birth certificate, divorce decree, or death certificate).

- ✔ **By mail:** Mail changes to the Defense Manpower Data Center Support Office. You must also mail supporting documentation if you are adding or removing a family member. The address is Defense Manpower Data Center Support Office, Attn: COA, 400 Gigling Road, Seaside, CA 93955-6771.

- ✔ **Online:** Visit the DEERS Web site at `https://www.dmdc.osd.mil/appj/address/index.jsp`, and follow the steps to update your mailing address, e-mail address, and phone numbers online. You can't add or remove family members online.

Getting Your Medication

Tricare eligible participants have a host of options for getting their meds. Depending on which option you select, your medications may be free or provided at the ridiculously low cost of $3 per prescription, or they may cost you big bucks.

If you get your medications from a military pharmacy, Tricare network pharmacy, or the mail-order pharmacy, you don't have to file a reimbursement claim. The provider automatically does this for you.

If you get your drugs from a non-network pharmacy, the pharmacy may not file a claim on your behalf. In that case, you have to file your own claim for reimbursement, using DD Form 2642, Patient's Request for Medical Payment. The form is available online at `www.tricare.mil/mybenefit/Download/Forms/dd2642.pdf`, or you can call 303-676-3400 and ask to have a copy mailed to you.

Meds on military bases

Picking up your prescriptions from an on-base pharmacy is the best option if you live close to a military base. Your prescriptions filled at these pharmacies are completely free!

However, your nearby on-base pharmacy may not stock all the medications you need. Whether it does depends on the size of the military base, and therefore on the size of the military medical facility that supports that base.

Military regulations require each on-base military pharmacy to stock medications that are on a list called the Basic Corps Formula (BCF) listing. Depending on the size of the military pharmacy, it may stock medications on the Extended Core Formula (ECF) list as well. To see a current listing of medications on both lists, visit `www.pec.ha.osd.mil/BCF/BCFclass.htm`.

Choosing your own pharmacy

You can elect to fill your prescriptions at any civilian pharmacy. If you're smart enough to use one of the 54,000 pharmacies in the Tricare network, your prescriptions will only cost you $3 per prescription or refill (up to a 30-day supply) for generic drugs and $9 for name-brand items.

If you choose to use a commercial pharmacy that isn't part of the Tricare network, be prepared to pay more — possibly a lot more. Additionally, you'll probably have to pay the full amount of your prescription upfront, and then file a claim with Tricare to get your covered costs back. Tricare will reimburse you $9 or 20 percent of the authorized cost for the medication, whichever is greater.

If you're enrolled in Tricare Prime and elect to use a commercial non-network pharmacy (why would you?), there's an annual deductible of $300 per person or $600 per family before you receive any reimbursement. If you use Tricare Extra or Tricare Standard for your medical needs and elect to use a non-network pharmacy, the annual deductible is part of the Tricare Extra or Standard annual deductible.

Mail-order pharmacy: The med's in the mail

Using the mail-order pharmacy is a great option if your medication isn't urgent and you are lazy (I mean "physically conservative"), like me, and don't feel like going down the street to the pharmacy.

You can order your prescription or refill by mail or online, and Tricare's mail-order pharmacy will send your meds right to your door. Your cost-share is the same as using a Tricare network pharmacy — $3 for a generic drug and $9 for name-brand pharmaceuticals. However, you get more bang for your buck by using the mail-order service because you can receive a 90-day supply for that price, instead of a 30-day supply, with this option.

You can enroll in the mail-order pharmacy online at www.express-scripts.com/custom/dod/ben_message. You can also enroll by going to the Web site and printing out the mail-order registration form. Then mail it to Express Scripts Inc., P.O. Box 52150, Phoenix, AZ 85072; or fax it to 877-895-1900.

How Much Does All of This Cost?

Your costs under Tricare depend on which Tricare program you elect to participate in (see the "Tricare: Pick a Plan, any Plan" section). In the following sections, I give you the approximate prices you can expect for each program.

Looking at the plans' costs side by side

You know you're eligible for Tricare, and you know you want to use one of the plans. But in terms of cost, which one is right for your pocketbook? Table 5-1 shows you how the costs line up for Tricare Prime, Extra, and Standard. Because Tricare for Life works in conjunction with Medicare, I address the costs of that plan in the next section. (If you want to know how much you'd pay for prescription drugs, see the "Getting Your Medication" section.) *Note:* The costs for services under Tricare Extra and Tricare Prime are what you pay after you've met your deductible.

Table 5-1	Cost Comparisons for Tricare Prime, Extra, and Standard		
	Under Tricare Prime, You Pay	*Under Tricare Extra, You Pay*	*Under Tricare Standard, You Pay*
Annual enrollment	$230 for individuals; $460 per family	$0	$0
Annual deductible	$0	$150 for individuals; $300 per family	$150 for individuals; $300 per family
Outpatient visit	$12	20% of the Tricare allowable fee	25% of the Tricare allowable fee
Clinical preventive services (vaccinations, so on)	No charge	20% of the Tricare allowable fee	25% of the Tricare allowable fee
Hospitalization	$11 per day with a $25 minimum; no additional costs for separately billed professional charges	$250 per day or 25% for institutional services, whichever is less, plus 20% for separately billed professional charges	$535 per day or 25% for institutional services, whichever is less, plus 25% for separately billed professional charges
Emergency services	$30 per visit	20% of the Tricare allowable fee	25% of the Tricare allowable fee
Outpatient mental health care	$25 for an individual visit and $17 for a group visit	20% of the Tricare allowable fee	25% of the Tricare allowable fee
Inpatient mental health care	$40 per day with a $25 minimum; no additional costs for separately billed professional charges	20% for institutional services, plus 20% for separately billed professional charges	25% for institutional services, plus 25% for separately billed professional charges
Inpatient skilled nursing care	$11 per day with a $25 minimum; no additional costs for separately billed professional charges	$250 per day or 25% for institutional services, whichever is less, plus 20% for separately billed professional charges	25% for institutional services, plus 25% for separately billed professional charges

Costs of services under Tricare for Life

Tricare for Life combines Medicare Part B benefits and Tricare benefits. Under this program, you pay a Medicare monthly Part B premium, which in 2009 is $96.40 per month. You must also pay the annual Tricare deductible, which is $150 per individual or $300 for a family, but you don't have to pay the Medicare annual deductible.

If you obtain your medical care from an authorized Medicare provider, Medicare covers a majority of the costs, and Tricare pays the remainder. The result is no additional cost to you. In effect, you're receiving complete and total healthcare coverage for the price of your monthly Medicare Part B payments and the annual Tricare deductible.

 There may be instances where a medical service is covered by Medicare but not Tricare, or vice versa (although these situations are rare). In such cases, if the service is covered by Medicare but not Tricare, you pay the standard Medicare co-pays. If the treatment is authorized by Tricare but not Medicare, you pay the co-pays listed under Tricare Extra or Tricare Standard, depending on whether you're receiving the treatment from a Tricare network provider.

Catastrophic cap

The maximum amount that you have to pay out-of-pocket per fiscal year (October 1–September 30) for Tricare-covered medical services is called the *catastrophic cap.* The cap applies to all covered services: annual deductibles, pharmacy co-payments, inpatient and outpatient cost-shares, and other costs based on Tricare allowable charges.

After you meet the catastrophic cap, Tricare pays your portion of the Tricare allowable amount for all covered services for the rest of the fiscal year. This protection keeps you from going into the poorhouse in the event of long-term illness or injury.

What Isn't Covered by Tricare?

Tricare covers most inpatient and outpatient care that's medically necessary and considered proven. However, there are special rules or limits on certain types of care, while other types of care aren't covered at all. Some services or treatments require prior authorization.

A few examples of medical procedures that aren't covered are

- ✔ Abortions (unless the mother's life is at risk).

- ✔ Condoms. However, other forms of birth control that require a prescription, such as birth control pills, are covered.

- ✔ Cosmetic surgery or drugs used for cosmetic purposes (such as Botox). However, cosmetic surgery to correct a disfigurement, such as the result of an accident or burn, is covered.

- ✔ Nonsurgical treatment for obesity or weight control.

- ✔ Smoking cessation products and treatment.

- ✔ Most dental work. (The military has a separate insurance program for dental care — see the "Smiling about Dental Care" section.) However, dental care that is medically necessary in the treatment of an otherwise covered medical (not dental) condition is covered.

Using Tricare Overseas

The only Tricare program that can be used in foreign countries (by eligible veterans and their family members) is Tricare Standard. Tricare Prime can be used overseas by current military members and their families, but Tricare Prime isn't available overseas to others. Tricare Extra can't be used in foreign countries because there are no Tricare network providers outside of the United States. You can't use Tricare for Life in non-U.S. states and territories overseas because of Medicare restrictions.

Under Tricare Standard, the military pays 75 percent of the authorized cost. If the overseas provider charges more than what Tricare authorizes for the procedure, you have to pay the difference out of your own pocket.

If you're age 65 or older, you must still enroll in Medicare Part B and pay the monthly Medicare premiums to use Tricare Standard overseas.

Smiling about Dental Care

The Tricare Retiree Dental Program (TRDP) is a separate, voluntary coverage program available to eligible users of Tricare (see the "Checking Your Tricare Eligibility" section earlier in this chapter). Under this program, you pay a monthly premium in exchange for dental care benefits, which are managed by a company called Delta Dental.

If after you read the following sections you decide you want to enroll, go to www.trdp.org/pro/index.html. You can get more information about the dental program there. You can also enroll by calling 888-838-8737 between 6 a.m. and 6 p.m. (Pacific time) Monday through Friday.

Counting the costs

The dental program is a separate, voluntary benefit, and it isn't free. If you elect to participate, you pay a monthly premium in exchange for dental coverage. How much you pay depends on where you live and the number of people in your family that you elect to have covered.

For example, using the 2009 rates, if you live in Daytona Beach, Florida, your monthly premium would be $31.46 per person, or $102.55 for a family of three or more. If you live the good life in Los Angeles, your monthly premium would be $46.46 or 150.83 for a family of three or more. To search for premium rates where you live, visit www.trdp.org/pro/premiumSrch.html.

Using a desirable dentist

Delta Dental has a listing of more than 100,000 network providers. If you use a network provider, the provider files your insurance claims for you and doesn't charge more than the plan's authorized amount.

You can, of course, use any dentist you want, but your coverage is based on the authorized amount. If your non-network dentist charges more than this, you'll have to dig into your pocket to pay the difference. You can find a list of Delta Dental network providers online at www.trdp.org/findadentist.html.

Covering your coverage

Under the Tricare dental program, you have to pay an annual deductible. For the TRDP, the deductible is $50 per person with a $150 cap per family. After the deductible is met, you receive the coverage shown in Table 5-2.

Table 5-2	Dental Benefits Provided and Their Costs
Benefits Available during the First 12 Months of Enrollment	*Delta Dental Pays*
Diagnostic services (such as exams)	100%
Preventive services (such as cleanings)	100%
Basic restorative services (such as fillings, including tooth-colored fillings on back teeth)	80%
Endodontics (such as root canals)	60%
Periodontics (such as gum treatment)	60%
Oral surgery (such as extractions)	60%
Emergency (such as treatment for minor pain)	80%
Dental accident coverage	100%
Additional Services Available after 12 Months of Continuous Enrollment or if Enrolled within 4 Months after Military Retirement	Delta Dental Pays
Cast crowns, onlays, and bridges	50%
Partial/full dentures	50%
Dental implant services	50%
Orthodontics	50%
Maximums per Benefit Year (October 1– September 30)	
Annual maximum (per person, per benefit year)	$1,200
Orthodontic maximum (per person, per lifetime)	$1,500
Dental accident maximum (per person, per benefit year)	$1,000

The coverage shown in Table 5-2 is based on the Delta Dental allowable rates. If you decide to use a dentist outside of the Delta Dental network, you may have to pay extra. See the "Using a desirable dentist" section.

Like everything else in life, the cost-shares and fees in Table 5-2 are subject to change. For the latest information, visit www.trdp.org/pro/overview.html.

Using dental benefits overseas

Here's some good news for military retirees and their family members who live overseas. While you and I were sitting around picking our teeth (pun intended), your friendly neighborhood Congress critters decided to expand retiree dental benefits to those living in foreign countries. How cool is that? This expansion of benefits became effective October 1, 2008.

You should carefully weigh your options when considering whether to enroll in the TRDP overseas. In some cases, you may not get back what you pay into it. Generally, the monthly premiums are significantly higher than the amount charged for those who live in the United States. For instance, average out-of-pocket expenses for dental care in the Philippines are generally much less than monthly insurance premiums. In some countries, if you're married to a citizen of that country, you may be eligible for national healthcare, which may include free dental care. So do a little bit of homework before you enroll.

Looking Into Vision Care

Veterans enrolled in Tricare Prime are allowed one comprehensive eye examination every two years. Veterans who use Tricare Standard, Tricare Extra, and Tricare for Life do not qualify for free or reduced-cost eye examinations.

Regardless of the plan, Tricare only pays for eyeglasses and contacts for the following conditions:

- ✔ Infantile glaucoma
- ✔ Keratoconus
- ✔ Dry eyes
- ✔ Irregularities in the shape of the eye
- ✔ Loss of human lens function resulting from eye surgery or congenital absence

Chapter 6

Disability Compensation and Pensions

Military service is not the safest job in the world. In addition to the dangers of combat, military members often travel to corners of the world where they can be exposed to all kinds of nasty environments and icky germs. Sometimes this results in a lifelong medical condition or disability that can interfere with a veteran's ability to get and hold a good job.

The U.S. government takes care of veterans who have disabilities and medical conditions that were caused or worsened by military service by providing monthly disability compensation. It also takes care of low-income veterans who are totally and permanently disabled due to non-service-connected medical conditions and disabilities by providing a monthly disability pension. Finally, the Department of Veterans Affairs (VA) provides a lifelong pension to veterans who have earned our nation's highest military decoration — the Medal of Honor. Keep reading for more details.

Checking Your Eligibility for Disability Compensation

The VA provides monthly disability compensation to certain veterans. To be eligible

✔ Your disability or medical condition must have been caused or made worse by your service in the military, as determined by the VA. The VA makes determinations based on service connection and presumed service connection (see the upcoming sections for more on these).

✔ You must have a disability or a medical condition that the VA has assigned a disability rating to. The amount of monthly tax-free disability compensation you can receive is based primarily on the disability rating you receive from the VA. The VA rates medical conditions and disabilities on a scale of 10 percent to 100 percent in 10-percentage-point intervals (in other words, 10 percent, 20 percent, 30 percent, 40 percent, and so on).

✔ You must have either an honorable or general discharge. If you have any other kind of a discharge, such as an other than honorable conditions (OTHC) or a bad-conduct discharge awarded by a special court-martial, then the VA must determine that your discharge wasn't under dishonorable conditions. (You can read about discharge characterizations in Chapter 2.)

Establishing the service connection

To qualify for VA disability compensation, the VA must determine that your medical condition was caused or aggravated by your military service. *Service connection* for a disability or death can be established through many ways. The four most common are

✔ **The disability or condition was incurred in military service.** These determinations are usually cut and dry because the evidence should be in your military medical records. An example would be if you were shot or were wounded by an explosion during combat.

✔ **The aggravation of a before-service disability during service.** This can be harder to determine because it precludes prior-service conditions that get worse due to the natural progression of the disease or condition.

For example, if you had mild asthma when you joined the military, and then you spent four years of service working behind a desk in Maryland during which time your asthma got worse, it's unlikely that the VA would conclude this had anything to do with your military service. On the other hand, if you were deployed to Kuwait when all those oil wells were on fire, it would be easy for the VA to conclude that your condition was aggravated due to your service.

When making a determination, the VA considers the places, types, and circumstances of your military service as documented in your service records (see Chapter 2 for information about service records). The VA gives particular weight to combat duty and other hardships of service.

✔ **Because of a service-connected disability, a secondary condition has occurred.** It's been scientifically proven that some medical conditions can cause other medical conditions. For example, it's medically known that individuals who have had an amputation of the leg at or above the ankle are prone to develop heart disease. In such cases, the condition (heart disease) caused by the service-connected disability (amputation) can be rated as a service-connected disability by the VA.

✔ **Presumption that the disease or disability was incurred in military service.** In certain cases, the VA can make a presumption that a medical condition or disability is service connected. You can read more about this in the next section.

In all cases, there must be evidence of a *current* disability.

Making a presumptive service connection

The VA presumes that specific disabilities diagnosed in certain veterans were caused by their military service, so it issues a *presumptive service-connection* determination. The VA does this because of the unique circumstances of the veteran's military service. If you fit into one of the following groups and are diagnosed with one of the listed conditions, the VA presumes that the circumstances of your service caused the condition, and it awards disability compensation.

✔ **Veterans within one year of release from active duty:** If you are diagnosed with a chronic disease (such as arthritis, diabetes, or hypertension), the VA can presume the condition is service connected, even in the absence of any evidence of service connection.

✔ **Veterans with ALS:** If you served in the Persian Gulf (Iraq, Kuwait, Saudi Arabia, or other nearby locations) from August 2, 1990, to July 31, 1991, and are diagnosed with amyotrophic lateral sclerosis, otherwise known as ALS or Lou Gehrig's disease, the VA considers that condition to be service connected. Additionally, the VA presumes a service connection if you served on active duty (anywhere) for 90 or more days and are diagnosed with ALS.

✔ **Former prisoners of war for any length of time:** If you were a POW for any length of time and are diagnosed with a disability that's at least 10 percent disabling for any of the following conditions, your condition is considered service connected:

   • Dysthymic disorder (clinical depression)

   • Heart disease or hypertensive vascular disease and its complications

   • Mental health conditions

- The aftereffects of frostbite

- Post-traumatic osteoarthritis (degenerative joint disease)

- Stroke and its aftereffects

✔ **Former prisoners of war for at least 30 days:** If you were a POW for at least 30 days and are diagnosed with a disability that's at least 10 percent disabling for any of the following conditions, your condition is considered service connected:

- Avitaminosis (any disease caused by chronic or long-term vitamin deficiency)

- Beriberi (a nervous system ailment caused by thiamine deficiency)

- Pellagra (disease caused by lack of niacin)

- Any other nutritional deficiency

- Chronic dysentery (severe, bloody diarrhea)

- Cirrhosis of the liver

- Helminthiasis (infested with worms)

- Irritable bowel syndrome

- Malnutrition

- Peptic ulcer disease

- Peripheral neuropathy (numbness of the fingers, toes, hands, or feet)

✔ **Vietnam veterans:** If you served in Vietnam between January 9, 1962, and May 7, 1975, and were exposed to the herbicide known as Agent Orange, the VA assumes service connection for the following medical conditions:

- Peripheral neuropathy (numbness of the fingers, toes, hands, or feet) if it manifests within one year of exposure to Agent Orange

- Chloracne (acne-like eruption of blackheads and cysts caused by over-exposure to chemicals) or other diseases similar to chloracne if it manifests within one year of exposure to Agent Orange

- Chronic lymphocytic leukemia

- Hodgkin's disease (type of lymphoma cancer)

- Multiple myeloma (cancer of plasma cells)

- Non-Hodgkin's lymphoma

- Porphyria cutanea tarda (blistering of the skin) if it manifests within one year of exposure to Agent Orange

- Primary amyloidosis (protein fibers imbedded in tissues and organs, causing them harm)

- Prostate cancer

- Respiratory cancers (lung, bronchus, larynx, trachea)

- Soft-tissue sarcomas (cancer of the soft tissues of the body)

- Type 2 diabetes

✔ **Gulf War veterans:** If you served in the Persian Gulf and have developed any of the following conditions (it must be diagnosed before December 31, 2011), the VA will assume you have Gulf War Syndrome, which is considered to be service connected:

- Chronic fatigue syndrome

- Fibromyalgia (widespread pain)

- Irritable bowel syndrome

- Any diagnosed or undiagnosed illness that the secretary of Veterans Affairs determines warrants a presumption of service connection

At the present time, signs or symptoms of an undiagnosed illness include fatigue, skin symptoms, headaches, muscle pain, joint pain, neurological symptoms, respiratory symptoms, sleep disturbance, GI symptoms, cardiovascular symptoms, weight loss, and menstrual disorders.

✔ **Other presumptive conditions:** The VA may presume a condition is service connected in many other situations, based on the date and place of military service. The complete list is contained in Title 38 of the Code of Federal Regulations (CFR), in sections 3.307, 3.308, and 3.309:

- Section 3.307 can be read online at www.warms.vba.va.gov/regs/38CFR/BOOKB/PART3/S3_307.DOC.

- Section 3.308 can be viewed at www.warms.vba.va.gov/regs/38CFR/BOOKB/PART3/S3_308.DOC.

- You can read Section 3.309 at www.warms.vba.va.gov/regs/38CFR/BOOKB/PART3/S3_309.DOC.

Determining your disability rating

The VA has a massive (and I do mean massive!) listing of medical conditions and disabilities, along with rules and conditions, and more rules and more conditions, and required rules and required conditions that ultimately result in the assignment of a disability rating.

To reprint the VA's entire Schedule for Rating Disabilities, I would need to persuade my publisher to print a second volume of this book several hundred pages long. Good thing I invented the Internet a few years ago. You can see the entire list online at www.warms.vba.va.gov/bookc.html. The Schedule for Ratings Disabilities can be found in Part 4 of Title 38. (Okay, I really didn't personally invent the Internet, but I would have if somebody else hadn't beaten me to it.)

Employability matters

The ability to overcome a disability varies widely among individuals. The VA rating schedule is based primarily on how much the earning capacity is reduced due to the disability. The VA doesn't consider the veteran's personal ability to overcome the disability when it determines employability and compensation.

Sometimes the disability rating schedule calls for a disability rating of less than 100 percent disabled, but due to individual circumstances, the VA determines that the veteran is unemployable. In such cases, the VA may award disability compensation equal to 100 percent. This can be done only under certain circumstances however. The basic rules are:

- ✔ In the VA's opinion, the veteran's service-connected disability must prevent him from landing or keeping a decent-paying job.

- ✔ If a veteran has only one service-connected disability, it must be rated at 60 percent or more.

- ✔ If a veteran has two or more service-connected disabilities, at least one of the disabilities must be rated at 40 percent or more, and the combined disability rating (see the next section) must be at least 70 percent or more.

Combined ratings

It's possible that you could have more than one service-connected medical condition or disability, each with its own rating. How does the VA determine what your total rating is in such cases? You'd think they would simply add the ratings together. But, no — that would be too simple for the government. If it were that easy, then anyone could do it.

I should probably mention here that, as far as the VA is concerned, you can't be more than 100 percent disabled. That's true even if you have multiple disabilities, each rated at 100 percent. Remember, the VA rates a disability or combination of disabilities based on how it would affect the average person's employability. Someone with a 100 percent disability rating is considered to be completely unemployable, and you can't be more unemployable than that.

The VA uses a chart that, when properly used, results in a *combined disability rating.* I've reproduced the VA's chart in Table 6-1.

The chart may look a bit complicated, but it's not too hard to follow. To find the combined disability rating when multiple ratings are involved, take the highest rating and locate it at the top of the chart. Then take the next highest rating and locate it on the left side of the chart. Where the two lines intersect is the combined disability rating.

If there are more than two disabilities, take the next highest disability rating (not including the combined rating) and locate it at the top of the chart. Then take the previous combined rating and find it on the left side. Where the lines intersect is the combined rating for the three disabilities. You continue this process until all the ratings are combined. After you've combined all the ratings, you round the final result to the nearest multiple of 10. This final number is your combined disability rating.

Table 6-1			Combined Disability Ratings						
	10	**20**	**30**	**40**	**50**	**60**	**70**	**80**	**90**
19	27	35	43	51	60	68	76	84	92
20	28	36	44	52	60	68	76	84	92
21	29	37	45	53	61	68	76	84	92
22	30	38	45	53	61	69	77	84	92
23	31	38	46	54	62	69	77	85	92
24	32	39	47	54	62	70	77	85	92
25	33	40	48	55	63	70	78	85	93
26	33	41	48	56	63	70	78	85	93
27	34	42	49	56	64	71	78	85	93
28	35	42	50	57	64	71	78	86	93
29	36	43	50	57	65	72	79	86	93
30	37	44	51	58	65	72	79	86	93
31	38	45	52	59	66	72	79	86	93
32	39	46	52	59	66	73	80	86	93
33	40	46	53	60	67	73	80	87	93
34	41	47	54	60	67	74	80	87	93
35	42	48	55	61	68	74	81	87	94
36	42	49	55	62	68	74	81	87	94
37	43	50	56	62	69	75	81	87	94
38	44	50	57	63	69	75	81	88	94

(continued)

Table 6-1 *(continued)*

	10	20	30	40	50	60	70	80	90
39	45	51	57	63	70	76	82	88	94
40	46	52	58	64	70	76	82	88	94
41	47	53	59	65	71	76	82	88	94
42	48	54	59	65	71	77	83	88	94
43	49	54	60	66	72	77	83	89	94
44	50	55	61	66	72	78	83	89	94
45	51	56	62	67	73	78	84	89	95
46	51	57	62	68	73	78	84	89	95
47	52	58	63	68	74	79	84	89	95
48	53	58	64	69	74	79	84	90	95
49	54	59	64	69	75	80	85	90	95
50	55	60	65	70	75	80	85	90	95
51	56	61	66	71	76	80	85	90	95
52	57	62	66	71	76	81	86	90	95
53	58	62	67	72	77	81	86	91	95
54	59	63	68	72	77	82	86	91	95
55	60	64	69	73	78	82	87	91	96
56	60	65	69	74	78	82	87	91	96
57	61	66	70	74	79	83	87	91	96
58	62	66	71	75	79	83	87	92	96
59	63	67	71	75	80	84	88	92	96
60	64	68	72	76	80	84	88	92	96
61	65	69	73	77	81	84	88	92	96
62	66	70	73	77	81	85	89	92	96
63	67	70	74	78	82	85	89	93	96
64	68	71	75	78	82	86	89	93	96
65	69	72	76	79	83	86	90	93	97
66	69	73	76	80	83	86	90	93	97
67	70	74	77	80	84	87	90	93	97
68	71	74	78	81	84	87	90	94	97
69	72	75	78	81	85	88	91	94	97

	10	20	30	40	50	60	70	80	90
70	73	76	79	82	85	88	91	94	97
71	74	77	80	83	86	88	91	94	97
72	75	78	80	83	86	89	92	94	97
73	76	78	81	84	87	89	92	95	97
74	77	79	82	84	87	90	92	95	97
75	78	80	83	85	88	90	93	95	98
76	78	81	83	86	88	90	93	95	98
77	79	82	84	86	89	91	93	95	98
78	80	82	85	87	89	91	93	96	98
79	81	83	85	87	90	92	94	96	98
80	82	84	86	88	90	92	94	96	98
81	83	85	87	89	91	92	94	96	98
82	84	86	87	89	91	93	95	96	98
83	85	86	88	90	92	93	95	97	98
84	86	87	89	90	92	94	95	97	98
85	87	88	90	91	93	94	96	97	99
86	87	89	90	92	93	94	96	97	99
87	88	90	91	92	94	95	96	97	99
88	89	90	92	93	94	95	96	98	99
89	90	91	92	93	95	96	87	38	99
90	91	92	93	94	95	96	97	98	99
91	92	93	94	95	96	96	97	98	99
92	93	94	94	95	96	97	98	98	99
93	94	94	95	96	97	97	98	99	99
94	95	95	96	96	97	98	98	99	99

How about an example? Assume you've been granted a rating of 10 percent for one condition, a rating of 20 percent for another condition, and a rating of 40 percent for still another disability:

1. **Take the highest rating (40), and locate it at the top of the chart.**

2. **Take the next highest rating (20), and locate it at the left of the chart.**

   The lines for these two ratings intersect at a combined rating of 52.

3. **Now take the final rating (10) and locate it at the top of the chart.**

4. Locate the combined rating (52) on the left side.

The combined rating for all three conditions is 57. Rounding to the nearest multiple of 10 gives you a combined disability rating of 60 percent.

Although not depicted in Table 6-1, a disability rating of 10 percent plus a disability rating of 10 percent equals a combined disability rating of 19 percent.

Don't round to the nearest multiple of 10 until all the disability ratings have been combined.

How Much Is Your Disability Compensation?

If you have a disability rating awarded by the VA for a service-connected condition (see "Determining your disability rating" earlier in the chapter), you are eligible for monthly (tax-free) disability compensation from the government. The amount of basic benefits paid ranges from $117 to $2,527 per month (2008 rates), depending on how disabled you are.

Unless you're rated as 10 or 20 percent disabled, you receive even higher compensation for dependents (spouse, children, and dependent parents), and even more if your spouse is seriously disabled and requires special aid and assistance (A/A) in the home.

Figuring monthly rates

Your monthly disability compensation depends primarily on your disability rating. For those rated at 30 percent or more, rates increase based on the number of dependents you have.

If you're rated at 10 percent disabled, your 2008 monthly disability rate is $117 per month. If you're 20 percent disabled, it's $230 per month.

If you're rated as 30 percent disabled or more, the 2008 monthly entitlements are shown in Table 6-2 and Table 6-3. Table 6-2 shows the rates for veterans who don't have children, while Table 6-3 displays the rates for veterans with children.

Table 6-2	Disability Compensation for Veterans without Children (2008)							
Dependent Status	*30%*	*40%*	*50%*	*60%*	*70%*	*80%*	*90%*	*100%*
Veteran alone	$356	$512	$728	$921	$1,161	$1,349	$1,517	$2,527
Veteran with spouse only	$398	$568	$799	$1,006	$1,260	$1,462	$1,644	$2,669
Veteran with spouse and one dependent parent	$432	$613	$856	$1,074	$1,339	$1,553	$1,746	$2,783
Veteran with spouse and two dependent parents	$466	$658	$913	$1,142	$1,418	$1,644	$1,848	$2,897
Veteran with one dependent parent	$390	$557	$785	$989	$1,240	$1,440	$1,619	$2,641
Veteran with two dependent parents	$424	$602	$842	$1,057	$1,319	$1,531	$1,721	$2,755
Additional for A/A spouse	$39	$52	$64	$77	$90	$103	$116	$129

Table 6-3	Disability Compensation for Veterans with Children (2008)							
Dependent Status	*30%*	*40%*	*50%*	*60%*	*70%*	*80%*	*90%*	*100%*
Veteran with spouse and child	$429	$610	$850	$1,068	$1,332	$1,545	$1,737	$2,772
Veteran with child only	$384	$550	$776	$978	$1,228	$1,425	$1,603	$2,623

(continued)

Table 6-3 *(continued)*

Dependent Status	30%	40%	50%	60%	70%	80%	90%	100%
Veteran with spouse, one dependent parent, and child	$463	$655	$907	$1,136	$1,411	$1,636	$1,839	$2,886
Veteran with spouse, two dependent parents, and child	$497	$700	$964	$1,204	$1,490	$1,727	$1,941	$3,000
Veteran with one dependent parent and child	$418	$595	$833	$1,046	$1,307	$1,516	$1,705	$2,737
Veteran with two dependent parents and child	$452	$640	$890	$1,114	$1,386	$1,607	$1,807	$2,851
Add for each additional child under age 18	$21	$28	$35	$42	$49	$56	$63	$71
Each additional school child age 18-22	$68	$90	$113	$136	$158	$181	$204	$227
Additional for A/A spouse	$39	$52	$64	$77	$90	$103	$116	$129

As with most veterans benefits, *children* are considered to be those under the age of 18, or under the age of 23 if attending a college or university as a full-time student. Also included are children who are incapable of self-care if the incapability happened before the age of 18 (or 23 if enrolled in school).

The rates shown in Tables 6-2 and 6-3 are for the year 2008. The VA adjusts the rates on December 1 of each year to account for inflation. For the latest rates, visit the VA's Web site at www.vba.va.gov/bln/21/Rates.

Special monthly compensation

Through *special monthly compensation (SMC),* the VA can pay additional compensation to a veteran who, as a result of military service, incurred the loss or loss of use of specific organs or extremities. The additional compensation can range from $3,145 per month to $7,556 per month (2008 rates). The exact amount payable depends on several factors, including the exact medical condition (or combination of conditions) and number of dependents.

Loss, or *loss of use,* is described as either an amputation or having no effective remaining function of an extremity or organ. The disabilities that the VA can consider for SMC include:

- Loss or loss of use of a hand or foot
- Immobility of a joint or paralysis
- Loss of sight or an eye (having only light perception)
- Loss or loss of use of a reproductive organ
- Complete loss or loss of use of both buttocks
- Deafness in both ears (having absence of air and bone conduction)
- Inability to communicate by speech (complete organic aphonia)
- Loss of a percentage of tissue from a single breast or both breasts from mastectomy or radiation treatment

The VA will pay higher rates for combinations of these disabilities, such as loss or loss of use of the feet, legs, hands, and arms, in specific monetary increments, based on the particular combination of the disabilities. There are also higher payments for various combinations of severe deafness with bilateral blindness.

If you have a service-connected disability rated at 100 percent, and you are housebound, bedridden, or so helpless that you need the aid and attendance of another person, you can also receive SMC.

Current SMC rates can be found on the VA's Web site at `www.vba.va.gov/bln/21/Rates/comp02.htm`.

As you read through the charts online, you'll note that the particular conditions are coded, such as SMC L, SMC N, or SMC L. These correspond to specific disabilities listed under federal law in United States Code (USC), Title 38, Section 1114. You can look up these definitions online at `www4.law.cornell.edu/uscode`.

Concurrent receipt: Military retired pay and disability compensation

It used to be that in order to receive VA disability compensation, a military retiree was forced to waive an equivalent amount of her retirement pay. After years and years and years of veteran complaints, Congress finally agreed that this was a bummer and changed the law in 2004 to allow concurrent receipt. Simply put, *concurrent receipt* means you can receive the full amount of your military retired pay (as explained in Chapter 7) and the full amount of any VA disability compensation you may be entitled to.

However, veterans didn't get everything they asked for (when do they?). The change only applies to veterans who have service-connected disability ratings of 50 percent or more. Veterans who have disability ratings of less than 50 percent must still waive an equivalent amount of their military retirement pay to receive VA disability compensation

Waiving military retirement pay to receive VA disability compensation is a good choice because military retirement pay is taxable, while disability compensation is not.

Also, the change hasn't been fully implemented yet. To save money (Congress critters often use that as an excuse), the change is being phased in. Each year, the percentage of military retirement pay exempt from concurrent receipt restrictions is increased. The phase-in will be complete in 2014, when the full amount of military retirement pay will be exempt.

Combat-Related Special Compensation

Veteran lobby groups really hoped that Congress would expand the concurrent receipt law (see the preceding section) to include veterans with service-connected disabilities of less than 50 percent.

But Washington's waskely wabbits had a different idea. They created a new program called *Combat-Related Special Compensation,* or *CRSC.* Under this program, any veteran with a combat-related disability can be paid a monthly special pay that is intended to reduce or eliminate the offset of military retirement pay.

For the purpose of this program, the individual military service, not the VA, decides whether a disability is considered combat related.

You're eligible for monthly CRSC payments if you receive military retirement pay, as explained in Chapter 7, and you have a disability incurred as a direct result of

- ✔ Armed conflict (gunshot wounds, Purple Heart, so on)
- ✔ Training that simulates war (exercises, field training, so on)
- ✔ Hazardous duty (flight, diving, parachute duty)
- ✔ An instrumentality of war (combat vehicles, weapons, Agent Orange, so on)

Table 6-4 shows the authorized amounts of monthly CRSC payments for 2008. Like VA disability compensation, CRSC payments aren't subject to income taxes.

Table 6-4	Monthly CRSC Payments (2008)
Combat-Related VA Disability Rating	*Monthly CRSC*
100%	$2,527
90%	$1,517
80%	$1,349
70%	$1,161
60%	$921
50%	$728
40%	$512
30%	$356
20%	$230
10%	$117

CRSC is intended to reduce or eliminate the concurrent receipt restrictions. Therefore, the amount of CRSC plus the amount of retirement pay you receive can't exceed the amount of full retirement pay you would be authorized to receive if not for the offset.

Updating Your Home to Accommodate Your Disability

If you suffered a disability while you were serving, chances are you need to make some structural changes to your home. The good news is that the government has put some programs in place to help you. The VA has four main grant programs designed to assist disabled veterans with necessary home modifications:

✔ The Specially Adapted Housing (SAH) grant

✔ The Special Home Adaptation (SHA) grant

✔ The Temporary Residence Adaption (TRA) grant

✔ The Home Improvements and Structural Alterations (HISA) grant

To find out how to apply for any of these grants, flip to the "Adaptive housing grants" section at the end of the chapter.

Specially Adapted Housing (SAH) grant

The goal of the Specially Adapted Housing (SAH) Grant Program is to provide a barrier-free living environment that gives a disabled veteran a level of independent living that he may otherwise not enjoy. This grant is available if you have a service-connected disability for any of the following:

✔ The loss or loss of use of both legs so that you can't move without the aid of braces, crutches, canes, or a wheelchair

✔ Blindness in both eyes, having only light perception, plus the loss or loss of use of one leg

✔ The loss or loss of use of one leg together with (1) residuals of organic disease or injury, or (2) the loss or loss of use of one arm, which affects your balance or movement so that you can't get around without the aid of braces, crutches, canes, or a wheelchair

A *residual* is doctor-talk for aftereffects. For example, if you had lung cancer that was cured by surgery or radiation, your lungs may still have scarring, which could affect your ability to breathe. Doctors would call this condition a residual of the lung cancer.

✔ The loss or loss of use of both arms at or above the elbow

The grant can be used to pay for the construction of an adapted home or modification of an existing home to meet your adaptive needs. The SAH grant is generally used to create a wheelchair-accessible home. This grant is currently limited to $60,000.

Special Home Adaptation (SHA) grant

If you are permanently and totally (100 percent) disabled with a service-connected disability for blindness (vision of no better than 5/200 when corrected with glasses), or you suffer from the anatomical loss or loss of use of both hands or arms below the elbow, you may be eligible to receive a Special Home Adaptation (SHA) grant of up to $12,000.

This grant is generally used to assist veterans with mobility throughout their homes.

Temporary Residence Adaptation (TRA) grant

If you're eligible for SAH or SHA, you can use part of that money to modify a family member's home to fit your needs if you're temporarily living with her. You can use up to $14,000 of the maximum SAH assistance or up to $2,000 of the maximum SHA assistance for this purpose.

Under current law, the Temporary Residence Adaption (TRA) Grant Program ends June 15, 2011. Of course, Congress could decide to extend this deadline in future legislation.

Home Improvements and Structural Alterations (HISA) grant

The Home Improvements and Structural Alterations (HISA) grant is available to veterans with service-connected disabilities and those with non-service-connected disabilities. The purpose of the grant is to make any home improvement necessary for the continuation of treatment or for disability access to the home and bathroom facilities.

To be eligible, a VA doctor must indicate that improvements and structural alterations are necessary or appropriate for the effective and economical treatment of your disability (see Chapter 4). You can receive up to $4,100 if you have a service-connected disability and up to $1,200 if you have a non-service-connected disability.

Clothing Allowance: Replacing Your Wardrobe

Any veteran who is entitled to receive disability compensation for a service-connected disability for which he uses prosthetic or orthopedic appliances may receive an annual clothing allowance.

The allowance also is available to any veteran whose service-connected skin condition requires prescribed medication that damages the veteran's outer garments. The clothing allowance rate as of 2008 is $641 per year.

To find out how to apply for this allowance, flip to the later "Clothing allowance" section.

Looking into VA Pensions

A VA pension is a benefit paid to wartime veterans who have limited or no income and are age 65 or older, or if under 65, are permanently and totally disabled.

VA disability compensation (see the "How Much Is Your Disability Compensation?" section) is payable to veterans who have service-connected disabilities that have been rated by the VA to be at least 10 percent disabling (see the "Checking Your Eligibility for Disability Compensation" section). You can't receive VA disability compensation for disabilities that aren't service-connected.

VA pensions, on the other hand, are payable to many veterans who have at least one day of wartime service, even if they don't have a service-connected disability.

Generally, you may be eligible for the VA pension if you meet all the following criteria:

✔ You were discharged from service under conditions other than dishonorable (see Chapter 2 for information about how the VA makes this determination).

✔ You served at least 90 days of active military service, one day of which was during a wartime period. If you entered active duty after September 7, 1980, generally you must have served at least 24 months or — if you're a member of the Reserves or National Guard — the full period for which called or ordered to active duty.

✔ Your countable family income is below a yearly limit set by law (the yearly limit on income is set by Congress).

✔ You are age 65 or older, *or* you are permanently and totally disabled, not due to your own willful misconduct. The disability doesn't have to be service connected.

To receive a VA pension, you must have an annual household income below the limits shown in Table 6-5.

Table 6-5	Household Income Limits for the Year 2008
If You Are a . . .	*Your Yearly Income Must Be Less Than . . .*
Veteran with no dependents	$11,181
Veteran with a spouse or a child	$14,643
Housebound veteran with no dependents	$13,664
Housebound veteran with one dependent	$17,126
Veteran who needs aid and attendance and has no dependents	$18,654
Veteran who needs aid and attendance and has one dependent	$22,113
Note: For each additional child	Add $1,909 to the limit

Congress usually changes these limits on December 1 of each year to account for inflation. For the current limits, see www.vba.va.gov/bln/21/Rates.

Counting your income

Your *countable income* includes income received by you or your dependents, if any, from most sources. It includes earnings, disability and retirement payments, interest and dividends, and net income from farming or business.

There is a presumption that all your child's income is available to or for you. However, you can exclude a portion of your child's income. For 2008, the annual exclusion limit is $8,950.

Some income is not counted toward the yearly limit. For example, welfare benefits, food stamps, and Supplemental Security Income (SSI) aren't counted. Additionally, you're allowed to deduct certain medical and educational expenses. When you apply for a VA pension (see the "Applying in All the Right Places" section), you should include all income and deductions. The VA will exclude any income and include all deductions allowed by law when computing your annual family income.

Receiving payment

Assuming you qualify, your annual pension is the difference between your countable family income (after exclusions and deductions) and the income limits shown in Table 6-5. This amount is then divided by 12 and rounded down to the nearest dollar. This gives you the amount of your monthly pension payment. VA pensions are exempt from income taxes.

You can't receive a VA non-service-connected pension and service-connected disability compensation (see the "How Much Is Your Disability Compensation?" section) at the same time. However, if you apply for the pension and are awarded payments, the VA will pay you whichever benefit is the greater amount.

Medal of Honor pensions

Veterans who have earned our nation's highest military decoration, the Medal of Honor, receive a lifelong pension, beginning when they retire or separate from the military. This pension is paid in addition to any other monetary benefits they may be entitled to, such as military retirement (see Chapter 7) or VA disability compensation (see the section "How Much Is Your Disability Compensation?").

The pension rate for 2008 is $1,129 per month. The Medal of Honor pension is not subject to income taxes.

Congress generally changes this rate on December 1 of each year to account for inflation. For the current rates, see www.vba.va.gov/bln/21/Rates/special1.htm.

Applying in All the Right Places

You guessed it. You can't get any of the goodies described in this chapter without paperwork. Exactly what paperwork, where you get it, and where you send it depend on the specific benefit that you're applying for.

VA disability compensation or pension

To apply for either VA disability compensation or a VA pension, use VA Form 21-526, Veteran's Application for Compensation and/or Pension. If available, attach copies of dependency records (marriage and children's birth certificates), as well as proof of military service and discharge characterization (see Chapter 2).

You can obtain the form from any VA regional office (see Appendix B) or download it from the VA's Web site at www.vba.va.gov/pubs/forms/ VBA-21-526-ARE.pdf. Return the completed application, along with the supporting evidence, to your closest VA office.

Combat-Related Special Compensation

To receive this benefit, you must apply through your individual military service. The application is made on DD Form 2860, Claim for Combat-Related Special Compensation (CRSC). The form is available at the Military Pay and Finance section on any military base, or you can download it online at www. dtic.mil/whs/directives/infomgt/forms/eforms/dd2860.pdf.

Along with the application, include any documentation that you feel is relevant. Examples of documentation you may want to send include copies of the following:

- ✔ Retirement orders
- ✔ 20-year letter or statement of service (for reservists)
- ✔ Relevant pages in your VA or military medical records
- ✔ VA ratings determinations
- ✔ Purple Heart decoration award citations (if applicable)
- ✔ Retirement Form DD Form 214 (see Chapter 2)

The Department of Defense (DOD) guidance doesn't provide an exhaustive list of relevant documentation but instead states that decisions will be made on the significance of available documents. Keep in mind that the quality of the information is more important than the quantity.

Be sure to send copies — not original documents. Original documents won't be returned.

Mail the completed application to the appropriate address (of the military service you retired from), listed on page 1 of the application form.

After a final decision is made, your branch of service will notify you in writing of approval or denial of your application. If approved, a copy of your approval letter will be forwarded to the Defense Finance and Accounting Service, which will start your monthly CRSC payments.

Adaptive housing grants

You can apply for Specially Adapted Housing (SAH) and Special Home Adaptation (SHA) grants by completing VA Form 26-4555, Veterans Application in Acquiring Specially Adapted Housing or Special Home Adaptation Grant. The form is available at any VA regional office (see Appendix B) or online at www.vba.va.gov/pubs/forms/VBA-26-4555-ARE.pdf. Return the completed form to your closest VA regional office.

You can apply for the Home Improvement and Structural Alterations (HISA) grant by completing VA Form 10-0103, Veterans Application for Assistance in Acquiring Home Improvement and Structural Alterations. This form is available from your VA medical center (see Appendix C). It's also available from the VA's Web site at www.prosthetics.va.gov/docs/vha-10-0103-fill.pdf. Return this completed form to the VA medical center that you receive your VA medical care from (see Chapter 4).

Clothing allowance

Application for a clothing allowance is made by completing VA Form 10-8678, Application for Annual Clothing Allowance. This form is available at VA medical centers (see Appendix C) or online at www.va.gov/vaforms/medical/pdf/vha-10-8678-fill.pdf. Upon completion, submit the form to the VA medical center that provides your medical treatment.

Chapter 7

Getting Your Military Retirement Pay

Military service is a tough life. Sure, it has advantages. You get to travel and see the world — lovely garden spots such as Kuwait, Afghanistan, Bosnia, and Kosovo. Hours are often long, but on the bright side, the work is hard. There's no overtime pay. You uproot your family every couple of years and move to another location. If you lose it and yell at your boss, you not only will be fired (discharged), but you could wind up in jail as well. And it seems as if someone is always shooting at you. Ah, how I miss it all.

Those who can adjust to this rigorous lifestyle and live it 20 or more years are rewarded for the rest of their lives with a monthly military retirement check.

Military retirement pay is unlike civilian retirement pay systems. There's no vesting, no matching funds, no interest, and no special retirement accounts. A retired military member is subject to the Uniform Code of Military Justice (UCMJ), that code of laws that applies only to military members. That means, for example, that a military retired member can be court-martialed for misconduct committed as a retired member. Additionally, a military member can be involuntarily "un-retired" (that is, returned to active duty) for any reason that the military feels is appropriate. Other than these minor inconveniences, getting a monthly check for the rest of your life is a pretty sweet deal.

Understanding Retainer versus Retired

After you've put in so many years of military service, you can retire. However, the number of years you have to serve differs between the branches. (As I'm sure you're well aware, nothing's ever simple with the military.)

If you serve in the Army, Air Force, or Coast Guard, you can retire after 20 years of military service. After you pick up your retirement orders and have that final farewell bash with your buddies, you're called a *retired member*.

Of course, the Navy and the Marine Corps have elected to be different. For Navy and Marine Corps members, you are considered to be a *retired member* for classification purposes if you are

- An enlisted member with more than 30 years of service
- A warrant or commissioned officer with 20 or more years of military service

Enlisted Navy and Marine Corps members with less than 30 years of service but more than 20 years are transferred to the Fleet Reserve/Fleet Marine Corps Reserve, and their pay is referred to as *retainer pay*.

When an enlisted Navy or Marine Corps member completes 30 years, including time on the retired rolls in receipt of retainer pay, the Fleet Reserve status is changed to retired status, and he begins receiving *retired pay*.

Don't get confused about this. A rose by any other name . . . The law treats retired pay and retainer pay exactly the same way. The amount of retainer pay you receive is the exact same amount as retired pay.

So why do these two branches insist on calling it "retainer pay" for some of their members? Good question! Keep reading for the answer.

Becoming "unretired:" Recall to active duty

One of the reasons that the Navy and Marine Corps use the term "retainer" for some of their retirees is that they want to emphasize to the member, to Congress, and to the general public that the military retirement system is different. Members — especially those who have recently retired — can be recalled to active duty anytime the service wants them. For this reason, military officials often refer to military retirement/retainer pay as "reduced pay for reduced services."

Younger retirees who are healthy are more likely to be recalled to active duty in times of need than older retirees or those with a disability.

Department of Defense (DOD) Directive 1352.1 places retirees into one of three categories, with Category I the most likely to be recalled during times of war, national emergency, or "needs of the service":

✔ **Category I:** Nondisabled military retirees under age 60 who have been retired less than five years.

✔ **Category II:** Nondisabled military retirees under age 60 who have been retired five years or more.

✔ **Category III:** Military retirees, age 60 or older, and those retired for disability.

Military retired members of any age can be recalled to active duty to face court-martial charges. I should emphasize, however, that this doesn't happen very often. In most cases, the military allows the civilian justice system to process military retirees who engage in misconduct.

Retirement versus discharge

Another difference between the military retirement program and most civilian retirement systems is that there is no vesting. In other words, it's all or nothing. You either qualify for retirement by honorably serving at least 20 years in the military, or you do not.

If you're discharged from the military with 19 years, 11 months, and 27 days of service, for example, you don't qualify for retirement pay (other than a few early retirement programs offered during the 1980s and 1990s, which were designed to reduce the size of the armed forces).

Additionally, to be entitled to receive retirement pay from the military, your service must be characterized as honorable. A general discharge under honorable conditions won't hack it (see Chapter 2 for information about service characterizations).

Figuring Out Your Retirement Pay

Military members receive all kinds of pay, depending on their job, assignment, and other individual factors. As a member of the military, you may receive combat pay, subsistence allowance, housing allowance, hazardous duty pay, flight pay, jump pay, sea pay, submarine duty pay, and more. When it comes to retirement pay calculation, however, only basic pay counts. Everyone in the military receives basic pay. The amount of monthly basic pay you receive is based on your rank and how many years of military service you have.

In the vast majority of cases, your retirement rank is the same as the rank you held at the time you retired. However, if you spent part of your military career as a commissioned officer, this may not be the case. To retire in your commissioned rank, the law requires that you have at least 10 years of service as a commissioned officer.

This won't affect your retirement pay if you're under the High 36 program (see "The High 36 Retirement Program" later in the chapter) because it's computed using your highest 36 months of basic pay. But if you entered the military before September 8, 1980, the amount of time you spent as a commissioned officer could have a significant impact on your retirement pay.

A military member who entered the service prior to September 8, 1980, and first enlisted and later became commissioned, but has less than 10 years of commissioned service, would retire using the basic pay of the highest *enlisted* rank he held. Because enlisted members generally make much less in basic pay than commissioned officers, this could put a serious dent in your retirement wallet.

Basic pay rates from 1949 to present can be found on the Defense Finance and Accounting Web site at www.dfas.mil/militarypay/military paytables.html.

Retirement pay is calculated differently for those who retire from active duty and for those who retire from the National Guard or reserves. That's because folks on active duty serve full time, while those in the Guard and Reserves serve a mixture of full-time and part-time duty. Chapter 2 provides more information about active-duty vs. Guard/Reserve service. I go into more detail on how service time relates to retirement pay later in the chapter.

Calculating active-duty retirement

To retire from active duty you must have at least 20 years of active-duty military service. The basic formula to calculate your retirement pay is

Basic Pay × Number of Years Active-Duty Service × 2.5%

Imagine that you're an E-6 with 20 years of military service, earning a basic pay of $3,243.30 per month. Here's how you'd calculate your retirement pay:

$3,243.30 × 20 years = $64,866
$64,866 × 2.5% = $1,621.65

My, how times have changed

Every year, Congress passes a Defense Authorization Act and a Defense Appropriations Act, which — among other things — set the military basic pay rates for the upcoming year. It's interesting to see how times have changed over the years.

My uncle retired from the Army in 1949 in the pay grade of E-6 with 20 years of service.

In 1949, an enlisted member in the pay grade of E-6 with 20 years of service took home $249.90 per month in basic pay. A commissioned officer in the pay grade of O-6 with 20 years of service made $612.75 per month.

In 2008, that same E-6 would have earned $3,243.30 per month in basic pay, and the O-6 would have made a whopping $8,075.10 per month.

I retired from the Air Force in 1998 as an E-8 with 23 years of service. At the time of my retirement, my basic pay was $2,873.10 per month. Just in case you were wondering.

Hold on, you're not done yet. Whether you receive this amount or a slightly less *averaged* amount, casually referred to as "High 3," depends on when you joined the military. You can get all the details on High 3 in the "The High 36 Retirement Program" section.

Active-duty members begin receiving their retirement pay on the first day of the month after their official date of retirement. Unlike active-duty pay, in which the monthly earned pay is equally divided between two paydays (the 1st and the 15th of each month), you receive your retirement pay only on the 1st of the month. If the 1st falls on a weekend or holiday, you receive your monthly retirement pay on the first business day after the 1st.

Computing reserve retirement points and pay

The formula used to compute National Guard and Reserve retirement pay is the same as for active duty, with one major exception: Because active-duty service is full time and Guard/Reserve service is a mixture of part-time and full-time duty, you first have to calculate *equivalent active-duty time*. After all, fair is fair, right?

Members of the National Guard and Reserves receive *retirement points*. At a minimum, they're required to perform one weekend of drill per month, plus two weeks of active-duty training per year. Sometimes they spend extra time on active duty, such as if they need to attend a military training school or if they're called for deployment.

Guard/Reserve members receive 4 points for each weekend drill and 1 point for each day spent on active duty, such as deployments, active duty for training (ADT) (including the two weeks of training per year), and attending military school.

Qualifying years

Like active-duty members, Guard/Reserve individuals must have at least 20 years of service to qualify for retirement. However, those years must be *qualifying years*. A qualifying year is one in which you earn a minimum of 50 retirement points.

If you perform the minimum required duty (one weekend per month of drill, plus two weeks per year of active-duty training) for a year, you receive a total of 62 points, making that a qualifying year for retirement. That actually gives you a little buffer zone in case you have to miss a weekend drill or two during the year.

60/75 point rule

Can you persuade your commander to let you work every weekend, and thereby increase your retirement points for the year? To a point, yes. Weekend drill is *inactive duty time*. That's an important distinction because the law only allows you to accumulate a total of 60 points per year of inactive duty time for service prior to 1996, and 75 points per year for duty performed after 1996. What a bummer!

Full-time duty you spend in military schools and during deployments is active-duty time, not inactive-duty time, and isn't subject to the 60/75 point rule. For example, if you were deployed to Iraq for a year, you'd earn 365 retirement points (366 retirement points if you deployed during a leap year).

Converting points to years

To determine how much retired pay you may be eligible to receive, the first step is to calculate the number of equivalent years of service. The formula for computing equivalent years of service for Guard/Reserve retired pay is fairly simple:

Total Number of Retirement Points ÷ 360

The formula computes the number of equivalent years of service the soldier has completed (comparable to full-time active-duty service). For example, 3,600 points equals 10 years of equivalent active-duty service.

The formula to compute your pay is then the same as for active-duty retirement pay:

Basic Pay × Number of Years Equivalent Active-Duty Service × 2.5%

As with active-duty retirement pay, whether you receive this amount or a lesser, averaged amount depends on when you first joined the military. See the "The High 36 Retirement Program" section.

Knowing when to expect your first check

Members who retire from the National Guard and Reserves don't receive their retirement pay immediately upon retirement. They receive their first pay when they reach the age of 60.

That's the bad news. The good news is that Congress fiddled a little with Guard/Reserve retirement in 2008. Under the 2008 National Defense Authorization Act, Congress reduced the age for receipt of Guard/Reserve retired pay by three months for each 90 days of specified duty performed in any fiscal year after January 28, 2008. *Specified duty* includes active duty for deployment to a combat zone and when called to active duty in response to a national emergency declared by the president or supported by federal funds. Your retired pay eligibility age, however, can't be reduced below the age of 50.

The High 36 Retirement Program

During the 1980s, Congress decided that military retirement pay benefits were too generous, so they did something about it while trimming the federal budget a bit along the way. Congress enacted a provision, the *High 36 Retirement Program,* that could affect the final retirement pay you receive. Some folks call this the "High 3" program because 36 months equals 3 years.

If you joined the military before September 8, 1980, you're not affected by the High 36 program. Your retirement pay is your final base pay multiplied by the number of years of active-duty service multiplied by 2.5 percent.

On the other hand, if you joined the military on or after September 8, 1980, your retirement pay will be reduced significantly under High 36.

Under High 36, instead of using your final base pay in the formula, you use the average of your highest 36 months of basic pay. The exact amount of retired pay varies with each individual because of pay increase factors during the member's final 36 months of service. For example, military members receive a cost of living allowance (COLA) every January, which increases their basic pay. Also, their basic pay increases when they have more time-in-service. Finally, if they get promoted during their final 36 months of service, that increases their basic pay. On average, High 36 retirement pay is about 10 percent less than retirement pay for those who aren't subject to High 36.

Is it taxable?

I run into civilians all the time who think that my military retirement pay is tax free. Not so, folks. Military retirees pay their fair share of the costs of running our government.

Military retirement pay is subject to federal income tax. The amount deducted from your pay for federal withholding tax each month is based on the number of exemptions you indicate on your W-4 after retirement. Whether your retirement pay is subject to state income tax depends on your state's laws. Some states exempt military retired pay from state income taxes. Contact your state's veterans office (see Appendix B) for more information about state taxes and military retirement pay.

You can change the amount of tax withheld from your retirement pay each month by completing a new W-4 at any time. See "Keeping DFAS Up-to-Date."

Although military retirement pay is subject to federal income tax, it's not subject to FICA (Social Security) deductions.

Medical retirement pay is tax free if you joined the military before September 24, 1975. It's also tax free if the military makes a determination that your medical condition is combat related.

How retired pay fits with Social Security and other money matters

The question I'm probably asked the most from military retirees who have not yet reached the age of 65 is, "Will military retired pay affect my Social Security benefits?" The answer, thankfully, is no. Your military retirement pay isn't reduced when you receive Social Security, nor are your Social Security benefits reduced because you receive military retirement pay.

If you're receiving disability compensation from the Department of Veterans Affairs (VA), your military retirement pay is reduced by the amount of VA disability compensation you receive, unless you qualify for an offset because your disability rating is 50 percent or more, or you're eligible for Combat-Related Special Compensation. Both of these program are explained in Chapter 6.

Unlike active-duty and National Guard/Reserve pay, military retired pay can't be garnished for commercial debts (credit cards, automobile loans, and the like). Military retirement pay can, however, be garnished for alimony, child support, IRS tax levies, and debts owed to the government.

Also, if you retire from the military and elect to get a federal government job (see Chapter 12), you may continue to receive your military retirement pay during your federal employment. However, if or when you retire from federal civil service, you can waive your future military retired pay to include your military service in the computation of your civil service annuity. Depending on which of the dozens of civil service retirement programs you fall under, this could be a good deal.

If you elect to combine your military retirement with your civil service retirement, you no longer qualify for the disability compensation offset or the Combat-Related Special Compensation programs explained in Chapter 6.

Taking the bonus

In 2001, Congress made another significant change to the military retirement system. The program is called *Career Status Bonus* (and is commonly referred to as *Redux*). Under Redux, active-duty military members can elect to take a lump-sum bonus of $30,000 when they have 15 years of military service, in exchange for an agreement to accept a decreased retirement pay amount.

This is a good deal — for the government, not for the veteran. Congress's goal in establishing this program was to save hundreds of millions of dollars in future retirement obligations. It works well, but at the veteran's expense. In fact, it could be argued that no payday lender has ever ripped off a military member as the government has done with this program.

For a 20-year military career, High 3 provides retirement pay equal to 50 percent of your average basic pay over your three highest income years (see the section "The High 36 Retirement Program" for details). Redux pays only 40 percent for a 20-year retiree. The percentage gap narrows for each year of military service performed past 20 years, so that for 30 years of service, both plans pay 75 percent of the average of 36 months of basic pay. But most members don't serve 30-year careers. Redux also includes a cap on annual retirement pay cost of living allowances (COLA). See the "Getting a yearly pay raise" section.

While other military retirees receive an annual COLA equal to the cost of inflation, Redux retirees have their COLA capped by a full percentage point below the inflation rate. Redux does provide a one-time catch-up in purchasing power at age 62, but then the capped COLAs continue until death.

Several military and government think tanks have dissected this program north and south. Their conclusions? It's a bad deal. The average loss in retirement pay over a normal life span is about $300,000.

Consider a typical enlisted member who takes the $30,000 bonus at 15 years of service. The amount received, after taxes, is actually about $25,500. If you retired at 20 years in the pay grade of E-7 at age 38, the lifetime retirement loss would be $344,400, or 13 times the value of the bonus.

Look at it this way: If you finance a home for 30 years, you'd typically pay the mortgage lender about 2¹/₂ times the loan's value. However, in accepting the Redux bonus, you would be agreeing to pay back 13 times the amount of money you "borrowed." Take my advice: Walk away from this particular bribe.

Getting a yearly pay raise

A military member in the pay grade of E-7 who retired after 20 years of service in 1980 earned about $609.60 per month in retirement pay. How would you like to try to live on that today?

Fortunately for the retiree in the example, he doesn't have to. Military retirees receive an *annual cost of living adjustment,* or *COLA,* on December 1 of each year.

The amount of the COLA is equal to the inflation rate for that year, based on the consumer price index (CPI). The purpose of the annual COLA is to help retirees maintain the same purchasing power from year to year.

If you accepted the Career Status Bonus (also known as Redux), your COLA will be capped at one full percentage point below the rate of inflation. See the "Taking the bonus" section earlier in this chapter.

Getting a Handle on Medical Retirement

Military service is a dangerous business. Sometimes a serious injury or illness may interrupt a successful military career. In such cases, military medical authorities may decide that medical retirement is appropriate if the medical condition is severe enough to interfere with the proper performance of your military duties.

Medical evaluation boards

When a military doctor determines that you have a medical condition that may interfere with the performance of your military duties, he refers the case to a *Physical Evaluation Board (PEB).* This medical board consists of active-duty physicians (not personally involved in your medical care) who review the clinical case file and decide whether you should be returned to duty or medically separated or retired using the published medical standards for continued military service.

You can see the list of medical conditions that are generally considered incompatible with continued military service online at usmilitary.about.com/od/theorderlyroom/l/blmedstandards.htm.

The PEB's recommendations are forwarded to a central medical board that uses four factors to determine whether your disposition is fit for duty, separation, permanent retirement, or temporary retirement (see the next section for more on disposition types):

- Whether you can perform your military job
- Your assigned disability rating
- The stability of your medical condition
- Years of active-duty service in the case of preexisting conditions

You can appeal the central medical board's decision, and you're allowed to have legal counsel at these hearings.

The military is required by law to rate your disability using the "Department of Veterans Affairs Schedule for Rating Disabilities." However, DOD Instruction 1332.39 allows the military to modify the rating schedule, based on conditions that are unique to the military. Ratings can range from 0 to 100 percent, rising in increments of 10.

Don't confuse disability ratings granted by the military with disability ratings awarded by the VA (see Chapter 6). While both the DOD and the VA use the "Department of Veterans Affairs Schedule for Rating Disabilities," not all the general policy provisions set forth in the rating schedule apply to the military. Consequently, disability ratings may vary between the two. The military rates only conditions determined to be physically unfitting, compensating for loss of a military career. The VA may rate any service-connected impairment, thus compensating for loss of civilian employability.

Types of disposition

Depending on several factors, the central medical board may order that you be returned to duty, medically separated without severance pay, medically separated with severance pay, permanently medically retired, or temporarily medically retired. Here's the lowdown on each of these:

✔ **Fit for duty:** The board judges you to be fit for duty when you can reasonably perform the duties of rank and military job. If the board finds you to be medically unfit to perform the duties of your current military job, it can order medical retraining into a job you are medically qualified to perform.

✔ **Separated without severance pay:** Separation without severance benefits occurs if your medical condition existed prior to service, wasn't permanently aggravated by military service, and you have less than eight years of active-duty service (or equivalent Guard/Reserve retirement points).

It is also imposed if you suffered your disability while you were absent without leave (AWOL) or while engaged in an act of misconduct or willful negligence.

✔ **Separated with severance pay:** Medical separation with severance pay occurs if you're found unfit for duty, have fewer than 20 years of service, and the board awards a disability rating of less than 30 percent. Disability severance pay equals 2 months of basic pay for each year of service not to exceed 12 years of service. You may also be eligible to apply for monthly disability compensation from the VA if it determines your disability is service connected. See Chapter 6 for details.

If you are approved for disability compensation from the VA, the law requires the VA to recoup your military severance pay before paying your disability compensation benefits.

✔ **Permanent medical retirement:** Permanent disability retirement occurs if you are found unfit, and your disability is determined permanent and stable and is rated at a minimum of 30 percent. You may also be eligible for VA disability compensation if the VA determines your medical condition constitutes a service-connected disability. (Chapter 6 provides complete information about VA disability compensation.)

You can also be medically retired if you have 20 or more years of military service, regardless of disability rating. For National Guard and Reserve members, this means at least 7,200 retirement points. See "Computing reserve retirement points and pay" earlier in this chapter.

✔ **Temporary medical retirement:** Temporary medical retirement occurs if the board finds you are unfit and entitled to permanent medical retirement except that your disability is not stable for rating purposes. *Stable for rating purposes* refers to whether the condition will change within the next five years so as to warrant a different disability rating. When this happens, you are placed on the *temporary disability retirement list (TDRL)*. When on the TDRL, you are subject to medical reevaluation every 18 months and limited to 5 years max on the TDRL. At the 5-year point, if not sooner during a reevaluation, you are removed from the TDRL and either found fit and returned to duty, or permanently medically retired.

Medical retirement pay compensation

For permanent retirement or placement on the TDRL, your compensation is based on the higher of two computations: Disability rating × retired pay base; or 2.5 × years of service × retired pay base. Veterans on the TDRL receive no less than 50 percent of their retired pay base.

The computation of your retired pay base depends on when you joined the military. If you joined prior to September 8, 1980, retired pay base is computed from your military basic pay at the time of medical retirement. For those who entered after September 7, 1980, it's the average of the high 36 months of basic pay. See "The High 36 Retirement Program."

Divorce and Its Effects on Military Retirement Pay

If you're married, I hope you're living the "happily ever after" part. Unfortunately, the military divorce rate is about the same as the U.S. civilian divorce rate: about 50 percent.

In 1981, the U.S. Supreme Court ruled that military retirement pay couldn't be divided as community property by state divorce courts. When the decision was announced, military retirees shouted for joy, while ex-spouses sent up cries of protest.

In its decision, however, the court was very clear that division of military retired pay wasn't necessarily unconstitutional, but that current federal laws (at the time) prohibited treating military retired pay as joint property.

Once again, Congress came to the rescue. In 1982, Congress passed the Uniformed Services Former Spouse Protection Act (USFSPA). This act allows state courts to treat disposable retired pay either as property solely of the member, or as property of the member and his spouse in accordance with the laws of the state court.

Contrary to popular belief, there is no "magic formula" contained in the act to determine the appropriate division of retired pay. A state court can divide retired pay in any way it chooses (subject to state laws). For example, it would be perfectly legal for a court to divide military retired pay fifty-fifty for a marriage that only lasted two months (again, subject to the laws of that state). A state could also decide to award a majority of the retired pay to the former spouse if the state laws allowed such a division. Conversely, a court may also choose to treat retired pay as the exclusive property of the military member.

The myth of a "magic formula" derives from a section of the law that allows the DOD to pay the ex-spouse directly, but only under specific circumstances:

✔ The ex-spouse must have been married to the military member for a period of at least ten years, with at least ten years of the marriage over-lapping a period of military service creditable to retired pay.

✔ Direct payments won't be made for division of retired pay in excess of 50 percent. (If there is more than one divorce, it's first come, first served — no more than 50 percent will be paid as division of retired pay. For example, if a court awards ex-spouse number one 40 percent of retired pay, and another court awards ex-spouse number two 40 percent of retired pay, DOD Finance will directly pay ex-spouse number one 40 percent and will directly pay ex-spouse number two 10 percent.)

However, these guidelines only restrict when the DOD can pay the ex-spouse directly. In other situations, the member receives the retirement pay and must directly pay the ex-spouse her share or otherwise face a contempt of court charge.

The moral of the story is don't get divorced. The only ones who get rich are the lawyers.

Keeping DFAS Up-to-Date

After you're retired, you need to keep the Defense Finance and Accounting Service (DFAS) informed of any changes in your account, such as change of address or number of exemptions you'd like to claim for tax withholding purposes.

The toll-free number that may be used for any calls made within the United States, including Alaska and Hawaii, is 800-321-1080. The commercial number for calls made from outside these areas is 216-522-5955.

All telephone lines are staffed Monday through Friday from 7:00 a.m. to 7:30 p.m. (eastern time).

These telephone numbers can be used for general questions about your account and for notifications, such as a change of address. You must sign requests that involve monetary changes. Therefore, you can't make monetary changes over the telephone. You can make monetary changes by mail or by using DFAS's secured myPay Web site at `mypay.dfas.mil`.

The address for requesting monetary changes is Defense Finance & Accounting Service, Cleveland Center Retired Pay Operations (Code PPR), P.O. Box 99191, Cleveland, OH 44199-1126.

Chapter 8

Carrying On: Payments and Benefits for Survivors

In This Chapter

▶ Categorizing your life insurance

▶ Paying the bills with pensions and compensation programs

▶ Getting smart about education programs

▶ Staying healthy with VA medical care

*L*ife goes on, and — in some cases — so do veterans benefits. Many federal benefits are available to survivors of certain veterans. For the most part, "certain veterans" means those who have died on active duty, died as a result of a service-connected medical condition, or have been rated as totally and permanently disabled by the Department of Veterans Affairs (VA). However, that's not true in all cases, so please read through this chapter to see which benefits may be applicable to you.

Veterans benefits for survivors are offered by both the VA and the Department of Defense (DOD). They range from life insurance programs to educational benefits to monthly compensation to medical care. Some surviving spouses can even finance a home through the VA. I touch on all these topics in this chapter.

Ensuring the Family Future: Veterans Life Insurance Programs

Veterans life insurance programs are valuable benefits offered by the government to qualified veterans. The government has established these programs because military members and veterans may find it hard to enroll in civilian life insurance programs because of the risks of military service and the possibility of service-connected disabilities and medical conditions. Depending on your status, you can choose from several programs.

Servicemembers' Group Life Insurance (SGLI)

Members of active duty, the Reserves, and National Guard are automatically enrolled in the Servicemembers' Group Life Insurance (SGLI) program at the maximum coverage, unless they elect (in writing) a reduced amount or no coverage at all.

SGLI premiums are currently $0.065 per $1,000 of insurance, regardless of the member's age, up to a maximum of $400,000 worth of coverage. That means the full coverage costs $27 per month. That's quite a deal.

SGLI rates are subject to change. Check out www.insurance.va.gov/sgliSite/SGLI/sgliPremiums.htm for the current rates.

As an added bonus, coverage of $10,000 is also automatically provided for dependent children of members insured under SGLI with no premium required.

Unfortunately, in most cases SGLI coverage ends 120 days after release from the military. Service members with SGLI coverage have two options upon their release from service:

- ✔ They can convert their SGLI coverage to term insurance under the Veterans' Group Life Insurance program (see the "Veterans' Group Life Insurance [VGLI]" section).

- ✔ They can convert to a permanent plan of insurance with a participating commercial insurance company. For a list of commercial insurance companies that work with the VA, see www.insurance.va.gov/sgliSite/forms/ParticList.htm.

As a result of a law passed by Congress in 2005, service members who have an SGLI policy and are totally disabled when they separate from service can now keep their SGLI coverage for up to two years after separation at no cost.

Traumatic Servicemembers' Group Life Insurance (TSGLI)

All service members and veterans who are enrolled in the Servicemembers' Group Life Insurance (SGLI) program are automatically covered for Traumatic Servicemembers' Group Life Insurance (TSGLI) and pay a monthly premium of $1. TSGLI provides financial assistance to covered members during their recovery period from a serious traumatic injury. Coverage ranges from $25,000 to $100,000, depending on the nature of the injury. For a list of payments, see www.insurance.va.gov/sgliSite/popups/ScheduleOfLosses.htm.

Coverage ends when the SGLI terminates, which in most cases is 120 days after separation from the military. See the "Servicemembers' Group Life Insurance (SGLI)" section.

You don't have to apply for this separate coverage. If you're enrolled in SGLI, you're enrolled in TSGLI automatically.

For a deceased member to be eligible for payment under the TSGLI program, he must have suffered a qualifying traumatic injury and survived for at least seven full days from the date of the traumatic injury. Insurance proceeds will then be paid to the beneficiary named by the member on his SGLI application.

Family Servicemembers' Group Life Insurance (FSGLI)

Family Servicemembers' Group Life Insurance (FSGLI) is a program extended to the spouses and dependent children of members insured under the SGLI program. (See the "Servicemembers' Group Life Insurance [SGLI]" section.)

FSGLI provides a maximum of $100,000 of insurance coverage for spouses, not to exceed the amount of SGLI the insured member has, and $10,000 for dependent children.

FSGLI is a service member benefit for which the member pays the premium and is the beneficiary of the policy. Monthly rates depend on the amount of coverage selected and the age of the spouse. See www.insurance.va.gov/sgliSite/FSGLI/fsgliPremiums.htm for a table of current rates.

FSGLI is only available for family members of those currently in the military. To enroll your family members, contact your unit or base personnel office.

Veterans' Group Life Insurance (VGLI)

Veterans' Group Life Insurance (VGLI) is a program of post-separation insurance that allows a veteran to convert his SGLI coverage to renewable term insurance. You can convert your SGLI coverage to VGLI upon your discharge from the military or within 485 days of discharge. If you convert within 120 days of separation, you don't have to show proof of health. However, if you wait longer to enroll in VGLI, you'll need to show evidence of good health.

VGLI coverage is issued in multiples of $10,000 up to $400,000. However, your VGLI coverage amount can't exceed the amount of SGLI you had at the time of separation from the military.

Monthly premium rates depend on your age and the amount of coverage you elect. Premiums can range from as low as $0.80 per month to a whopping $1,800 per month. That's not a typo, folks. A veteran over the age of 75 would have to pay $1,800 per month for the maximum coverage under VGLI. For this reason, many veterans don't consider VGLI to be such a good deal, unless you plan on dying soon after you get out of the military. For a list of current premium rates, see www.insurance.va.gov/sgliSite/VGLI/VGLI%20rates.htm.

You can apply for VGLI coverage at the time of your military discharge through your unit or base personnel office, or online at giosgli.prudential.com/osgli/web/OSGLIMenu.html.

Although VGLI may not be the best choice for most veterans, it's a very valuable benefit for those who are medically discharged or retired from the military due to a potentially life-threatening condition, because most civilian life insurance plans won't cover such pre-existing conditions.

Service-Disabled Veterans' Insurance (S-DVI)

Service-Disabled Veterans' Insurance (S-DVI) is designed specifically for veterans with service-connected disabilities. (See Chapter 6 for information about service-connected disabilities and disability ratings.) S-DVI is available as term insurance and in a variety of permanent plans as well. The maximum amount of coverage is $10,000.

You can apply for S-DVI if you meet the following four criteria:

✔ You were released from active duty on or after April 25, 1951, with a discharge that the VA considers to be other than dishonorable. (See Chapter 2 for information about discharge characterizations.)

✔ You were rated for a service-connected disability.

✔ You are in good health except for any service-connected conditions.

✔ You apply within two years from the date the VA grants your service-connected disability.

Monthly premiums depend on your age, the amount of coverage you elect, and the specific insurance plan you choose. You can review the current rates at www.insurance.va.gov/inForceGliSite/forms/29-9.pdf.

If you're eligible, you can apply for S-DVI by completing a VA Form 29-4364, Application for Service-Disabled Veterans Life Insurance. You can obtain this form from any VA regional office (see Appendix B for locations). You can also download the form from the VA's Web site at www.insurance.va.gov/inForceGliSite/forms/29-4364.pdf.

Veterans' Mortgage Life Insurance (VMLI)

Veterans' Mortgage Life Insurance (VMLI) is a life insurance program designed to pay off the home mortgages of severely disabled veterans in the event of their death.

Only veterans who have received a Specially Adapted Housing Grant from the VA are eligible for VMLI. This grant helps a disabled veteran build or modify a home to accommodate his disabilities. Chapter 6 has more information about this program.

The amount of VMLI coverage equals the amount of the outstanding mortgage balance still owed by the veteran or $90,000, whichever is the lesser amount. VMLI is term insurance that decreases as the mortgage balance is reduced by regular payments.

Premiums are based on age, the outstanding balance of the mortgage at the time of application, and the number of years remaining on the mortgage. The VA has an online premium calculator at `insurance.va.gov/inForce GliSite/VMLICalc/VMLICalc.asp`.

If you're an eligible veteran (that is, you've received a Specially Adapted Housing Grant from the VA), you can apply for this insurance program by completing VA Form 29-8636, Application for Veterans' Mortgage Life Insurance. You can obtain this form at any VA regional office (see Appendix B), or online at `www.insurance.va.gov/inForceGliSite/forms/ 29-8636.pdf`.

Survivor Benefit Program (SBP)

The Department of Defense (DOD), not the VA, manages the Survivor Benefit Program (SBP). When a retired member of the military dies, his retirement pay stops. (See Chapter 7 for information about the military retirement program.)

At the time of retirement, military members can enroll in the Survivor Benefit Program. Under this program, a retiree forfeits 6.5 percent of "covered" retirement pay each month in premiums. In return, when the retiree dies, the surviving spouse or minor children get an annuity equal to 55 percent of the covered retirement pay.

You can elect to have any portion, up to 100 percent of your military retired pay, covered under SBP. Assume your military retirement pay is $2,000 per month. If you want, you can cover 100 percent of that, meaning you would have 6.5 percent of the entire $2,000 ($130) deducted from your retirement pay each month, and your spouse or children would receive 55 percent of the $2,000 ($1,100) per month upon your death. On the other hand, you could elect to cover only 50 percent of your retired pay under SBP. In that case, your retired pay would be reduced by 6.5 percent of that $1,000 amount ($65), but your family would only receive 55 percent of $1,000, or $550 per month, upon your demise.

At the time you out-process from the military for retirement, you must sign a form either accepting or declining the SBP option (your friendly neighborhood military personnel clerk will make sure you do so).

If you are married and you decline SBP, your spouse must also sign, agreeing to the declination. Otherwise, you'll be automatically enrolled in the SBP.

If your spouse remarries before age 55, SBP payments stop. However, if the remarriage ends, SBP payments can be reestablished.

Under the law, SBP payments are reduced by any amount of Dependency and Indemnity Compensation received (see the "Dependency and Indemnity Compensation [DIC]" section of this chapter). Many members of Congress want to eliminate this offset. However, even Congress critters don't always get everything they want. Some members tried to eliminate the offset in 2007 but accepted a compromise instead. As part of the 2008 Defense Authorization Act, a new payment called "Special Survivor Indemnity Allowance" was created.

The VA pays $50 a month to a surviving spouse who is eligible for both DIC and SBP. The $50 allowance is set to increase by $10 a year on October 1 each year through 2012 — and then cease on February 28, 2016, unless Congress takes action to make the allowance permanent or to eliminate the offset altogether.

Filing a life insurance claim

Claims for veterans life insurance programs are filed with the VA. You file a claim for SBP with the DOD.

Veterans life insurance claims

To file a death claim for a veterans life insurance program, you need to complete VA Form 29-4125, Claim for One Sum Payment. The form is available at any VA regional office (see Appendix B) and online at www.insurance.va.gov/inForceGliSite/forms/29-4125.pdf.

Submit the claim, along with a copy of the death certificate showing date and cause of death, by mail to Department of Veterans Affairs, Regional Office and Insurance Center, P.O. Box 7208, Philadelphia, PA 19101, or fax it to 888-748-5822.

You can call 800-669-8477 for assistance in completing VA insurance claims.

SBP claims

To report the death of a military retiree and make a claim for SBP, you should contact the Annuitant Pay section of the Defense Finance and Accounting Service (DFAS). The contact information is Defense Finance and Accounting Service, U.S. Military Annuitant Pay, P.O. Box 7131, London, KY 40742-7131; phone 800-321-1080 or 216-522-5955; fax 800-982-8459.

Understanding Death Pensions

The VA will pay a death pension to a spouse who has not remarried or to an unmarried child of a deceased wartime veteran. This is a needs-based benefit and is payable only to eligible dependents who have annual income below a yearly limit set by law.

You may be eligible to receive a VA death pension if all the following conditions are met:

✔ You are the unmarried spouse or unmarried child of a deceased veteran. To be eligible, a child must be under the age of 18, be in school and under 23, or have been incapable of self support before the age of 18.

✔ You have an annual "countable income" less than the limit set by law (see the next two sections for more on countable income).

✔ The deceased veteran served at least one day during a period of war. For the purposes of this benefit, periods of war include:

- World War I: April 6, 1917, through July 2, 1921

- World War II: December 7, 1941, through December 31, 1946

- Korean conflict: June 27, 1950, through January 31, 1955

- Vietnam era: The period beginning February 28, 1961, and ending May 7, 1975, for service within Vietnam, and August 5, 1964, through May 7, 1975, in all other cases

- Persian Gulf War: August 2, 1990, through a date yet to be determined

✔ The deceased veteran joined the military on or before September 7, 1980, and served on active duty for at least 90 days, or joined the military after September 7, 1980, and served on active duty for at least 24 months or (for National Guard and Reserve members) for the full period called to active duty.

✔ The deceased veteran was discharged from the military with a discharge characterization that the VA does not consider dishonorable (see Chapter 2 for information about military discharge characterizations).

To apply for the VA death pension, you need to complete VA Form 21-534, Application for Dependency and Indemnity Compensation, Death Pension and Accrued Benefits by Surviving Spouse or Child. The form is available at any VA regional office (see Appendix B) or online at www.vba.va.gov/pubs/forms/VBA-21-534-ARE.pdf.

Mail the completed form to the VA regional office which has responsibility for the state in which you live. Appendix B lists the addresses. If available, attach copies of dependency records (marriage or children's birth certificates).

Checking the rates and income limits

To be eligible, the surviving spouse or dependent child must have *countable income* less than that prescribed by Congress (the "Deciphering your countable income" section lists what is and isn't considered countable). Table 8-1 shows the income limits for 2008. The VA pays you the difference between your countable income and the yearly income limit for your situation. This difference is generally paid in 12 equal monthly payments rounded down to the nearest dollar.

Table 8-1	Annual Death Pension Income Limits for 2008
If You Are a . . .	*Your Yearly Income Must Be Less Than . . .*
Surviving spouse with no dependent children	$7,498
Surviving spouse with one dependent child	$9,815
Housebound surviving spouse with no dependents	$9,164
Housebound surviving spouse with one dependent	$11,478
Surviving spouse who needs aid and attendance with no dependents	$11,985
Surviving spouse who needs aid and attendance with one dependent	$14,298
Surviving child (no eligible parent)	$1,909
Note: For each additional child	Add $1,909 to the limit

For example, using the rates shown in Table 8-1, a surviving spouse with one child with a countable annual income of $3,000 would be paid an annual death pension of $6,815, or $567 per month.

Congress generally changes the annual income limits once a year to account for inflation. For the latest rates, visit www.vba.va.gov/bln/21/Rates/pen02.htm.

Deciphering your countable income

Countable income includes income received from most sources by the surviving spouse and any eligible children. It includes earnings, disability and retirement payments, Dependency and Indemnity Compensation (DIC), Survivor Benefit Program (SBP) payments, interest and dividends, and net income from farming or business. Also, the VA presumes that all of a child's income is available to or for the surviving spouse. The VA may grant an exception in hardship cases.

Watch out for exclusions and deductions

Some income doesn't count when computing your countable income, and some expenses may be deducted.

Examples of noncountable income include public assistance, such as Supplemental Security Income (SSI), food stamps, or welfare. Deductions that you may take to decrease your countable income include medical expenses, final expenses relating to the deceased veteran's last illness paid by the survivor, burial expenses paid by the survivor, and certain educational expenses for the surviving spouse and children.

Examining your net worth

Net worth means the net value of the assets of the surviving spouse and her children. It includes such assets as bank accounts, stocks, bonds, mutual funds, and any property other than the surviving spouse's residence.

There is no set limit on how much net worth you can have for this benefit, but under the law, net worth can't be excessive. The VA makes this determination on a case-by-case basis. When making this decision, the VA decides whether your assets are sufficiently large that you could live off them for a reasonable period of time. Remember, the death pension is a needs-based program, and it's not intended to protect substantial assets or build up an estate for the benefit of heirs.

Dependency and Indemnity Compensation (DIC)

Dependency Indemnity Compensation, or DIC, is a monthly benefit paid to eligible survivors — the spouse, unmarried child, and in some cases, parent — of certain deceased veterans.

The deceased veteran must meet one of the following criteria:

✔ A veteran who died on active duty

✔ A veteran whose death resulted from a service-related injury or disease

✔ A veteran whose death resulted from a non-service-related injury or disease, and who was receiving, or was entitled to receive, VA compensation for a service-connected disability that was rated as totally disabling (this includes veterans who were receiving 100 percent disability compensation due to "unemployability," as explained in Chapter 6)

  • For at least 10 years immediately before death

  • Since the veteran's release from active duty and for at least five years immediately preceding death

  • For at least one year before death if the veteran was a former prisoner of war who died after September 30, 1999

Eligible spouses include those who meet one of the following conditions:

✔ Married the veteran before January 1, 1957

✔ Was married to a service member who died on active duty

✔ Married the veteran within 15 years of discharge from the period of military service in which the disease or injury that caused the veteran's death began or was aggravated

✔ Was married to the veteran for at least one year

✔ Had a child with the veteran and lived with the veteran continuously until the veteran's death or, if separated, was not at fault for the separation

Spouses who remarry before the age of 57 lose their entitlement to benefits, unless that marriage ends. However, due to a change in the law, this doesn't apply to those who remarry on or after December 16, 2003.

If there is no eligible spouse, surviving children of the deceased veteran are eligible for DIC in their own right. Eligible children include unmarried children under the age of 18, or age 23 if attending school. Also eligible are unmarried children who became physically or mentally incapable of self-care before age 18.

Surviving parents with low incomes may be eligible to receive DIC payments. The term *parent* includes biological, adoptive, and foster parents. A foster parent is a person who stood in the relationship of a parent to the veteran for at least one year before the veteran's last entry into active duty.

Like the death pension benefit, this program is needs-based, and only parents with a countable income less than the limit established by law are eligible. (See the "Understanding Death Pensions" section of this chapter for an explanation of countable income.)

Payment rates and income limits for DIC

DIC payment rates depend on several factors, the most significant being when the veteran died. The 2008 basic monthly rate for surviving spouses of eligible veterans who died on or after January 1, 1993, is $1,091. The rate is increased for each dependent child, and also if the surviving spouse is housebound or in need of aid and attendance. See Table 8-2 for 2008 rates.

Table 8-2	2008 DIC Rates for Veterans Who Died on or after January 1, 1993
If You Are a . . .	*Monthly DIC Rate Is*
Surviving spouse with no dependent children	$1,091
Surviving spouse with one dependent child	$1,362
Housebound surviving spouse with no dependents	$1,219
Housebound surviving spouse with one dependent	$1,347
Surviving spouse who needs aid and attendance with no dependents	$1,362
Surviving spouse who needs aid and attendance with one dependent	$1,633
Note: For each additional qualifying child	Add $271

In addition to the rates shown in Table 8-2, the VA pays a transitional benefit of $250 to the surviving spouse's monthly DIC if there are children under age 18. The amount is based on a family unit, not on the number of children.

An additional allowance of $233 per month is also paid if, at the time of death, the veteran was entitled to receive 100 percent disability compensation for a service-connected disability (including a rating based on individual unemployability) for a continuous period of at least eight years immediately preceding death *and* the surviving spouse was married to the veteran for those same eight years. (See Chapter 6 for information about the VA disability compensation program.)

When there is no surviving spouse, eligible children are entitled to DIC, payable in equal shares, at the following monthly rates divided by the number of children:

- ✔ One child, $462
- ✔ Two children, $663
- ✔ Three children, $865
- ✔ More than three children, $865, plus $165 for each child in excess of three

DIC rates for veterans who died before January 1, 1993, vary according to the military rank the veteran held at the time of discharge from the military. Current rates can be found on the VA's Web site at `www.vba.va.gov/bln/21/Rates/comp03.htm`.

The DIC is a needs-based program, and a veteran's parents are eligible only if their annual income is below established levels. Monthly DIC rates depend on the parents' annual countable income. Current rates can be read online at `www.vba.va.gov/bln/21/Rates/comp04.htm`.

For 2008 the income limits are

- ✔ Sole surviving parent unmarried or remarried living with spouse: $7,449
- ✔ One of two parents not living with spouse: $5,649
- ✔ One of two parents living with spouse or other parent: $6,362

Applying for DIC

The magic wand for applying for DIC is VA Form 21-534, Application for Dependency and Indemnity Compensation, Death Pension and Accrued Benefits by Surviving Spouse or Child. You can pick up this form at any VA regional office (see Appendix B) or download it from the VA's Web site at `www.vba.va.gov/pubs/forms/VBA-21-534-ARE.pdf`.

Mail the completed form to the VA regional office that has responsibility for the state where you live. Appendix B has addresses for all VA regional offices.

Making Use of Education Benefits

Survivors' & Dependents' Educational Assistance is an education benefit for eligible spouses and children of certain veterans. Unlike most other benefits in this chapter, the veteran does not have to be deceased for dependents to take advantage of the VA's generosity.

Eligible persons can receive up to 45 months of full-time or equivalent benefits for

- ✔ College, business, technical, or vocational courses; high school diploma or GED; independent study; or distance learning courses

- ✔ Correspondence courses (spouses only); apprenticeship/on-the-job training

- ✔ Remedial, deficiency, and refresher training (in some cases)

- ✔ The cost of tests for licenses or certifications needed to get, keep, or advance in a job

To be eligible for this education program, you must be the son, daughter, or spouse of

- ✔ A veteran who is rated by the VA with a 100 percent service-connected disability. (See Chapter 6 for information about disability ratings and service-connection.)

- ✔ A veteran who died from any cause while such a service-connected disability was in existence.

- ✔ A service member missing in action or captured in the line of duty by a hostile force.

- ✔ A service member forcibly detained or interned in the line of duty by a foreign government or power.

- ✔ A service member who is hospitalized or receiving outpatient treatment for a service-connected, 100 percent permanent disability and is likely to be discharged for that disability.

After finding a program approved for VA training, complete VA Form 22-5490, Application for Survivors' and Dependents' Educational Assistance. The form is available at VA regional offices (see Appendix B) and online at www.vba.va.gov/pubs/forms/VBA-22-5490-ARE.pdf.

You should submit the form to the VA regional office that serves the state where you will train. Appendix B has the addresses.

How much does the VA pay?

The amount the VA pays is based on the type of training program and training time (full time, half time, so on). This program works much like the military GI Bill explained in Chapter 10. You receive 45 months of full-time benefits. If you go to school half time, you receive 90 months of half-time benefits, and so on. Tables 8-3 through 8-5 show the education rates, effective October 1, 2008, depending on the type of training.

Table 8-3	Education Rates for Institutionalized Training
Training Time	*Monthly Rate*
Full time	$915.00
Three-quarters time	$686.00
Half time	$456.00
Less than half time, more than one-quarter time	$456.00
One-quarter time or less	$227.75

Note: When you train at less than half time, you'll be reimbursed for tuition and fees only, up to the maximum monthly amounts shown on the chart. When you are enrolled in college at least half time, you're paid the monthly amount shown, regardless of the cost of your college courses.

Table 8-4	Farm Cooperative Training Rates
Training Time	*Monthly Rate*
Full time	$737
Three-quarters time	$553
Half time	$368

Full time means taking at least 12 credit hours in a term, or 24 clock hours per week. Three-quarters time is defined as at least 9 credit hours in a term, or 18 clock hours per week. Half time means taking at least 6 credit hours in a term, or 12 clock hours per week. One-quarter time means taking at least 3 credit hours in a term, or 6 clock hours per week.

Table 8-5	Apprenticeship and On-Job Training Rates
Training Period	*Monthly Rate*
First six months of training	$666
Second six months of training	$499
Third six months of training	$329
Remaining pursuit of training	$166

Rates change October 1 of each year. For current rates, see www.gibill.va.gov/GI_Bill_Info/rates.htm.

Expiration of benefits

Spouses and surviving spouses have ten years from the date VA establishes eligibility to use the benefit. Surviving spouses of veterans who died while on active duty have 20 years from the date of the veteran's death to use the benefit.

Children may use the benefit while they are between the ages of 18 and 26.

VA Medical Care for Your Family

Family members of certain veterans may be eligible for a medical insurance program managed by the VA. The program is called the *Civilian Health and Medical Program of the Department of Veterans Affairs*. Because that's a mouthful, it is generally just referred to as *CHAMPVA*.

CHAMPVA works a whole lot like Medicare. After you're enrolled, you pay an annual deductible and a co-pay for medical care you obtain.

In general, the CHAMPVA program covers most healthcare services and supplies that are medically and psychologically necessary. Though not a complete list, the program covers ambulance, ambulatory surgery, durable medical equipment (DME), family planning and maternity, hospice, inpatient services, mental health services, outpatient services, pharmacy, skilled nursing care, and transplants.

The program doesn't cover all medical procedures. Remember, the VA must consider the treatment to be medically or psychologically necessary. A few examples of non-covered services are most dental work, private hospital rooms, abortion counseling, cosmetic surgery, cosmetic drugs, artificial insemination, custodial care (such as bathing and feeding), routine eye and hearing examinations, eyeglasses and contact lenses, hypnosis, and pre-employment physicals.

Long-term care is not a covered CHAMPVA benefit. Long-term care is also known as *custodial care* and is usually provided in nursing homes, assisted-living facilities, or adult day care, or at a patient's home. It involves assistance with activities of daily living or supervision of someone who is cognitively impaired. Because CHAMPVA doesn't cover custodial long-term care and it can be very expensive, you should consider obtaining long-term-care insurance.

To be eligible for CHAMPVA, you must be in one of these categories:

- ✔ The spouse or child of a veteran who has been rated as permanently 100 percent disabled for a service-connected disability (see Chapter 6)
- ✔ The surviving spouse or child of a veteran who died from a VA-rated service-connected disability
- ✔ The surviving spouse or child of a veteran who was at the time of death rated permanently and totally disabled from a service-connected disability
- ✔ The surviving spouse or child of a military member who died in the line of duty, not due to misconduct

Eligible children include those unmarried children who are under the age of 18, or age 23 if attending school, and those who became mentally or physically incapable of self-care prior to age 18.

As with most survivor benefits, surviving spouses who remarry before age 55 lose eligibility for this benefit. However, if the new marriage ends, you may reestablish eligibility.

If you're eligible for Tricare, the medical program for military retirees and their family members, you're not eligible for CHAMPVA. For details about Tricare, see Chapter 5.

If you are eligible for Medicare (age 65 or older), you must enroll in Medicare Part B (where you pay monthly premiums) to remain eligible to participate in CHAMPVA. Medicare then becomes your primary insurer, and CHAMPVA picks up any costs that Medicare doesn't pay for.

If you meet the eligibility criteria, you can enroll in CHAMPVA by completing VA Form 10-10d, Application for CHAMPVA Benefits. The form can be obtained from any VA regional office (see Appendix B) or downloaded online at www.va.gov/vaforms/medical/pdf/vha-10-10d-fill.pdf.

Deductibles and co-pay

CHAMPVA is an excellent healthcare program, but it's not free. Like Medicare, there is an annual deductible, and you pay a co-pay for any medical treatment you receive. The annual deductible is $50 per family member, not to exceed $100 for an entire family.

There is no deductible for inpatient services, ambulatory surgery facility services, partial psychiatric day programs, hospice services, or services provided by VA medical facilities.

After the annual deductible has been paid, the VA will pay 75 percent of the "allowable cost" for the medical treatment. You pay a co-pay of 25 percent. The VA sets a maximum amount for each type of medical treatment covered under CHAMPVA. Some medical providers agree not to charge more than the allowable cost, and other medical providers charge whatever the market will bear. If you use one of the latter providers, the VA pays 75 percent of the allowable amount, and you pay the remainder of the bill. More about this in the "Understanding how medical providers work with CHAMPVA" section.

To provide financial protection against the impact of a long-term illness or serious injury, the VA has established an annual limit for out-of-pocket expenses for covered services paid by you. This is the maximum out-of-pocket expense you and your family can incur for CHAMPVA-covered services and supplies in a calendar year. Upon meeting the limit, you or your family's co-pay for covered services for the remainder of the calendar year is waived, and the VA pays 100 percent of the CHAMPVA allowable amount for covered services for the remainder of the calendar year.

Understanding how medical providers work with CHAMPVA

When you are accepted for enrollment in CHAMPVA, you receive a CHAMPVA insurance card. This is your passport to CHAMPVA medical benefits. When you obtain medical care, you present this card to the provider you're seeing. What happens next depends on the type of medical provider you're using.

You have three options: You can obtain medical care from a provider who agrees to accept CHAMPVA assignments; you can obtain care from any other provider; or you can (in some cases) receive care from a VA medical facility.

CHAMPVA assignments

When you go to a medical provider, find out if the provider accepts CHAMPVA. Providers most often refer to it as *accepting assignment*. What that means is the provider will bill CHAMPVA directly for covered services, items, and supplies. They do all the paperwork and submit the claim for you. What's even better is that doctors or providers who agree to accept assignment are agreeing to accept the CHAMPVA allowable amount and can't charge more than that amount for the services provided to you.

Unfortunately, the VA doesn't maintain a network of providers who have agreed to accept CHAMPVA assignments. However, most Medicare providers also accept CHAMPVA. Also, most Tricare (the military retiree healthcare system) providers also accept CHAMPVA assignments. You can find

Medicare providers on the Medicare Web site at www.medicare.gov/
Physician/Search/chooseprovider.asp. See Chapter 5 for information
about locating a Tricare provider.

Other providers

If assignment isn't accepted, you can still see the medical provider. But
if you do, you will likely have to pay the entire charge at the time of service. Additionally, you may be charged more than the CHAMPVA allowable
amount. To obtain reimbursement, you'll have to submit the itemized bill
from the provider with a CHAMPVA claim form (see the "Submitting claims"
section). When the claim is processed, the VA will send you 75 percent of the
allowable amount. So when the medical provider doesn't accept assignment,
your cost will be not only for your share of the CHAMPVA allowable amount
but also for any charges over your allowable amount.

VA medical facilities

Many VA medical centers (VAMCs) participate in a program called the
CHAMPVA Inhouse Treatment Initiative, or *CITI* (pronounced "city") for short.
Depending on the CITI programs a VAMC has available, you may be able to
receive all or a portion of your medical care through the CITI program. The
care may include inpatient, outpatient, pharmacy, durable medical equipment, and mental health services. Over half of all VA medical facilities participate in the CITI program, so there's a good chance that a VAMC near you is a
participant. See Appendix C for addresses and phone numbers for VA medical centers.

Covering your medication

CHAMPVA also covers medication prescribed by your doctor. The catch is,
however, that to use the CHAMPVA pharmacy program, you can't have any
other type of medical insurance (including Medicare Part D) that provides
for pharmacy coverage. If you are enrolled in CHAMPVA and don't have such
additional insurance, you have three options: VA network pharmacies, non-
network pharmacies, or the Meds by Mail program.

You may find this information very similar to the Tricare pharmacy program
explained in Chapter 5. They are similar because Congress designed this program using the Tricare system as a model. However, don't confuse the two.
The Tricare program is managed by the Department of Defense (DOD), while
this program is managed by the VA. Although they're similar, they are separate programs with separate pharmacies, contacts, and required forms.

VA network pharmacies

The VA maintains a network of more than 45,000 pharmacies. It does this through a contract with a pharmacy network company called SXC Health Solutions Inc. If you don't have another health insurance plan that includes pharmacy coverage and you're enrolled in CHAMPVA, you can use this network of pharmacies. You only pay your co-pay for the medication (after your outpatient deductible has been met), and there are no claims for you to file.

You can find out if a pharmacy near you is a network provider by calling 800-880-1377. You can also search for network providers near you on the SXC Health Solutions Web site at `https://vahac.rxportal.sxc.com/rxclaim/VAH/index.html`.

Non-network pharmacies

You can choose any pharmacy. The CHAMPVA insurance card is your proof of coverage, but you need to tell the pharmacy that CHAMPVA currently doesn't have a special drug coverage card for prescriptions. When using a pharmacy that's not part of the network, the pharmacy most likely will ask you to pay the full amount of the prescription. In that case, you need to request reimbursement from the VA by submitting a claim form (see the "Submitting claims" section) along with an itemized pharmacy statement.

Meds by Mail

This is by far the most cost-effective way for you to receive your non-urgent, maintenance medications if you're enrolled in CHAMPVA and don't have another health insurance plan with pharmacy coverage (to include Medicare Part D). There are no co-payments, no deductible requirements, and no claims to file. Your medication is free and is mailed to your home. The disadvantage is that, being a mail program, it's not very fast, so it's not suitable for use for urgent medications. You can still use your local pharmacy for urgent care medications.

To begin using Meds by Mail, fill out the Meds by Mail Order Form and Patient Profile form available by visiting the VA Web site at `www.va.gov/hac/forms/forms.asp`. You can also call 800-733-8387 and select the self-service option to request that forms be mailed to you.

Submitting claims

To submit a claim for reimbursement for medical services under CHAMPVA, use VA Form 10-7959a, CHAMPVA Claim Form, which is available online at `www.va.gov/vaforms/medical/pdf/vha-10-7959a-fill_061507.pdf`.

You can also request a copy of the form to be mailed to you by calling 800-733-8387. When submitting your claim, make sure you include an itemized bill for services received. Mail the completed form to VA Health Administration Center, CHAMPVA, P.O. Box 65024, Denver, CO 80206-9024.

Claims must be filed no later than one year after the date of service or, in the case of inpatient care, within one year of the discharge date.

If you use a provider who accepts CHAMPVA assignment or one of the VA's network pharmacies, it will file the claim form for you.

Home Loan Guarantees

Surviving spouses of certain veterans are eligible to obtain loans under the VA Home Loan program. So I don't have to explain the home loan program all over again, please refer to Chapter 13 for details about this program.

You're eligible for a VA home loan if you

- ✔ Are an unmarried spouse of a veteran who died while in service or from a service-connected disability (see Chapter 6 for information about disabilities)
- ✔ Are a spouse of a serviceperson missing in action or who is a prisoner of war

A surviving spouse who remarried before December 16, 2003, and on or after reaching age 57 loses eligibility for the VA Home Loan program. However, if that marriage ends, eligibility may be reestablished.

Chapter 9

Burial and Memorial Benefits

• •

In This Chapter

▶ Determining eligibility

▶ Choosing a place to rest

▶ Marking the final resting place

▶ Getting a certificate from the president

▶ Providing honors for those who served

• •

*H*ave you ever attended a military funeral? If so, I think you'll agree when I say it's one of the most dignified and respectful ways to be laid to rest. It's an experience you never forget.

When taps is played and the members of the honor guard give the final salute to their fallen comrade, it's impossible not to reflect on this solemn final tribute offered to our veteran loved ones who were not only heroes in our hearts, but heroes to our nation's freedom as well. When the United States flag is folded and respectfully presented to the next of kin, you hear the words, "As a representative of the United States Army (Air Force/Navy/Marine Corps/ Coast Guard), it is my high privilege to present you this flag. Let it be a symbol of the grateful appreciation this nation feels for the distinguished service rendered to our country and our flag by your loved one."

We all pass on at some time. That's the universal truth of life. A funeral can cost thousands of dollars, and a huge funeral bill isn't the final gift I want to give my daughters. I would rather they use the money to throw a huge party in my honor — to celebrate my life, not mourn my passing. However, I do want to be placed in my final resting place with a modicum of dignity and respect. To that end, I plan to make sure they keep a copy of this book handy, so when the time comes (hopefully not soon), they can turn to this chapter and take advantage of the free burial and memorial benefits available to veterans.

Eligibility for Military Burial

Most, but not all, veterans are eligible for veterans burial and memorial benefits. You're eligible if you fall into one of the following categories:

✔ President or former presidents of the United States, based on their service as commander in chief. If you've ever been president of the U.S., you probably don't need to read any further in this chapter. Presumably, someone will take care of your funeral arrangements for you.

✔ Veterans who die while on active duty. This includes active duty for training for members of the reserves and National Guard. See Chapter 2 for information about Guard and Reserve duty.

✔ Veterans who have active-duty service on or before September 7, 1980 (enlisted), and on or before October 16, 1981 (officers), and have a discharge characterization that the Department of Veterans Affairs (VA) doesn't consider dishonorable. See Chapter 2 for information about discharge characterizations.

✔ Veterans with service beginning after September 7, 1980, as an enlisted person, and service after October 16, 1981, as an officer, with at least 24 months of continuous, active-duty service. Again, such veterans must have a discharge characterization that the VA doesn't consider dishonorable, as explained in Chapter 2.

✔ Members of the National Guard or Reserves who were called to active duty for less than 24 months and served during the entire period of the call-up. These veterans must also have a discharge characterization that the VA doesn't consider dishonorable, according the criteria listed in Chapter 2.

✔ Reservists and National Guard members who, at the time of death, were entitled to retired pay, or would have been entitled, but for being under the age of 60. Chapter 7 has information about the military retirement system.

✔ Reservists who die due to an injury or illness incurred or aggravated by military service.

Meeting conditions for burial expenses

If a veteran is buried or inurned in a private cemetery, the government is willing to pick up some of the expenses, as long as the veteran meets certain criteria. In addition to the eligibility criteria for burial listed in the preceding section, at least *one* of the following conditions must be met:

✔ The veteran died because of a service-related disability.

✔ The veteran was receiving VA pension or compensation at the time of death.

- The veteran was entitled to receive VA pension or compensation, but decided not to reduce his military retirement or disability pay.

- The veteran died while hospitalized by the VA or while receiving care under VA contract at a non-VA facility.

- The veteran died while traveling under proper authorization and at VA expense to or from a specified place for the purpose of examination, treatment, or care.

- The veteran had an original or reopened claim pending at the time of death, and the VA ruled he was entitled to compensation or pension from a date before the date of death.

- The veteran died on or after October 9, 1996, while a patient at a VA-approved state nursing home.

Getting into Arlington

Arlington National Cemetery has strict eligibility criteria. For one thing, eligible veterans must have a fully honorable discharge, not just a discharge that the VA considers to be other than dishonorable. (For details about discharge characterizations, see Chapter 2.)

Burial at Arlington National Cemetery is an exclusive honor, restricted to those who fit one of the following categories:

- Service members who die on active duty, except those on duty-for-training purposes only.

- Active-duty retirees. See Chapter 7 for information about the military retirement system.

- Reserve and National Guard retirees age 60 and older who are drawing retired pay at the time of death and who have served a period of active duty for more than training purposes. Again, Chapter 7 has complete information about military retirement.

- Veterans who have been awarded the Medal of Honor, Distinguished Service Cross, Air Force Cross, Navy Cross, Distinguished Service Medal, Silver Star, or Purple Heart.

- Former prisoners of war who died on or after November 30, 1993.

- Widows and widowers of service members who are officially determined missing in action.

- Spouses, widows, widowers, minor children, permanently dependent children, and certain unmarried adult children of eligible veterans. (When spouses or children die first, service members must agree in writing to be buried at the same site.)

A Final Place to Rest: Selecting a Cemetery

The VA operates 141 national cemeteries throughout the United States and its territories. Take a look at Appendix E for locations and contact information for all national cemeteries.

The United States has been doing this for quite a while now. On July 17, 1862, Congress enacted legislation that authorized the president to purchase "cemetery grounds" to be used as national cemeteries "for soldiers who shall have died in the service of the country." Fourteen cemeteries were established that first year. To date, more than 3 million Americans, including veterans of every war and conflict — from the Revolutionary War to the Gulf War — are honored by burial in U.S. national cemeteries. Approximately 17,000 acres of land from Hawaii to Maine, and from Alaska to Puerto Rico are devoted to the memory of those who served our nation. More than 300 recipients of the Medal of Honor (our nation's highest military medal) are buried in U.S. national cemeteries.

Most states operate one or more cemeteries dedicated or reserved for military veterans. Eligibility criteria, services provided, and costs can vary greatly from one state to another. For a complete list of state-sponsored veterans cemeteries, including links to eligibility criteria, services, and an application, see www.cem.va.gov/cem/scg/lsvc.asp.

In addition to national and state cemeteries, certain veterans may be eligible for burial in other veterans cemeteries, such as Arlington or National Park Service cemeteries, as well. I explain more in the following sections.

Who can be buried where?

Eligible veterans (see the "Eligibility for Military Burial" section) can be buried for free in any of the 141 national cemeteries with available space. Services include opening and closing of the grave, perpetual care, a government headstone or marker, a burial flag, and a presidential memorial certificate at no cost to the family.

Cremated remains are buried or inurned in national cemeteries in the same manner and with the same honors (see the "Giving a Final Salute with Military Funeral Honors" section) as casketed remains.

Spouses and dependents of eligible veterans are also eligible for burial in national cemeteries. This is true even if they predecease the veteran. Benefits include burial with the veteran and perpetual care. The spouse or dependent's name and date of birth and death are inscribed on the veteran's headstone. Again, there is no cost to the family for these services.

The spouse or surviving spouse of an eligible veteran can be buried in a national cemetery, even if that veteran isn't buried or memorialized in a national cemetery. In addition, the surviving spouse of a member of the armed forces whose remains are unavailable for burial is also eligible for burial. In this case, the spouse would be eligible for a free headstone from the VA.

A surviving spouse who remarries a nonveteran may be buried in a national cemetery, as long as the death of the veteran's surviving spouse occurred after January 1, 2000.

For the most part, eligible dependents are unmarried children under the age of 21. If the child is a full-time student, the cutoff age is 23.

Also eligible are the unmarried adult children of eligible veterans if the individual is permanently physically or mentally disabled and incapable of self-support. The disability must have occurred before the age of 21 (or age 23 if a full-time student).

When certain conditions are met, service members may be buried in the same grave with a close relative already buried at some cemeteries, including Arlington. This generally requires approval of the cemetery staff and approval by the next of kin of the previously deceased relative.

National Park Service cemeteries

The National Park Service (NPS), under the U.S. Department of Interior, maintains 14 cemeteries nationwide. These include

- ✔ Andersonville National Historic Site, Andersonville, Georgia
- ✔ Andrew Johnson National Historic Site, Greenville, Tennessee
- ✔ Antietam National Cemetery, Sharpsburg, Maryland
- ✔ Battleground National Cemetery, Washington, D.C.
- ✔ Colonial National Historical Park, Yorktown, Virginia
- ✔ Fort Donelson National Battlefield, Dover, Tennessee

- ✔ Fredericksburg and Spotsylvania County Battlefield Memorial National Military Park, Fredericksburg, Virginia

- ✔ Gettysburg National Military Park, Gettysburg, Pennsylvania

- ✔ Jean Lafitte National Historical Park, New Orleans, Louisiana

- ✔ Little Bighorn Battle National Monument, Crow Agency, Montana

- ✔ Petersburg National Cemetery, Petersburg, Virginia

- ✔ Shiloh National Military Park, Shiloh, Tennessee

- ✔ Stones River National Battlefield, Murfreesboro, Tennessee

- ✔ Vicksburg National Military Park, Vicksburg, Mississippi

Only two of these NPS cemeteries, Andersonville National Historic Site and Andrew Johnson National Historic Site, are classified as active, meaning they continue to bury veterans and their dependents.

Veterans who meet the eligibility criteria (see the "Eligibility for Military Burial" section) and their dependents may elect to be buried in either of these cemeteries. As with national cemeteries, there's no cost to the family.

To apply for burial benefits at Andersonville National Historic Site or Andrew Johnson National Historic Site, contact the Department of Interior at Department of the Interior, National Park Service, 1849 C St., NW, Washington, DC 20240, or phone 202-208-4747.

Arlington National Cemetery: A special case

More than 285,000 people have been laid to rest at Arlington National Cemetery. Across its rolling hills stand the unadorned headstones of veterans from the Revolutionary War to the current struggles in Iraq and Afghanistan.

Arlington may be a national cemetery, but it's not managed by the VA. Arlington is managed and operated by the U.S. Army and has additional eligibility criteria (see the "Getting into Arlington" section earlier in the chapter). For information about making burial arrangements at Arlington, see the "Applying for Arlington" section later in the chapter.

Those eligible for burial can also opt for inurnment. Also eligible for inurnment are any veterans with a fully honorable discharge, their spouses, and their dependent children. Each niche has room for two urns and is sealed with a marble plaque that bears the names and years of birth and death of those within.

What the VA Does and Doesn't Cover

When a veteran or his qualifying dependents are buried or inurned in a national cemetery, Arlington, or a National Park cemetery, the government will pay for opening and closing of the grave, perpetual care, a headstone or marker, and a burial flag.

If the veteran or his qualifying dependents are buried in a state veterans cemetery, burial services are provided by the individual state, not by the VA, and available services can vary widely from one state to another, and even from one state veterans cemetery to another within the same state. But what if the veteran is buried or inurned in a private cemetery? Will the government pick up the cost?

The government probably won't cover all the costs, but you may be eligible for reimbursement from the VA for burial expenses if you paid for a veteran's burial or funeral *and* you have not been reimbursed by another government agency or some other source, such as burial insurance or the deceased veteran's employer. The VA also provides headstones and markers, presidential memorial certificates (PMCs), and burial flags. More on those later in this section.

What the VA doesn't cover

Regardless of where a veteran or eligible family member is buried, the VA doesn't pay for cremation, preparation of the deceased (embalming), casket or urn, or transportation to the cemetery. Of course, some of these expenses may be reimbursed if the veteran meets the eligibility criteria listed in the next section. However, in certain situations, the government will cover some of these costs. Here are the exceptions:

✔ When a military member dies while on active duty, the military service (not the VA) will pick up most of the costs, including cremation, embalming, casket or urn, funeral director services, and transportation of remains. In fact, the military will even pay for a family member to accompany the remains from the place of death to the funeral home. For Reserve and National Guard members, this includes active duty for training (ADT) and inactive duty training (IDT), as explained in Chapter 2.

✔ The military will pay to transfer the remains of military retirees and their family members who die while admitted to a military hospital, provided the place of burial is no farther than the deceased's last residence.

✔ If a veteran dies while admitted to a VA facility, such as a VA medical center or nursing home, the VA will pay the cost of transporting the remains to a national cemetery, provided the cemetery is no farther than the deceased's last residence.

How much does the VA pay?

The costs covered by the VA depend on whether the death was related to the veteran's military service. The VA pays more for veterans who die because of a service-related medical condition or injury than it does for non-service-related deaths. When the cause of death is not service related, the reimbursements are generally described as two payments:

- ✔ A burial and funeral expense allowance
- ✔ A plot or interment allowance

For a service-related death, the VA will pay up to $2,000 toward burial expenses for deaths on or after September 11, 2001. The VA will pay up to $1,500 for deaths prior to September 10, 2001. If the veteran is buried in a VA national cemetery, some or all of the cost of transporting the deceased may be reimbursed.

For a non-service-related death, the VA will pay up to $300 toward burial and funeral expenses and a $300 plot-interment allowance for deaths on or after December 1, 2001. The plot-interment allowance is $150 for deaths prior to December 1, 2001. If the death happened while the veteran was in a VA hospital or under VA-contracted nursing home care, some or all of the costs for transporting the veteran's remains may be reimbursed.

The VA doesn't pay these benefits in advance. You must have copies of the funeral bills, and they must show that they have been paid in full to qualify for reimbursement. Additionally, if the cause of death wasn't service-related, you must file your claim within two years from the date of death. There is no time limit for service-connected claims.

Furnishing markers and headstones

When someone is buried or memorialized in a national cemetery, state veterans cemetery, or National Park cemetery, a headstone or marker is part of the package. However, the VA also furnishes, upon request, a government headstone or marker for the unmarked grave of any deceased eligible veteran in any cemetery around the world. (See the "Eligibility for Military Burial" section for eligibility criteria.)

Because of a change in the law, the VA also provides for eligible veterans who died on or after November 1, 1990, a headstone or marker for graves already marked with a private headstone or marker.

As with other veteran burial benefits, the VA doesn't charge for the headstones or markers it provides. However, like all things governmental, you need to submit the proper paperwork. See the "Obtaining markers and headstones" section later in the chapter for details.

Although there's no charge for the headstone or marker itself, arrangements for placing it in a private cemetery are the applicant's responsibility, and all setting fees are at private expense.

The VA offers several types of markers and headstones, including upright headstones, flat grave markers, bronze niche markers, and a new headstone medallion that the VA plans to have available in 2009:

- ✔ **Upright headstones:** These headstones are 42 inches high, 13 inches wide, and 4 inches thick. They weigh about 230 pounds and are available in marble or granite.

- ✔ **Flat grave markers:** The flat grave markers are available in bronze, marble, or granite. The flat bronze grave marker is 24 inches long and 12 inches wide, with a $^3/_4$-inch rise, and weighs about 18 pounds. The flat granite and flat marble grave markers are 24 inches long, 12 inches wide, and 4 inches thick. Weight is approximately 130 pounds.

  Anchor bolts, nuts, and washers for fastening to a base are furnished with the marker. However, the government doesn't furnish a base.

- ✔ **Bronze niche marker:** This niche marker is $8^1/_2$ inches long and $5^1/_2$ inches wide, with a $^7/_{16}$-inch rise, and weighs approximately 3 pounds. As with the flat grave markers, mounting bolts and washers are furnished with the marker.

The VA is also developing a medallion to be affixed to an existing privately purchased headstone or marker to signify the deceased's status as a veteran. When available, it can be furnished in lieu of a traditional government headstone or marker to those veterans who died on or after November 1, 1990, and whose grave is marked with a privately purchased headstone or marker.

Spouses and dependents aren't eligible for a government-furnished headstone or marker unless they are buried in a national cemetery, National Park Service cemetery, Arlington, or state veterans cemetery.

Adding an inscription

Mandatory items of inscription on government-furnished headstones at government expense are legal name, branch of service, year of birth, and year of death.

In addition to the mandatory facts, you can request that optional information be included at government expense. Optional items include month and day of birth; month and day of death; highest rank attained; medals earned; war service; and emblem of belief.

War service includes active-duty service during a recognized period of war, but the individual does not have to have served in the actual place of war. For example, "Vietnam" may be inscribed if the veteran served during the Vietnam War period, even though the individual never served in Vietnam itself.

You can also request that space be reserved for future inscriptions at private expense, such as a spouse or dependent's data. Only two lines of space may be reserved on flat markers due to space limitations. Reserved space is unnecessary on upright marble or granite headstones because the reverse side is available for future inscriptions.

You may request additional items on the headstone or marker if space is available. Examples of acceptable items include terms of endearment, nicknames (in expressions such as "Our beloved Poppy"), and military or civilian credentials or accomplishments, such as "Doctor," "Reverend," and so on. All requests for additional items at government expense are subject to approval by the VA.

Replacing headstones and markers

Headstones and markers previously furnished by the government may be replaced at government expense if badly deteriorated, illegible, stolen, or vandalized. The VA will also replace the headstone or marker if the inscription is incorrect, if it was damaged during shipping, or if the material or workmanship doesn't meet government contract specifications.

If a government headstone or marker in a private cemetery is damaged by cemetery personnel, the cemetery should pay all replacement costs.

Providing presidential memorial certificates

A *presidential memorial certificate (PMC)* is an engraved paper certificate, signed by the current president, to honor the memory of honorably discharged veterans. The certificate is available in memory of any deceased veteran, as long as he received a military discharge that the VA doesn't consider dishonorable. (See Chapter 2 for information about discharge characterizations.)

This program was initiated in March 1962 by President John F. Kennedy and has been continued by all subsequent presidents.

If you're the next-of-kin, family member, loved one, or even a friend of an eligible deceased veteran, you may request a PCM from the VA. More than one certificate may be issued, and there is no time limit for requesting one. To find out how to obtain a certificate, see the "Requesting a presidential memorial certificate" section later in the chapter.

Receiving a burial flag

The VA provides a United States flag, at no cost, to drape the casket or accompany the urn of a deceased eligible veteran (See the "Eligibility for Military Burials" section). It is furnished to honor the memory of a veteran's military service to his country.

Generally, the flag is given to the next of kin as a keepsake after its use during the funeral service (see the "Giving a Final Salute with Military Funeral Honors" section). When there is no next of kin, the VA can furnish the flag to a friend who requests it.

Memorial flags can't be replaced at government expense if they are lost, damaged, or stolen. The law allows for only one burial flag to be furnished at government expense.

Most family members elect to display the memorial flag in a specially constructed flag case. Several varieties are available in military surplus stores and for purchase on the Internet.

The memorial flag isn't suitable for flying on a flag pole or displaying outdoors because of its size and fabric. It's made of cotton and can easily be damaged by weather.

Giving a Final Salute with Military Funeral Honors

Military funeral honors aren't provided by the VA, but rather by the Department of Defense (DOD). The military services have a long tradition of providing funeral honors for fallen veterans of their branches. However, during the military drawdowns of the late '80s and '90s, as resources began to stretch, the DOD found this harder and harder to do.

That's when various veteran organizations, such as the Veterans of Foreign Wars (VFW) and the American Legion, stepped in to pick up the slack. These organizations volunteered to conduct funeral honors for fallen deceased veterans when the DOD was forced to decline due to lack of manpower and resources.

Many members of Congress thought this was atrocious (even though the congressionally mandated downsizing of the military caused the problem in the first place). In 1999, Congress passed a law requiring the military services to provide funeral honors for eligible veterans (see the "Eligibility for Military Burial" section).

Under the law, the DOD must provide, upon request, an honor guard consisting of at least two military members to provide funeral honors for fallen eligible veterans. The law requires that at least one member of the detail be a representative of the parent armed service of the deceased veteran. The honor detail must, at a minimum, perform a ceremony that includes the folding and presenting of the American flag to the next of kin and the playing of taps.

For information about requesting an honor guard at a veteran's funeral, see the later section "Setting up military funeral honors."

Meeting military honor guards

Almost every military installation has an honor guard team. Members of the honor guard are trained in military drill and ceremonies, and provide memorial honors, upon request, at the funerals of eligible veterans.

It may surprise you to know that military honor guard teams are comprised almost exclusively of volunteers who practice, drill, and perform funeral honors in their off-duty time. Although the military pays for their honor guard uniforms, equipment, and transportation expenses, most of these dedicated individuals also have other full-time military jobs.

Each of the services do have one or two full-time honor guard units. These are the teams you often see on TV at major ceremonial events or in front of the White House to welcome distinguished visitors. They also often perform funeral honors for deceased U.S. presidents and other high-ranking officials.

However, most military funeral honors are performed by individual honor guard teams stationed at most military bases. My hat is off to these silent heroes, who dedicate their own time to honor our fallen military comrades.

The law requires the DOD to provide a minimum of two honor guard members to conduct honors at a veteran's funeral. However, usually a funeral detail consists of between four and seven members. Much depends on the capabilities of the local honor guard unit, available resources, and manpower. Other factors, such as if there are other veteran funerals occurring in the area at the same time, may also affect availability.

Knowing what honors are provided

The law requires the DOD to play taps, fold the U.S. flag, and present the flag to the next of kin. However, other honors, such as honor guard pallbearers and a rifle volley, may be offered, depending on the resources available to the honor guard unit and desires of the family. Here are the specifics of what's involved:

- ✓ **Taps:** Taps is the customary bugle call played at military funerals. The law requires taps to be played by a bugler, if available, but very few buglers are in the military these days, so it's usually played by electronic means. During the playing of taps, the honor guard presents a final salute to the deceased veteran.

- ✓ **Flag folding:** The U.S. flag is carefully removed from the coffin and solemnly folded by members of the honor guard team. When completely folded, the flag forms a triangle, which is representative of the tricornered hats worn by colonial soldiers during the Revolutionary War. The procedure involves 13 folds, representing the original colonies. When all the folds have been made, no red or white stripes are visible, leaving only the honor field of blue and stars.

- ✓ **Flag presentation:** The folded flag is given to an honor guard member who is in the same military branch as the deceased veteran. The service representative marches slowly to the next of kin and presents the flag with the words, "As a representative of the United States Army (Air Force/Navy/Marine Corps/Coast Guard), it is my high privilege to present you this flag. Let it be a symbol of the grateful appreciation this nation feels for the distinguished service rendered to our country and our flag by your loved one."

    If there is no next of kin, the flag may be presented to a friend of the deceased.

- ✓ **Pallbearers:** If manpower is available, family members can request that members of the honor guard act as pallbearers, in addition to providing other funeral honors.

✔ **Rifle volley:** At military funerals, you often see three volleys of shots fired in honor of the deceased veteran. This tradition is performed by honor guard teams, based on family desires and available resources. The rifle volley is often mistaken by nonmilitary folks as a 21-gun salute, although it's entirely different. In the military, a gun is a large-caliber weapon. The three volleys are fired from rifles, not guns. Therefore, the three volleys aren't any kind of gun salute at all. The firing team can consist of any number, but it's usually made up of seven or eight members. Whether the team consists of three, eight, or ten, each member fires three times (three volleys).

The three volleys come from an old battlefield custom. The warring sides would cease hostilities to clear their dead from the battlefield, and the firing of three volleys meant that the dead had been properly cared for and the side was ready to resume the battle.

The honor guard often slips three shell-casings into the folded flag before presenting the flag to the family. Each casing represents one volley.

Arranging Military Funerals

When it's time to lay a veteran to rest, you have a couple of options. Your choice affects how arrangements are made:

✔ A veteran can be buried in a national cemetery, Arlington, a National Park Service cemetery, or a state veterans cemetery (see Appendix E for contact information for national cemeteries). If one of these resting places is chosen, the funeral director will take care of most of the arrangements for you, and the government will handle most of the expenses. However, proof of the veteran's eligibility, such as DD Form 214 (see Chapter 2), must be presented.

✔ If the veteran is buried in a private cemetery, the funeral director can help you set up the military arrangements, and you will have to seek reimbursement for the expenses. You will have to provide proof of the veteran's eligibility, such as DD Form 214 (see Chapter 2), to receive military funeral honors.

When supplying proof of eligibility or other official records, do not send original documents because they will not be returned.

The following sections explain how to arrange for specific details of a military funeral service and burial.

Seeking reimbursement for private funeral expenses

If you choose to have your loved one buried in a private cemetery and you want to be reimbursed for funeral and burial expenses, you can apply by filling out VA Form 21-530, Application for Burial Benefits. You may download the form from the VA's Web site at www.vba.va.gov/pubs/forms/VBA-21-530-ARE.pdf. You should attach a copy of the veteran's military discharge document, death certificate, and funeral/burial bills. The bills should show that they have been paid in full. The completed form may be submitted to any VA regional office. See Appendix B for office locations.

A claim for non-service-connected burial expenses or plot allowance must be filed with the VA within two years of the date of the veteran's permanent burial or cremation. There is no time limit for service-connected deaths.

Setting up military funeral honors

You can arrange for military funeral honors by contacting the honor guard representative for the branch of the military in which the deceased served. Table 9-1 gives the phone numbers for each branch's honor guard teams, arranged by state or U.S. territory.

Veteran service organizations, such as the American Legion or Veterans of Foreign Wars (VFW), can often assist with arranging military funeral honors. This is especially true if the deceased veteran was a member of the organization.

Table 9-1	Contact Information for Funeral Honors				
Location	*Army*	*Navy*	*Air Force*	*Marine Corps*	*Coast Guard*
Alabama	334-255-9081	904-542-9807	334-953-4545	866-826-3628	504-253-6361
Alaska	907-384-3811	360-315-5132	907-552-4600	866-826-3628	907-463-2169
Arizona	520-533-2229	800-326-9631	520-228-4189	866-826-3628	510-437-3712
Arkansas	580-442-8592	877-478-3988	501-987-6317	866-826-3628	314-269-2321

(continued)

Table 9-1 *(continued)*

Location	Army	Navy	Air Force	Marine Corps	Coast Guard
California	520-533-2229	800-326-9631	707-424-5252	866-826-3628	510-437-3712
Colorado	719-526-5613	800-326-9631	719-556-8226	866-826-3628	314-269-2321
Connecticut	888-325-1601	866-203-7791	609-754-4117	866-826-3628	617-223-3476
Delaware	301-677-2206	866-203-7791	800-565-1398	866-826-3628	757-686-4032
District of Columbia	703-696-3237	202-433-4589	202-767-5631	866-826-3628	202-372-4010
Florida	800-557-7408	904-542-9807	813-828-5191	866-826-3628	305-535-4584
Georgia	706-545-4116	904-542-9807	478-926-9775	866-826-3628	305-535-4584
Guam	808-655-5261	671-339-4315	671-366-5178	866-826-3628	808-842-2012
Hawaii	808-655-5261	808-472-0020	808-448-0955	866-826-3628	808-842-2012
Idaho	888-634-7496	360-315-5132	208-828-2874	866-826-3628	206-217-6513
Illinois	573-596-0134	877-478-3988	618-256-4586	866-826-3628	314-269-2321
Indiana	502-624-6051	877-478-3988	618-256-4586	866-826-3628	314-269-2321
Iowa	913-684-3557	877-478-3988	402-294-6667	866-826-3628	314-269-2321
Kansas	785-239-3741	877-478-3988	316-759-3991	866-826-3628	314-269-2321
Kentucky	502-624-6051	877-478-3988	937-257-8964	866-826-3628	314-269-2321
Louisiana	888-474-0377	904-542-9807	228-377-1986	866-826-3628	504-253-6361
Maine	888-325-1601	866-203-7791	866-835-9240	516-228-5666	617-223-3476
Maryland	301-677-2206	202-433-4589	202-767-5631	866-826-3628	757-686-4032

Location	Army	Navy	Air Force	Marine Corps	Coast Guard
Massachusetts	888-325-1601	866-203-7791	866-835-9240	866-826-3628	617-223-3476
Michigan	502-624-6051	877-478-3988	937-257-8964	866-826-3628	216-902-6117
Minnesota	913-684-3557	877-478-3988	701-747-3272	866-826-3628	314-269-2321
Mississippi	888-474-0377	904-542-9807	662-434-2311	866-826-3628	504-253-6361
Missouri	573-596-0134	877-478-3988	660-687-6532	866-826-3628	314-269-2321
Montana	888-634-7496	360-315-5132	406-731-2831	866-826-3628	206-217-6513
Nebraska	785-239-3741	877-478-3988	402-294-6667	866-826-3628	314-269-2321
Nevada	520-533-2229	800-326-9631	530-634-5700	866-826-3628	510-437-3712
New Hampshire	888-325-1601	866-203-7791	866-835-9240	866-826-3628	617-223-3476
New Jersey	609-562-4453	866-203-7791	609-754-4117	866-826-3628	617-223-3476
New Mexico	915-568-2903	800-326-9631	505-846-1804	866-826-3628	504-253-6361
New York	888-325-1601	866-203-7791	609-754-4117	866-826-3628	617-223-3476
North Carolina	800-682-6973	866-203-7791	919-722-7019	866-826-3628	757-686-4032
North Dakota	719-526-5613	877-478-3988	701-723-4503	866-826-3628	314-269-2321
Ohio	502-624-6051	877-478-3988	937-257-8964	866-826-3628	314-269-2321
Oklahoma	580-442-8592	877-478-3988	405-734-4226	866-826-3628	504-253-6361
Oregon	888-634-7496	360-315-5132	253-982-2700	866-826-3628	206-217-6513
Pennsylvania	301-677-2206	866-203-7791	202-767-5631	866-826-3628	757-686-4032
Puerto Rico	787-707-3245	904-542-9807	787-253-5272	866-826-3628	787-729-6800

(continued)

Table 9-1 *(continued)*

Location	Army	Navy	Air Force	Marine Corps	Coast Guard
Rhode Island	888-325-1601	866-203-7791	866-835-9240	866-826-3628	617-223-3476
South Carolina	803-751-4519	904-542-9807	843-963-3398	866-826-3628	305-535-4584
South Dakota	719-526-5613	877-478-3988	605-385-1186	866-826-3628	314-269-2321
Tennessee	270-798-4729	877-478-3988	478-926-9775	866-826-3628	314-269-2321
Texas	254-287-7200	904-542-9807	210-652-3604	866-826-3628	504-253-6361
U.S. Virgin Islands	787-707-3245	904-542-9807	340-778-1280	866-826-3628	787-729-6800
Utah	719-526-5613	800-326-9631	801-777-3967	866-826-3628	510-437-3712
Vermont	888-325-1601	866-203-7791	866-835-9240	866-826-3628	617-223-3476
Virginia	804-734-6606	866-203-7791	202-767-5631	866-826-3628	757-686-4032
Washington	888-634-7496	360-315-5132	253-982-2700	866-826-3628	206-217-6513
West Virginia	502-624-6051	866-203-7791	937-257-8964	866-826-3628	757-686-4032
Wisconsin	719-526-5613	360-315-5132	307-773-2686	866-826-3628	314-269-2321

If you have difficulty reaching the appropriate point of contact, call 877-MIL-HONR (877-645-4667). A service representative will help you get in touch with the appropriate honor guard unit.

Applying for Arlington

When a veteran wants to be buried in Arlington National Cemetery, arrangements, including burial site selection, are made only upon the individual's death. Arrangements are typically coordinated between staffs at the deceased's funeral home and the cemetery. Cemetery staff can also help schedule use of the nearby Fort Myer Chapel, as well as arrange for a military chaplain when a family minister isn't preferred.

Upon the veteran's death, you should contact a local funeral home to arrange for any desired services in the hometown. The funeral director should call the Interment Office at Arlington (703-607-8585) to arrange for the burial. Before scheduling the service, the cemetery staff will need to determine the veteran's eligibility (see the earlier "Getting into Arlington" section), so you need to have proof of the veteran's service, such as a DD Form 214, on hand. You can fax any documents that prove eligibility to the cemetery at 703-607-8583. Upon verification of eligibility, the Arlington cemetery staff will schedule the funeral.

The next available gravesite or niche is assigned on the afternoon before the burial service. The Arlington cemetery staff assigns graves and niches without regard to the veteran's military rank, race, color, creed, or gender. The family may request a burial location close to other family members buried or inurned within the cemetery; however, limited space may prevent the cemetery from accommodating such requests.

Obtaining markers and headstones

When burial is in a national cemetery, National Park cemetery, or state veterans cemetery, the cemetery officials order a headstone or marker and use inscription information provided by the next of kin.

When burial is in a private cemetery, the next of kin or a representative, such as a funeral director, must submit VA Form 40-1330, Application for Standard Government Headstone or Marker for Installation in a Private Cemetery or a State Veterans Cemetery, along with the veteran's military discharge documents, to request a government-provided headstone or marker.

You can obtain VA Form 40-1330 from any VA regional office (see Appendix B for contact information). The form is also available online at www.va.gov/vaforms/va/pdf/40-1330.pdf. Send the completed form and proof of military service by mail to Memorial Programs Service (41A1), Department of Veterans Affairs, 5109 Russell Road, Quantico, VA 22134-3903; or fax to 800-455-7143.

Requesting a presidential memorial certificate

To request a presidential memorial certificate, you'll need a copy of the deceased's death certificate and proof of honorable military service, such as the veteran's DD Form 214.

Complete a VA Form 40-0247, Presidential Memorial Certificate Request Form, which is available from any VA regional office (see Appendix B) and online at www.va.gov/vaforms/va/pdf/VA40-0247.pdf. Mail it, along with proof of honorable service and a copy of the death certificate, to Presidential Memorial Certificates (41A1C), National Cemetery Administration, 5109 Russell Road, Quantico, VA 22134-3903. You may also fax the required documents to 800-455-7143.

The funeral home may order a certificate for you. Additionally, some state veterans cemeteries automatically order a PMC, so you'll want to check with the cemetery administrator before ordering.

Obtaining a burial flag

You may apply for the flag by completing VA Form 21-2008, Application for United States Flag for Burial Purposes, which is available online at www.vba.va.gov/pubs/forms/VBA21-2008.pdf. The form is also available from VA regional offices (see Appendix B) and any United States Post Office. You may take the completed form, along with proof of military service, such as a DD Form 214, to any VA regional office or U.S. Post Office and receive the flag.

Generally, the funeral director will help you obtain the flag. If burial is in a national cemetery, National Park Service cemetery, or state veterans cemetery, the flag will usually be obtained by the cemetery staff.

Part III

Understanding Education and Employment Programs

The 5th Wave   By Rich Tennant

"I've been working over 80 hours a week for the past two years preparing for retirement, and it hasn't bothered me OR my wife, what's-her-name."

In this part . . .

*W*ant a free college education? How about vocational training? Thanks to veterans benefits, not only can you get a free college degree, you may be able to get special vocational training. And after you've earned a degree or completed a training program, you can get help entering the real world and earning a living.

Many veterans qualify for special preference when applying for federal government jobs, so the information in this part also tells you how qualify for one of these positions. Or, if you'd rather work for yourself, you can obtain a small business loan guarantee from the Small Business Administration. Read on to find out how!

Chapter 10

Advancing Your Education through the GI Bill

Have I got a deal for you! What would you say if I asked you to give me $1,200, and in exchange I would give you $47,556 to go to college? Or, if you don't like that deal, how about if you give me nothing, and I provide you with $11,844 worth of education benefits?

Still not excited? How about if you pay nothing, and I pay your full tuition, a monthly housing stipend, and up to $1,000 per academic year for books and fees?

These deals describe the Active-Duty and Selected Reserve Montgomery GI bills and the new GI Bill of the 21st Century, in a nutshell. Of course, to get the money, you may have to agree to forgo some of your military pay, serve for so many months, and choose an educational program that the military deems acceptable. And if you have active-duty service after September 11, 2001, you may qualify for the mega-bonuses offered by the GI Bill of the 21st Century.

Okay, using the GI Bill in any one of its forms is not really as simple as it sounds. After all, these are government-administered programs, and under the rules of bureaucracy, it's not allowed to be that simple. Don't worry. I'm here to uncomplicate the complicated.

Getting Cash for College: The Active-Duty GI Bill

Under the Active-Duty Montgomery GI Bill (ADMGIB), active-duty members forfeit $100 per month of their military pay for their first 12 months of active-duty service. In exchange, they receive 36 months of full-time education benefits.

If you enlist on active duty on or after August 1, 2009, you'll no longer be allowed to enroll in the ADMGIB. Your educational entitlements will be covered under the brand-new GI Bill of the 21st Century. For details, see the "GI Bill of the 21st Century" section later in this chapter.

You must either accept or decline the ADMGIB in writing during the first couple of weeks of military basic training. If you accept the ADMGIB, your military pay is reduced by $100 per month for the first 12 months of active-duty service, and then you can receive education benefits if you otherwise qualify. More about that in the following sections.

If you decline the ADMGIB in basic training, that's it. No second chances. Well, that's not entirely true. Every once in a while, Congress makes an exception. During the late '80s, Congress offered an open period during which service members and veterans who originally elected not to participate could change their minds. In the late '80s and early '90s, veterans who were discharged as part of the military's drawdown were offered ADMGIB benefits as part of their incentive package.

Doing the time and double-checking other eligibility requirements

The original GI Bill only required you to perform a minimum of 90 days of active-duty service to establish eligibility. Times change.

If your initial service obligation (enlistment contract, commissioning agreement, and so on) is for three or more years of active-duty service, you must serve on active duty for at least three years before establishing eligibility to use your ADMGIB benefits. If your initial service obligation is for less than three years, you must serve on active duty for at least two years before you're eligible to apply for benefits.

If you separate before performing the minimum required active-duty service, you may still be eligible for partial or even full benefits, depending on the reason for your active-duty discharge. For details, see "Meeting your service obligation" later in this section.

Setting up the modern GI Bill

The active-duty GI Bill — fondly referred to as ADMGIB — has been around in one form or another since 1944. The Servicemen's Readjustment Act of 1944 — commonly known as the *GI Bill of Rights* — provided up to $500 per school year to honorably discharged veterans. The program was a dramatic success. By 1947, military veterans accounted for 49 percent of all college admissions in the United States. As of 1956, 7.8 million of 16 million World War II veterans had participated in an education or training program under the GI Bill.

In 1952, the original GI Bill was replaced by the Veterans' Readjustment Act, providing education benefits for veterans of the Korean conflict. This benefit, in turn, was updated in 1966, by what is commonly referred to as the "Vietnam-era GI Bill." This version provided not only education benefits, but also living expenses for the veteran and his dependents while attending college.

In 1976, the Vietnam-era GI Bill was replaced by the Veterans Educational Assistance Program (VEAP). This marked the first time that service members were required to contribute funds in order to receive education benefits. Under VEAP, service members could deposit $100 per month (up to a total of $2,700) into a fund and receive 36 months of full-time education benefits.

In 1984, former Mississippi Congressman Gillespie V. "Sonny" Montgomery sponsored legislation to replace VEAP with a new GI Bill, which has been known as the "Active Duty Montgomery GI Bill" ever since.

In June 2008, Congress enacted new legislation that dramatically expanded the GI Bill. Congress called this new GI Bill the "GI Bill of the 21st Century." You, lucky reader, are going to be among the first to read about this new program.

Don't drop out: The need for a high school education

You don't need a high school education to enroll in the ADMGIB, but before you can apply for benefits under the program, you must first obtain a high school diploma or equivalency certificate, or complete a minimum of 12 hours toward a college degree.

Congress made a change in eligibility rules that took effect November 1, 2000. If you weren't previously eligible because you didn't meet the high school diploma requirement, the change may provide a second chance. You may be eligible if you now meet the high school requirement and reapply for ADMGIB benefits. If eligible, you have until November 2, 2010, or ten years from the date of your last discharge from active duty, whichever is later, to use your benefits.

Checking your discharge characterization

Most veterans benefits managed by the Department of Veterans Affairs (VA) don't require an honorable discharge. As long as the VA determines that your service was not other than honorable, you may be eligible for benefits. I explain this in detail in Chapter 2.

Eligibility for the ADMGIB, on the other hand, is an exception to this general rule. To use ADMGIB after you're separated from active duty, your discharge must be fully honorable. Discharges under honorable conditions and general discharges don't establish eligibility for ADMGIB.

However, if you have more than one period of service and receive an other-than-honorable discharge from one period, you may be able to qualify for ADMGIB if you receive an honorable discharge from another period of service. (A period from which you were discharged in order to reenlist may meet the eligibility requirements.)

Meeting your service obligation

If your initial active-duty service obligation is for three or more years, you must serve on active duty for at least three years to retain your ADMGIB eligibility. If your active-duty contract is for less than three years, you must serve at least two of those years on active duty to keep your benefits.

However, there are certain exceptions to the minimum service rule. If you don't complete the required period of service, you may still be eligible if you were separated early for one of the following reasons:

- **Convenience of the government:** Discharge reasons that fall under this category include early release to further education, early release to accept public office, pregnancy or childbirth, parenthood, conscientious objection, and surviving family member.

  To retain your full ADMGIB benefits (36 months) if you were discharged under this category, you must have 30 months of continuous active duty if your obligation was 3 or more years, or 20 months of continuous active duty if your obligation was less than 3 years.

- **Service-connected disability:** You'd think that veterans who were discharged early because of a disability they suffered because of active-duty service would retain full ADMGIB benefits, but — for reasons known only to lawmakers — that's not the way Congress worded the ADMGIB law. Veterans discharged early with a service-connected disability receive one month's ADMGIB benefit for each month served on active duty (up to the maximum entitlement of 36 months).

- **Hardship:** If you request it and Uncle Sam agrees, you can be discharged early when genuine dependency or undue hardship exists. Veterans discharged early for approved hardships receive reduced ADMGIB benefits at the rate of one month's education benefit for each month served on active duty (up to 36 months).

- ✔ **Previously existing medical conditions:** Sometimes a military member is discharged before the end of his term because he has a medical condition that existed prior to joining the military, and it's later determined that the condition interferes with properly performing military duties. Veterans discharged for this reason retain one month's worth of ADMGIB benefits for each month they served on active duty prior to discharge (up to 36 months).

- ✔ **Other medical or mental health conditions:** Veterans who are discharged early for medical or mental health conditions that interfered with their duties are eligible for partial benefits, even if the condition doesn't amount to a disability. Such veterans receive one month's worth of education benefits for each month served on active duty (up to 36 months).

- ✔ **Sole survivor:** If you were discharged after September 11, 2001, under the Sole Survivor program, you're eligible for one month's worth of education benefits for each month you served on active duty (up to 36 months). Sole survivors are those who request and receive an honorable discharge because they had an immediate family member killed or seriously disabled due to military service.

- ✔ **Reduction-in-force (RIF):** A RIF can occur if a particular military service branch has more people on active duty than the law allows. Only certain RIFs qualify for partial benefits. If you were separated due to a reduction-in-force, check with the VA regional office that serves your state to see if you qualify. See Appendix B for VA regional office locations.

You must receive an honorable discharge to retain your ADMGIB benefits. See the "Checking your discharge characterization" section for more details.

Your reason for discharge can be found on your DD Form 214, Certificate of Release or Discharge From Active Duty, in block 23. See Chapter 2 for complete information about the DD Form 214.

If you're currently on active duty and plan to leave early, don't assume your separation reason meets the requirements for the ADMGIB! Check with your education services officer or education counselor well in advance of separating to make sure you don't lose your ADMGIB benefits!

Officers beware: The effects of commissioning programs

The military services have several programs in which they will pay for your college education so you can become a commissioned officer. If you received a commission by attending a service academy (such as the U.S. Military Academy at West Point, the Naval Academy, or the Air Force Academy), you're not eligible for ADMGIB benefits unless you're already eligible because of prior military service.

Likewise, if you were commissioned through a Reserve Officer Training Corps (ROTC) scholarship program, you're also ineligible unless your eligibility was established by service before you entered the scholarship program.

If you received a commission as an ROTC scholarship graduate after September 30, 1996, and received $3,400 or less during any one year of your scholarship program, you're still eligible to participate in the ADMGIB.

Knowing your costs: This isn't a free deal!

To enroll in the ADMGIB, you must agree to give up $1,200 of your military pay at the rate of $100 per month for your first 12 months of active-duty service. You're required to make this decision during the first couple of weeks of military basic training (or officer accession training).

Your decision whether to enroll in the ADMGIB is a one-shot deal. You can't change your mind later. If you elect to enroll in the ADMGIB and later fail to qualify (such as if you receive a general discharge), you don't get your $1,200 back.

ADMGIB rates are automatically adjusted for inflation at the beginning of each fiscal year (October 1). The rates I list in the following sections reflect the FY2008 rates which were in effect at the time this book went to press. You can find the current rates on the VA's Web site at www.gibill.va.gov/GI_Bill_Info/rates.htm.

The effects of college loan repayments

Each of the military services offers a college loan repayment program to certain enlistees as an enlistment incentive. Under these programs, the military pays all or part of qualifying student loans obtained before joining the military. The amounts vary, from a maximum of $65,000 for certain Army and Navy active-duty enlistment programs to $10,000 for some Air Force active-duty enlistments.

Here's the rub: The law doesn't allow you to participate in the college loan repayment program and qualify for benefits under the ADMGIB during the same enlistment period.

To participate in the college loan repayment program, the services require recruits in basic training to sign a statement declining participation in the ADMGIB. Remember when I said earlier that accepting or declining the ADMGIB is a one-shot deal?

However, thousands of service members fell through the cracks. The services didn't require them to sign a statement declining the ADMGIB in basic training, and they still participated in the service's college loan repayment program.

If you didn't decline ADMGIB and received loan repayments, you can still be eligible for ADMGIB. But the number of months made on your loan repayment will be subtracted from your total months of ADMGIB benefits.

The maximum number of months you receive under ADMGIB is 36. So if the military service made three annual payments toward your college loan, you would have no ADMGIB entitlement. If the military made two annual payments toward your loan repayment, you could still have 12 months of ADMGIB entitlement.

However, if you received loan repayment for one period of active duty, you can still be eligible for up to 36 months of benefits based on a second period of active duty as long as you haven't declined ADMGIB.

Deciphering entitlements and rates

I think that to work for the federal government, employees must take a special course in how to make things sound more complicated than they actually are.

When the VA explains ADMGIB rates, they use the term *entitlement* to mean the number of months of benefits you may receive. Under the ADMGIB, you're entitled to 36 months worth of full-time benefits at the rate of $1,321 per month (if your active-duty contract was for three or more years) or $1,073 per month (for those who joined for less than three years of active duty).

If you go to college full time and receive $1,321 ($1,073), you use one month's worth of entitlement. If you go to college half time, you receive half of the maximum monthly amount, or $660.50 ($536.50), and use a half month's entitlement.

In other words, if you attend college full time, you receive the full monthly benefit for each month you attend courses, up to 36 months. If you attend college half time, you receive half of the full monthly benefits each month for up to 72 months. If you attend college one quarter of the time, you receive one quarter of the maximum monthly benefit for up to 144 months.

Good thing I don't work for the federal government. There's a much simpler way to look at it: If you served active duty for three or more years, your ADMGIB benefit totals $47,556. If your active-duty contract was for less than three years, your benefits total $38,628. When you go to college, you'll receive a monthly amount, as explained in the following section. When you've used up all the money, your benefits stop. Simple, huh?

Rates for institutional training

When the VA talks about paying for education at a college or university, it refers to rates for "institutional training." Sounds like you've been committed to an asylum, doesn't it? Come to think of it, many colleges could probably be considered asylums, especially if you live in the dormitories.

Table 10-1 shows the monthly ADMGIB benefit for those attending colleges and universities. For the latest rates, check out the VA's Web site at www.gibill.va.gov/GI_Bill_Info/rates.htm.

Table 10-1	ADMGIB Education Rates (Effective October 1, 2008)	
Training Time	*Monthly Rate (3-Year or Longer Enlistment)*	*Monthly Rate (Less Than 3-Year Enlistment)*
Full time	$1,321.00	$1,073.00
Three-quarters time	$990.75	$804.75
Half time	$660.50	$536.50
Less than half time, more than one-quarter time	$660.50	$536.50
One-quarter time or less	$330.25	$268.25

Note: When you enroll at less than half time, you're reimbursed only for tuition and fees, up to the maximum monthly amounts shown in Table 10-1. When you enroll at least half time, you're paid the monthly amount shown, regardless of the cost of your college courses.

Full time means taking at least 12 credit hours in a term, or 24 clock hours per week. Three-quarters time is defined as at least 9 credit hours in a term, or 18 clock hours per week. Half time means taking at least 6 credit hours in a term, or 12 clock hours per week. One-quarter time means taking at least 3 credit hours in a term, or 6 clock hours per week.

The rates shown in the table are for veterans using their ADMGIB benefits after they leave the military. Using the ADMGIB while still on active duty pays substantially less, as explained in the "Using the program while still in the military: Not a good deal" section later in this chapter.

Rates for apprenticeship and on-the-job training

The ADMGIB also pays for apprenticeship and on-the-job training programs (see the section "The GI Bill Is a Terrible Thing to Waste: Where You Can Use It" later in the chapter for details). However, these benefits are less than the amount paid for attending college full time (see the preceding section). Rates as of late 2008 are shown in Table 10-2. (For rate updates, go to the VA's Web site at www.gibill.va.gov/GI_Bill_Info/rates.htm.)

Table 10-2	Apprenticeship and On-the-job Training Rates (Effective October 1, 2008)	
Training Period	*Monthly Rate (3-Year or Longer Enlistment)*	*Monthly Rate (Less Than 3-Year Enlistment)*
First six months of training	$990.75	$804.75
Second six months of training	$726.55	$590.15
Remaining pursuit of training	$426.35	$375.55

Correspondence courses, tests for licenses or certifications, and flight training

In these cyberspace days, I doubt that very many people study by mail anymore. But if you choose to do so, the ADMGIB will pay for 55 percent of the approved charges for the course, up to your ADMGIB entitlement (see the "Deciphering entitlements and rates" section for the specific amounts). Payments for correspondence courses are made quarterly (every three months), instead of monthly.

If you require a license or certification, such as a state teaching certification, to get a job, the ADMGIB will pay up to $2,000 for each test or certification, up to your ADMGIB entitlement. There is no limit to the number of tests or re-tests you can take. However, the ADMGIB doesn't pay for tests (or college courses) that you fail, nor does it pay for license renewals.

Unfortunately, the ADMGIB won't pay for you to obtain your private pilot license. However, the program will make monthly payments based on 60 percent of the approved charges for advanced flight training courses, such as a commercial flight license, instrument rating, instructor pilot rating, and so on, up to the maximum monthly amounts shown in Table 10-2.

Before taking flight training, tests for licenses or certifications, or costly high-tech programs, consider carefully your remaining entitlement to ADMGIB benefits. For example, assume you have ten months ($13,210) of ADMGIB benefits remaining, and you decide to enroll in flight training for an instrument rating and commercial pilot license. The total cost of the approved course charges is $20,210. Sixty percent of the approved charges is $12,126. Your ADMGIB would pay $13,210 (10 × $1,321). You would have to pay the remaining $6,790 out of your own pocket. Can you say "ouch"?

Getting the most for your money: Increases above the basic rates

Two programs allow active-duty members to increase their ADMGIB benefits:

- ✓ **The contribution program:** Members on active duty can contribute up to an additional $600 to their ADMGIB. For every $20 you contribute, you receive an additional $5 on your monthly ADMGIB full-time rate. If you're eligible for the maximum 36 months of ADMGIB benefits, contributing the total $600 increases your total benefit by $5,400.

  You must make these contributions while you're on active duty. Neither VA nor the military can collect them after you've left active duty.

- ✓ **The College Fund:** Many of the services offer a college fund as an enlistment incentive. Usually, to be eligible for a college fund, you must agree to enlist in a critical occupation specialty. A *critical occupation specialty* is a military job that your service branch considers to be critically undermanned. Each recruiting service maintains its own listing of critical occupation specialties. The amount of the fund varies according to the current occupational needs of the service, but it can range from $5,000 to $50,000. You don't receive your College Fund money in one lump-sum payment. Instead, it's divided into monthly payments that are added to your basic ADMGIB rate. It's prorated for part-time training, just as the basic ADMGIB benefit is.

You can't receive your College Fund money without receiving the ADMGIB. The college fund isn't a separate benefit, but an add-on, or *kicker,* to your ADMGIB benefit.

If you lose eligibility to the ADMGIB, you also lose the college fund! Check with your education service officer or education counselor before separating to make sure you don't lose your ADMGIB (including College Fund) eligibility!

You aren't limited to one type of increase. For example, if eligible, you can receive both the College Fund money and the increase based on contributions.

Using the program while still in the military: Not a good deal

You can begin using your ADMGIB benefits while still in the military for off-duty college courses. To be eligible, you must first complete two years of active-duty service. However, going to college on the ADMGIB while still on active duty is not a wise move because your benefits are reduced dramatically.

For active-duty members going to school, the VA only pays the cost of tuition and fees (up to your allowed monthly amount). However, if tuition and fees for the course cost less than your monthly benefit, the VA subtracts the entire maximum monthly amount from your benefit entitlements.

For example, assume you're enrolled in three college courses (a total of 9 credit hours) for a three-month term. The tuition and fee costs for the three courses total $1,500. If you use your ADMGIB benefits for these courses after you get out of the military, you would receive a total of $2,972.25 from your ADMGIB benefits (three-quarter enrollment at a rate of $990.75 per month for three months). If you take these same courses while still on active duty, the VA only reimburses $1,500 (the cost of tuition and fees), but $2,972.25 is still subtracted from your ADMGIB benefits. Now that's a bum deal if I ever heard one!

You don't have to use your ADMGIB entitlements to attend college while still on active duty. Each of the services has a tuition assistance program, which pays 100 percent of tuition (up to $250 per semester hour and $4,500 per year) for college courses taken by military members on active duty. For this reason, most active-duty members use tuition assistance while still in the military and save their ADMGIB benefits for after they separate from the service.

Transferring your benefits

In 2001, Congress amended the ADMGIB law to allow the individual active-duty branches to let their members transfer up to half of their ADMGIB benefits to their spouses and/or dependent children. Congress didn't mandate the establishment of such programs, but allowed the services to do so if they wished.

In 2002, the Air Force offered a pilot (meaning trial, not someone who flies a plane) program for transferring ADMGIB benefits to a spouse and/or children. The program was available to a limited number of participants and was ended in 2003.

At press time, the Army is the only branch with an ADMGIB transfer program. It implemented the transfer of entitlement option effective July 21, 2006. The Army is offering transfer of entitlement as a reenlistment incentive option for service members reenlisting after 6 years of service and with less than 14 years of service. The Army's program allows for transfer of entitlement to an individual's spouse *only* and doesn't allow transfer to dependent children.

Under an Army test program, effective November 1, 2007, certain enlisted soldiers can transfer up to 18 months of their ADMGIB to their spouse and/or dependent children. To be eligible, the soldier must have served at least six years on active duty and agree to reenlist for at least four years in an occupational field that the Army considers critical.

For many years, Congress has debated requiring all the military branches to develop programs for transferring benefits, but that's now a dead issue because the new GI Bill of the 21st Century makes such a requirement. Therefore, Congress is unlikely to make further changes to the ADMGIB.

GI Bills aren't forever: Expiration of benefits

Your eligibility for the ADMGIB (including the College Fund if you qualify for it) generally ends ten years from the date of your last separation from active duty, or when you use all your months of entitlement, whichever is earlier.

The VA can extend your ten-year period by the amount of time you were prevented from taking classes during that period because of a disability or because you were held by a foreign government or power.

The VA can also extend your ten-year period if you reenter active duty for 90 continuous days or more (not counting any period of active duty for training). Your new ten-year eligibility period begins after your last separation from active duty.

If you serve two or more years on active duty and serve four or more years in the Selected Reserve, you have ten years from your release from active duty or ten years from the completion of the four-year Selected Reserve obligation to use your benefits, whichever is later.

If your benefits expire but you still have ADMGIB money available while still attending school, the VA can extend your entitlement to the end of a term, quarter, or semester if the ending date of your entitlement falls within a term, quarter, or semester. If the school doesn't operate on a term basis and you've completed at least one-half of your program, the VA can extend your entitlement for 12 weeks.

The Selected Reserve Montgomery GI Bill: A Free Cash Cow

The Reserve GI Bill, otherwise known as the Selected Reserve Montgomery GI Bill (SRMGIB), is an educational assistance program enacted by Congress in 1984 to attract high-quality men and women into the Reserve branch of the armed forces. This program is for members of the Selected Reserve of the Army, Navy, Air Force, Marine Corps, and Coast Guard, and the Army and Air National Guard. The SRMGIB doesn't require service in the active armed forces to qualify.

The ADMGIB is being phased out, in favor of the new GI Bill of the 21st Century (for details, see the "GI Bill of the 21st Century" section later in this chapter). Active-duty recruits who enlist on or after August 1, 2009, will no longer be eligible for the ADMGIB. At press time, there has still been no announcement as to whether the SRMGIB will follow suit. Because the SRMGIB doesn't require any active-duty time to participate, and the new GI Bill of the 21st Century requires at least 90 days of active duty in order to be eligible, there's a good chance that the SRMGIB will remain.

Eligibility: Who can play on this ball field?

A primary difference between the ADMGIB and the SRMGIB is that while the VA determines benefit eligibility for those who participate in the active-duty program, the agency does not determine eligibility for the SRMGIB.

Your Reserve or Guard component determines your eligibility and, if you qualify, will code your eligibility into the Department of Defense (DOD) personnel system. The VA makes the payments, but it can't pay benefits without eligibility information from your Reserve or Guard component.

Here are the eligibility requirements you must meet to qualify for SRMGIB benefits:

- **Service commitment:** You must enter into a six-year obligation to serve in the Selected Reserve. If you're an officer, you must agree to serve six years in addition to any service obligation you agreed to when you became an officer.

- **Selected Reserve status:** To use your benefits, you must serve in a drilling Selected Reserve unit and remain in good standing (by participating in all required weekend drills and training periods). If your component notifies you that you have failed to participate satisfactorily in the Selected Reserve, your eligibility is suspended. It can be restored only when your component determines that you have participated satisfactorily.

- **Military scholarships:** You can't receive the SRMGIB when you're receiving a scholarship through the Senior Reserve Officers' Training Corps (SROTC) program to become an active-duty officer. If you receive only a monthly stipend (versus a scholarship), you're still eligible for SRMGIB benefits. If you receive an ROTC scholarship under section 2107a of Title 10, U.S. Code, you're still eligible for the SRMGIB. Individuals receiving this type of ROTC scholarship agree to serve as officers in either the Army Reserve or the Army National Guard.

  Interestingly, although officers who graduate from military service academies are ineligible for active-duty MGIB benefits, nothing in the law makes them ineligible for the SRMGIB.

- **Active Guard and Reserve:** Your SRMGIB benefits are suspended if you enter AGR (Active Guard and Reserve) status. You can resume SRMGIB eligibility after your AGR status ends if you return to the Selected Reserve within one year. You can be eligible for the ADMGIB based on your AGR service.

If you disagree with a decision about your basic eligibility, the VA can't help you. You must contact your Reserve or Guard unit's education officer for assistance.

Rates: Pays less, but heck, it's free

The great news for Reservists is that you don't have to pay anything to participate in the SRMGIB (unlike the ADMGIB, which requires a reduction in pay of $1,200). On the negative side, the reserve program pays significantly less than the active-duty program.

You're entitled to 36 months of full-time education benefits under the SRMGIB, at the rate of $329 per month, which means you can receive up to $11,844 toward your college education.

SRMGIB rates are automatically adjusted for inflation at the beginning of each fiscal year (October 1). The rates I include in the following sections reflect the FY2008 rates, which were in effect when this book went to press. You can find the current rates on the VA's Web site at `www.gibill.va.gov/GI_Bill_Info/rates.htm`.

Institutional training

What you and I would call traditional attendance at a four-year college or university, the VA calls "institutional training." But who cares what it's called when the government is willing to pay for it, right? Table 10-3 shows the monthly benefit rates for SRMGIB participants who are enrolled in college or university courses.

Table 10-3 SRMGIB Education Rates (Effective October 1, 2008)

Training Time	Monthly Rate
Full time	$329.00
Three-quarters time	$246.00
Half time	$163.00
Less than half time	$82.25

Full time means taking at least 12 credit hours in a term, or 24 clock hours per week. Three-quarters time is defined as at least 9 credit hours in a term, or 18 clock hours per week. Half time means taking at least 6 credit hours in a term, or 12 clock hours per week.

As with the ADMGIB, you are charged for a month of entitlement for each month of full-time benefits you receive. If you attend school part time, the VA adjusts your entitlement charge according to your course load. For example, if you receive full-time benefits for 12 months, the charge is 12 months of entitlement. If you receive half-time benefits for 12 months, the charge is only 6 months.

Apprenticeship and on-the-job training

You can use your SRMGIB benefits to pay for apprenticeship and on-the-job training programs. The amount of benefits you receive depends on what stage of the program you're in, as shown in Table 10-4.

Table 10-4	Apprenticeship and On-the-job Training Rates (Effective October 1, 2008)
Training Period	*Monthly Rates*
First six months of training	$246.75
Second six months of training	$180.95
Remaining pursuit of training	$115.15

Correspondence courses, tests for licenses or certifications, and flight training

Just like the ADMGIB, you can use the SRMGIB to enroll in correspondence courses. The SRMGIB will pay for 55 percent of the approved charges for the course, up to your SRMGIB entitlement.

In January 2006, Congress amended the law to allow participants in the SRMGIB to be reimbursed for approved licenses or certifications. Prior to this, only those in the active-duty program could use this benefit.

You can receive reimbursement from your SRMGIB entitlement for the cost of a license or certification test, up to $2,000 per test. You may take as many tests as you need, and you don't have to pass a test to receive benefits. You can receive benefits to retake a test you failed and to renew or update your license or certificate.

The SRMGIB won't pay for you to get a private pilot's license. But if you already have a license, the SRMGIB will pay up to 60 percent of approved advanced flight training (up to your SRMGIB entitlement), such as commercial flight license, instrument rating, instructor pilot rating, and so on, up to the maximum monthly amounts shown in Table 10-4.

Patience, Grasshopper: When you can start using the benefits

You officially become eligible for the SRMGIB and can begin using the benefits when you complete initial entry training for the Selected Reserves. Your training generally is considered complete after you finish basic training and school for your military job, and return to your unit for monthly drills.

Some people join the National Guard or Reserves under a program called *split option*. Under this program, a person enlists in the National Guard or Reserves, attends basic training, and then returns to drill with her unit for up to one year before attending military job training. If you enlisted under this program, you're not entitled to SRMGIB benefits until you've completed the job portion of your military training.

Converting to the Active-Duty GI Bill

If you're called up to active duty under Title 10 of the United States Code (federal duty), you can convert your SRMGIB benefits to the ADMGIB, as long as you're called up for two years or more and you don't decline the ADMGIB in writing. Of course, if you elect this option, you have to request it (see your local education office) and agree to have your pay reduced by $100 per month for your first 12 months of active-duty service. (To find out the details of the ADMGIB, check out the earlier section "Getting Cash for College: The Active-Duty GI Bill.")

A call-up to full-time National Guard duty under Title 32, U.S. Code (state authority) won't qualify you for the ADMGIB, unless the purpose of the duty is for organizing, administering, recruiting, instructing, or training the National Guard. Duty under Title 32, U.S. Code for the purpose of performing operations (such as drug interdiction or disaster relief) isn't qualifying duty for the ADMGIB.

When time runs out: Expiration of benefits

In most cases, you must use your SRMGIB while you're still in the Selected Reserves. If you leave the Selected Reserves, generally your benefits end the day you separate. However, there are a couple of exceptions to this general rule.

If you leave the Selected Reserve and you meet the following requirements, you generally are still eligible for a full 14 years from the date you became eligible:

✔ You were separated because you had a disability that wasn't caused by misconduct, or

✔ Your unit was inactivated or you were otherwise involuntarily separated between October 1, 1991, and December 31, 2001.

Even if you stay in the Selected Reserves, there is a time limit for using your SRMGIB benefits. Your benefits expire 14 years from your eligibility date.

If you stay in the Selected Reserves and you're called up for federal active duty under Title 10 of the U.S. Code, the VA will extend your eligibility for the length of your active duty, plus four months. You'll receive a separate extension for each call-up. Unfortunately, the law doesn't permit the VA to grant extensions for call-ups under Title 32 (state authority).

Additionally, the VA can extend your eligibility if it expires while you're enrolled in classes or a program. Eligibility is usually extended to the end of a term, quarter, or semester. If the school doesn't operate on a term basis, the VA can generally extend your eligibility for 12 weeks.

Finally, the VA can extend your eligibility if you couldn't train because of a disability caused by Selected Reserves service.

The GI Bill of the 21st Century

If you're a veteran with at least 90 days of active-duty service after September 11, 2001, have I got great news for you! On June 20, 2008, Congress stopped bickering long enough to pass a new GI Bill with significantly expanded benefits, including up to 100 percent tuition, payment for books and fees, and even a monthly housing allowance while you attend college!

Congress is calling this the GI Bill of the 21st Century (GIB21C), and it goes into effect August 1, 2009. Actually, the new program is technically in effect now, but Congress has given the VA until August 1, 2009, to come up with the new rate tables.

The GIB21C doesn't change where or how education benefits can be used (see the "The GI Bill Is a Terrible Thing to Waste: Where You Can Use It" section later in this chapter), but boy, oh, boy does it change the amount of money available to you for your education.

The new law requires the military services to establish a program to allow military members to transfer a portion of their GI Bill benefits to their spouses or dependent children. However, the law doesn't go into specifics. How various military service branches will implement this provision is still unknown at press time. Most likely, you'll be required to reenlist to be eligible to transfer benefits.

Claiming what's yours: Eligibility

You're eligible for the new benefit if you have performed active-duty service after September 11, 2001, for

✔ At least 90 continuous days, or

✔ Six or more months of total days

If you have post-9/11 active-duty service of less than 24 months, you can't use your initial entry training (IET) time to qualify. *IET active duty* means active duty you performed in basic training or initial military job training school. If you have 24 or more months of post-9/11 active-duty service, your time in IET does count when computing benefit entitlement and how much you'll receive (see the upcoming "Post-9/11 active-duty time" section).

Good news for officers: Everyone who meets the post-9/11 active-duty requirements is eligible for the GIB21C. However, officers can't use their active-duty time while in initial training status to qualify. (Under the ADMGIB, officers who obtained their commission through a military service academy or ROTC scholarship weren't eligible, unless they qualified for benefits for previous active-duty service.)

As with the ADMGIB and the SRMGIB, you must first have a high school diploma or GED to begin using benefits under the GIB21C.

No more contributions

Unlike the ADMGIB, you don't have to contribute $1,200 of your military pay to participate in the new program. If you're currently on active duty and paying into the ADMGIB, you can stop. You'll still be eligible for the GIB21C program on August 1, 2009 (assuming you have the prerequisite active-duty time; see the earlier "Claiming what's yours: Eligibility" section).

Unfortunately, the new law doesn't provide for refunds. If you've already contributed to the ADMGIB, you won't get your money back.

Converting to the new GI Bill

If, on August 1, 2009, you are eligible for the ADMGIB and/or the SRMGIB and you qualify for the GIB21C, you may make an irrevocable election to receive benefits under the GIB21C. After you elect to receive benefits under the GIB21C, you're no longer eligible to receive benefits under the program(s) from which you elected the GIB21C.

Before you elect to convert, carefully consider your education objectives and how you plan to achieve them. For example, if you plan to receive your degree online, the ADMGIB may actually pay more. That's because the GIB21C doesn't pay the housing allowance component for online education.

Assuming you're eligible for the new program and you elect to convert, you only receive the number of months of education benefits you had available under your old program. For example, if you have 22 months of ADMGIB benefits remaining at the time you convert, you would receive 22 months of benefits under the new program.

Entitlements: More cash for college

Your education benefits under the GIB21C vary, according to several factors, but — on the whole — the new program pays a whole lot more than does the ADMGIB and SRMGIB.

Like the other GI Bill programs, you're entitled to 36 months of full-time education benefits. If you go to school half time, you'd receive 72 months of half benefits.

If you've already used some of your benefits under the ADMGIB or SRMGIB, the amount will be subtracted from your total benefits when you convert to the GIB21C. For example, if you've already used 12 months of your ADMGIB benefits, you will have only 24 months of GIB21C benefits when you convert.

Post-9/11 active-duty time

The percentage of the total authorized benefits you receive depends on the amount of post-9/11 active-duty time you have under your belt. The percentages are

- 100 percent for 36 or more total months
- 100 percent for 30 or more consecutive days with a disability-related discharge
- 90 percent for 30 total months
- 80 percent for 24 total months
- 70 percent for 18 total months
- 60 percent for 12 total months
- 50 percent for 6 total months
- 40 percent for 90 or more consecutive days

Tuition

The GIB21C pays 100 percent of the full tuition rate set by your state for public schools (subject to the percentage restrictions shown in the preceding section). An added feature of this tuition payment plan is that the tuition will be paid directly to the school, relieving you of the responsibility.

At press time, the tuition rates weren't available because the VA has until August 1, 2009, to produce tuition rate charts for each state. When available, you can view the rates on the VA's GI Bill Web site at www.gibill.va.gov.

Books and fees

The GIB21C pays $1,000 per academic year for books and fees (subject to the percentage restrictions shown in the "Post-9/11 active-duty time" section). You'll receive a lump-sum payment the first month of each quarter, semester, or term, depending on how your school divides the academic year.

Housing stipend

A very attractive feature of the new GI Bill is payment of a monthly housing stipend. Subject to the percentage restrictions shown in the "Post-9/11 active-duty time" section, the amount payable is the same as the housing allowance given to active-duty enlistment members in the pay grade of E-5 at the "with dependent" rate. The military's active-duty housing allowance depends on location, and it changes each January 1, depending on the rise or fall of average housing costs. Current rates can be found on the Department of Defense Per Diem Web site at perdiem.hqda.pentagon.mil/perdiem/bah.html.

The average housing allowance for an E-5 with dependents in 2008 was $1,400 per month.

Veterans who attend school through distance learning don't receive the housing stipend. Additionally, military members who use the benefit while still on active duty don't receive the housing stipend because their housing needs are already being taken care of by the military.

More time to use the benefits

The ADMGIB expires ten years after your last discharge from the military. The SRMGIB expires upon your discharge from the Reserves. If you're eligible for the new GI Bill, you retain your benefits until you use them up or for 15 years after your last discharge from the military, whichever occurs first.

The GI Bill Is a Terrible Thing to Waste: Where You Can Use It

You can use your GI Bill benefits to pay for almost any education program that leads to an accredited college degree or to an occupational objective.

Benefits under the new GIB21C can only be used for programs offered by schools in the United States that are authorized to grant an associate's degree or higher. That means, for example, you can't use the new program to pay for overseas college educations, nor for apprenticeship and on-the-job training programs, unless those programs are offered by a degree-granting institution in the United States. The ADMGIB and the SRMGIB can often be used for these purposes. This is another factor you should consider before deciding whether to convert to the GIB21C.

The programs listed here are examples of the types of approved training programs for which GI Bill benefits are payable:

✔ An undergraduate or graduate degree at a college or university, including

- An accredited independent study program (which may be offered through distance education) leading to a standard college degree.

- A cooperative (co-op) training program (a full-time program alternating school instruction and job training in a business or industrial establishment).

✔ A certificate or diploma from a business, technical, or vocational school, including co-op programs.

✔ An accredited independent study course leading to a certificate from a college, university, or other degree-granting educational institution.

✔ An apprenticeship or on-the-job training (OJT) program offered by a company or union. Apprenticeships or OJT programs offer an alternative to college or vocational school for helping you gain experience in the field you choose.

✔ A correspondence course.

✔ Flight training. You must have a private pilot certificate and meet the medical requirements for the desired certificate when you begin training.

✔ Qualified programs overseas that lead to a college degree.

A state agency or the VA must approve each program offered by a school or company.

Although the GI Bills can be used to pay for a variety of education and training programs, there are certain restrictions on where or how the benefits can be used. You may not receive benefits for the following courses:

✔ Bartending and personality development courses

✔ Nonaccredited independent study courses

✔ Any course given by radio

✔ Self-improvement courses such as reading, speaking, woodworking, basic seamanship, and English as a second language

✔ Farm cooperative courses

✔ Audited courses

✔ Courses paid in whole or in part by the military tuition assistance or other armed forces program

✔ Courses that are recreational in character

✔ Courses that don't lead to an educational, professional, or vocational objective

✔ Courses you've taken before and successfully completed

✔ Courses you take as a federal employee under the Government Employees' Training Act

In addition to the course restrictions, you can't use the ADMGIB or SRMGIB under the following circumstances:

✔ **Imprisonment:** Individuals who are in a federal, state, or local prison after being convicted of a felony may receive only the cost of tuition, fees, necessary books, equipment, and supplies (up to your maximum monthly entitlement). I guess Congress figured that's all you need if you're in prison, because your bed and breakfast are already being taken care of.

✔ **Denial of admission to degree program:** If you seek a college degree, the school must admit you to a degree program by the start of your third term.

✔ **Position of influence at a proprietary school:** You can't use VA education benefits if you're an owner or official of the school.

✔ **Fugitive felon status:** The VA can't pay education benefits for any period during which federal or state law enforcement identifies you as a fugitive felon. A person is considered a *fugitive felon* if he has an outstanding warrant for a felony.

Dual Duty: Combining the GI Bills

If you're eligible for both the ADMGIB and the SRMGIB, you may receive a maximum of 48 months of benefits. However, you can't use both benefits at the same time. You must choose which program you want to use.

For example, if you're eligible for both benefits and elect to use the ADMGIB, you would have 12 months of SRMGIB benefits remaining when your ADMGIB benefits are used up.

You can't combine the ADMGIB or the SRMGIB with the new GIB21C. However, you can convert any remaining entitlements under the ADMGIB and/or the SRMGIB to GIB21C benefits. See the "Converting to the new GI Bill" section earlier in this chapter.

Get That Cap and Gown Ready: Applying for the Benefits

Applying for ADMGIB, SRMGIB, and GIB21C benefits is rather easy, considering this is a program administered by the federal government. Just follow these steps:

1. **Find out if the program you want to participate in is approved for VA education benefits.**

   You can check with the school's financial aid office or training facility employment office, or contact the VA (see Appendix B). If the facility hasn't requested approval before, ask the school or training facility official to contact the VA to request approval.

2. **Complete VA Form 22-1990 and submit it to the appropriate VA regional office (see Appendix B).**

   You can get the application form in several ways:

   - If the school or facility you want to attend is already approved for VA education benefits, the financial aid office will likely have copies.

   - You can also get the form online. Just go to www.gibill.va.gov and click "Education Benefits," then "How to Apply for Benefits." From here, you can print the form and mail it, or you can fill it out online and submit it electronically.

   If you apply online, you must still print the signature page and send it to the VA, because the agency needs your original signature to begin payments. If you're on active duty, your education services officer must also sign your application.

   - You can call 888-GIBILL-1 (888-442-4551) and request an application. (You may have difficulty getting through quickly, especially when school enrollments are heavy. You may have more success by going to the Internet site.)

3. **Ask the school or training official to certify your enrollment to VA.**

   If the program has been approved for VA benefits, check in with the school or training facility official who certifies enrollments for VA benefits. At a school, this certifying official may be in one of the following offices: financial aid, veterans affairs, registrar, admissions, counseling, or others. For on-the-job training or an apprenticeship, the official may be in the training, finance, personnel, or other office.

   The certifying official at the school or education facility isn't a VA employee and can't make decisions about your eligibility for VA benefits.

4. **The VA will review your application and let you know whether anything else is needed to begin payments.**

If you haven't decided on a program or simply want a determination of your eligibility for the GI Bill, just submit the application to the appropriate VA regional office. If you're eligible, you'll receive a Certificate of Eligibility showing how long you're eligible and how many months of benefits you can receive. See Appendix B for VA regional office locations.

Chapter 11

Aid and Vocational Training for Disabled and Homeless Veterans

* *

* *

*I*f you're a military veteran who has a disability that was caused or aggravated by your military service, and your disability prevents you from landing a steady job, don't despair (for too long, anyway). The U.S. Department of Veterans Affairs (VA) has a program designed to fit your needs.

The VA has helped thousands of disabled veterans prepare for and find jobs. It can help you determine what kind of job you're best suited for, assist you in preparing your resume and applying for jobs, and — in certain cases — even pay for you to get a college degree or receive job-related training in order to become employable. In some cases, the VA even helps pay your living expenses while you're improving your mind in a training program.

In addition to helping disabled veterans, Congress has established several programs within the VA to address homelessness among veterans. The primary goal for these programs is to return homeless veterans to self-sufficiency and stable independent living. The VA provides healthcare to about 100,000 homeless veterans, and compensation and pensions to nearly 40,000 annually. The department also offers homeless veterans employment assistance and help obtaining foreclosed homes and excess federal property, including clothes, footwear, blankets, and other items. In this chapter, I give you an overview of who the homeless veterans are and explain available programs and what they provide.

In addition to the programs detailed in this chapter, many states operate separate programs to assist homeless veterans. For details, contact the appropriate state veterans affairs office (see Appendix A).

The Chapter 31 Program: What It Offers

The VA's Vocational Rehabilitation and Employment (VR&E) Program helps veterans who have service-connected disabilities get and keep a job. The program has placed vets in positions ranging from sales associate at the mega-superstore up the road to production manager at an international corporation. The program is a result of a law enacted by Congress under Title 38, Code of Federal Regulations, Chapter 31. Because of this, the program is commonly referred to as the Chapter 31 Program.

The program offers a variety of services that can help fit you into the right job, including:

- **Interest and aptitude testing:** Remember when you took the Armed Services Vocational Aptitude Battery (ASVAB) when you first joined the military? That test measured your aptitude for learning various military jobs. The VA offers a similar test that can tell you where your aptitude lies in civilian job fields. Who knows? Maybe you have the makings of an electronic engineer!

- **Occupational exploration:** There are thousands of jobs out there in job land. The VA can help you explore those opportunities to determine what the qualifications are, where the jobs are located, how much they pay, and what particular fields have the greatest need.

- **Setting occupational goals:** Sometimes you may know what kind of career you want, but you may not know how to get from here to there. The VA can help you establish a set of goals, ultimately leading to your dream job.

- **Locating the right type of training program:** You may require additional training to qualify for your career choice. The VA can help you determine the training program that is best suited to your needs and capabilities. In some cases, the VA can even pay for your tuition and fees.

- **Exploring education and training facilities:** After you know the type of training program you require, the next step is finding a school or training facility that offers what you need. The VA can help you locate schools that fit your budget, time, location, and capabilities to achieve your occupational goal.

Examining Your Eligibility for Chapter 31

Not all veterans are eligible for the Chapter 31 Program (see the previous section for details on this program). In fact, you may meet the basic eligibility criteria but still not be *entitled* to benefits under the VR&E program. Even if the VA finds you're entitled to other benefits under the program (I list these additional benefits in the "Using Benefits beyond Education and Training" section later in this chapter), a counselor may decide you're not entitled to vocational training or education. I cover this in more detail in the "Knowing what you're entitled to," section a little later in this chapter.

Meeting the basic requirements

Three factors determine whether you meet the basic eligibility requirements to participate in the VR&E program:

- **Service characterization:** You must have been discharged (or will soon be discharged) from the military under circumstances that the VA doesn't determine to be dishonorable. See Chapter 2 for information about how the VA makes this determination.

- **Disability rating:** The VA must have awarded you a disability rating of at least 10 percent. If you have not yet been discharged from the military, your *expected* disability rating must be at least 20 percent. Additionally, the disability must be *service-connected* (a result of your military service). Read Chapter 6 for more information about VA disability ratings.

- **Time period:** You have a limited time in which you can apply for benefits under the VR&E program. This is generally 12 years from the date the VA notified you that you had at least a 10 percent service-connected disability.

Knowing what you're entitled to

After you submit your application (see "Applying for Chapter 31 Benefits" later in this chapter), you meet with a VA *vocational rehabilitation counselor (VRC)* who determines if you're entitled to program benefits.

In order to be entitled to benefits, the VRC must find that you have at least a 20 percent service-connected disability with an *employment handicap,* or you have at least a 10 percent service-connected disability with a *serious employment handicap.* Here's how the VA defines these two terms:

- **Employment handicap:** This means your disability impairs your ability to get a job in the field where your interests, experience, and aptitude lie. Your disability may not preclude you from all employment in this field, but it may limit advancements and promotions, or impact your ability to perform some tasks in the field.

- **Serious employment handicap:** Your disability severely limits or completely prevents you from obtaining employment in the job field that you have experience, training, and aptitude in.

I know these definitions sound subjective. That's because they are. There isn't any go/no-go list that the VRC uses to establish your degree of employment handicap. Each and every case is evaluated on an individual basis. The VRC uses many individual factors, including the exact nature of the disability, your previous training and work experience, your interests and occupational goals, and so on, in establishing your degree of employment handicap. Of course, like most VA programs, if you disagree with the VRC's determination, you can file an appeal. Chapter 3 includes information about filing an appeal.

Although the VRC determines your degree of employment handicap, your disability rating and whether it's service connected are established by the VA under a separate process. I discuss disability rates and service connection in Chapter 6.

I'm afraid that's not the end of it. Even if the VRC determines that you're entitled to benefits under Chapter 31, she may determine that you don't require education or vocational training programs to become employable. In that case, you'd be entitled to other benefits under the VR&E program, including vocational counseling, rehabilitation planning, and job referral services. See the "Using Benefits beyond Education and Training" section later in this chapter.

Footing the Bill: What the VA Pays For

Assuming the VRC determines you're entitled to Chapter 31 benefits and that you require education or vocational training to help you become employable (see the previous sections), the VA will pay for a variety of education and training programs.

If a VA counselor determines that you need training to reach your vocational goal, you may train in a vocational school, a special rehabilitation facility, an apprenticeship program, an on-the-job training position, a college, or a university. In addition to covering the costs or tuition of your training program, the VA may pay for fees, books, equipment, tools, or other supplies you need to succeed in your program.

You may be breathing a sigh of relief that the government picks up the costs for much of this training. But wait! I've got more good news. During your program, you may qualify for a monthly *subsistence allowance* to help you meet your living expenses. The allowance you receive depends on

✔ The type of training you receive and where you receive it

✔ Your rate of attendance (full-time versus part-time enrollment)

✔ The number of dependents you have

See the "Monthly subsistence allowance rates" section in this chapter for more details about how much money Uncle Sam will kick in to help you cover other expenses. You'll receive this allowance in addition to any VA compensation or military retired pay you may receive. Additionally, the VA will provide medical and dental care while you're enrolled in a training program. I'm afraid that your dependents aren't covered for medical care or dental care under this program, however.

You can't use more than one VA education program at a time. If you're going to college on the GI Bill (see Chapter 10), the VA can't pay education benefits under Chapter 31. Additionally, if you have remaining GI Bill benefits, you can't receive free education under this program. You have to use your GI Bill benefits first.

Monthly subsistence allowance rates

In addition to paying for fees, tuition, books, tools, supplies, and other equipment while you're participating in a training program, the VA may determine that you qualify for a monthly subsistence allowance. You don't apply separately for this benefit. If you're approved for VA-funded education, the VA determines whether you need the subsistence allowance, based on your household income. The rates vary depending on where you train, your enrollment status, and the number of dependents you have. You can use this money however you need to while you're training for your new gig.

The subsistence allowance is paid monthly, via direct deposit to your bank account on the first of every month, and it's not subject to income taxes.

The rates listed in the tables in the following sections are as of October 1, 2007. For the latest rates, go to www.vba.va.gov/bln/vre/sa.htm.

Institutional training

These subsistence allowance rates are paid if you are enrolled in an institution of higher learning, such as a college or university. Table 11-1 shows the monthly subsistence rates you may receive if you are enrolled in college or university courses.

Table 11-1   Institutional Training Rates (Effective October 1, 2007)

Number of Dependents	Full Time	Three-quarters Time	Half Time
0	$520.74	$391.27	$261.81
1	$645.94	$485.15	$324.38
2	$761.18	$569.09	$381.30
Each additional	$55.49	$42.67	$28.47

Full time means taking at least 12 credit hours in a term, or 24 clock hours per week. Three-quarters time is defined as at least 9 credit hours in a term, or 18 clock hours per week. Half time means taking at least 6 credit hours in a term, or 12 clock hours per week.

Work-experience programs

If you enroll in a nonpay or nominal-pay work experience program in a federal, state, local, or federally recognized Indian tribe agency, the monthly rates are the same as the institutional training rates shown in Table 11-1.

Public Law 102-477 allows federal, state, or local recognized Indian tribes to use federal grants to establish work-experience programs for members of their tribe. Of course, to participate in one of these work-education programs and receive the subsistence rates shown in Table 11-1, you would have to be a veteran entitled to Chapter 31 benefits and also be a member of the tribe.

When computing entitlement for such work-experience programs, full time equates to 40 hours per week, three-quarters time means 30 hours per week, and half time is equal to 20 hours of work per week.

Nonpay on-the-job training programs

The government pays a monthly subsistence allowance only for full-time training in the following training programs:

- ✔ **Nonpay or nominal pay on-the-job training in a federal, state, or local program or a federally recognized Indian tribe agency.**

- ✔ **Training in the home:** This includes distance learning courses and correspondence courses that aren't part of an accredited college or university program.

- ✔ **Vocational course in a rehabilitation facility or sheltered workshop:** As an essential part of their programs, many shelters and rehabilitation facilities include vocational courses. Training received in these types of facilities may qualify you for the monthly subsistence allowance.

- ✔ **Institutional nonfarm cooperative:** A *cooperative* is a business that is owned and controlled equally by the people who use its services or who work at it. They are often referred to as a *co-op*.

You may be confused about what constitutes a work-experience program (see the preceding section) and what an on-the-job training (OJT) program is. A work-experience program provides you with job experience that you can then put on a resume or job application to make you more employable. OJT, on the other hand, is a formal training program that leads to a job in the same agency after the OJT period is complete.

The monthly rates for subsistence allowance when you're in a nonpay on-the-job training program are shown in Table 11-2.

Table 11-2	Nonpay On-the-Job Training Program Rates (Effective October 1, 2007)
Number of Dependents	***Monthly Rates***
0	$520.74
1	$645.94
2	$761.18
Each additional	$55.49

Farm cooperative, apprenticeship, or other on-the-job training

Monthly subsistence rates for farm cooperative, apprenticeship, or other on-the-job training programs are reduced because you receive a salary to participate in such programs. Rates, shown in Table 11-3, are paid for full-time enrollment only.

Table 11-3	Farm Cooperative, Apprenticeship, or Other On-the-Job Training Program Rates (Effective October 1, 2007)
Number of Dependents	**Monthly Rate**
0	$455.29
1	$550.69
2	$634.55
Each additional	$41.28

Farm cooperatives are just like nonfarm cooperatives (see the preceding section), except they exist in the fields of agriculture and livestock. The majority of America's 2 million farmers and ranchers belong to one or more farm cooperatives. Because of the tax breaks these cooperatives receive, they are required to pay salaries to Chapter 31 Program veterans who are training with them.

Apprenticeship and OJT programs lead to full-time employment after the apprenticeship or OJT period is completed.

Other types of programs

Subsistence allowance is also paid for nonfarm cooperative institutional training and nonfarm cooperative on-the-job training that's not operated by a recognized Indian tribe. If you're enrolled in a nonfarm cooperative institutional training program, you'll receive the full-time rates listed in Table 11-1, but only full-time rates apply. Those enrolled in a nonfarm cooperative on-the-job training program receive the rates listed in Table 11-3.

Buckling down and participating in a VA work-study program

Veterans who are participating in the Chapter 31 Program and training at the three-quarters or full-time rate may participate in the VA's *work-study program.* In this type of program, you work during or between periods of enrollment in your vocational training or education program. When you participate in the VA's work-study program, you're working both sides of the fence, so to speak. You're using the VA's benefits to master a new skill or knowledge (that's the study part). As far as the work half of the program goes, you may provide VA outreach services, prepare and process VA paperwork, work at a VA medical facility, or perform other VA-approved activities.

Under this program, you earn an hourly wage equal to the federal minimum wage or your state's minimum wage, whichever is greater. As much as 40 percent of the total of your work-study allowance may be paid in advance.

You can arrange with the VA to work any number of hours you want during your enrollment, but the total number of hours you work can't be more than 25 times the number of weeks in your enrollment period.

Applying for Chapter 31 Benefits

Unlike many other VA programs, you can't apply online for Chapter 31 training benefits. You can, however, download VA Form 28-1900, Disabled Veterans Application for Vocational Rehabilitation, from the VA's Web site at www.vba.va.gov/pubs/forms/VBA-28-1900-ARE.pdf.

After you complete the application, sign it and mail it to your nearest VA regional office (found in Appendix B). The VA will review your application and arrange for you to meet with a vocational rehabilitation counselor.

You can apply for the program while you're still in the military. If you are pending medical discharge from the military for a condition that is reasonably expected to be 20 percent or more disabling, you can submit your application before discharge.

Using Benefits beyond Education and Training

As I mention in the "Examining Your Eligibility for Chapter 31" section, the VA may determine that you're entitled to participate in the program but that you don't need education or vocational training to meet your employment objectives. In such cases, the program offers several other valuable benefits:

- ✔ **Comprehensive rehabilitation evaluation to determine abilities, skills, interests, and needs:** These include tests and interviews designed to help you discover what occupational field you may be best suited for.

- ✔ **Vocational counseling and rehabilitation planning:** VA counselors can help you plan a course of action and a set of goals, leading to your dream job.

✔ **Employment services such as job-seeking skills, resume development, and other work readiness assistance:** To find a job, you need to know where to look, and VA counselors can help with that. They can also assist you with preparing that perfect resume in order to land the job of your choice.

✔ **Assistance finding and keeping a job, including the use of special employer incentives:** Some employers give special job preference to veterans. The federal government is the perfect example (see Chapter 12). The VA can help you locate employers who prefer to hire veterans.

✔ **Supportive rehabilitation services, including case management, counseling, and referral:** While enrolled in the Chapter 31 Program, you receive ongoing support, counseling, and feedback from the VA, leading to the day when you cash that first paycheck.

✔ **Independent living services:** If you're a veteran with a serious disability, one severe enough to require assistance to perform your daily living activities, the VA has programs that can help you transition to an independent living status.

Giving Homeless Veterans a Helping Hand

About 250 community-based organizations are dedicated to helping the homeless veteran. Most of these organizations work with the VA, other government agencies, veterans organizations, and community groups to help provide support, resources, and opportunities to America's homeless veterans. The services offered by these organizations vary widely, limited only by available funds and the imagination of the organizers. Some of them offer traditional homeless services, such as overnight shelters and soup kitchens, while others provide counseling and referral services, and still others offer medical screenings and limited medical care.

For a list of these community-based service providers, see the National Coalition for Homeless Veterans Web site at www.nchv.org/network.cfm.

The VA has established homeless veteran coordinators in every state. The coordinators work with local community-based organizations to provide services to homeless veterans, but the coordinators are available to answer questions and provide referrals to individual veterans as well.

You can find your state's homeless veteran coordinator by visiting the VA's Web site at www1.va.gov/homeless/page.cfm?pg=21, or by calling the VA's toll-free services line at 800-827-1000.

Examining the plight of the homeless veteran

According to the VA, in urban, suburban, and rural communities throughout America, one of every three adult males sleeping under bridges, in alleys, and in abandoned buildings or living in shelters or other community-based organizations has served our nation in the armed forces.

If I knew all the answers, I'd be the king of the authors. Unfortunately, nobody knows for sure why there are so many homeless veterans. Many veterans are homeless because of the complex set of factors that affect all homeless people: extreme shortage of affordable housing, livable income, limited access to healthcare, and a lack of family and social support networks.

A large number of homeless veterans live with the lingering effects of post traumatic stress disorder (PTSD) and substance abuse, and that's likely the key. PTSD is an insidious thing; it creeps into the mind. It doesn't always affect the veteran right away, nor are veterans necessarily homeless right after discharge. Many times, it takes years for depression, anxiety, substance abuse, and bad economic situations to take their toll, driving veterans to the street.

A person doesn't always know that he's suffering from PTSD. If you know a veteran who is suffering from depression, drug or alcohol abuse, or mental health issues, please try to get them to seek help at a VA medical center. See Chapter 4 for information about receiving medical care from the VA.

The vast majority of homeless veterans are single men, although service providers are reporting an increased number of veterans, both women and men, with children seeking their assistance. Beyond that, the statistics for homeless veterans are alarming:

- 23 percent of America's homeless are veterans
- 33 percent of all male homeless in America are veterans
- 47 percent served during the Vietnam era
- 17 percent served after Vietnam
- 15 percent served before the Vietnam era
- 67 percent served three or more years
- 33 percent were stationed in war zones
- 25 percent have used VA homeless services
- 85 percent have completed high school or received their GED compared with 56 percent of nonveteran homeless
- 89 percent received an honorable discharge
- 79 percent reside in central cities
- 16 percent reside in suburban areas
- 5 percent reside in rural areas
- 76 percent experience alcohol, drug, or mental health problems
- 46 percent are white males compared with 34 percent of nonveteran homeless
- 54 percent are people of color
- 46 percent are age 45 or older compared with 20 percent of nonveteran homeless

I explain some of the services available to homeless veterans in the following sections.

The grant and per diem program

This program doesn't provide money to the individual veteran. Instead, the VA's Homeless Providers Grant and Per Diem Program provides funding to community-based agencies so they can provide essential services to homeless veterans.

In order to be eligible, organizations must provide supportive housing (up to 24 months) to homeless veterans or must offer support services that

- Help homeless veterans achieve residential stability
- Increase their skill levels and/or income
- Obtain greater self-determination

Such services include, but are not limited to

- Case management
- Education
- Crisis intervention
- Counseling

Grants

The VA provides grants to organizations to pay for the cost of constructing, renovating, or acquiring a facility to use for homeless veterans transitional housing, or establishing a homeless veterans service center.

The grant limit is 65 percent of the cost. Organizations must find other sources for the remaining 35 percent of the costs.

The number of grants issued each year depends in large part on the amount of funding that Congress approves for the program.

Grants can't be used to pay for operational costs or salaries. That's the purpose of the per diem portion of the program, as explained in the next section.

Per diem

Per diem may be paid by the VA to community-based agencies that provide services for homeless veterans to supplement salaries and operational costs. *Per diem* is simply a fancy VA word for additional funding that's based on the actual number of homeless veterans receiving service from the agency.

Organizations that received a grant (see the preceding section) get first priority to available per-diem funds.

For organizations that provide housing, the maximum amount of per diem paid is $33.01 per day for each veteran housed. These are the rates for 2008. The VA may adjust these rates periodically, based on the funding it receives each year from Congress. Organizations that provide support services only may receive one-eighth of the daily cost of care, not to exceed the current VA State Home rate for rehabilitation and treatment care, and not to exceed eight hours in any one day.

Applying for the program

Organizations interested in applying for the VA's Homeless Providers Grant and Per Diem Program should call 877-332-0334 or write to VA Homeless Providers Grant and Per Diem Program, Office of Mental Health Services (116E), VAHQ, 810 Vermont Ave., NW, Washington, DC 20420.

Stand Downs for homeless veterans

Stand Downs are usually organized by local veterans groups, with support from the VA. It's a case of veterans helping veterans. Since 1988, when the first Stand Down was organized in San Diego by a group of Vietnam veterans, the program has helped more than 200,000 homeless veterans and their families.

The name *Stand Down* comes from a program used during the Vietnam War to provide a safe retreat for troops returning from combat operations. Combat units would be relocated to a secure base camp area, where they could take care of personal hygiene, get clean uniforms, enjoy warm meals, receive medical and dental care, mail and receive letters, and enjoy the camaraderie of friends in a safe environment. Stand Downs gave weary soldiers the chance to renew their spirit, health, and overall sense of well-being.

This is also the purpose of the Stand Down programs for homeless veterans. Today's Stand Downs are organized by grass-roots, community-based organizations and are designed to give the homeless veteran a respite from "combat" life on the streets. Stand Downs can be a one-, two-, or three-day event. Although some are conducted indoors, the majority are held on football fields, in parks, or in other wide-open spaces. During Stand Downs, homeless veterans can simply show up and receive a broad range of services, including food and clothing; medical, legal, and mental health assistance; job counseling and referrals; and companionship and camaraderie.

The VA supports Homeless Veteran Stand Downs in major cities throughout the United States. If you're a homeless veteran, you don't have to register, sign up, apply, or fill out any forms to attend a Stand Down. Simply show up. If you know a homeless veteran, why don't you do him a big favor and take him to the next Stand Down hosted in your community?

To see a list of scheduled Stand Downs in your area, visit www1.va.gov/homeless/page.cfm?pg=6 or call 202-461-7401.

If you are part of a community-based organization and would like to conduct a Stand Down in your area, the National Coalition for Homeless Veterans would love to help you get started. You can contact them at National Coalition for Homeless Veterans, 333½ Pennsylvania Ave., SE, Washington, DC 20003-1148; phone 202-546-1969; e-mail nchv2@nchv.org; Web site www.nchv.org.

Veterans industry: Group homes

The VA operates a Compensated Work Therapy (CWT) program at 162 locations throughout the nation. This program allows at-risk, disadvantaged, and homeless veterans to live in supervised group homes while working for pay.

Professional CWT staff provides state-of-the-art vocational rehabilitation services; job matching and employment support; and case management for the transitioning veteran. The VA contracts with private companies and government agencies to provide jobs for these veterans. Participants learn new job skills and successful work habits, and they regain a sense of self-worth and self-esteem.

The average length of stay in the program is 174 days, and veterans work about 33 hours per week, earning approximately $732 per month. Out of that, the veteran pays an average of $186 per month for rent at the group home.

A list of program locations is available on the VA's Web site at www1.va.gov/vetind/page.cfm?pg=4. Veterans can apply for the program through their VA regional office (see Appendix B).

Drop-in centers

Drop-in centers aren't homeless shelters in the traditional sense. They don't provide overnight accommodations. They are community-organized programs, supported by the VA, that provide a daytime sanctuary where homeless veterans can clean up, wash their clothes, and participate in a variety of therapeutic and rehabilitative activities. Some facilities offer additional services, such as meals or an address where homeless veterans can have their mail sent. The centers can also provide referral services to longer-term assistance.

To find the location of your nearest drop-in center, check with your state's homeless veteran coordinator by visiting the VA's Web site at `www1.va.gov/homeless/page.cfm?pg=21` or by calling the VA's toll-free services line at 800-827-1000.

Donations of excess government property

The VA collects excess government personal property, such as hats, coats, parkas, socks, footwear, gloves, sleeping bags, and other items, and distributes them to homeless veteran programs throughout the United States. The program's name is a mouthful: the VA Excess Property for Homeless Veterans Initiative.

An interesting aspect of this program is that the main distribution center at the Medical Center in Lyons, New Jersey, is staffed entirely by formerly homeless veterans working there under a Compensated Work Therapy Program (see the "Veterans industry: Group homes" section for more details).

Foreclosure help and prevention

Housing foreclosures made big news in 2008. Perhaps you know a friend, relative, or neighbor who has lost her home through foreclosure. It's a fact of life with a volatile job and housing market. Fortunately, for veterans, help is available.

VA financial counselors at 11 regional loan centers throughout the United States can assist veterans in avoiding foreclosure through counseling and special financing arrangements. The centers are located at

- ✔ Atlanta, Georgia: 888-768-2132
- ✔ Cleveland, Ohio: 800-729-5772
- ✔ Denver, Colorado: 888-349-7541
- ✔ Honolulu, Hawaii: 808-433-0481
- ✔ Houston, Texas: 888-232-2571

   ✓ Manchester, New Hampshire: 800-827-6311

   ✓ Phoenix, Arizona: 888-869-0194

   ✓ Roanoke, Virginia: 800-933-5499

   ✓ St. Paul, Minnesota: 800-827-0611

   ✓ St. Petersburg, Florida: 888-611-5916

   ✓ Winston/Salem, North Carolina: 888-244-6711

The counseling isn't limited to veterans who have VA home loans (see Chapter 13); veterans with other types of home loans can also receive assistance. VA counselors have helped about 74,000 veterans, active-duty members, and survivors keep their homes since 2000.

To obtain help from a VA financial counselor, call the number listed for the center near you, or you can call the VA toll-free at 877-827-3702.

The Residential Rehabilitation and Treatment Program

The VA's Residential Rehabilitation and Treatment Program provides a full range of treatment and rehabilitation services to many homeless veterans. This program is designed for homeless veterans with health problems, including mental health conditions.

The average length of stay in the program is four months. In addition to health treatment, the facilities conduct outreach and referral; vocational counseling and rehabilitation; and post-discharge community support.

VA has established 34 rehab and treatment facilities, providing 1,873 beds. More than 71,000 homeless veterans have received medical treatment through this program since 1987.

To locate a facility, contact your state's homeless veterans coordinator by visiting the VA's Web site at www1.va.gov/homeless/page.cfm?pg=21 or by calling the VA's toll-free services line at 800-827-1000.

Homeless veterans, like other veterans, may also be eligible for the VA health-care program, as explained in Chapter 4, and disability and pension programs, as detailed in Chapter 6.

Chapter 12

Veterans' Job Preference & Small Business Loans

. . . .

In This Chapter

▶ Boosting your chances of working for the man

▶ Pointing out the main points of the points system

▶ Special appointments for special veterans

▶ Taking care of business with a small business loan

▶ Planning for a great business plan

▶ Locating a lender

. . . .

*T*here is a working life after the military. Every single person I know who got out of uniform, even if he retired after 20 or more years of service, got a civilian job sooner or later. Unless you're lucky enough to win the lottery while you're in the military, you're not going to make enough money from your military service to set you up for life. (Don't laugh about the lottery thing, though; I know three people who won the lottery while in the service.)

Fortunately for veterans who don't have a rich, dying relative, two veterans benefits can help you get on with your life — your working life, that is.

The first is the *veterans' preference system,* which gives certain veterans a head start when applying for many federal government jobs. The program gives veterans bonus points in the job-hiring process, just for being a veteran. Unfortunately, it doesn't apply to all federal jobs, and there are a few catches (when isn't there a catch or two?). More on that later in this chapter.

Second is the Patriot Express Small Business Loan Initiative, which was established in June 2007. It provides loan guarantees of up to $500,000 for veterans and certain family members who want to start a small business. It also provides small business loans to those who already own a small business. Read on for more information!

Veterans' Preference: A Leg Up for Federal Jobs

Did you know that veterans hold a far higher percentage of jobs in the government than they do in private industry? It's true. This is due in large part to a conglomerate of federal laws that together form the *veterans' preference system.*

Unlike most veterans benefit programs, this benefit isn't managed by the Department of Veterans Affairs (VA). It's run by the Office of Personnel Management (OPM), which is the government organization in charge of hiring and firing for most federal jobs.

Veterans' preference doesn't mean a veteran is placed in every vacant federal job. The program doesn't guarantee a job for veterans. It simply gives veterans a slight advantage over nonveterans who apply for the same job.

Why veterans get preference

Military veterans have been given some degree of preference in appointments to federal jobs ever since the Civil War. Recognizing their sacrifice, Congress enacted laws to prevent veterans seeking federal employment from being penalized for their time in military service. Veterans' preference

✔ Recognizes the economic loss suffered by citizens who have served their country in uniform

✔ Restores veterans to a favorable competitive position for government employment

✔ Acknowledges the larger obligation owed to disabled veterans

Veterans' preference is not so much a reward for being in uniform as it is a way to help make up for the economic loss suffered by those who answered the nation's call to arms. Historically, preference has been reserved by Congress for those who have been disabled or who served in combat areas.

Qualifying: The veterans' preference point system

Not all military veterans qualify for preference. To qualify, you must meet the criteria established by law. Assuming you're eligible for veterans' preference and you meet the minimum qualification requirements of the position, 5 or 10 points are added to your score on the civil service examination.

Entitlement to veterans' preference doesn't guarantee a job. An agency has many ways to fill a vacancy other than by appointment from a list of candidates.

Military retirees at or above the rank of major or equivalent aren't entitled to preference unless they qualify for 10-point preference as disabled veterans.

5-point preference

If you're an honorably discharged veteran and you served on active duty during certain periods of time or during certain campaigns, you may qualify for 5-point veterans' preference. In this case, an honorable discharge means you must have received an honorable or general discharge (see Chapter 2 for a description of military discharge characterizations). Additionally, active duty for training (such as weekend Guard or Reserve duty) doesn't count. To qualify, you must have served during any one of the following periods:

✔ During any war (this means a war declared by Congress, the last of which was World War II).

✔ Between April 28, 1952, and July 1, 1955 (the Korean War).

✔ For more than 180 consecutive days, any part of which occurred after January 31, 1955, and before October 15, 1976 (the Vietnam War).

✔ During the Gulf War period beginning August 2, 1990, and ending January 2, 1992.

✔ For more than 180 consecutive days, any part of which occurred during the period beginning September 11, 2001, and ending on the date prescribed by presidential proclamation or by law as the last day of Operation Iraqi Freedom.

✔ In a campaign or expedition for which a campaign medal has been authorized, such as El Salvador, Lebanon, Granada, Panama, Southwest Asia, Somalia, and Haiti. (See the nearby sidebar for a complete listing.)

If you are a medal holder or Gulf War veteran who originally enlisted after September 7, 1980, or entered active duty on or after October 14, 1982, you must have completed at least 24 months of continuous active duty to qualify for 5-point preference.

10-point preference

To qualify for 10-point preference, you must have an honorable or general discharge and be one of the following:

✔ A disabled veteran with a present service-connected disability

✔ A Purple Heart medal recipient

✔ The spouse of a veteran who is unable to work because of a service-connected disability

> ✔ The unmarried widow of a veteran who died in service or from a service-connected disability

> ✔ The mother of a veteran who died in service or is permanently and totally disabled

---

U.S. military campaigns and expeditions

The United States military has participated in many combat campaigns and expeditions over the years. The campaigns and expeditions listed here qualify for 5-point veterans' preference:

✔ **Armed Forces Expeditionary Medal (AFEM):** A veteran's DD Form 214 showing the award of any Armed Forces Expeditionary Medal is acceptable proof. The DD Form 214 doesn't have to show the name of the theater or country of service for which the medal was awarded.

✔ **Army Occupation of Austria,** May 9, 1945, to July 27, 1955; Occupation of Berlin, May 9, 1945, to October 2, 1990; Occupation of Germany (exclusive of Berlin), May 9, 1945, to May 5, 1955; Occupation of Japan, September 3, 1945, to April 27, 1952

✔ **Afghanistan:** Operation Enduring Freedom, September 11, 2001, to date to be determined; Operation Iraqi Freedom, March 19, 2003, to date to be determined

✔ **Berlin,** August 14, 1961, to June 1, 1963

✔ **Bosnia:** Operation Joint Endeavor, November 20, 1995, to December 20, 1996; Operation Joint Guard, December 20, 1996, to June 20, 1998; Operation Joint Forge, June 21, 1998, to present

✔ **Cambodia,** March 29, 1973, to August 15, 1973

✔ **Cambodia Evacuation** (Operation Eagle Pull), April 11–13, 1975

✔ **Chinese Service Medal** (Extended), September 2, 1945, to April 1, 1957

✔ **Congo,** July 14, 1960, to September 1, 1962, and November 23–27, 1964

✔ **Cuba,** October 24, 1962, to June 1, 1963

✔ **Dominican Republic,** April 28, 1965, to September 21, 1966

✔ **El Salvador,** January 1, 1981, to February 1, 1992

✔ **Global War on Terrorism,** September 11, 2001, to date to be determined

✔ **Grenada** (Operation Urgent Fury), October 23, 1983, to November 21, 1983

✔ **Haiti** (Operation Uphold Democracy), September 16, 1994, to March 31, 1995

✔ **Iraq:** Operations Northern Watch and Desert Spring, January 1, 1997, to date to be determined; Operation Enduring Freedom, September 11, 2001, to date to be determined; Operation Iraqi Freedom, March 19, 2003, to date to be determined

✔ **Korea,** October 1, 1966, to June 30, 1974

✔ **Korea Defense Service Medal,** July 28, 1954, to date to be determined

✔ **Korean Service,** June 27, 1950, to July 27, 1954

✔ **Kosovo,** March 24, 1999, to date to be determined

✔ **Kosovo Campaign Medal (KCM):** Operation Allied Force, March 24, 1999, to June 10, 1999; Operation Joint Guardian, June 11, 1999, to date to be determined; Operation Allied Harbor, April 4, 1999, to September 1, 1999; Operation Sustain Hope/Shining Hope,

April 4, 1999, to July 10, 1999; Operation Noble Anvil, March 24, 1999, to July 20, 1999; Task Force Hawk, April 5, 1999, to June 24, 1999; Task Force Saber, March 31, 1999, to July 8, 1999; Task Force Falcon, June 11, 1999, to date to be determined; Task Force Hunter, April 1, 1999, to November 1, 1999

- Laos, April 19, 1961, to October 7, 1962
- Lebanon, July 1, 1958, to November 1, 1958, and June 1, 1983, to December 1, 1987
- Mayaguez Operation, May 15, 1975
- Navy Occupation of Austria, May 8, 1945, to October 25, 1954; Occupation of Trieste, May 8, 1945, to October 25, 1954
- Operations in the Libyan Area (Operation Eldorado Canyon), April 12–17, 1986
- Panama (Operation Just Cause), December 20, 1989, to January 31, 1990
- Persian Gulf Operation: Operation Earnest Will, July 24, 1987, to August 1, 1990; Operation Southern Watch, December 1, 1995, to present; Operation Vigilant Sentinel, December 1, 1995, to February 1, 1997; Operation Desert Thunder, November 11, 1998, to December 22, 1998; Operation Desert Fox, December 16–22, 1998

- Persian Gulf Intercept Operation, December 1, 1995, to date to be determined
- Quemoy and Matsu Islands, August 23, 1958, to June 1, 1963
- Rwanda (Operation Distant Runner), April 7–18, 1994
- Somalia: Operations Restore Hope and United Shield, December 5, 1992, to March 31, 1995
- Southwest Asia Service Medal (SWASM): Operations Desert Shield and Desert Storm, August 2, 1990, to November 30, 1995
- Taiwan Straits, August 23, 1958, to January 1, 1959
- Thailand, May 16, 1962, to August 10, 1962
- Units of the Sixth Fleet (Navy), May 9, 1945, to October 25, 1955
- Vietnam (including Thailand), July 1, 1958, to July 3, 1965
- Vietnam Evacuation (Operation Frequent Wind), April 29–30, 1975
- Vietnam Service Medal (VSM), July 4, 1965, to March 28, 1973

How candidates are chosen

When the government wants to hire a new employee, several factors are considered. For scientific and professional positions in grade GS-9 or higher (see the "How the VRA works" section for more on job grades), names of all candidates are listed in order of their total ratings (civil service examination, qualifications, work experience, and so on). For all other positions, the names of 10-point preference candidates who have a service-connected disability of 10 percent or more are placed ahead of the names of all other applicants. Other candidates are then listed in order of their total earned ratings. A preference-eligible candidate is listed ahead of a nonpreference-eligible candidate with the same score.

The federal agency doing the hiring must select from the top three candidates. This is known as the Rule of 3 (creative, eh?). The agency may not pass over a preference eligible in favor of a lower-ranking nonpreference eligible without sound reasons that relate directly to the veteran's fitness for employment. The agency may, however, select a lower-ranking preference eligible over a disabled veteran within the Rule of 3.

If you're preference eligible and are passed over for a federal position, you can request a copy of the agency's reasons for the pass-over and the examining office's response.

If the preference-eligible veteran is 30 percent or more disabled, the agency must notify the veteran and the Office of Personnel Management (OPM) of the proposed pass-over. The veteran has 15 days from the date of notification to respond to the OPM. The OPM then decides whether to approve the pass-over based on all the facts available and notifies the agency and the veteran.

Finding and filling federal jobs

One way to find a federal job is to directly contact the agency where you want to work and inquire about opportunities. For example, if your dream is to work in rain, snow, sleet, or gloom of night, you should contact the United States Postal Agency's personnel office. If you qualify for one of the special appointing authorities (such as the VRA; see the section "Veterans Recruitment Appointment" later in this chapter), be sure to let the agency personnel office know.

Federal law also requires OPM to list all competitive vacancies with state employment offices. So if you're looking for federal employment in your particular state, this would be the place to start.

The federal government's Employment Information System is a wonderful employment resource. Available at www.usajobs.gov, this online site gives you access to federal job vacancies, employment information fact sheets, and job applications and forms. It also has online resume development and electronic transmission capabilities, so you can apply for many federal jobs online.

Two categories of federal jobs

Virtually all federal jobs can be divided into one of two categories: competitive civil service and excepted service. Veterans can be given preference for both types of jobs:

✔ **Competitive civil service:** This type of job is exactly what it sounds like. Individuals compete with other individuals for a specific job vacancy, and the one with the best overall qualifications is supposed to get the job. Points are granted for various factors, including experience, qualifications, and score achieved on the civil service examination.

When considering whom to hire, government agencies are bound by complicated federal laws. Some jobs must be filled by candidates who are already in the civil service (merit promotion); some jobs can be filled by applicants outside the civil service (competitive); and some jobs must be filled under one of the special appointing authorities (special appointments; see the "Veterans Recruitment Appointment" section for more on special appointments that apply to veterans).

- **Merit promotion appointment:** This type of appointment happens when a particular government agency plans to fill a vacancy by promoting from within. Sometimes the agency promotes from within the agency, and at other times it opens the appointment to employees of other federal agencies. When an agency decides on the latter, veterans can apply for the vacancy, even if they aren't currently civil service employees. However, when competing for merit promotion vacancies, veterans don't receive veterans' preference points. They compete on a merit-to-merit basis with the other candidates. The advantage to veterans, under this type of appointment, is that veterans who aren't current civil service employees can apply, while nonveterans/noncivil service employees are ineligible.

- **Competitive appointment:** A competitive appointment is one in which the veteran competes with others from a list of eligible candidates. This is the normal entry route into the civil service for most employees. Before a job is filled by competitive appointment, OPM must announce the job opening to the public. Veterans' preference applies in this situation, and those veterans who qualify for veterans' preference have 5 or 10 extra points added to their passing score on a civil service examination. Therefore, the veteran has a slight advantage over nonveteran applicants.

✔ **Excepted service:** Excepted service jobs, as the name suggests, are excepted from most or all of the civil service laws for various reasons. Positions are excepted by law, by presidential executive order, or by federal regulations. For example, certain entire agencies, such as the Postal Service, the Federal Bureau of Investigation, and the Central Intelligence Agency, are excepted by law. In other cases, certain jobs or classes of jobs in an agency are excepted by federal regulations. These include attorneys, chaplains, student trainees, and others. Veterans may or may not receive veterans' preference, depending on the specific hiring practices of the agency or program.

Applying for the job

You can apply for most jobs with a resume or the Optional Application for Federal Employment (OF-612), which can be downloaded at `www.opm.gov/ FORMS/pdf_fill/of612.pdf`.

If you decide to apply using a resume, make sure you include the following information, as a minimum:

- ✔ **Job information:** Announcement number, title, and grade.

- ✔ **Personal information:** Full name, mailing address (with zip code), day and evening phone numbers (with area code), Social Security number, country of citizenship, veterans' preference, reinstatement eligibility, highest federal civilian grade held.

- ✔ **Education:** High school name, city, and state; college or university name, city, and state; majors and type and year of any degrees received (if you didn't earn a degree, show the total credits earned and indicate whether they were semester or quarter hours).

- ✔ **Work experience:** Job title, duties and accomplishments, employer's name and address, supervisor's name and phone number, starting and ending dates (month and year), hours per week, salary, and whether your current supervisor may be contacted. Prepare a separate entry for each job.

- ✔ **Other qualifications:** Job-related training courses (title and year), skills, certificates and licenses, honors, awards, and special accomplishments.

Veterans Recruitment Appointment

Congress has written a slew of laws that, in some cases, allow a government agency to noncompetitively hire under a *special appointment authority*. In other words, the agency directors can pretty much hire anyone they want to, as long as the candidate falls within the scope of that particular special appointment authority.

One such authority is known as the Veterans Recruitment Appointment (VRA) authority. Veterans who are disabled or who served in certain campaigns may be hired if an agency elects to select a candidate under this authority. Veterans who are eligible under this special authority have a significant advantage over others who want to work for the government — the veterans don't have to compete against anyone for the job (this is called a *noncompetitive appointment*).

An agency that wants to hire through the VRA can simply appoint the eligible veteran to any position for which the veteran is qualified. There is no red tape or special appointment procedure.

How the VRA works

The Veterans Recruitment Appointment allows a federal agency to appoint an eligible veteran without competition. This appointment can only be made to a position that would otherwise be a competitive appointment (see the "Two categories of federal jobs" section for more on this type of appointment). If you're hired for a federal job under this authority, you convert to a career appointment in the competitive service after two years of satisfactory performance as a government employee.

When two or more VRA applicants are preference eligible, the agency must apply veterans' preference points before deciding whom to hire. (Just because you may qualify for VRA, doesn't necessarily mean you qualify for veterans' preference points; see the next section for details on qualifying for VRA.)

VRA candidates may be appointed to any position up to GS-11 or equivalent. Of course, you must be able to meet the qualification requirements for the position. The good news is that for GS-3 positions or equivalent, any military service experience is considered qualifying.

Once onboard, VRA appointees are treated like any other competitive service employee and may be promoted, reassigned, or transferred. VRA appointees with less than 15 years of education must complete a training program established by the agency.

Just as the military has ranks, civil service also has a rank system (sort of). Blue-collar workers fall under a pay scale called *wage grade,* or *WG.* Federal employees considered to be white-collar workers — such as professional, technical, administrative, and clerical positions — are under the *general schedule (GS).* There are 15 grades of GS, ranging from GS-1 to GS-15. Higher numbers mean higher rank (and more pay).

VRA eligibility criteria

Up until recently, only veterans who had a 30 percent or greater service-connected disability could qualify for a VRA appointment. This changed in 2007 when Congress passed the Jobs for Veterans Act. Under this law, you now qualify if you

- ✔ Are a disabled veteran
- ✔ Served on active duty in the armed forces during a war, or in a campaign or expedition for which a campaign badge has been authorized

> ✔ Participated on active duty in a U.S. military operation for which an Armed Forces Service Medal was awarded
>
> ✔ Have been separated from active duty for less than 180 days

If you claim eligibility on the basis of service in a campaign or expedition for which a medal was awarded, you must be able to prove that you earned the campaign badge or medal.

Your DD Form 214, Certificate of Release or Discharge from Active Duty, lists your earned medals in Block 13. See Chapter 2 for more information.

In addition to meeting the listed criteria, you must have been separated under honorable conditions (that is, received either an honorable or general discharge).

To maximize your opportunities, if you're eligible for both preference and noncompetitive appointments you should, where possible, make sure you are being considered both competitively through a civil service examination and noncompetitively under special authority such as the VRA.

Patriot Express Veterans Small Business Loans

Maybe you don't want a cushy government job. Perhaps, after years of listening to superiors giving you orders, you don't want any job in which you're not the boss. Maybe your post-military dream is to own your own business. In most cases, however, starting a small business requires money, sometimes lots of money. Where can you get the bucks to start your dream business?

The answer may be the Patriot Express Veterans Small Business Loan program. This program provides loans for veterans who want to start a small business or expand a small business they already own. Patriot Express isn't managed by the VA; it's administered by the U.S. Small Business Administration (SBA).

Patriot Express is a pilot program that officially started in June 2007, but it didn't really get off the ground and start making loans until February 2008. Because it's a pilot program, nobody knows how long it will last, but it will continue at least until December 31, 2010. At that time, the SBA will evaluate the program and determine whether it should be retained, modified, or eliminated. If you're thinking of starting your own small business, you may want to get in while the getting is good.

The SBA definition of a small business

When the U.S. Congress first established SBA, the fundamental question was just what numerical definition SBA should use to define small businesses, industry by industry, to determine what businesses were eligible for SBA's programs. Over the years SBA has established and revised numerical definitions for all for-profit industries, and this numerical definition is called a *size standard*.

The most common size standards are as follows:

- ✔ 500 employees or fewer for most manufacturing and mining industries
- ✔ 100 employees or fewer for all wholesale trade industries
- ✔ $6.5 million or less for most retail and service industries
- ✔ $31 million or less for most general and heavy construction industries
- ✔ $13 million or less for all special trade contractors
- ✔ $750,000 or less for most agricultural industries

If you plan to apply for a loan through the Patriot Express program, your business must meet one of these standards.

Borrowing up to a half a million bucks!

You can borrow up to $500,000 under the Patriot Express program. The SBA will guarantee up to 85 percent of the borrowed amount for loans of $150,000 or less and up to 75 percent for loans over $150,000 up to $500,000.

The U.S. government doesn't actually lend you the money. Instead, it guarantees a large percentage of your loan to the lender. In other words, if you default, the government repays the lender the lion's share of the loan. Think of it as having your favorite Uncle Sam as your co-signer. (This is also how the VA Home Loan program is set up. You can read more about that in Chapter 13.)

You don't need to provide collateral for many loans, but for loans above $350,000, lenders are required to take all available collateral.

Interest rates can vary, depending on certain factors, but the SBA guarantees it will use its lowest small business loan rates under the Patriot Express program. These rates are generally 2.25 to 4.75 percent over prime, depending on the loan's size and time to maturity. Interest rates are usually on the high end for larger loans and loans with a longer repayment period.

Checking your eligibility

Most veterans, and even some spouses of veterans, are eligible for the Patriot Express program. Eligibility includes

- ✔ Veterans (except those with a dishonorable discharge). See Chapter 2 for information about discharge characterizations.
- ✔ Service-disabled veterans. You can find out more about service-connected disabilities in Chapter 6.
- ✔ Active-duty members eligible for the military's Transition Assistance Program. This includes military retirees within 24 months of separation and other active-duty members within 12 months of separation.
- ✔ Reservists and National Guard members.
- ✔ Current spouses of any of these folks.
- ✔ The widowed spouse of a service member or veteran who died during service or of a service-connected disability.

Making your business plan

You can't just walk into a lender and get a small business loan, even under the guarantees of programs such as Patriot Express. The lender wants to know that your business is likely to succeed and that you'll be able to repay the loan. In other words, they want to see a solid business plan.

A *business plan* precisely defines your business, identifies your goals, and serves as your firm's resume. Its basic components include a current and pro forma balance sheet, an income statement, and a cash flow analysis. A business plan helps you allocate resources properly, handle unforeseen complications, and make the right decisions. Because it provides specific and organized information about your company and how you will repay borrowed money, a good business plan is a crucial part of any loan package. Additionally, it tells your sales personnel, suppliers, and others about your operations and goals.

Writing a solid business plan isn't an easy task and is beyond the scope of this book. The SBA has an excellent tutorial on writing the perfect business plan for your small business. You can access the tutorial online at www.sba. gov/smallbusinessplanner/plan/index.html. (You can also check out *Business Plans For Dummies* or *Business Plan Kits For Dummies,* both published by Wiley.)

Finding a lender

Patriot Express is a new program, and as such, at press time only a handful of lending institutions were on the approved lending list. The approved lenders under this program (as of October 12, 2008) are as follows:

CedarStone Bank
Lebanon, Tennessee
Phone 615-443-1411
Web site www.cedarstonebank.com

First State Bank of Bloomington
Bloomington, Illinois
Phone 309-662-0411
Web site www.firststatebloomington.com

Indiana Bank & Trust
Columbus, Indiana
Phone 812-376-3323
Web site www.myindianabank.com

Manufacturers Bank & Trust Company
Forest City, Iowa
Phone 641-585-2825
Web site www.mbtbank.com

Whitney National Bank
Jefferson, Louisiana
Phone 800-844-4450
Web site www.whitneybank.com

Willow Financial Bank
Wayne, Pennsylvania
Phone 610-995-1700
Web site www.ffbonline.com

Wilmington Trust Company
Wilmington, Delaware
Phone 800-814-8386
Web site www.wilmingtontrust.com

Wilson & Muir Bank & Trust Company
Bardstown, Kentucky
Phone 502-348-5996
Web site www.wilsonmuirbank.com

Winona National Bank
Winona, Minnesota
Phone 800-546-4392
Web site www.winonanationalbank.com

Woodsville Guaranty Savings Bank
Woodsville, New Hampshire
Phone 800-564-2735
Web site www.theguarantybank.com

Wright Patt Credit Union Inc.
Fairborn, Ohio
Phone 800-762-0047
Web site www.wpcu.coop

Wyoming Bank & Trust
Cheyenne, Wyoming
Phone 307-632-7733
Web site www.wyomingbank.com

Wyoming National Bank
Riverton, Wyoming
Phone 888-662-5645
Web site www.wyomingnationalbank.com

Yellowstone Bank
Billings, Montana
Phone 406-248-3600
Web site www.yellowstonebank.com

York State Bank & Trust
York, Nebraska
Phone 402-362-4411
Web site www.yorkstatebank.com

Zions First National Bank
Sacramento, California
Phone 866-761-8349
Web site www.zionsbank.com

The preceding list was current when this book went to press. For updates, see the SBA's Web site at www.sba.gov/patriotexpress/sba_patriotexp_lenderlist.html.

Part IV

Home Is Where the Heart Is — Except When You're Traveling!

The 5th Wave   By Rich Tennant

"Let's see if we can determine your capacity for assuming risk. Now, how familiar are you with snake handling?"

In this part . . .

Are high prices, expensive airline flights, and outrageous hotel rates holding you back from your dream of owning a home, traveling, or just owning nice things? If you fall into that special category of military veteran or family member, privileged to possess the enchanted military identification card, you've got a distinct advantage over many other people.

In this part, I take you on a trip through the home loan program, military shopping, and the wonderful world of military veterans travel benefits. Here you can discover how to travel for free on military aircraft to almost any country in the world. You also find out how to stay cheap at military motels, rest and relax at luxurious military vacation resorts, or even rent a condominium at more than 3,500 locations for the unbelievably low price of $329 per week. So what are you waiting for? Take a ride with me on the veterans travel train!

Chapter 13

Financing Your Dream House: VA Home Loan Guarantees

*P*art of the American Dream includes buying your own home. Owning your own home can give you a sense of security and stability, and it makes a whole lot more sense than putting money into a landlord's pocket each month.

The Department of Veterans Affairs (VA) has made this dream come true for countless veterans over the years. Since 1944, when the program was first established by law, the VA Home Loan Program has guaranteed more than 18 million loans to veterans to purchase or construct a home or to refinance another home loan on more favorable terms.

Under the foundation law — Public Law 78-346 — the maximum amount of guaranty was limited to 50 percent of the loan, not to exceed $2,000. That wouldn't pay for a bathroom in a mobile home today!

Fortunately, the program has kept up with the times. Today, eligible veterans can finance as much as $417,000 ($729,000 in some high-cost areas) without a down payment.

Despite the benefits of the VA Home Loan Program, many people who qualify don't use it. If you plan to purchase a home in the future, you can't afford not to educate yourself about this valuable veteran benefit. This chapter contains the basics of what you need to know.

It's Not a Loan, but Guaranteed Financing

Despite its name, VA Home Loan Program, the VA doesn't actually lend you the money to buy a house. You don't get a dime from Uncle Sam. Instead, the VA guarantees a portion of the loan amount to the lender, making you a much more favorable candidate for a loan in the lender's eyes.

Because the lender is protected against financial loss in the event that you stop making mortgage payments and the lender is forced to foreclose on your house, credit and income standards are generally not as strict as they can be with other home loan programs. Additionally, having a portion of the loan guaranteed gives you much more flexibility in negotiating the best possible interest rate. (See the "Knowing How Much Uncle Sam Will Guarantee" section for details about amounts.)

You may use VA-guaranteed financing

- ✔ To buy a home
- ✔ To buy a townhouse or condominium unit in a project that has been approved by the VA
- ✔ To build a home
- ✔ To repair, alter, or improve a home
- ✔ To simultaneously purchase and improve a home
- ✔ To refinance an existing mortgage under more favorable terms
- ✔ To improve a home through installment of a solar heating and/or cooling system or other energy-efficient improvements
- ✔ To buy a manufactured (mobile) home and/or lot
- ✔ To buy and improve a lot on which to place a manufactured home that you already own and occupy
- ✔ To refinance a manufactured home loan in order to acquire a lot

You can also use the VA Home Loan Program to buy or construct a residential property containing more than one family unit. But there are restrictions. The total number of separate units can't be more than four if one veteran is buying. If more than one veteran is buying, then one additional family unit may be added to the basic four for each veteran participating; thus, one veteran could buy four units; two veterans, six units; three veterans, seven units; and so on.

In addition, if the veteran must depend on rental income from the property to qualify for the loan, the veteran must

> ✔ Show that she has the background or qualifications to be successful as a landlord. For example, the VA would want to know if the veteran has been a successful landlord in the past or has experience working with a rental agency.
>
> ✔ Have enough cash reserves to make the loan payments for at least six months without help from the rental income.

Knowing How Much Uncle Sam Will Guarantee

If you meet the eligibility requirements for a VA Home Loan (see the "Military Service Requirements for a VA Home Loan" section), your basic entitlement is $36,000. That means the VA will guarantee up to $36,000 of your home loan for loans of $417,000 or less. That's the same as making a $36,000 down payment from the lender's point of view. If you need less than $36,000, then the VA will only guarantee the amount you borrow.

If you need to borrow more than $417,000, the VA guarantees 25 percent of what a company called Freddie Mac (which, as of September 2008, had been taken over by the federal government) says is the *conforming loan limit* for the county in which your new home is located.

The conforming loan limit is the amount that Freddie Mac (now the federal government) advises banks to limit mortgage loans to for homes located in specific parts of the country. In 2008, the limit was $417,000 in the continental United States and $625,000 in Hawaii, Alaska, Guam, and the U.S. Virgin Islands. Now that the Feds are running things, the Federal Housing Administration (FHA) is picking up the ball and will publish new rates on January 1 of each year. Beginning January 1, 2010, rates should be available on the FHA's Web site at `portal.hud.gov`.

So if the FHA says the maximum conforming loan limit for the area where your new dream house is located is $550,000, the VA would guarantee 25 percent, or $137,500, of that amount.

Under current law, the maximum amount that the VA can guarantee is 25 percent of $729,000, no matter what.

Of course, other types of mortgages are available. To find out more about them and for help determining which one is right for your situation, pick up a copy of *Mortgages For Dummies,* 2nd Edition, by Eric Tyson and Ray Brown (Wiley).

Military Service Requirements for a VA Home Loan

The U.S. government believes it's so important for its current and former service members (and their spouses in certain situations) to own their own homes that it's almost impossible to be ineligible for the home loan program. To confirm your eligibility, check out the following categories of service.

Regardless of category (unless you're still in the military), you must have a discharge that the VA does not consider "dishonorable." Chapter 2 explains how the VA makes such determinations.

The categories for eligibility include:

✓ **Wartime service:** Veterans who served at least 90 days on active duty during the periods listed here are eligible. For these periods, the active-duty time is not required to be continuous.

- **World War II:** September 16, 1940, to July 25, 1947

- **Korean War:** June 27, 1950, to January 31, 1955

- **Vietnam War:** August 5, 1964, to May 7, 1975

✓ **Peacetime service:** To qualify for the VA Home Loan Program for peacetime service, you must have served at least 181 days of *continuous* active duty during the following periods. Active duty for training doesn't count.

- July 26, 1947, to June 26, 1950

- February 1, 1955, to August 4, 1964

- May 8, 1975, to September 7, 1980 (enlisted)

- May 8, 1975, to October 16, 1981 (officer)

✓ **September 7, 1980 (enlisted) or October 16, 1981 (officer):** If you are a veteran who joined the military for the first time after these dates, you must meet certain minimum active-duty requirements to qualify. You qualify if at least one of the following points applies to your time of service:

- Completed 24 months of continuous active duty

- Served the full period (at least 181 days) for which you were ordered or called to active duty from the reserves or National Guard

- Completed at least 181 days of active duty and were discharged for a hardship or a voluntary early-separation program

- Were discharged with less than 181 days of service due to an involuntary reduction in force, certain medical conditions, or in some instances, for the convenience of the government

✔ **Gulf War service:** If you served on active duty during the Gulf War (October 2, 1990, to a date yet to be determined), you're eligible if you meet any of the following conditions:

- Completed 24 months of continuous active duty

- Served the full period (at least 90 days) for which you were ordered or called to active duty from the Reserves or National Guard

- Completed at least 90 days of active duty and were discharged for a hardship or a voluntary early-separation program

- Were discharged with less than 90 days of service due to an involuntary reduction in force, certain medical conditions, or in some instances, for the convenience of the government

✔ **Reserves and National Guard:** If you have completed a total of six years in the Selected Reserves or National Guard (that means you were a member of an active unit and attended required weekend drills and the annual two-week training), you're eligible if you

- Received an honorable discharge

- Were placed on the retired list

- Were transferred to the Standby Reserve or an element of the Ready Reserve other than the Selected Reserve after service characterized as honorable service

- Continue to serve in the Selected Reserves

If you qualify based solely on your Reserve or National Guard service as shown here and you're no longer in the Guard/Reserves, you must have an honorable discharge. See Chapter 2 for information about discharge characterizations.

If you were discharged in any of these first five categories due to a service-connected disability before you completed the required time, you're still eligible for the VA Home Loan Program. Chapter 6 provides more information about service-connected disabilities.

✔ **Active-duty members:** If you're still in the military, you can benefit from the VA Home Loan Program before discharge. To qualify, you must have served at least 90 days. This will change to at least 181 days after the president establishes an end period for Gulf War service.

✔ **Spouses:** Spouses of certain veterans, including veterans of the Reserves and National Guard, are also eligible to receive a VA Home Loan guarantee. You're eligible if you are

- An unmarried spouse of a veteran who died while in service or from a service-connected disability

- A spouse of a serviceperson missing in action or a prisoner of war

The law concerning surviving widows changed in 2003. A surviving spouse who remarries upon or after turning 57 and on or after December 16, 2003, retains her eligibility for the VA Home Loan Program. However, a surviving spouse who remarried before December 16, 2003, and upon or after reaching age 57, is not eligible.

Using the VA Home Loan Program, Step by Step

It's actually easier to finance a home under the VA Home Loan Program than it is under many commercial loan programs. Imagine that! A government-managed program that's relatively easy! What will they think of next? (If you want more details about the home-buying process in general, check out *Home Buying For Dummies* by Eric Tyson and Ray Brown [Wiley].)

Here's how it works:

1. **Obtain counseling.**

   This isn't required under the VA Home Loan Program, but it's certainly a good idea — especially for the first-time home buyer. Prepurchase counseling gives you information on

   - The process of buying a home
   - The key players in the home-buying process
   - Debt management

   Housing counseling is usually free. The Department of Housing and Urban Development (HUD) maintains a toll-free number and Web site for this purpose. To locate a nearby housing counseling office, call 800-569-4287, or visit HUD's Web site at www.hud.gov/offices/hsg/sfh/hcc/hccprof14.cfm.

2. **Find a home.**

   Some people love the hunt for a new home; others hate it. But regardless of which camp you fall into, you can't proceed until you find that potential home, sweet home. After you've found the place, discuss the purchase with the seller or selling agent. It's perfectly okay to sign a purchase contract at this point, as long as it's conditioned on approval of your VA home loan.

3. **Select a lender.**

   Finding a lender who participates in the VA Home Loan Program isn't difficult because virtually all of them do. It's a good idea to shop around to find the best possible terms. Remember, all lenders are not created equal.

4. Obtain a Certificate of Eligibility.

To obtain a VA home loan, the VA must first certify that you're eligible for the program. This is done by issuing a *Certificate of Eligibility*.

Maybe you think I should have listed this step first, but there's a method to my madness. Many lenders can obtain this certificate for you, easily and almost instantly, through the Automated Certificate of Eligibility (ACE) system. This Internet-based application can establish eligibility and issue an online Certificate of Eligibility in a matter of seconds. Not all cases can be processed through ACE — only those for which the VA has sufficient data about the applicant in its records. However, I strongly encourage you to ask your lender about this method because it can save weeks of time.

If your lender doesn't have access to ACE, you can apply for a Certificate of Eligibility by submitting a completed VA Form 26-1880. You can obtain this form from any VA regional center (see Appendix B) or print it from the VA's Web site at `www.vba.va.gov/pubs/forms/vba-26-1880-ARE.pdf`.

You should also include proof of your military service (see Chapter 2) along with your request. In some cases it may be possible for the VA to establish eligibility without your proof of service. However, to avoid any possible delays, it's best to provide such evidence. Mail the completed application to VA Loan Eligibility Center, P.O. Box 20729, Winston-Salem, NC 27120. For overnight delivery, VA Loan Eligibility Center, 251 N. Main St., Winston-Salem, NC 27155.

5. Get a VA appraisal.

The lender will ask the VA to assign a licensed appraiser to determine the reasonable value for the property. The appraiser will issue a Certificate of Reasonable Value.

Although the VA appraiser must view the property from both the exterior and the interior to determine its overall condition, the appraisal process isn't an inspection of the property. You should hire your own licensed inspector to satisfy yourself that the home you intend to purchase is in a condition that is acceptable to you. The VA guarantees only the loan, *not* the condition of the property. It's your responsibility to be an informed buyer and assure yourself that what you are buying is satisfactory to you in all respects.

You may be required to pay for the appraisal unless the seller agrees to pay. However, many lenders allow you to include this fee as part of the loan.

6. Play the waiting game.

The lender will let you know the decision on the loan. You should be approved if the home's established value and your credit and income are acceptable.

Sometimes it may take longer than you expect for the lender or VA to process your loan application. For instance, your current or former employer may be slow in returning an employment verification form, or it may take some time to obtain a credit rating from out-of-state creditors. Ordinarily, you should plan on four to six weeks to obtain a decision on your application.

Do not make any commitments based on an expected approval of your loan. You should not, for example, give notice to your landlord until the loan is approved by the lender and the VA. If you jump the gun, you may find yourself without a place to live.

7. **Attend the loan closing.**

You (and your spouse) need to attend the loan closing. The lender or closing attorney will explain the loan terms and requirements, as well as where and how to make the monthly payments. During this meeting, you sign the note, mortgage, and other related papers.

8. **Move in!**

You can now move into your new property. The loan is sent to the VA for guaranty. The VA annotates your Certificate of Eligibility to reflect the use of entitlement (the $36,000 or whatever amount was approved; see the "Knowing How Much Uncle Sam Will Guarantee" section for details) and returns it to you. Congratulations! You're now a homeowner.

Before You Sign up: VA Home Loan Restrictions

The VA Home Loan Program sounds pretty nifty, doesn't it? Unfortunately, it's not all a bed of roses. You should be aware of several factors when deciding whether a VA home loan is the best option for you.

✔ **Defaulting is a no-no.** Just because the VA guarantees a portion of your loan doesn't mean that guarantee is a gift to you. It must be repaid, just as you must repay any money you borrow. The VA guaranty, which protects the lender against loss, encourages the lender to make a loan with terms favorable to the veteran. If you fail to make the payments you agreed to make, you may lose your home through foreclosure, and you and your family would probably lose all the time and money you had invested in the house. If the lender does take a loss, VA must pay the guaranty to the lender, and you then owe that amount to the federal government.

Trust me, owing the government money is not a situation you want to be in. It can result in liens against property and bank accounts, garnishment of wages, and forfeiture of any future income tax refunds.

If your loan closed on or after January 1, 1990, you will only owe the government if the default involved fraud, misrepresentation, or bad faith on your part. The VA makes the determination on a case-by-case basis. For example, if you're still in the military and you knew you had change of assignment orders that would preclude you from meeting the initial occupancy requirements, the VA considers that "bad faith." Of course, if you disagree with the VA's decision, you can appeal it using the procedures explained in Chapter 3.

If you default on a VA home loan, you can't get another one until you repay the VA for its losses. This is true even if the VA determines you aren't required to repay the government.

✔ **You can't use the benefit again until your loan is paid in full.** You can reestablish your eligibility to use the VA Home Loan Program as long as the property you previously financed under the program has been sold and the loan has been paid in full. Alternatively, if you sell the home to another qualified veteran, and that veteran agrees to assume the remaining loan balance using her VA home loan eligibility, you can use the benefit again.

If you have repaid the prior VA loan in full and you still own the property, you can get another loan guaranteed by the VA. You can use this special provision only once in a lifetime.

Any loss suffered by the VA (for example, a claim paid to a lender if a loan goes to foreclosure) must be repaid in full before the entitlement used on the loan can be restored.

✔ **You have to pay a funding fee.** A principle disadvantage of the VA Home Loan Program is that the law requires you to pay a *funding fee.* The fee you pay goes toward the cost of this benefit, reducing the cost to taxpayers.

Often a lender will roll this fee into the amount of the loan. The amount of the fee depends on your status and the amount of down payment for the loan. Take a look at the following table to see what the funding fee will run you.

Status	*Down Payment*	*Funding Fee*
Active duty	0	2.15%
Active duty	5% to 10%	1.50%
Active duty	10% or more	1.25%
Guard/Reserves	0	2.4%
Guard/Reserves	5% to 10%	1.75%
Guard/Reserves	10% or more	1.50%

✔ **You have to buy American.** The VA home loan can't be used to purchase homes or properties outside of the United States and its territories (Puerto Rico, Guam, Virgin Islands, American Samoa, and Northern Mariana Islands).

✔ **You must live on the property, at least for a while.** The purpose of the VA Home Loan Program isn't to provide veterans with an avenue for purchasing investment property. One of the program's rules is that you or your spouse must occupy the property within a reasonable time after closing. *Reasonable time* is defined as within 60 days after closing. In unusual cases, this time period can be extended with VA approval; however, anything beyond 12 months will not be considered reasonable.

This doesn't mean you have to live on the property for the duration of the loan, but you must be the first ones to live there. The law doesn't prevent you from moving out and renting the property after the initial period of occupancy. The law doesn't define how long you have to live there, but keep in mind that if you move out too quickly, the VA may consider this bad faith on your part if it determines that the certification you signed stating your intent to occupy the home was a sham.

Chapter 14

There's No Place Like
(A Military Retirement) Home

The U.S. government operates two retirement homes for certain military veterans. The Gulfport campus, located in Gulfport, Mississippi, was originally established as the Naval Asylum in 1834, until the name was changed to the Naval Home in 1880. Primarily, its residents were veteran enlisted sailors and marines. The Soldiers' Home in Washington, D.C., was established in 1851 as an "asylum for old and disabled veterans." In 1947, when the Air Force became a separate service, the name was changed to the Soldiers' and Airmen's Home. Most who lived there were veteran enlisted Army soldiers and enlisted Air Force members.

Today these two retirement facilities are known as the Armed Forces Retirement Home – Gulfport and the Armed Forces Retirement Home – Washington. In this chapter, I describe the Washington, D.C., facility and let you know what you can expect from it — and how to apply!

I wish I could give you a tour of the Gulfport facility as well, but at press time, this new facility was still under construction after being damaged by Hurricane Katrina in 2005, and nobody yet knows what it will offer. The Gulfport home is scheduled to reopen in late 2010 or early 2011. You can track the progress of the home's reconstruction on the Armed Forces Retirement Home – Gulfport Web site at www.afrh.gov/afrh/gulf/gulf campus.htm.

What's a retired officer to do?

Those who have spent more than 50 percent of their military careers as an officer aren't eligible to reside at the Armed Forces Retirement Home.

In fact, there are no federally operated military retirement homes for veteran military officers. However, a few nonprofit agencies offer retirement communities specifically for former officers:

✔ **Air Force Village West:** This community is located adjacent to March Field in Riverside, California. This nonprofit community accepts career, reserve, or honorably discharged officers, as well as widows or widowers of officers from any service branch. For complete information, visit `www.afvw.com`.

✔ **The Air Force Villages:** This nonprofit retirement community, located in San Antonio, Texas, accepts retired and honorably separated officers of *all* uniformed services and their spouses, widows, widowers, and senior family members, age 62 and up. You can visit its Web site at `www.airforcevillages.com`.

✔ **Falcons Landing:** This nonprofit community accepts retired military officers, their spouses, and surviving spouses who haven't remarried. The retirement home is located in Washington, D.C. More information is available at `www.falconslanding.org`.

✔ **Knollwood:** Also located in Washington, D.C., this unique retirement community is for male and female officers and their female relatives. Regular and reserve male and female military officers of all uniformed services, their spouses, sisters, daughters, mothers, and mothers-in-law are eligible for residency. Visit the Knollwood Web site at `www.armydistaff.org`.

✔ **Vinson Hall:** This home is located just three miles from the nation's capital in McLean, Virginia. Eligibility includes those who have served as a commissioned officer (including warrant officer) in the uniformed services, and the widows, widowers, former spouses, dependents, or immediate family members of such officers. For details, visit `www.vinsonhall.org`.

In addition to the programs explained in this chapter, most states have one or more state-operated veterans retirement homes. These are often called "VA Homes." For more information, contact the appropriate state veterans agency listed in Appendix A.

Moving In: Do You Qualify?

Not all military veterans are eligible to reside at the AFRH. Eligibility factors include your military rank, military status, age, physical and mental health at the time of admission, and criminal history.

Here are the basics on each qualification:

- ✔ **Military rank:** The Armed Forces Retirement Homes are not for commissioned officers. Only those who spent at least 50 percent of their military service as an enlisted member, warrant officer, or what the Navy and Marines call a "limited-duty officer" are eligible. I list retirement home options for commissioned officers in the nearby sidebar "What's a retired officer to do?"

- ✔ **Military status:** Your status as a veteran also plays a role in your eligibility. You can move into an AFRH if you're a

  - Veteran with 20 years or more of active-duty service and at least 60 years old

  - Veteran unable to earn a livelihood due to a service-connected disability (see Chapter 6)

  - Veteran unable to earn a livelihood due to injuries, disease, or disability, and who served in a war theater or received hostile-fire pay

  - Female veteran who served prior to 1948

- ✔ **Staying fit for admission:** At the time of admission, you need to be capable of self-care. That means

  - Full mental competency (in other words, able to make rational decisions)

  - Able to take care of your own personal needs

  - Able to attend a central dining facility for meals

  - Able to keep all medical appointments

  - An ability to speak, hear, and see (with or without aids) to perform basic functions

  - The ability to care for your own room (for example, make the bed and clean the bathroom, floors, and windows)

  - Freedom from alcoholism, drug addictions, or mental disorders

If you have a history of excessive alcohol or drug use, you'll have to prove you've been sober for at least one continuous year. The sobriety must be documented in the form of three letters from rehab professionals, Alcoholics Anonymous (AA) staff, or medical personnel (not from friends or neighbors). These letters must indicate that your treatment was successful and you are maintaining sobriety. Even so, such documentation doesn't guarantee your acceptance at the AFRH. The admission staff decides on a case-by-case basis.

If you qualify and are interested in residing at the AFRH, make your decision early. Don't wait until it's too late. If you wait until you develop a serious illness or are unable to take care of yourself, it's too late to apply to live at the AFRH.

If you require increased healthcare after you become a resident, assisted-living and long-term care are available at the campus.

You need some kind of medical insurance to live at the AFRH, be it Medicare, Tricare (military healthcare; see Chapter 5), or a commercial insurance program. For more details, see the "Factoring in medical insurance" section.

✔ **Married couples:** Married couples are welcome at the AFRH, but both must be eligible in their own right.

✔ **Criminal history:** If you've been convicted of a felony, whether by civilian or military court, at any time in your life, you're not eligible to reside at the AFRH. A *felony* is defined as any state, federal, or military offense in which the *maximum* permissible punishment exceeds one year in prison.

Two Homes, No Waiting

Members of Congress have long felt it was inefficient for the military services to operate their own retirement homes. (Remember when the Department of Defense was spending $500 on hammers and $2,000 on toilet seats?) In 1999, having nothing better to do that particular legislative year, Congress moved the responsibility for operations and maintenance of the two homes from the Department of the Navy and Department of the Army to an independent establishment in the executive branch of the federal government known as the Armed Forces Retirement Home (AFRH).

Not through fiddling with it, two years later Congress declared it wasn't right having soldiers and airmen living in Washington, D.C., and sailors and marines living on the Gulf Coast of Mississippi. Why can't we all just get along? Again, they waived their magical legislative wands and renamed the U.S. Naval Home and the U.S. Soldiers' and Airmen's Home as the Armed Forces Retirement Home – Gulfport and the Armed Forces Retirement Home – Washington, respectively. Now eligible veterans of any branch can live in either home. Of course, that was true before, but with the name changes, it's more evident.

All retirement homes are not created the same

When you think of a retirement home, maybe you envision a cross between a hospital and a jail: plain, unimpressive facilities consisting of white walls, devoid of décor and personality; long, gleaming corridors of shining, yellow tile; the entire structure smelling of stale disinfectant. Inmates — I mean, residents — are told when to sleep, when to wake up, when to eat, and what "fun," rigidly organized activities they will endure that particular day of the week.

My grandmother lived for several years in such a facility. When I would visit on one of my infrequent trips to my hometown, it was always easy to find her; she would be in her room (which she shared with two other residents), the dining room, or the organized activities room. I hated that she had to live there, but when your only income is Social Security, what are the alternatives?

One time on a business trip to our nation's capital, at my mother's insistence, I visited my Uncle Tim, a military veteran who resides at the Armed Forces Retirement Home. While I most certainly love my uncle and wanted to see him, I dreaded the visit because of the dark, gloomy mood I knew the facility would leave me in. Was I ever in for a shock! When I first entered the campus, I was stunned by the majestic buildings, rolling hills, and tranquil lakes that adorn the 272 acres of pristine grounds.

Want to know where I finally found my beloved uncle? He was on the second hole of the facility's private, nine-hole golf course. The only gloomy mood I was in for that day was when my 76-year-old uncle beat me by three strokes.

Gulfport: Whacked by a Hurricane, but on the Road to Recovery

Unfortunately, the Gulfport facility isn't there right now. But don't worry, it'll be back! On August 29, 2005, Hurricane Katrina visited her destructive fury on the Gulf Coast, decimating the 44-acre Gulfport campus. More than 150 years of history and tradition were wiped out in a single day as the massive storm roared through. Like many in that devastated part of the country, the 416 veteran residents of the Gulfport AFRH were left homeless.

Plans were implemented immediately to rescue the stranded veterans. The independent-living residents were bused to the Washington campus, while those who required assisted care were flown there from nearby Maxwell Air Force Base. Long-term care residents were relocated to Lynnwood Nursing Home in Mobile, Alabama.

For more than a year, Congress debated the future of the Gulfport home. Many lawmakers wanted to close the Gulfport campus, expand the Washington facility, and operate just one military retirement home. A few wanted to repair the existing facilities. Congress finally agreed that the best option was to completely rebuild on the existing grounds.

In October 2007, the storm-damaged facility was imploded. Army engineers really love it when they get to set off explosives. In February 2008, construction began on the $140 million, 660,000-square-foot main facility. When the project is completed in late 2010 or early 2011, the Gulfport campus will have space for 584 residents, including independent living, assisted care, and long-term care. The new grounds will feature controlled parking and complete landscaping of the entire site, including walking paths, outdoor areas, and recreation areas.

Visiting the Washington Campus

The Washington campus of the Armed Forces Retirement Home is located on 272 acres, smack-dab in the heart of our nation's capital. The campus is just minutes away from the White House, the Capitol, and many other national monuments. The main building has housed four U.S. presidents, so if you see a sign that says, "Lincoln slept here," it's really true!

I can't possibly cover everything about the Washington AFRH in these pages. To see photos of the campus and to get more details about what it offers, check out www.afrh.gov/afrh/wash/washcampus.htm.

Living the high life in retirement

I live in a fairly upscale private community. In other words, they charge me an arm and a leg to live here. I wish we had even a tenth of the amenities offered by the Armed Forces Retirement Home. The Washington campus is actually a city within a city, featuring everything you could need for daily living. Check out the following sections for the lowdown on the luxuries.

The necessities

When it comes down to what you need from a retirement home, you want a place to lay your head and have a meal. Having someone to take care of you when you're under the weather is nice, too. Here's what the AFRH offers:

- **1,021 private rooms for independent living:** Each room is air conditioned and equipped with a twin bed, desk, chair, and a reading lamp. If you want, you can even bring some of your own furniture so you won't miss that favorite recliner.

All new residents are assigned to the Scott Building, in which the average room size is about 130 square feet of living space, plus a private bathroom, shower, and walk-in closet. After you become a resident, you can put your name on the waiting list to reside in the Sheridan Building, where the rooms are 180 square feet. The rooms are wired for cable and telephone, but if you want such services, you'll have to arrange that yourself with local cable and telephone companies. The home also provides linens and towels, which are laundered by a private contractor. Don't expect maid service, though. You have to keep your own room clean, just like Mom made you do when you were a kid. This isn't a hotel, after all.

✔ **Dining facilities:** The AFRH features not one, but two full-service dining facilities, both serving three meals a day, planned by licensed nutritionists. Nutritional counseling is available.

The meals are served buffet style (all-you-can-eat — like a cruise ship). You can choose which line to go through — the regular one for home-style meals or the diet line for those who prefer low-calorie choices. If you don't like the entrée on the buffet, the short-order station is happy to take your order for hamburgers, hot dogs, grilled chicken sandwiches, grilled cheese, and fries. And if you're a diabetic, you can head to a separate meal station for specialized food for your condition.

The staff provides individual table service for those who can't serve themselves through the buffet stations. Each meal period lasts about three hours, and you can come and go as you please.

If you get a case of the munchies or want to join your friends for a tall, cold one, you can hit the lounge, which stays open late into the evening hours and serves beer and snacks.

✔ **Medical facilities:** You can receive basic medical, dental, and vision care and physical therapy on campus. Services that aren't available on campus are offered at nearby facilities. You can also get your prescriptions filled at the campus pharmacy. I cover the specifics of medical care in the "Examining Your Healthcare Options" section later in this chapter.

Exercise and outdoor activities

You can keep up your active lifestyle after you move into the Armed Forces Retirement Home. Whether you want to fish, join a fitness class, or take quiet walks by yourself, you can find an activity that suits your interests.

✔ **Golf course:** There's nothing quite like sinking the first putt on a lush, green golf course on a perfect balmy day. The AFRH features a nine-hole golf course nestled among its grounds. At 2,530 yards, the course isn't long, but it's challenging. The course plays to a par of 35; the first hole is a 460-yard par 5, and then you tee off on two challenging par 3s and six par 4s that range from 225 to 370 yards. You can even play the golf course twice from two sets of tees to make an 18-hole round.

If one day you don't feel like moving around the course, you can take a few swings at the driving range instead. Clubs and golf carts are available to residents.

✔ **Bowling alley:** How many retirement homes have their own bowling alleys? The AFRH most certainly does. It's not very large, consisting of only six lanes, but how many lanes do you need, really? The center hosts bowling leagues almost nightly and tournaments throughout the year for the community's residents.

✔ **Fitness center:** If the legendary Jack LaLanne were a resident of the AFRH, he would certainly be impressed by the modern fitness center. The spacious center includes several treadmills, stationary bikes, resistance training equipment, and much more. In addition to the many pieces of exercise equipment, you can also take advantage of fitness classes, personal trainers, and free weights.

If indoor fitness isn't your cup of sports drink, you can take your exercise regimen outside to several walking trails, including a *life trail*. (This is a walking/jogging trail with various low-impact exercise stations interspersed along the trail.)

After an energizing workout, you can take a few minutes to relax those tired muscles and clear the stress from your mind in the fitness center sauna.

✔ **Fishing ponds:** Have you heard about the big one that got away? Well, there's nowhere for the fish to run in AFRH's two fishing ponds. The ponds are generously stocked with crappie, bass, bream, and catfish, which means you won't have to wait too long between bites.

Want to prove you're the champion fisherman? Fishing rodeos are conducted frequently throughout the year. Be nice to the kitchen staff and maybe they'll even agree to cook up your catch for lunch.

Entertainment and educational resources

If you like to be entertained and educated, you won't be disappointed by the AFRH's offerings. You can catch the latest movie, borrow the newest bestseller, and hit your favorite Web sites.

✔ **Movie theater:** No need to go out and spend 50 bucks for a movie and stale gummi bears. The AFRH has its own movie theater. This 667-seat, fully equipped theater not only hosts the latest movies, but also serves as the gathering place for periodic community meetings, bingo, special events, and live entertainment.

✔ **Library:** Unlike many commercial retirement homes, this isn't just a room in the corner with a few old paperbacks. The AFRH boasts a huge, full-service library with thousands of books, and it even employs a full-time librarian to keep things organized and help you find what you need. Maybe you'll even find a copy of *Veterans Benefits For Dummies* there. Also available for checkout are all kinds of movies in both VHS and DVD format.

✔ **Computer room:** It seems as if none of us can live without our computers these days. At the AFRH, you don't have to. Residents are welcome to bring their own computers to surf the Internet from their rooms via DSL, or you can take advantage of the facility's 24-hour computer room. There's also a computer lab where you can learn to become a professional driver on the information superhighway.

Everything else

It would take this entire book to fully describe all the amenities offered to residents at the AFRH (and then I'd have to change the title of the book). The list of goodies available goes on and on:

✔ Art studio

✔ Auto hobby shop

✔ Bank

✔ Barber shop

✔ Beauty salon

✔ Bike shop

✔ Card rooms

✔ Ceramics studio

✔ Chapel

✔ Convenience store

✔ Craft cottage

✔ Garden plots

✔ Ham radio room

✔ Listening room

✔ Puzzle room

✔ Sports lounge

✔ Woodshop

Is smoking allowed?

If you smoke, you should quit. All the doctors say so, and we want to keep you around so you can read more great *For Dummies* books, like this one.

However, if you're unwilling or unable to quit, the AFRH offers smoking rooms, as well as designated smoking areas within the facility. Nonsmokers can request to be assigned to a nonsmoking room or even a nonsmoking floor.

Going out and about: Cars and transportation

Residents at the AFRH are free to come and go as they please. If you've got a hot date and don't get home until 2 a.m., no problem. Some residents have jobs in the area and spend all day off campus. Many others choose to enjoy the world-class theaters, museums, restaurants, and attractions in the metropolitan area. Some even periodically jaunt over to nearby Andrews Air Force Base and jump on a military aircraft for space-available, free flights to Europe.

If you're medically capable of driving and have a valid driver's license, you can have your own car at the AFRH. The facility has plenty of free parking for residents. If you're handy with a wrench, you can even change the oil at the auto hobby shop.

If you don't have a car or don't want to hassle with driving in the city's traffic, you can catch the Washington, D.C., Metrobus, which stops right outside of the front gate. From there it's just a short ride to the D.C. Metrorail stations at Fort Totten and Brookland. From those two stations, you can travel to almost anywhere in the D.C. area.

In addition, the AFRH provides scheduled daily transportation to nearby hospitals, including Walter Reed Army Medical Center and the Washington VA Medical Center.

Trips and special events are planned each month. Residents can sign up for daytrips to local events and attractions almost any day of the week, as well as take advantage of overnight trips. Not long ago, the staff of the AFRH Recreation Services Division hosted an eight-day cruise to the Caribbean.

Getting there

The folks at the AFRH love it when prospective residents come to visit. In fact, you, as a retired veteran considering taking up residence there, and your family are entitled to complimentary lodging in a guest room for two nights and a limited number of meals at the Washington campus. You can schedule a visit by calling 800-422-9988 and making an appointment.

Guest rooms are not available just for prospective residents. Friends and family visiting residents at the Washington campus can also reserve guest rooms. The prices range from $25 to $40 per night, depending on the type of room. Try to match that price anywhere else in Washington, D.C.! Meals are very reasonable too, at $6 per meal (all-you-can-eat), and children under 3 eat free. Call 202-730-3014 for a reservation.

The Washington campus is located in Washington, D.C., at the corner of Rock Creek Church Road, NW, and Upshur Street, NW.

From I-95 north of D.C.: Take I-95 southbound to the I-495 westbound exit. Stay on I-495 ("The Beltway") westbound. Take Exit 31 for Silver Spring. Stay on Georgia Avenue through Silver Spring and past Walter Reed Army Medical Center. Turn left on Upshur Street (between the 4200 and 4100 blocks of Georgia Avenue). Cross Rock Creek Church Road into the AFRH "Eagle Gate" at Upshur Avenue.

From I-95 south of D.C.: From I-95 northbound, exit at the I-395 exit. From I-395, stay on it when it ends at New York Avenue. Turn right on New York Avenue. Go two blocks and make a right onto M Street. Go to the second traffic light and make a left onto North Capitol Street, NW. Continue on North Capitol, past the sign to the Armed Forces Retirement Home – Washington. At Allison Street, make a left turn. Make another left turn onto Rock Creek Church Road, and make another left into the AFRH "Eagle Gate" at Upshur Avenue.

From the Annapolis (Route 50) area: Take Route 50, which becomes New York Avenue. Take the South Dakota Avenue exit. Continue on South Dakota and make a left onto Taylor Street, NE. Continue on Taylor and make a right onto North Capitol Street, NE. At the second stop light, turn left on Allison Street. Make another left turn onto Rock Creek Church Road, and make another left into the AFRH "Eagle Gate" at Upshur Avenue.

Paying for Your New Home

The cost of residing at the AFRH depends on how much money you make each month — both taxable and nontaxable income.

- ✔ **Taxable income** means all income reportable as adjusted gross income (AGI) on your U.S. income tax return.
- ✔ **Nontaxable income** includes benefits administered by the Department of Veterans Affairs, Social Security Administration, disability retired pay, pensions, annuities, and IRA distributions that aren't included in your AGI.

Actual cost is based on a percentage of your income and the level of care you require:

- ✔ **Independent-living residents:** 35 percent of total current income, but not to exceed $1,170 each month
- ✔ **Assisted-living residents:** 40 percent of total current income, but not to exceed $1,754 each month
- ✔ **Long-term care residents:** 65 percent of total current income, but not to exceed $2,924 each month

Like anything else in life, these rates are subject to change. For the latest rates, visit www.afrh.gov/afrh/newres/elig/elig_fees.htm.

When you first move in to the AFRH, you must be capable of independent care (see the earlier section "Moving In: Do You Qualify"). When and if your care needs change, your cost will increase accordingly.

Believe it or not, no taxpayer money is used in the operations of the AFRH. How do the administrators offer such an array of amenities at such a modest cost? The AFRH is one of the few veteran benefits that potential future recipients pay for while they're still in the military. Fifty cents per month is deducted from the military pay of all active-duty enlisted members. The mandatory deduction, along with funds garnered from fines and forfeitures of military disciplinary actions, are placed in the AFRH trust fund.

Examining Your Healthcare Options

The AFRH provides a continuum of care, including outpatient, dental, and medical services; hospital care; and long-term nursing care.

Staying on campus for treatment

Services for primary care and basic dental, vision, and podiatry services are available on the campus. Additionally, there are on-campus programs in urology, psychiatry, internal medicine, and COPD. There's even a pharmacy on the campus.

For those requiring special treatment for a disability, the home has trained and licensed therapists for physical therapy, occupational therapy, recreational therapy, and speech-language pathology.

The on-site, 200-bed King Health Center for primary, intermediate, and skilled healthcare is accredited by the Joint Commission on Accreditation of Healthcare Organizations (JCAHO).

Going off campus for care

Off-site care is provided by the renowned Washington Hospital Center, the Washington VA Medical Center, the George Washington Hospital, and Walter Reed Army Medical Center. Of course, the AFRH provides free transportation to these facilities, which certainly helps with your gas, taxi, or bus budget.

Factoring in medical insurance

There's no such thing as a free lunch. The same is true of medical care offered at the AFRH. It's not free. You'll need some type of medical insurance to be accepted as a resident. The exact type depends on your status:

✔ Medicare A & B are mandatory prior to admission to AFRH for those who qualify.

✔ Military retirees under 65 with no Medicare benefits are required to obtain Tricare Prime at their cost. See Chapter 5 for more information about Tricare.

✔ Military retirees under 65 with Medicare benefits must obtain Tricare Prime as secondary coverage. There's no cost for this coverage.

✔ Military retirees over 65 with no Medicare benefits are required to obtain Tricare Prime.

✔ Nonmilitary retirees with Medicare benefits are required to have a Medicare supplement, enroll in a Medicare HMO if available, or enroll in Medicaid if eligible.

✔ Nonmilitary retirees with a 100 percent service-connected disability are required to use the nearby VA or military facilities, which support the AFRH.

✔ Nonmilitary retirees under 65 with no Medicare and VA benefits and who are ineligible for Medicaid would need to purchase a major medical insurance policy.

What Are You Waiting For? Apply Now!

At the time of this publication, there was no waiting list for the Armed Forces Retirement Home in Washington, D.C. Assuming you qualify, you can apply now and be enjoying luxury retirement living in three or four weeks.

The application process involves three basic steps: gathering your documents, obtaining a physical, and completing your application.

Gathering the required documents

The Armed Forces Retirement Home is, of course, a government organization, which means it can't operate without paperwork. Here are the documents you should gather before submitting your application:

✔ DD Form 214, Record of Military Service, or Statement of Service summary. See Chapter 1 for more information.

- ✔ A copy of your federal tax return for the most recent tax year. If you're exempt from filing, you must provide verification of all income for the most recent year (W-2s, 1099s, all investments and savings).

- ✔ Documentation of the gross amount you're entitled to from all federal payments (civil service retired pay, military retired pay, Social Security, VA compensation or pension, and so on).

- ✔ Verification of current year Medicare Part B premium and supplemental insurance payment (or proof of Tricare enrollment).

- ✔ Proof of payment for other health insurance.

Obtaining a medical physical

As mentioned in the "Moving In: Do You Qualify?" section earlier in this chapter, you must be capable of self-care when you first move into the AFRH. To certify that you meet the minimum medical standards for admission, you must obtain a physical from your doctor.

You can download a copy of the medical examination form at the AFRH Web site at www.afrh.gov/afrh/forms/forms_medical.pdf, or call 800-422-9988 and ask for an application packet.

The physical must include a PPD screening test for tuberculosis. A positive result won't necessarily deny you residency, but a chest X-ray will be required.

Completing your application

You can download the six-page application for admission at www.afrh.gov/afrh/forms/forms_app.pdf, or obtain one by calling 800-422-9988. To avoid delays, make sure you provide thorough and accurate information. Mail the completed application and supporting documents to AFRH, PAO/Marketing #1305, 3700 N. Capitol St., NW, Washington, DC 20011-8400.

The online application form is interactive. You can complete the application while online, and then print and sign it to include in your application packet.

Upon receipt of your packet, the AFRH takes four to six days to process the application and make a decision. That's pretty darn fast for a government agency.

After the decision is made, the staff at the Armed Forces Retirement Home will call you and follow up in writing with an official notification. Then all you have to do is pack your bags, notify your friends and relatives of your new address, and move into your new home. Good luck!

Chapter 15

Shopping Until You Drop

In This Chapter

▶ Taking stock of the inventory at the BX and PX

▶ Eliminating your hunger pangs

▶ Fueling up your vehicle

▶ Gearing up for grocery shopping

▶ ID cards for shopping and a whole lot more

My girlfriend loves this chapter because it's all about shopping. That woman treats shopping like it's a full-time career. *Shopping For Dummies*? I think I need to give my publisher a call.

Everyone loves a good bargain. Even in times of high gas prices, I know people who will drive halfway across town because soda is on sale.

Some of the best bargains around can be found on military bases. Established primarily for active-duty members and their dependents, on-base *exchanges* and *commissaries* sell goods and services at a substantial discount over their civilian competitors.

But you don't have to be a current member of the military to share in this shopping bonanza. Certain categories of veterans and family members are also entitled to shop on military installations. In this chapter, I tell you more about this military perk and who is qualified to use it.

Getting Familiar with the Military Exchange System

I run into civilians all the time who think, as a military retiree, I can buy a suit at the Base Exchange for $20 or pick up a $2,000 stereo system for $500. Although military exchanges can save you money, they certainly don't produce the gigantic savings that many civilians think they do. However, savings can be especially substantial for large-ticket items because they're located on federal military bases, and sales are not subject to state sales tax.

The *military exchange system* is most certainly the king of *nonappropriated fund activities*. Nonappropriated fund activities are government activities that don't use taxpayer money. The exchange systems fund their operating budgets (civilian employee salaries, inventory investments, utilities, and capital investments for equipment, vehicles, and facilities) from the sale of merchandise, food, and services to customers.

There are four exchange systems:

- The Army and Air Force Exchange Service (AAFES)
- The Navy Exchange Service (NEXCOM)
- The Marine Corps Exchange (MCX)
- The Coast Guard Exchange (CGX)

Why four? Because it's always been that way. There has been some talk about combining the four systems into one exchange service, but so far that's all it's been, just talk. Even though there are four separate exchanges, qualified veterans and family members can use any of them. In other words, if you're an Air Force veteran, you can still shop in Marine Corps exchanges and vice versa.

The exchange systems operate most of the shopping activities on military installations, including the BXs, PXs, gas stations, movie theaters, food concessions, uniform sales, and liquor stores. More on those in the following sections.

Exchanges are located on military bases. Even tiny little military bases will have an exchange, although it may be the size of a 7-Eleven gas station. The general rule is the bigger the military base, the larger the exchange. A listing of major military bases located in the United States can be found at usmilitary.about.com/od/theorderlyroom/l/blstatefacts.htm.

Saving money at BX's, PX's, and other X's

A rose by any other name would still require fertilizer, and the same holds true for a military store's name. Soldiers call it a *PX*, which is short for *post exchange*. Airmen say *BX*, for *base exchange*. Sailors call it a *ship's store* when afloat and *NEX* when in port. Marines say *MCX*; to the Coast Guardsmen, it's *CGX*. I mention all of these so if you need to ask for directions, you can call the store by its military name. That way some snooty person won't correct your use of terminology.

Not a fly-by-night operation

The exchange services aren't minor-league players in the field of retail sales. The Army and Air Force Exchange System alone (AAFES; the largest of the four exchange systems) operates more than 3,000 facilities worldwide, in more than 30 countries, 5 U.S. territories, and 49 states. (Oregon doesn't have any Army or Air Force bases. It does, however, have Navy and Coast Guard bases, so veterans can still get their shopping fix.) AAFES operates some 143 retail stores and more than 2,200 fast-food restaurants, such as Taco Bell, Burger King, Popeyes, and Cinnabon.

The Navy Exchange (NEXCOM) oversees 107 Navy Exchange facilities, 344 stores worldwide, and 45 Navy Lodges, as well as Ship Stores, the Navy Uniform Program, and Navy Family Support Program.

The Marine Corps Exchange (MCX) currently operates 17 main exchanges, 96 branch and convenience stores, 17 package stores, 27 services stations, 13 military clothing stores, and services like vending machines, dry cleaning, and rentals.

The Coast Guard, our nation's smallest military branch, operates exchanges in 23 states and one U.S. territory (Puerto Rico). On average,

Coast Guard exchanges are much smaller than their sister-service counterparts. However, because Coast Guard bases are often in remote locations, their exchanges often offer merchandise at little or no profit to the exchange. Some of the best deals can be found in these exchanges.

In fiscal year 2007, AAFES revenues totaled $9.7 billion and earnings totaled $441.7 million. NEXCOM garnered $2.5 billion in sales and more than $40 million in profits. MCX sales totaled $774 million and resulted in profits exceeding $45 million.

So what do the exchanges do with all those profits? The majority of it (roughly two-thirds) is used to fund various military morale, welfare, and recreation (MWR) quality-of-life programs, such as youth services, Armed Forces Recreation Centers, swimming pools, arts and crafts, military social functions, and golf courses.

The remaining earnings are used to build new stores or renovate existing facilities. Funds to build these new or replacement facilities come entirely from the sale of merchandise and services, not taxpayer money.

Regardless of whether it's called a BX or PX, the stores are the military's version of Wal-Mart. Exchanges can be very, very large, or relatively modest, depending on the size and type of community (active duty, retired, and dependent) they are designed to support.

The military claims that customers who shop at BXs and PXs save an average of 17 to 20 percent compared with off-base stores. That is over and above the savings derived from the exclusion of sales taxes. From time to time, you can find off-base establishments selling an item on sale, cheaper than the BX/PX, but the exchanges combat this with a program called *price matching*. If an exchange customer finds an identical item in the local community selling for a price lower than the BX/PX's price, the exchange will match the price.

BXs and PXs accept MasterCard, Visa, American Express, and Discover credit cards. Exchanges also offer their own credit plan through the joint-exchange Military Star Card. Exchanges also cash personal checks at no charge with a valid military or dependent ID card. More on ID cards later in the chapter.

Name brands galore

The BXs and PXs sell famous name-brand merchandise like American West, Babies 1st, Bobby Jones, Dreamgirl, Coach, Gucci, Island Surf, Hot Topic, Magic Silk, Panasonic, Sony, Toshiba, and Wearguard at bargain prices.

A common complaint about the BX/PX I've heard over the years is that they may lean too much toward high-priced, name-brand items. Many low-ranking enlisted folks, retirees, and other veterans can't afford Dooney & Bourke handbags, no matter how good the savings. They would rather buy an off-brand purse from Wal-Mart at half the price. Over the past few years, the exchanges have addressed this criticism by offering private-label merchandise, found exclusively at military exchanges, with the same quality as national brands at significant savings.

Your mileage may vary. I took my girlfriend shopping with me at the Keesler Air Force Base exchange a couple of years ago. She was absolutely thrilled with the selections and prices in the BX. That one shopping trip set me back several hundred dollars, but I was assured by my sweetie that we scored the bargains of the century.

Carousing through the catalog

I remember as a young airman anxiously awaiting the arrival of the annual exchange mail-order catalogs. The pages of these giant volumes contained thousands of items you could purchase from the exchange, many of which were not carried on the shelves of the local BX/PX.

The exchange services still publish the annual mail-order catalogs. Authorized shoppers can browse through the color pages and order merchandise to be shipped to their homes. This is handy for veterans who don't have a computer and don't live close to a military base. Of course, you usually have to pay for shipping, but think of the gas you'll save. Like other exchange sales, there's no sales tax.

Catalogs cost five bucks but include a coupon for $10 off your first order. To order an exchange catalog, call 800-527-2345. You can also order exchange catalogs online. See the next section.

Unveiling merchandise online

I know what you're thinking. Who shops by mail order these days (see the preceding section)? Online shopping is the thing now. Don't worry. The exchanges have kept up with the times. Anything you can buy in the catalogs, you can also purchase through the exchange's online sites. Like catalog sales, you'll usually have to pay for shipping, but there's no sales tax.

The secure sites will verify your exchange privileges against the Defense Enrollment Eligibility Reporting System (DEERS) database. To begin your online shopping spree, visit:

- Army and Air Force Exchange: www.aafes.com
- Navy Exchange: www.navy-nex.com
- Marine Corps Exchange: www.usmc-mccs.org/shopping
- Coast Guard Exchange: www.cg-exchange.com

Giving the gift of shopping

The exchanges sell gift cards in their stores and through their online sites. The military exchange system offers a program called *Gifts from the Home-front,* through which individuals can buy gift cards for donation to deployed troops, who can then use the cards to shop at exchanges in their theater of operation.

You don't have to be an authorized exchange shopper to purchase a gift card for deployed service members through the Gifts from the Homefront program.

You can't have everything

One thing you won't get a great deal on in the BXs and PXs is tobacco products. The prices for these products are only marginally cheaper than retail stores off-base. This is because of an ongoing Department of Defense program to reduce smoking in the military. Under DOD regulations, the maximum discount for tobacco products is 5 percent less than the most competitive price in the local community for BXs/PXs located in the United States. For overseas exchanges, tobacco prices must fall within the range of the average U.S. prices.

Also, over the years, Congress has passed various laws that restrict what can be sold in military exchanges. This is to protect selected retail industries from what they view as "unfair competition." These restrictions apply mostly to BXs and PXs located in the United States. (Apparently Congress doesn't care much about the exchange system competing with overseas retail establishments.) Stateside exchanges can't sell cars, fur coats, or major appliances, for example. Congress has also limited the size of diamonds and types of furniture that can be sold in exchanges located in the United States. Exchanges can sell some finished furniture, although any one piece can't cost more than $900.

Feasting at eating establishments

After you wander around the BX/PX looking at all the stuff you can buy (see the preceding section), you'll probably start to get hungry. It's most certainly not hard to find something to eat on a military base, and I'm not talking about the chow halls. The exchanges operate a variety of eating establishments on military installations.

Almost every BX and PX sports a food court, just like the food courts in American malls. Here you can satisfy your hunger pangs with salads, submarine sandwiches, burgers, hot dogs, pizza, ice cream, and more. You may even find a Taco Bell here and there. In my humble opinion, a hot meatball sub from Robin Hood (a submarine sandwich shop that operates in many BX/PX food courts) can't be beat.

Outside of the food courts, you'll find familiar fast-food establishments, such as McDonald's, Popeyes, and Burger King, scattered throughout the base. These franchises operate through subcontracts with the military exchange system.

Shave and a haircut, and dental care, too!

Military bases are like small cities, so they have barber shops, beauty shops, video rental stores, one-hour photo shops, laundromats and dry cleaners, tailor shops, bookstores, florists, and other essential services for day-to-day living. On military bases, these activities are operated by subcontractors that are managed by the exchange system.

Several bases have optometry and audiology clinics operated as concessions. These clinics are run by private contractors that are overseen by local military medical officials. Navy clinics are run by private contractors with no military medical oversight.

AAFES even operates a dental clinic for family members at Fort Hood, Texas, and the Marine Corps offers the same at Camp Pendleton, California, to help relieve a shortage of dental staff there. Fees are comparable to those under the Tricare Dental Program (see Chapter 5).

Military clothing: Getting your uniform ready for the parade

The military services have regulations that allow certain veterans to wear their uniforms at certain times, such as when attending a patriotic event. But what's a veteran going to do if he discovers his valued uniform, which has been hanging in the closet for the past 15 years, doesn't fit quite the way it used to? Never fear — a clothing sales store may be near!

The exchange services operate military clothing stores on military bases where authorized shoppers can purchase military uniforms and accessories. Uniform items can also be purchased through the online exchange sites (see the "Unveiling merchandise online" section).

Clothing stores base their inventory on the primary population on that particular base. In other words, it's going to be hard to find an Air Force uniform item on a Marine Corps base. If you need to purchase a new uniform or uniform item, it's best to visit the branch base that corresponds with the item needed. If you need an Army uniform, visit an Army post; veteran sailors should visit a Navy base clothing store; and so on.

Gassing up at military gas stations

The exchange services also operate the gas stations on military bases. Many of these operations also include a car-care center where you can get your car fixed if it breaks down

Unfortunately, you won't find bargain fuel prices at military gas stations. Although the exchange services aren't subject to sales taxes on other items, the Hayden Cartwright Act does require the exchanges to pay fuel taxes. Additionally, this is another one of those "unfair competition" deals. Department of Defense regulations require the exchanges to periodically survey local off-base service stations and set their fuel prices competitively. As such, fuel sold to military personnel, veterans, and family members on military installations is often sold at nearly the same rate as the rates at nearby civilian locations.

Because surveys are generally performed only once or twice per month, it's not uncommon to find stations in surrounding communities selling fuel for several cents less per gallon than at the military gas stations.

Locating the liquor

The exchange services also operate liquor stores on military bases. These are sometimes called *package stores,* or *Class 6 stores,* a tradition carried on from before the mid-1980s, when the exchange services took over base liquor stores from appropriated fund activities.

Like tobacco products (see the earlier section "You can't have everything"), you're not going to get a substantial discount on liquor sales on military bases. This is because of the ongoing Department of Defense program to deglamorize alcohol use by military personnel. Alcohol sold at exchanges can be sold for no less than 10 percent below the best price in Alcohol Beverage Control states, and no less than 5 percent below the competitive rate at non–Alcohol Beverage Control states.

Alcoholic Beverage Control states are those that have a state monopoly over the wholesaling and/or retailing of some or all of the categories of alcoholic beverages. *Non–Alcoholic Beverage Control states* are those that leave the regulation of alcohol sales to the local community, such as counties and cities. The 18 ABC states are Alabama, Idaho, Iowa, Maine, Michigan, Mississippi, Montana, New Hampshire, North Carolina, Ohio, Oregon, Pennsylvania, Utah, Vermont, Virginia, Washington, West Virginia, and Wyoming.

Taking in a movie at the base theater

If you'd rather kick back and relax while you're on-base, you can check out the base's movie theater, which is operated by the exchange service. It wasn't that many years ago when seeing a movie on a military installation wasn't worth the time, unless you didn't have any transportation or were stationed overseas. Back then, movies weren't distributed to military bases until about the same time they were available at video rental stores.

Then the exchange services took over the operation of on-base movie theaters. The exchanges now operate their own brand-name chain of theaters, called Reel Time Theaters.

Movies seen at theaters on military bases today are the same as the ones shown at off-base cinemas. For a night at the movies on a military base, expect to pay about 20 percent less, on average, than you would off-base. A few bases still offer movies for free, and others may occasionally sponsor free movie nights.

To see what's playing near you, visit www.aafes.com/ems/default.asp.

Commissaries: The Military Supermarket

Seems like the military exchange system has its hand in just about everything, doesn't it? Not quite. Military grocery stores aren't operated by the exchange system. In fact, unlike military exchanges, the Defense Commissary Agency (DeCA) commissaries are appropriated fund activities. By that, I mean they are allowed to use taxpayer dollars for their operation and construction.

DeCA operates 258 commissaries on military installations around the world. You can find super grocery savings near you by visiting DeCA's Web site at www.commissaries.com.

Substantial savings on groceries

Commissaries operate under guidelines and procedures incorporated into federal law. Unlike the exchange services, which are allowed to make a profit, commissaries must sell their items for the same price they purchase them. A 5 percent surcharge is added to your purchase to help pay for normal operating costs and facility maintenance and construction.

Overall you save about 30 percent for grocery items over off-base retail stores. That means a family of four, shopping regularly, can save about $3,000 per year, and a single member can save about $1,000 per year in grocery costs. The savings can be even greater if you live in a state that charges sales tax for groceries. Like exchange shopping, the commissary doesn't charge sales tax.

Bragging about bagging

A welcome sight at military commissaries, especially to the older and disabled veterans, is the folks who bag the groceries. Baggers are often military dependents, off duty military personnel trying to make a few extra bucks, and military retirees. They not only bag your groceries, but also take them out and load them into your car! How many supermarkets still do that?

Baggers don't work for, nor are they paid by, the commissary. Instead, they work solely for tips. The average tip is between 5 and 10 percent of your grocery purchase.

Baggers aren't paid by the commissary. If you don't plan to tip, please decline the service while at the checkout line and bag your own purchases.

Online grocery shopping?

I wish I could order bread, milk, and snacks online. I hate grocery shopping, and I look forward to the day when DeCA will allow me to purchase my groceries online and have them delivered to my house.

While that day hasn't yet arrived, authorized shoppers can purchase gourmet food gift packages, such as cheeses, baked goods, and chocolates, online through the "virtual commissary." Simply visit www.commissaries.com, choose "Shopping" from the pull-down menu, and select "Virtual

Commissary." You'll be required to log in with your last name, Social Security number, and date of birth. Your data will then be compared with the DEERS database to ensure that you're an eligible shopper.

Qualifying for ID Cards

Not all veterans are authorized to participate in shopping opportunities on military bases. Congress makes the laws concerning who can and can't shop at military exchanges, commissaries, and other nonappropriated fund activities. However, there are numerous categories of military members, veterans, family members, and others who can enjoy the benefits of shopping on military installations.

Authorized customers must possess a military or dependent identification card. These are the same ID cards issued for other military benefits, including travel (see Chapter 16) and Tricare (see Chapter 5). Customers who can have cards are current military members, certain veterans, and family members, including

- Military members on active duty.

- Members of the active (drilling) National Guard or reserves.

- Retired active-duty members. Active-duty members can retire after performing at least 20 years of active-duty service. See Chapter 7 for details.

- Retired National Guard and Reserve members who are receiving retired pay. Members of the Guard and Reserve generally begin receiving retired pay at age 60. Chapter 7 explains this in more detail.

- Veterans who have received the Medal of Honor.

- Honorably discharged veterans who have been rated as 100 percent disabled by the Department of Veterans Affairs (VA) due to a service-related injury. See Chapter 6 for information about how the VA rates disabilities.

- Dependents of those listed here. Dependents include a veteran's spouse and children. A spouse usually loses entitlement upon divorce, unless certain conditions are met (see the "Exceptions for former spouses" section). Children include the legitimate, adopted, stepchild, or illegitimate child of the member; illegitimate child of a spouse; or a ward. Children lose entitlement when they marry, or at age 21, unless they are incapable of self-care. This is extended to age 23 for children who are full-time students. It's also possible to designate a father, mother, father-in-law, mother-in-law, stepparent, or parent-by-adoption as a dependent, if the military member provides more than 50 percent of the relative's support.

Most BXs and PXs allow authorized shoppers to be accompanied by a guest. Such guests may not make any purchases, however. All purchases must be made by the authorized customer.

Exceptions for former spouses

In most cases of divorce between a military member and his spouse, the non-military spouse will lose her ID card and privileges when the divorce is final, with two exceptions, known as the "20/20/20" rule and the "10/20/10" rule.

Under the 20/20/20 rule, full benefits are extended to an unmarried former spouse when all the following conditions are met:

- ✔ The couple had been married for at least 20 years

- ✔ The member performed at least 20 years of service creditable for retired pay (see Chapter 7 for more on military retirement)

- ✔ There was at least a 20-year overlap of the marriage and the military service

With the 10/20/10 rule, the former spouse retains full benefits if the military member was discharged for *domestic abuse* and the following conditions are met:

- ✔ The couple had been married for at least 10 years

- ✔ The member performed at least 20 years of service creditable for retired pay

- ✔ There was at least a 10-year overlap of the marriage and the military service

If the former spouse remarries, she loses her on-base shopping privileges. However, if she becomes widowed or divorces again, she regains the privileges.

Surviving family members

Under certain conditions, surviving family members of deceased military personnel are authorized to retain their ID cards, and thereby their on-base shopping privileges. You qualify if you are a surviving dependent of any of the following:

- ✔ Members who died while on active duty under orders that specified a period of duty of more than 30 days or members who died while in a retired-with-pay status.

- National Guard and Reserve members who died from an injury or illness that happened or was aggravated while on active duty for a period of 30 days or less, on active duty for training, or on inactive-duty training, or while traveling to or from the place where the member was to perform, or performed, such duty.

- National Guard and Reserve members who qualified for retirement and were receiving retirement pay (turn to Chapter 7 for more on retiring).

- National Guard and Reserve members who qualified for retirement, but weren't receiving pay because they hadn't reached age 60. Dependents of these veterans can receive ID cards and begin their on-base shopping privileges on or after the date on which the member would have been 60 years old had he survived.

- Honorably discharged veterans rated by the VA as 100 percent disabled because of a service-connected injury or disease (head to Chapter 6 for more details on disability ratings).

- Medal of Honor recipients.

If you are a surviving spouse who has authorized privileges under one of these categories, you lose those privileges if you remarry. If you then become widowed or divorced, you regain your shopping privileges.

Other authorized shoppers

Individual military base commanders can authorize other people to shop on-base, if they determine that the base shopping capabilities won't be affected. Others who may be given shopping privileges include

- Members in the Delayed Enlistment Program (DEP), waiting to ship out to basic training

- Civilian employees of the military and Red Cross who are working overseas at U.S. military installations

- Members of NATO and other allied forces who are stationed at U.S. military bases

- Reserve Officer Training Corps (ROTC) cadets in their last two years of training

- United Seaman's Service (USS) personnel in foreign countries

- Dependents of anyone listed here (except DEP) when living in the same household

How to Apply for Your ID Card

Most people who are eligible to receive a military or dependent ID card receive theirs in person at a military installation. A list of major military installations located in the United States can be viewed at `usmilitary.about.com/od/theorderlyroom/l/blstatefacts.htm`.

When you arrive at the base, ask the guard at the gate to direct you to the ID card issuing facility. On most military bases, this is the customer service section of the base's personnel function. Some bases may call this the "Pass and ID" section.

Make sure you bring any supporting documentation with you, such as proof of military service and disability status, applicable marriage certificates, birth certificates, divorce decrees, or expired military ID cards.

You may want to call the ID card issuing facility before making the trip to the base to ensure you have all the supporting documentation for your particular situation. Unfortunately, there's no easy way to reach the right folks on base. The best way is to call information (411 in most places) and ask for the number for the base operator for that particular military installation. Ask the base operator for the phone number for the base's ID card issuing facility.

When you receive your military or dependent ID card, you'll be simultaneously enrolled in the Defense Enrollment Eligibility Reporting System (DEERS). DEERS includes more than 23 million records pertaining to active-duty and reserve military and their family members, military retired, Department of Defense (DOD) civil service personnel, and DOD contractors. DEERS is comprised of the National Enrollment Database (NED), the Person Data Repository (PDR), and several satellite databases. After you're enrolled in DEERS, you'll no longer have to provide proof of eligibility to obtain a military or dependent ID card, or replacement in the future.

Signing on the dotted line

Military regulations require the *sponsor* (the military member or veteran) to sign the application for her own or a dependent's ID card before the card can be issued. The sponsor can visit the ID card issuing facility, apply for his or the dependent's ID card, and sign the application.

If you're applying for a dependent's card, you can mail the application to the dependent, who can then visit a military base for the card to be issued. In fact, this is done all the time for new recruits in basic training who have dependents.

Procedures are in place that allow the services to issue dependent ID cards in cases where the spouse is unable or unwilling to sign the application, but this process usually takes more time. Contact the ID card issuing facility on any military base for assistance.

If the folks at the ID card issuing facility tell you that they can't issue a card without your sponsor's signature, refer them to the Uniformed Services Identification Card regulation, page 92, paragraph 8-2.

Even though military regulations require the sponsor to sign the ID card application for dependents, the sponsor can't deny ID cards or authorized privileges to his dependents. It's Congress who gets to decide who is and is not entitled to benefits, not the individual military member or veteran.

What if you can't travel?

Sometimes entitled individuals can't travel to a nearby military installation to apply for their ID cards in person. These include

- ✔ People who live far from a military facility
- ✔ Those who are physically handicapped
- ✔ Individuals with no means of transportation
- ✔ People who are hospitalized or sick

In such cases, you can call the nearest ID card issuing facility (see the preceding section) to obtain its mailing address. You'll need to provide proof of entitlement, an 8-x-10-inch or 5-x-7-inch portrait-type photograph that is notarized on the back, along with a listing of your physical characteristics (your eye and hair color, weight, and height, for example).

This can take a while because it requires several exchanges via certified mail. Additionally, the ID card issuing facility may require verification of your inability to travel.

Because the by-mail procedure is relatively rare, the personnel at the ID card issuing facility may be unfamiliar with the process. In some cases, they may even tell you it can't be done. If this happens, refer them to the Uniformed Services Identification Card regulation, page 107, table 11.4. It's amazing how attitudes can change when officials discover that you know what's in the regulations!

Chapter 16

Things to Do, Places to See: Travel Benefits

I love to travel. I served 23 years in the Air Force and have traveled around the world — twice. In my second life as a retired military member and author, I continue to travel every chance I get. If I won the lottery tomorrow, I'd sell my condo and move onto a cruise ship.

Even though those winning numbers continue to elude me, I've been able to feed the travel monkey who lives on my back without breaking the bank. How? I've taken advantage of travel benefits offered to military members, retired military folks (like me), a few other lucky veterans, and their family members.

A select category of veterans and their dependents can travel for free on military aircraft, stay cheap in lodging facilities located on military bases, vacation at a military-operated recreation center, and even rent a luxury vacation condominium at an unbelievably low price. In this chapter, I tell you about your travel options and what you need to do to take advantage of them.

Leaving on a Jet Plane: Military Space Available (Space-A) Travel

As much as I love to travel, I hate flying. I know what you're thinking: "You spent 23 years in the Air Force, and you hate to fly?" Let me clarify: I hate the cost of flying, especially now that many major airlines are charging for checked baggage! "Fly with us, but leave your clothes at home?" I don't think so. Next thing you know, commercial airlines will start doing away with other "luxuries," such as maintenance, pilot training, and radar.

Fortunately, select veterans who have a flexible travel schedule and spare time can travel around the world on military aircraft for free when room is available to accommodate them. If I wanted to, I could possibly be on a flight to Europe tomorrow. Hmm . . . I wonder if my editor would give me an extension on my deadline? I could say it's research. . . .

Space available travel, or *space A,* as it's commonly referred to, is just that: space available. Passengers who have signed up for travel through this program board only after all duty cargo and required passengers have been accommodated. Military members traveling on official orders and cargo needed to perform military missions come first, and then — if there's any room left on the aircraft — others can fill that space.

The military services operate thousands of flights per week from military air terminals and commercial airports throughout the world. Your free flight may be on anything from a prop-driven C-130 cargo aircraft, sitting on "web seats" surrounded by cargo, to a modern commercial aircraft, such as a DC-9, 707, 747, or 767, complete with flight attendant, meals, and movie (the military often charters commercial aircraft to haul military members from assignment to assignment).

Of course, you can't just walk into a military airport and say, "Put me on the next flight to the Bahamas." You've got to jump through a few hoops first. But don't worry. I've traveled space A several times, and I'm glad to walk you through the process.

Although space-A travel is free, you must pay a *head tax* if you depart or arrive on a military contract flight at a commercial airport. The tax is $12.40 for departure, plus an $11.00 immigration/customs inspection fee for arrival. There are no fees for departure or arrival on military aircraft at military base air terminals.

Checking in: Are you eligible to fly the friendly skies?

The military allows all sorts of folks to fly space A on its aircraft. In fact, the Department of Defense (DOD) regulation for the space-A program includes several pages of eligibility categories, including certain veterans, DOD contractors and employees, Red Cross personnel, public health service, and even non-U.S. military personnel who are performing duty on U.S. military bases.

For brevity's sake and because this is a book about benefits available to veterans and their dependents, I list only those categories here. If you're interested in the complete list, you can read the DOD regulation that governs the program (all 113 pages of it) online at www.dtic.mil/whs/directives/corres/pdf/451513r.pdf.

Military members, veterans, and family members who are authorized to fill empty seats on military aircraft are

- **Active-duty members who are on official leave (vacation).** This includes members of the reserves and National Guard who are on active-duty status.

- **Reserve members not on active duty.** Members of the National Guard and Reserves who aren't on active-duty orders may fly space A on flights within the continental United States (CONUS) and between the CONUS, Alaska, Hawaii, Puerto Rico, the U.S. Virgin Islands, Guam, and American Samoa; or travel within Alaska, Hawaii, Puerto Rico, or the U.S. Virgin Islands.

- **Retired military members.** This includes active-duty members with 20 or more years of military service, and National Guard and Reserve members who have more than 20 years of service and are receiving retired pay, which usually begins when they turn 60. It also includes those who retired from the military early for medical reasons. (Chapter 7 explains retirement programs.)

- **Gray-area Reserve and National Guard members.** These are retired members of the Reserves and Guard who have not yet begun receiving retired pay (which usually happens at age 60 — see Chapter 7 for more information). If you fall into this category, you can only fly space A on flights within the CONUS and between the CONUS and Alaska, Hawaii, Puerto Rico, the U.S. Virgin Islands, Guam, and American Samoa; or travel within Alaska, Hawaii, Puerto Rico, or the U.S. Virgin Islands.

- **Veterans who have been awarded the Medal of Honor.**

- **Dependents of anyone listed here.** Unless otherwise indicated in the "Take a number: Priority travel categories" section, dependents must travel with the military member in order to jump onto a space-A seat.

Leave, pass, and temporary duty

Military members who leave their place of duty, without authorization, are considered *absent without leave (AWOL)*. That's a bad thing. However, that doesn't mean soldiers and sailors can't ever leave their duty assignment; they just have to have permission. Military members can travel away from their duty area when they are on leave (vacation), pass (time off), and when authorized to perform temporary duty (TDY).

✔ **Leave:** *Leave* is simply the military's word for *vacation.* Active-duty members earn 30 days of leave per year, at the rate of 2.5 days for each month of active-duty service. For space-A purposes, there are three types of leave: ordinary leave, emergency leave, and environmental morale leave (EML).

Military supervisors can allow their subordinates to take *ordinary leave* any time the military mission and unit workload allows. Members on ordinary leave travel space A in Category III.

Emergency leave is granted when there is a death, serious injury, or life-threatening illness in the military member's (or her spouse's) immediate family. Immediate family includes parents (including stepparents), brothers, sisters, sons, and daughters. It does not include aunts, uncles, or cousins. It also does not include grandparents unless the grandparent raised the member (or spouse) for at least five years *in loco parentis* (in place of a parent). The conditions requiring the emergency leave must be verified by the American Red Cross. Like ordinary leave, emergency leave is charged against the member's leave balance. Emergency leave is almost always granted, even if the member's absence will impact the unit mission accomplishment. Emergency leave is the highest space-A travel category.

Environmental morale leave (EML) is granted to members assigned to overseas installations where the Department of Defense has determined that adverse environmental conditions require special arrangements for leave in more desirable places at periodic intervals. Usually, such members receive one EML per year. Members on EML are placed in Category II for space-A travel. The EML program is one of the few exceptions when dependents can travel space A without the sponsor.

✔ **Pass:** *Pass* is time off in the military. When a military member gets off work, she is *on pass* until her next duty period. Commanders can grant three- and even four-day passes to members for outstanding achievement, and military members who aren't required to work on weekends and holidays are on pass during those times. Pass is not charged against a member's leave balance. Active-duty members on pass may not travel space A.

✔ **Temporary duty:** *Temporary duty (TDY)* occurs when military members are authorized to perform duties away from their home station. There are two types of TDY: official TDY and permissive TDY. *Official TDY* is when a member's travel is funded by the military, such as when attending a military school or training exercise. Those performing official TDY don't travel space A because their travel is funded by the military. They travel *space required.*

Permissive TDY isn't funded by the military, but — because the travel is considered advantageous to the military — it's not charged against a member's leave balance. One example of permissive TDY is house hunting. Members who are getting ready to move from one permanent duty station to another are authorized ten days of permissive TDY to visit their new duty station for the purposes of arranging living accommodations. Other examples of permissive TDY are travel to attend a professional conference or convention and travel to their hometown to participate in the military's recruiter assistance program. Under this program, military members get to return to their hometown without using any of their earned leave in exchange for assisting local recruiters in locating potential candidates for military service. Individuals traveling space A for permissive TDY house hunting are placed in Category III. Other permissive TDY travelers are assigned to Category IV.

Choosing a destination

You can choose not one, not two, but as many as five destinations when you sign up for space-A travel (see the later section "Finding a military air terminal and signing up for travel"). If you're really up for an impromptu adventure, you can choose *All* as one of your destination choices. That means you would go on the waiting list for all the flights departing that particular military air terminal.

Instead of listing a specific destination, you can also list countries as your destination choices. For example, if you listed Misawa Air Base in Japan as your destination choice, you would only be considered for flights to that particular military air terminal. But if you listed Japan as your destination choice, you would be placed on the space-A waiting list for all flights going to Japan. See the later section "Establishing a rigid policy of flexibility" for more on this idea.

Waiting on the waiting list

Active-duty members remain on the space-A register for the duration of their leave orders or until they reach their destination, whichever occurs first. Others, such as authorized veterans, remain on the space-A list for 60 days or until they complete travel to their listed destination, whichever comes first. If your name reaches the top of the waiting list a few days before you arrive at the terminal, you don't lose your place in line. The 60 days/completed travel conditions still apply.

Getting on the waiting list is a huge timesaver for non-active-duty folks. You can, for example, use the remote sign-up program (see the "Finding a military air terminal and signing up for travel" section) and get on the waiting list two or three weeks before you want to travel. Then when you arrive at the military air terminal, your name will be much closer to the top of the list.

Finding a military air terminal and signing up for travel

You sign up for space-A travel at a military air terminal or from the comfort of your own home. Following is a list of the major military air terminals, but any military base that has a runway will have an air terminal of one sort or another:

U.S. air terminals

Maxwell Air Force Base (AFB), Alabama, 334-953-7372

Eielson AFB, Alaska, 907-377-1854

Elmendorf AFB, Alaska, 907-552- 8588

Davis-Monthan AFB, Arizona, 520-228-2322

Little Rock AFB, Arkansas, 501-987-3342

NAS Lemoore, California, 559-998-1680

NAS Miramar, California, 858-577-4283

NAS North Island, California, 619-545-9567

NAS Point Mugu, California, 805-989-7731

Travis AFB, California, 707-424-5770

Peterson AFB, Colorado, 719-556-4521

Dover AFB, Delaware, 302-677-4088

Homestead AFB, Florida, 305-224-7518

MacDill AFB, Florida, 813-828-2440

NAS Jacksonville, Florida, 904-542- 3956

NAS Pensacola, Florida, 850-452-3311

Naval Air Station (NAS), Atlanta, Georgia, 678-655-6359

Robins AFB, Georgia, 478-926-3166

Hickam AFB, Hawaii, 808-449-1515

Scott AFB, Illinois, 618-256-2014

Forbes Field Air National Guard (ANG), Kansas, 785-861-4210

McConnell AFB, Kansas, 316-759-4810

NAS Brunswick, Maine, 207-921-2682

Andrews AFB, Maryland, 301-981-1854

Baltimore-Washington International Airport (IAP), Maryland, 410-918-6900

Westover ARB, Massachusetts, 413-557-3453

Jackson IAP, Mississippi, 601-936-8761

Keesler AFB, Mississippi, 228-377-2120

Offutt AFB, Nebraska 402-294-8510

Nellis AFB, Nevada, 702-652-2562

Pease ANGB, New Hampshire, 603-430-3323

McGuire AFB, New Jersey, 609-754-5023

Holloman AFB, New Mexico, 505-572-3150

Kirtland AFB, New Mexico, 505-846-7000

Stewart ANGB, New York, 914-563-2226

Pope AFB, North Carolina, 910-394-6527

Grand Forks AFB, North Dakota, 701-747-7105

Wright-Patterson AFB, Ohio, 937-257-7741

Altus AFB, Oklahoma, 580-481-6428

Tinker AFB, Oklahoma, 405-739-4339

Willow Grove Joint Reserve Base (JRB), Pennsylvania, 215-443-6217

Charleston AFB, South Carolina, 843-963-3083

Fort Worth JRB, Texas, 817-782-5677

Kelly Annex, Lackland AFB, Texas, 210-925-8715

NAS Corpus Christi, Texas, 361-961-2505

Randolph AFB, Texas, 210-652-3725

Hill AFB, Utah, 801-777-3089

Langley AFB, Virginia, 757-764-3531

Naval Station, Norfolk, Virginia, 757-444-4148

Fairchild AFB, Washington, 509-247-5435

McChord AFB, Washington, 253-982-7259

F. E. Warren AFB, Wyoming, 800-832-1959 (Option 7)

International air terminals

Lajes Air Base (AB), Azores, 351-295-57-3227

Souda Bay, Crete, 49-6565-61-8866

NAS Guantanamo Bay, Cuba, 011-53-99-6408

Diego Garcia, 678-655-4903

Cairo East AB, Egypt, 20-2-797-3212

Ramstein AB, Germany, 011-49-6371-47-4440-4299

Andersen AFB, Guam, 671-366-5165

Keflavik, Iceland, 354-228-6139

Ben Gurion IAP, Israel, 972-3-935-4333

Aviano AB, Italy, 39-434-66-7680

Naples, Italy (Capodichino Airport), 39-081-568-5247

Sigonella Airport, Sicily, Italy, 39-95-86-5576

Marine Corps Air Station (MCAS), Iwakuni Japan, 81-6117-53-5509

Kadena AB, Japan, 011-81-6117-34-2159

Misawa AB, Japan, 011-81-3117-66-2370

Yokota AB, Japan, 81-3117-55-5661

Kunsan AB, Korea,
82-63-470-4666

Osan AB, Korea,
011- 82-31-661- 1854

NAS Rota, Spain,
34-956-822411

Incirlik AB, Turkey,
90-322-216-6424

Royal Air Force (RAF),
Mildenhall, United Kingdom,
44-1638-54-2248

There's probably a military flight terminal near you. However, not all terminals have flights to all locations. You can call the terminals for flight schedules, availability of remote sign-up (mentioned later in this section), directions, or to check your status on the waiting list.

As a general rule, terminals located on the West Coast service the Pacific, such as Alaska, Hawaii, Korea, Japan, Australia, Guam, the Philippines, and so on. Terminals on the East Coast have more flights to Europe and the Middle East. All terminals offer flights to various locations in the continental United States.

The major air terminals are much like commercial airports. Facilities may include convenience stores, barber shops, snack bars, pay television (free television lounge in some military terminals), traveler assistance, baggage lockers or rooms, United Services Organization (USO) lounges, and nurseries. At smaller bases with limited air operations, the air terminal may be the size of a dentist's waiting room.

You can sign up for a space-A flight by using one of three methods:

- ✔ **In-person sign-up:** Many people sign up for space-A travel in person at the terminal they're departing from. This is generally not the best option, because it usually means standing in line. However, if you have questions about flights, your travel documents, or your eligibility to fly space A, a friendly passenger service representative will be waiting at the front of the line to help you.

- ✔ **Self sign-up:** Self sign-up allows you to sign up at a terminal without waiting in line. Most locations now provide self-sign-up counters with easy-to-follow instructions for registration. If your travel will take you to a foreign country, you'll want to ensure your border clearance documentation is up-to-date. If you're unsure, verify it with a passenger service representative on duty.

  If you're on active duty, you can't sign up until the effective date of your leave or pass.

- ✔ **Remote sign-up:** This is a relatively new program, and I love it. Remote sign-up allows you to put your name on the space-A waiting list by faxing copies of proper service documentation (such as your ID card), along with your desired destination(s) and family members' first names to the aerial port of departure. Some terminals now even accept e-mail sign-up. You can call the terminal to find out if it offers remote sign-up.

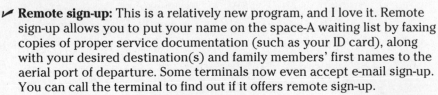

The fax data header (or e-mail) will establish the date and time of your sign-up; therefore, active-duty personnel must ensure the fax (or e-mail) is sent no earlier than the effective date of leave.

If applicable, you must include a statement that all required border clearance documents are current when using the remote sign-up program.

Take a number: Priority travel categories

When you sign up for space-A travel, you're assigned to one of six priority travel categories, depending on your status. By "status," I don't mean military rank; I mean a combination of factors that determine your place on the waiting list. Such factors include whether you are active duty, reserves, or retired; whether you are traveling for a family emergency; and other factors. One of the great things about space-A travel is that rank doesn't matter here. A four-star general receives the same treatment as a one-stripe private.

Category 1: Emergency leave

Travelers are placed in Category I when they are traveling on emergency leave due to the death or serious illness or injury of a family member (see the "Leave, pass, and temporary duty" sidebar).

- ✔ Military members may travel space A under this category from CONUS (continental United States) to CONUS, CONUS to overseas, overseas to overseas, or overseas to CONUS. Dependents may travel when accompanied by the sponsor.

- ✔ Dependents of military members who are stationed in the CONUS may travel space A unaccompanied under this category from CONUS to overseas or overseas to CONUS.

- ✔ Dependents of military members residing overseas with the sponsor may travel unaccompanied, one-way only, to the emergency destination. Return travel isn't authorized under space A.

- ✔ When retired uniformed services members die overseas, their dependents may travel unaccompanied under Category I. Travel is authorized for the purpose of accompanying the remains of the deceased from overseas to the CONUS. Return travel is authorized if accomplished within one year of arrival in the CONUS.

Category II: Environmental morale leave

Military members and their accompanying dependents who are traveling on approved EML (environmental morale leave) orders (see the "Leave, pass, and temporary duty" sidebar) may travel in Category II from CONUS to CONUS, CONUS to overseas, overseas to overseas, and overseas to CONUS.

Category III: Ordinary leave, house hunting permissive TDY, Medal of Honor holders, and others

Category III travelers include:

- Uniformed services members on a leave status other than emergency leave or EML, and their accompanying dependents. This includes members of the Reserves and National Guard on active duty. Travel is authorized from CONUS to CONUS, CONUS to overseas, overseas to overseas, and overseas to CONUS.

- Dependent spouses of military personnel who have officially been reported missing, and accompanying dependent children and parents, when traveling for humanitarian reasons and on approval on a case-by-case basis by the head of the service concerned. Travel is authorized from CONUS to CONUS, CONUS to overseas, overseas to overseas, and overseas to CONUS.

- Uniformed services members and one accompanying dependent traveling under permissive temporary duty orders for house hunting in anticipation of a pending assignment change. Travel can be from CONUS to CONUS, CONUS to overseas, overseas to overseas, and overseas to CONUS.

- Medal of Honor recipients and their accompanying dependents may travel in Category III from CONUS to CONUS, CONUS to overseas, overseas to overseas, and overseas to CONUS.

Category IV: Unaccompanied dependents on EML

Unaccompanied dependents traveling on the EML program (environmental morale leave; see the "Leave, pass, and temporary duty" sidebar) travel space A under the fourth priority travel category. Travel is authorized from overseas to CONUS, overseas to overseas, and CONUS to overseas. Dependents traveling unaccompanied for EML aren't authorized to travel space A from CONUS to CONUS.

Category V: Permissive TDY (non-house hunting) and students

Military members traveling on permissive TDY (temporary duty) and certain dependent children may travel space A under this category:

- Military personnel traveling on permissive TDY orders other than for house hunting may travel CONUS to CONUS, CONUS to overseas, overseas to overseas, and overseas to CONUS. Dependents aren't authorized to accompany sponsors during non-house-hunting permissive TDY space-A travel.

- Dependent children who are college students attending an overseas branch of an American university located in the same overseas area in which they reside with the sponsor can travel unaccompanied to and from their school under this category. Only one round trip each year is authorized.

✔ Unaccompanied spouses of military members stationed in overseas areas may travel space A, in response to written requests from school officials or when deemed essential by the sponsor's commander to address the needs of family members attending school at an overseas location. In this situation, the spouse doesn't need to be accompanied by the sponsor.

Category VI: Retired military, National Guard, and Reserves

This is the category I travel under when I decide to do it the space-A way:

✔ Retired military members and their accompanying dependents may travel from CONUS to CONUS, CONUS to overseas, overseas to overseas, and overseas to CONUS. This includes retired members of the National Guard and Reserves who are receiving retired pay (usually at age 60; Chapter 7 explains the military retirement program).

✔ Reserve and National Guard members who are not on active duty, and retired members of the Guard and Reserves who are not yet entitled to retired pay may travel space A in the CONUS; directly between the CONUS and Alaska, Hawaii, Puerto Rico, the U.S. Virgin Islands, Guam, and American Samoa; and within Alaska, Hawaii, Puerto Rico, or the U.S. Virgin Islands.

Calling all flights! Securing available seats

After you've signed up for space-A destinations and are assigned to a travel category, you compete against others on the waiting list for available seats. Category I passengers are assigned seats before Category II passengers, who get seats before Category III travelers, and so on.

Within a category, it's first come, first served. If you and I were both in Category VI, and you signed up before me, you would be ahead of me on the waiting list.

Space-A seats are normally identified as early as two to three hours and as late as 30 minutes prior to departure. You can call the passenger service center to find out the space-available showtime for each scheduled flight that meets your travel requirements. See "Finding a military air terminal and signing up for travel" for information about contacting the passenger service centers.

If your name is called and you're not there, you don't lose your place on the waiting list. This is a great feature of space-A travel because your name remains on the list until you reach your destination or for 60 days, whichever comes first. So you can sign up for space A weeks in advance and keep moving up on the waiting list before you even arrive at the terminal.

Active-duty members must be on official leave orders before they can sign up for space A.

Each terminal maintains a space-A register (organized alphabetically, by priority and the date and time of registration for travel) that is updated daily. The register is conveniently located in the terminal and is directly accessible to you. You can even call the terminal to find where you stand travel-wise. See "Finding a military air terminal and signing up for travel" for phone numbers.

The good news is that once you're assigned a space-A seat, you can't be bumped out of that seat by another space-A passenger, even if he's in a higher category.

The bad news is that you can be bumped at any point during your journey by *space-required* passengers — that is, those military members traveling on official orders. If you're removed en route, you may reregister using your original date and time of registration.

If you're removed en route and decide to change your destination, you don't get to keep your original date and time of registration. Passenger agents will assign a new date and time when you change or add a country to your itinerary.

Getting back home again

At some point after you've reached your travel destination, you'll probably want to return home. Or maybe you won't. I can think of several places I've visited that I haven't wanted to leave. In any event, if you're planning to return home at some point, it's a good idea to sign up for a return flight immediately after you reach your destination. Again, your name remains on the waiting list for up to 60 days. So while you're out seeing the sights of Europe or Japan, your name will be getting closer and closer to the top of the list for your return flight.

When traveling on a passport (family members, retired military, reserves, and so on), you may return to the continental United States only through authorized ports of entry where customs and immigration clearance is available. Although you may depart the United States from any military airfield, reentry locations for passport holders are limited. Active-duty passengers who don't require immigration clearance have more reentry options.

Packing right by packing light

The military lets you take quite a lot on space-A flights. Each passenger may check two pieces of baggage, which can be 70 pounds each, up to 62 linear inches (length + width + height) in size. Family members may even pool their baggage allowances. You are also allowed to hand-carry one article (small baggage, backpack, or such) and one personal item (purse, briefcase, teddy bear) for storage in the passenger cabin area. Hand-carried items can be no larger than 45 linear inches and must fit under your seat or in the overhead compartment (if available).

Although the military allows you to take everything but the kitchen sink, it's not a good idea. Space-A travel isn't exactly like commercial travel. There isn't going to be any curbside check-in or porters. You can't even check your bags until you've been called for a seat. That means you're going to have your bags with you in the terminal while waiting for your name to be called.

If you have to go to the bathroom, someone is going to have to watch your luggage, or you're going to have to haul everything to the bathroom with you. If your name isn't called that day, you'll have to cart your stuff out of the terminal to your overnight accommodations. The lighter you pack, the less you'll have to haul around.

 While packing light is a good idea, if you're traveling with young children, you may encounter delays in places where baby supplies may not be readily available, so make sure you have all the little ones' necessities on hand. It's also a good idea to bring a supply of games and books to keep the kiddies from getting too bored. "Are we there yet?"

Establishing a rigid policy of flexibility

Space-A travel success depends on flexibility and good timing. Although some travelers sign up and travel the same day, aircraft seats are space available, and you may have to wait several days for your name to be called for a seat on your flight of choice. You should make sure your finances permit for an overnight stay, because most military air terminals close at night. If you have to stay overnight, consider staying on-base in the military lodging facility. This can save you big bucks. Plus you'll be closer to the air terminal. See the "Sleeping Cheaply at Military Lodging" section for more information.

Be as flexible as possible in choosing a destination. For example, if you want to get to Ramstein Air Base, Germany, consider a flight to Spangdahlem Air Base, Germany, or even Royal Air Force (RAF) Base Mildenhall, United Kingdom, as an alternative. At Mildenhall, you can try for another flight bound for Germany. For more great tips on making your space-A adventure easier and less frustrating, see Chapter 19.

Sleeping Cheaply at Military Lodging

Bunking down at military lodging is another travel benefit I use all the time. I find it especially useful when driving cross-country or for short stays in locations that have military bases close by. Why pay $75 or more per night to stay in a small motel when you can get the military equivalent for about $35 per night?

All military bases operate temporary lodging facilities. Think of them as motels. The primary purpose of these operations is to provide a temporary place to stay for military folks on official business, such as visiting the base on official temporary duty or transitioning in or out of the base on official permanent change of station moves.

But after these individuals are accommodated, certain veterans and their family members can stay in these facilities, too. Like space-A air travel (see the "Leaving on a Jet Plane: Military Space Available (Space-A) Travel" section in this chapter), getting a room here is *space available.* That means folks traveling on official military business get first crack at available rooms.

Checking in on your eligibility

The key to getting a room, space available, at a military lodging facility lies with that all-magic document, the military ID card (see Chapter 15 for more on who qualifies for this handy piece of plastic and how to get one). Those eligible for this benefit include active-duty military members, members of the National Guard and Reserves, Medal of Honor holders, 100 percent disabled veterans, military retirees receiving retired pay, and dependents of these folks.

Although you must meet the eligibility criteria to make reservations and check in, guests of those eligible may stay at military lodging facilities provided the eligible patron is present at check-in.

Facility types and their rates

There are more types of lodging facilities scattered throughout U.S. military bases than you can shake a stick at. Every base is different. You may find yourself staying at a very modern, modular-construction, complete house-keeping unit that sleeps a family of five, or a modern low-rise or high-rise hotel. On the other hand, the base may feature reconstructed World War II barracks, which have been converted into single rooms with a bathroom shared between two rooms.

One time when traveling across Europe, I was placed space A for two nights in the VIP quarters at Ramstein Air Base in Germany. The room featured a separate bedroom, sitting room, and kitchen/dining room. It even had a minibar! At first I thought they recognized me from my many military books and articles, but I later discovered that I just got lucky, and that's what they had space available at the time.

Another time I stayed space available at a very small Army base in Korea and received a room about 400 square feet in size with a single steel bed, a small desk, and an even smaller dresser. The latrine (the Army word for bathroom) was down the hall and was shared by everyone on that floor.

Rates vary widely from place to place and usually reflect the type of accommodation. One thing is certain: Rates are always substantially cheaper than comparable accommodations off-base. For the privilege of being treated like a king during my stay at Ramstein, I paid $65 per night. My time in that prison cell in Korea only set me back $6 per night.

Not long ago, when traveling with my family in California, I stayed in the Temporary Lodging Facility (TLF) at Edwards Air Force Base. TLFs are intended for military families transitioning in to a new base or preparing to leave a base for their next assignment. My space-available TLF stay included two bedrooms, a living room, large bathroom, private laundry room, and full kitchen. Cost? $65 per night.

Reserving your right to rest

I remember the days when staying space available at military lodging facilities was no picnic. You generally would have to wait until 6 p.m., and then check with the lobby, in person, to see if any space-available accommodations were available for the night. If you wanted to stay for more than one night, you ran the risk of getting bumped out of your room each day by a *space-required* military member.

Thankfully, those days are long gone. Because of computerized central reservation systems, the military lodging facilities now have a handle on availability, even a couple of months in advance.

Active-duty members and their dependents who want space-available accommodations may make reservations up to 60 days in advance. Other authorized space-available participants may reserve rooms up to 30 days ahead of their visit. After your reservation is confirmed, you can't be bumped, even by those staying on official travel orders. How cool is that?

Centralized reservation systems for Army, Navy, and Air Force lodging

Three of the five military services operate *centralized reservation systems,* a single contact point for reservations at any of their lodging facilities:

- To make reservations on any Army post, call 866-363-5771.
- Reservations to stay on Navy bases can be made by calling 800-NAVY-INN (800-628-9466).
- You can reserve rooms at Air Force lodging facilities at 888-AF-LODGE (888-235-6343).

The Marine Corps and Coast Guard have to be different. They don't have centralized reservation systems, probably because they have far fewer bases than the other three branches.

Marine Corps reservations

To reserve lodging on a Marine Corps installation, you must call the lodging facility directly:

- Marine Corps Air Station (MCAS), Yuma, Arizona: 928-269-2262
- Marine Corps Base (MCB), Barstow, California: 760-577-6418
- MCB, Camp Pendleton, California: 760-725-5304
- MCB Twentynine, Palms, California: 760-830-6583
- MCAS Miramar, San Diego, California: 800-628-9466
- MCB Hawaii, Kaneohe Bay, Hawaii: 808-254-2806
- MCB, Camp Lejeune, North Carolina: 910-451-3041
- MCAS, Beaufort, South Carolina: 843-522-1663
- MCB, Quantico, Virginia: 800-965-9511
- MCB Camp Butler, Okinawa, Japan: 011-81-611-745-2455

Coast Guard reservations

To stay space available at a Coast Guard lodging facility, you must call the facility directly:

- Integrated Support Command (ISC), Kodiak, Alaska: 907-487-5446, ext. 1
- ISC, Alameda, California: 415-506-3130
- Coast Guard Station, Lake Tahoe, California: 530-583-7438
- Coast Guard Training Center, Petaluma, California: 707-765-7248

✔ Point Fermin Station, San Pedro, California: 310-521-6020

✔ Coast Guard Academy, New London, Connecticut: 860-444-8664

✔ Coast Guard Station, Marathon, Florida: 305-535-4565

✔ Coast Guard Yard, Baltimore, Maryland: 410-636-7497

✔ Air Station, Cape Cod, Massachusetts: 508-968-6461

✔ Loran Station, Siasconset Beach, Nantucket, Massachusetts: 508-968-6461

✔ Coast Guard Training Center, Cape May, New Jersey: 609-898-6922

✔ Fort Wadsworth, Staten Island, New York: 718-354-4407

✔ Coast Guard Support Center, Elizabeth City, North Carolina: 252-335-6482

✔ Coast Guard Reserve Training Center, Yorktown, Virginia: 757-856-2378

✔ Coast Guard Air Station, Borinquen, Aguadilla, Puerto Rico: 787-890-8492

✔ Coast Guard Station, San Juan, Puerto Rico: 787-774-0298

Getting Some R&R at Armed Forces Resorts

Sometimes a clean bed and a shower just aren't enough. Sometimes you need to splurge a little for some rest and recuperation at a luxury vacation resort. An Armed Forces Recreation Center (AFRC) may be just what you're looking for.

AFRC resorts are affordable Joint Service facilities operated by the U.S. Army Family, Morale, Welfare and Recreation Command and are located at ideal vacation destinations. AFRCs offer a full range of resort hotel opportunities for those who hold the magic ID card (see Chapter 14 for more on eligibility and obtaining one of these gems). If you're a military member (either active duty or reserve), retiree, veteran with a 100 percent service-connected disability, have won the Medal of Honor, or a dependent of one of these fine citizens, you're eligible for this perk.

Although not as cheap as military lodging facilities (see the "Sleeping Cheaply at Military Lodging" section earlier in this chapter), AFRC room rates are affordable. Rates are based on military rank (or the rank you held when you separated from the military), room size, and location. There's no "space available" here. Everyone with an ID card is equally eligible, regardless of duty status. However, these places are popular, and I mean *popular!* Reservations are required, often months in advance.

Cape Henry Inn and Beach Club

Ah, how I love the beach. The Cape Henry Inn and Beach Club is located on one of the finest beaches in the world — Fort Story near Virginia Beach, Virginia, nestled among protected sand dunes, overlooking Chesapeake Bay.

Facilities include 50 spacious hotel rooms with kitchenette and private balcony; multiple cottages, bungalows, and log cabins; handicapped-equipped rooms; two outdoor pools; and a fitness center. Activities range from boardwalk strolls, pristine beaches, hiking, whale watching, museums, shopping, and fine dining.

The Cape Henry Inn and Beach Club doesn't have its own restaurant on the property, but several dining choices are nearby. It does, however, have a large banquet facility that's suitable for weddings, group functions, events, and parties. Catering is available.

Like all AFRCs, rates are based on season, type of room, and your military rank (or the rank you held when you left military service), ranging from $75 to $175 per night.

Reservations can be made up to 52 weeks in advance. Reservations can be made by phone at 757-422-8818 or online at www.capehenryinn.com.

Shades of Green at Disney World

For many children, visiting Walt Disney World may be the Mecca of vacation spots. Taking pictures and getting autographs with Disney's finest is one thing they may very well remember for their whole lives. What do the parents remember, though? Expensive resorts, high-priced meals, and out-of-this-world attraction prices.

However, for those eligible to stay at AFRCs, there's an answer to these headaches: the Shades of Green Resort. Nestled between the Palm and Magnolia golf courses on Walt Disney World property, the Shades of Green boasts 586 guest rooms, 10 family and junior suites, two heated pools and a hot tub, state-of-the-art fitness center, and transportation to all of Orlando's many attractions. The resort also has an on-site ticket office, which provides discounted tickets to dozens of locations, including all Walt Disney World theme parks, Universal Studios, Sea World Orlando, and the Kennedy Space Center.

Exceptional dining options are available throughout the resort and include Mangino's, the Garden Gallery Restaurant, Evergreens Sports Bar and Grill, and the Express Cafe.

Nightly room rates run from $79 to $275, depending on the season, type of room, and your military rank. For reservations visit www.shadesofgreen.org, or call 888-593-2242.

Hale Koa in Hawaii

Who doesn't get excited about the prospect of a Hawaiian vacation? What? You say it's not in the budget? If you take advantage of the Armed Forces Recreation Center Hale Koa, located on the famous Waikiki Beach, it just may become an affordable option.

The Hale Koa's two towers, Maile and Ilima, house 817 spacious guest rooms. Most rooms are furnished with one king, two queen, or two double beds. Activities include beach services that rent surf and snorkel equipment, swimming pools, a fitness center, spa services with massage, tennis courts, sand volleyball, outdoor racquetball courts, and world-class golfing opportunities near the hotel.

You can enjoy culinary delights at Koko's Cafe, Bibas, or the Hale Koa Room restaurants, located on the property. Nightly entertainment features magic, songs and dances of Polynesia, and the best luau on Waikiki Beach. Okay, I've only been to one luau on Waikiki Beach, but it seemed like the best to me.

For a luxury beach resort located directly on the most famous beach in the world, rates are extremely reasonable, ranging from $87 to $277 per night, depending on your rank, the season, and the type of room. For reservations, call 800-367-6027, or you can make online reservations at www.halekoa.com.

Edelweiss in Germany

When I tell people about vacationing in the Bavarian Alps a couple of years ago, they often look me over as if trying to find out where I hide all my money. But when coupled with a free space-A military aircraft hop (see the "Leaving on a Jet Plane: Military Space Available (Space-A) Travel" section) and reservations at the AFRC Edelweiss Lodge, it was a sweet deal.

Edelweiss Lodge and Resort offers an array of guest amenities, entertainment, and recreation activities. You can enjoy a sightseeing tour of the area or spend a day on some of the best slopes ever. Afterward, perhaps a workout in the modern fitness club or a therapeutic massage is in order. For the water-inclined, there's an indoor pool and an outdoor hot tub. For your dining pleasure, the Edelweiss boasts four restaurants featuring foods from around the world, including regional cuisine and all-American favorites.

Depending on the season, type of room, and your military rank, a night at the Edelweiss will set you back about $84 to $239. Rustic cabins are available for $399 for seven nights, and deluxe cabins can be had for $1,113 for a week's stay. Reservations can be made by calling 011-49-8821-9440 or by visiting www.edelweisslodgeandresort.com.

Dragon Hill in South Korea

I spent seven years of my military career stationed in Korea. When I wanted to escape the pressures and stress of my duties, my first choice was always a stay at the Dragon Hill Lodge, located in the heart of Seoul.

Seoul, Korea, offers some of the best shopping opportunities in the world, and when you're finished getting world-class deals, the lodge provides you with a respite where you can enjoy a state-of-the-art health club and pool, travel and tour services, a gift store, flower shop, and beauty salon. Dining facilities include four full-service restaurants and a deli. There's even a Subway and a Pizza Hut for that fast-food taste of home.

Each of the 394 guest rooms and suites features a queen-size bed and a sleeper sofa, private bath, color television with satellite channels, direct-dial telephone, ironing board, mini refrigerator, coffee maker, and fireproof safe. Each room has high-speed Internet access.

Rates run from $59 to $139 per night, depending on your rank and the type of room you select. You can reserve a room at the Dragon Hill Lodge by calling 011-82-2-7918-222 or going to their Web site at www.dragonhilllodge.com.

Going Condo-Crazy with the Armed Forces Vacation Club

Sometimes I need a luxury vacation, but I don't want to travel to one of the five Armed Forces Recreation Centers, and I don't want to max out my credit cards. What do I do then? I take advantage of a little-known veteran travel benefit called the Armed Forces Vacation Club (AFVC).

As with staying at military lodging facilities (see the "Sleeping Cheaply at Military Lodging" section) or vacationing at one of the AFRCs (see the "Getting Some R&R at Armed Forces Resorts" section), you have to have an ID card to take advantage of this benefit. That means you have to be a military member, retiree receiving military retired pay, Medal of Honor holder, 100 percent disabled veteran, or a dependent.

These lucky veterans and family members can rent luxury condos at more than 3,500 locations around the world for the low cost of $329 per week. That comes out to $47 per day!

If you've got the time, they've got the place

Thousands of timeshare condos are located throughout the world. Often, someone buys a timeshare and then doesn't have an opportunity to use it. These unused timeshare weeks are sometimes rented out by the condo's management association, instead of allowing them to sit empty. The Department of Defense's Morale, Welfare, and Recreation Service has made a special deal with many of these management associations to offer unused timeshares to military members and eligible veterans and family members for the unbelievable price of $329 per week.

The AFVC has listings for virtually everywhere, including all states, Europe, Australia, the Bahamas, Africa, Canada, Mexico, Central and South America, India, the Pacific . . . pretty much anywhere you want to go.

Claiming your condo

Using the AFVC to locate and reserve a luxury condo for your next leave or vacation is simplicity itself. If you've never used the AFVC before, you must first call the club at 800-724-9988. The hours of operation are Monday through Friday 0700 to 2400 hours (7 a.m. to midnight), Saturday 0900 to 2000 hours (9 a.m. to 8 p.m.), and Sunday 0930 to 2000 hours (9:30 a.m. to 8 p.m.; all times are eastern time).

When you call the first time, the kind folks at the reservation center will issue you an account number and password. Write this down and keep it somewhere safe. You can then use this information to log onto the AFVC Web site at www.afvclub.com and make your reservations online.

If you prefer not to use the Internet to make reservations, you can use the Web site to locate available condo rentals, and then reserve the condo by calling 800-724-9988.

Condos may become available to AFVC members anywhere from 2 to 365 days in advance of the check-in date. As soon as they become available, they're listed on the Web site and can be reserved. After a reservation is made, the unit is taken out of the available reservation pool and the unit is yours. The reservation is guaranteed. Reservations are made on a first-come, first-served basis, so a high-demand location may be available in the morning but gone by that afternoon.

Some resorts in Mexico or the Caribbean are *all-inclusive* resorts. This means the resort provides all meals, beverages, entertainment, and sometimes day-trips, just like on a cruise ship. Anyone who stays at an all-inclusive resort pays a per-person fee for this service (in addition to the $329 per week rental fee). At some resorts, this is optional. At others, it's a mandatory fee. Even condo owners at these resorts must pay the fee when they stay in their own property. This fee can be very high, sometimes up to $1,000 for the week. All-inclusive conditions and rates are set by the resort, and the AFVC has no control over them. These resorts are well marked on the Web site, and vacation counselors will point out these fees if you make a reservation over the phone.

Part V
The Part of Tens

The 5th Wave   By Rich Tennant

"This option in the pension is a little tricky. You can start collecting benefits when you're 58 years old, as long as you look 58 years old."

In this part . . .

It's a sad fact of life that all too often with perks come irritations — minor irritations, to be sure, but irritations nonetheless. In this part I present you with three chapters containing short-but-sweet pointers on how to reduce or eliminate those irritations, just to make the benefits of handling your VA claims or traveling with the military a little more pleasant.

Chapter 17

Ten Places to Get Help with Veterans Benefits

In This Chapter

▶ Checking up on your pay

▶ Seeking education and employment help

▶ Visiting with a veterans service organization

*G*etting help with veterans benefits isn't all that difficult, and it's a wonder more veterans don't do so. Remember when you were in the military and were taught how team effort is the key to mission accomplishment? Well, the same is true when the "mission" involves applying for and receiving the veterans benefits you've earned and deserve.

Going it alone is not the best option. Two heads are better than one, and all that. You can get help from all sorts of places, and I list the top ten here.

American Legion

The American Legion was chartered by Congress in 1919 as a patriotic, wartime veterans organization devoted to mutual helpfulness. The organization has about 3 million members and nearly 15,000 American Legion Posts throughout the world. Many of these posts have accredited American Legion representatives to help veterans with their VA claims and appeals. These services are free, and you don't have to join the organization to receive these services.

Local American Legion posts are usually listed in the phone book. You can also contact the group at

American Legion National Headquarters
P.O. Box 1055
Indianapolis, IN 46206
Phone 317-630-1200
Web site www.legion.org

Defense Finance & Accounting Center

The folks at the Defense Finance & Accounting Center are the ones to contact if you need help with your military retired pay (see Chapter 7) or Combat Related Special Compensation (see Chapter 6). When you were in the military, you got help with your pay through the finance section on the military base you were assigned to, but that's not possible after you leave military service. Your pay matters are now handled by the Defense Finance & Accounting Center, located in Cleveland, Ohio. They maintain all pay accounts for military retirees.

You can contact the center at

DFAS Cleveland
Anthony J. Celebrezze Federal Building
1240 E. Ninth St.
Cleveland, OH 44199-2055
Phone 800-321-1080

The center also maintains a Web site at www.dfas.mil. The site has loads of detailed information about military retiree pay issues. It even supports an online system called MyPay, where you can make changes to your pay account, such as updates to your address, phone number, and tax information.

Disabled American Veterans

The Disabled American Veterans (DAV) is an organization of disabled veterans who are focused on building better lives for disabled veterans and their families. The DAV is a veterans service organization (VSO) that is chartered by Congress and is authorized by the Department of Veterans Affairs (VA) to represent and assist veterans with benefit claims and appeals. Like all VSOs, the DAV is a private organization funded by member dues and contributions; it's not an agency of the government.

The DAV staffs 88 offices with a corps of 260 volunteers who are certified and authorized to directly represent veterans with claims for benefits from the VA and Department of Defense. This free service is available to all veterans.

You can contact the DAV at

Disabled American Veterans National Headquarters
3725 Alexandria Pike
Cold Spring, KY 41076
Phone 877-I Am A Vet (877-426-2838) or 859-441-7300
Web site www.dav.org

National Veterans Legal Services Program

The National Veterans Legal Services Program (NVLSP) is an independent, nonprofit, charitable organization that recruits, trains, and assists thousands of volunteer lawyers and veterans advocates to help veterans with their VA claims and appeals. The organization also represents veterans and their dependents who are seeking benefits from the VA and in court.

The NVLSP manages the Veterans Consortium Pro Bono Program (explained in Chapter 3), a great program that can provide pro bono (free) attorneys to veterans who are appealing their case to the U.S. Court of Appeals for Veterans Claims.

Here's how to get in touch with the group:

National Veterans Legal Services Program
1600 K St., NW, Suite 500
Washington, DC 20006
Phone 202-265-8305
Web site www.nvlsp.org

Noncommissioned Officers Association

The Noncommissioned Officers Association (NCOA) was founded in 1960 to enhance and maintain the quality of life for noncommissioned and petty officers in all branches of the armed forces, National Guard, and Reserves. The

NCOA is well known among veterans and military members for employment programs. Through its Veterans Employment Assistance program, established in 1973, the NCOA has helped more than 60,000 veterans find employment.

Presently, the NCOA has two programs that assist veterans who are seeking employment throughout the world. These programs are the National Job Fair and the Internet job board located at www.MilitaryJobWorld.com or www. TheJobLeader.com. No membership requirements or fees are charged to veterans for the job assistance services.

You can contact the NCOA at

> Noncommissioned Officers Association
> 10635 IH 35 North
> San Antonio, TX 78233
> Phone 210-653-6161
> Web site www.ncoausa.org

State Veterans Offices

Every state and several U.S. territories have their own veterans affairs office, division, or bureau that is funded and managed by the individual state government. Although these offices are primarily responsible for processing veterans benefits for their residents, many of them have skilled counselors who can help veterans obtain federal veterans benefits as well. Often, state veterans offices can also assist in preparing for or obtaining employment in the state.

It's most certainly worth your time to find out more about your state's office. You can find a listing of state veterans offices, as well as contact and Web information, in Appendix A.

VA Regional Centers and Vet Centers

The VA isn't there just to process your paperwork. VA regional centers and vet centers have highly trained counselors who can help you put together a winning veterans benefit claims submission.

Under a law known as the "VA's duty to assist," explained further in Chapter 3, the VA is required to assist you by telling you exactly what supporting evidence you need to support your claim for benefits, as well as by doing everything in its power to help locate that evidence for you. The smart veteran will take advantage of this law by contacting his nearest VA regional center or vet center to sit down with a counselor before submitting his claim. You can find your nearest VA regional center or vet center in Appendix B.

Veterans Representatives on College Campuses

Most colleges and universities in the United States have a veterans affairs office. The folks in these offices are very helpful when you want to apply for veterans education benefits, as described in Chapters 10 and 11. Quite often, the individuals who work in such offices are veterans themselves, providing a "been there, done that" approach to helping veterans achieve their educational goals.

If you want help getting started with or continuing a college degree or training program, these are often the best folks to ask. Not only are they knowledgeable about federal benefits, but they have the latest information about state veterans education benefits as well. Call your local college or university and ask if it has a veterans office.

Veterans of Foreign Wars

The Veterans of Foreign Wars (VFW) was originally founded in 1899 as the American Veterans of Foreign Service. With 2.4 million members and more than 8,500 VFW posts located around the world, this VSO (veterans service organization) strives to be a voice for returning and currently deployed service members and their families.

The VFW maintains a nationwide network of service officers, which includes full-time professional veteran advocates and trained volunteer advocates, each of whom is certified by the VA to represent veterans on matters of claims and appeals. They assist more than 120,000 veterans and their families each year. These services are free, and you don't have to join the organization to take advantage of them.

Local VFW posts can be found in your phone book, or you can contact the national headquarters at

Veterans of Foreign Wars National Headquarters
406 W. 34th St.
Kansas City, MO 64111
Phone 816-756-3390
Web site www.vfw.org

Vietnam Veterans of America

The Vietnam Veterans of America (VVA) is the only national Vietnam veterans organization congressionally chartered and exclusively dedicated to Vietnam-era veterans and their families. Established in 1979, it has a national membership of approximately 50,000, with 635 chapters throughout the United States, Puerto Rico, the Virgin Islands, and Guam.

The VVA has a network of national service officers who are trained advocates to assist Vietnam veterans and their family members with VA claims and appeals. As with many other VSOs, their advocates are certified by the VA to represent veterans in such matters.

You can contact the VVA at

Vietnam Veterans of America
8605 Cameron St., Suite 400
Silver Spring, MD 20910
Phone 301-585-4000
Web site www.vva.org

Chapter 18

Ten Tips for Avoiding Problems with Your VA Benefit Claims

In This Chapter

▶ Instructions about instructions

▶ Communicating with the VA

▶ Dealing with deadlines

*W*orking with a government agency — any government agency — can be frustrating. It seems at times that government employees must attend a special school that teaches methods to make things more complicated. These well-meaning people don't do this on purpose, I'm sure they don't. It's just that they're saddled with a bunch of laws and regulations imposed on them by Congress and other high-ranking policy officials. They're required to make sure all the i's are dotted and all the t's are crossed. But if you follow some simple rules, you'll find that dealing with the Department of Veterans Affairs (VA) is much less frustrating.

Don't Try to Go It Alone

There are dozens of veterans benefits, and each one has different forms, procedures, and qualifications. This book helps you understand many of them, but it's still a good idea to get expert advice and help when preparing a claim for benefits.

Numerous people and organizations are able to help you, including veterans service organizations (VSOs), counselors at VA regional offices and vet centers, representatives at various state veteran offices, and even lawyers who specialize in veterans affairs. Chapter 17 includes a list of folks who can help with veterans benefit claims.

Read the Instructions Carefully

Yes, I know reading instructions isn't much fun. Half the time when I try to put something together, I skip reading the instructions, only to find out that I did it the hard way. Had I read the instructions in the first place, I would have saved hours. VA forms are much the same way. Taking a few extra minutes to read the instructions can save you loads of time. Sometimes a particular VA form is used to file for more than one benefit. The instructions will tell you which part(s) of the form to complete for which benefit(s).

For example, the same form is used to apply for both disability compensation and a VA pension (see Chapter 6), but the form has separate areas to fill out for each. Because the law says you can't receive both disability compensation and a VA pension at the same time, you only need to complete the section of the form that applies to the benefit you want. The instructions also usually include information about where to file the claim. Sending your claim to the wrong place can add months to the processing time.

Answer All the Questions

This may seem obvious, but many people leave a question field blank if they think it doesn't apply to them or they don't know the information. That's a mistake when dealing with the VA. When the VA employees review the claim, they don't know if you left the question blank on purpose or if you simply didn't see it or if you forgot to answer it. That means they'll probably stop the process and send the form back to you with a letter requesting more information. It's much better to write "Unknown" or "None" or "Not Applicable" on the form than to leave the area blank.

If you have an unusual situation that requires lengthy answers, feel free to attach separate sheets of paper. For example, if the form asks for your child's Social Security number and you don't have one yet because the child was recently born, explain that. Don't just leave the area blank.

Include Only Relevant Information

Make sure any evidence or information you include with your claim is directly related to the claim. Remember, it's the quality, not the quantity, that counts. Including information and background that has nothing to do with your claim just wastes time. The reviewing officials then have to sort through the irrelevant information to find the stuff that directly supports your claim. That's not only a bummer for them, but it can result in a significant delay of processing your claim.

Use Your Claim Number

When you file a claim for a VA benefit, you're issued a claim number. Everything is computerized these days, and this number is the VA's reference to the location where all of your claim information is located. Write your claim number on all correspondence and all forms you complete in relation to your existing claim. Otherwise, your information may wander around the halls of the VA for a time before it finally reaches the right place.

Don't make the rookie mistake of writing your claim number only on the envelope. Usually the envelopes are opened and discarded in the mailroom, so the number and the envelope's contents are forever separated.

Keep the VA Informed

The folks who work at the VA aren't psychic. They have no way of knowing if you moved, changed your phone number, had a kid, got married, got divorced, or whatever unless you tell them. Because many of these factors affect your eligibility for benefits and how much you may receive in benefits, you want to let the VA know about these changes as soon as possible so they can be included when considering your claim.

Don't assume that one section of the VA talks to another section. For example, if you're receiving healthcare at a VA medical center (see Chapter 4) and also have a claim pending for disability compensation with the VA regional office (see Chapter 6), don't assume that if you change your address at the VA medical center that the VA regional center will know about it. You need to notify both centers.

Meet the Time Limits

If you receive a letter from the VA about your claim and it states you have a certain amount of time to respond, you better take the deadline seriously. In most cases, these time limits are established by law. If you fail to respond in the required time frame, it may result in an automatic denial of your claim, and then you have to start the process all over.

Usually, the time frame (which is normally 30 or 60 days) is established from the date the VA mailed the request to you to the date your answer is post-marked. Remember, you don't have to wait until the last minute to respond. The quicker you respond, the less time your claim is delayed.

Read VA Correspondence Carefully

Correspondence from the VA is often loaded with useful information. For example, it may include a required time frame during which you must respond to keep your claim open, or it may provide you with information about how you can get even more goodies from the VA. Don't make the mistake of reading just the first page. Every page is important.

I knew a veteran who applied for and received VA disability compensation. He was excited when his claim was approved, but he failed to read beyond the first page of the approval letter, which stated how much money he would get. Had he read further, he would have known that if he ever got married (he was single at the time), he could apply for an increase in benefits. He didn't find out about that until I told him (several months after his marriage).

Establish a Filing System

Every piece of paper you receive from the VA is important. File a copy of everything in one place and arrange it chronologically. Make sure your loved ones know where the information is filed in case they have to carry on for you if you're sick or hospitalized. If a problem occurs with your claim, this correspondence (arranged chronologically) can help you form an appeal.

When you speak with someone on the phone about your claim, keep notes and make sure they're specific (date, time, subject, and the name of the person you talked to). Keep these notes in your filing system.

Keep Your Appointments

If you're scheduled for an appointment for a hearing on your claim or for a physical examination in support of your claim, do everything possible to be there. If you miss an appointment for a hearing, you may not get another chance to explain your side of the issue. If the VA does agree to reschedule the hearing, it could delay your claim or appeal by months. If you miss a medical examination in support of your claim, it can also take months to reschedule the exam.

Claims and appeals already take long enough to grind their way through the system. No need to add to this time just because you decide that you'd rather take in a movie instead of going to a boring hearing or medical examination.

Chapter 19

Ten Tips for Traveling via the Military

In This Chapter

▶ Planning your space-available travel

▶ Arriving at the terminal prepared for adventure

▶ Getting home again

Many veterans and their family members can travel for free on military aircraft by using the space-available travel program (often referred to as "space A"; I cover this program in more depth in Chapter 16). Although this is a valuable benefit, space-A travel can often be frustrating.

Take it from a space-A travel veteran: Maintaining a strong sense of humor and a rigid policy of flexibility is the key to a successful space-A experience. Here are some tips designed to keep you from pulling out your hair when trying to get from here to there when traveling with the military.

Choose Your Departure Terminal with Forethought

Generally speaking, military air terminals on the West Coast have more scheduled flights to Pacific locations, such as Japan, Hawaii, Alaska, Korea, Australia, and Guam, while terminals on the East Coast have the most flights to Europe and the Middle East. You need to plan your travel itinerary accordingly.

Also keep in mind that military terminals located in commercial airports are mostly contract flights, and the military generally fills those with space-required passengers. You have a much better chance of "catching a hop" (to use the common military phrase) from a terminal located on a military base than from a terminal located in a commercial airport.

Time Your Travel Wisely

If possible, travel during off-peak space-A travel periods. Historically, February through March and October through November are low travel periods, and your chances to get out quickly on a space-A hop are much greater. (Peak periods are the summer months when school is out and during the Christmas holiday season.)

Sign Up from the Comfort of Home

Don't waste your time standing in line at the terminal to sign up for a space-A flight. Most terminals now allow remote signup, which allows you to put your name on the space-A waiting list via fax, and sometimes even by e-mail. (Flip to Chapter 16 for contact information.) The advantage of this system is that your name stays on the waiting list for up to 60 days, getting closer and closer to the top every day.

I recommend signing up for a space-A flight three to four weeks before your desired date of travel. That way when you get to the terminal, you should get a seat fairly quickly. You can call the terminal at any time to find out where you stand on the waiting list.

Plan for Flexibility

When you want to travel around the world, you can often get where you want to go by any number and combination of routes and stops. You may feel like you're playing a game of connect the dots, but with a little patience and flexibility, you will reach your destination.

For example, if you want to get to Japan, consider listing Korea as one of your destination choices. You can then sign up for a flight to Japan at the military air terminal in Korea. Both Osan and Kunsan air bases in Korea generally have several flights per week to Japan.

Double-Check Your Travel Documents

Although active-duty military members can travel to most countries by using their military ID card and leave (vacation) orders, family members and veterans usually need a valid passport. Some countries require a visa or may require that certain vaccinations be current. Use the State Department's Web site at www.state.gov to check for required travel documents. Nothing is more frustrating than arriving at the military flight terminal, having your name called for a space-A flight, and then discovering that you can't board because you don't have the right travel documents.

Pack Lightly

As a space-A traveler, you can check two pieces of luggage, weighing up to 70 pounds each, per person. Family members traveling together can pool their baggage allowance as long as the total doesn't exceed the total allowance. However, I strongly recommend that you travel lightly. Take only what is essential for your trip. Why? Because you can't check your bags until your name is called for your flight. That means you have to haul your bags with you everywhere while you wait.

Although some terminals have baggage lockers, many don't. Additionally, because this is space-available travel, you may not get a flight on the same day you arrive at the terminal, so you and your bags will be stuck waiting overnight somewhere. Also, don't place valuables, medicine, or important documents in your checked baggage. That's good advice, no matter how you travel.

Arrive Ready to Go

Call the terminal to find out when the space-A showtime is for your flight. (Terminal phone numbers are listed in Chapter 16.) Don't confuse showtime with departure time. The space-A showtime is the listed time that they plan to select passengers from the space-A list. If you're not there to accept when your name is called, they move on to the next person on the list, and you miss your chance for that flight. Arrive at least one hour before the scheduled showtime. Sometimes they call for space A earlier than scheduled.

It can really make your blood pressure rise when you arrive at the terminal and lug all of your baggage in, just to find out that all the space-A seats have already been taken. When your name is called, sometimes it's only minutes until you go through security for boarding, so be all set and ready to go.

Be Financially Prepared

Remember, you may not travel on the same day you arrive at the terminal. You need to have funds available to stay overnight, or possibly for several days, because most military terminals close at night. Sometimes veterans can stay at an on-base lodging facility for a relatively inexpensive fee (I cover these options in Chapter 16). But you can't count on these being available, so you may need to seek commercial lodging off-base.

Additionally, if you have to return home before a certain date, remember that your return travel is also space available. If you can't get a return space-A flight that fits your schedule, you need to be prepared to purchase a commercial airline ticket.

Purchase an In-Flight Meal

Meals on most commercial airlines leave much to be desired these days. Thankfully, I can't say that about the in-flight meals available for a nominal fee on military aircraft.

Often called "boxed lunches" or "boxed meals," these munchies are very good, in my humble opinion. Options include a healthy-heart menu, breakfast menu, snacks, and a sandwich meal. Prices usually range from $1.35 to $5.00, depending on your choice. You can also bring your own food and drinks aboard. Sorry, alcoholic beverages aren't allowed.

Sign Up Immediately on Arrival for Your Return Flight

As soon as you get to your destination, take a few moments before you leave the terminal and sign up for your return flight. Your name remains on the waiting list for 60 days, which means that while you're out and about taking in the sights and eating too much rich food, you're getting closer and closer to the top of the list for your return flight.

It's often more difficult for veterans and family members to return to the United States than to depart from it. That's because those traveling on passports must enter the States through designated customs and immigration points, whereas active-duty members can enter the United States at virtually any military terminal.

Part VI
Appendixes

The 5th Wave   By Rich Tennant

"Can you explain your benefit program again, this time without using the phrase 'yada, yada, yada?'"

In this part . . .

All through this book, I tell you about various VA contacts and facilities that handle a multitude of benefits and tasks. For details on where and how to find these resources, look no further than the appendixes in this part.

Appendix A

Contacts for State & U.S. Territory Veterans Benefits

●●●

*1*n addition to the federal veterans benefits explained throughout this book, many states and U.S. territories offer a wide variety of benefits to their veteran residents.

Available benefits and eligibility criteria differ from one location to another. It depends on laws passed by individual state or territorial legislatures. Examples of benefits that may be offered include income and property tax breaks, education assistance, discount fishing and hunting licenses, special license plates, free vehicle registration, state veterans pensions, employment preference, housing assistance and home loans, passes to state parks and camping areas, free or reduced public transportation, and job training.

So what are you waiting for? There may be some great goodies just waiting for you to check them out!

ALABAMA
Department of Veterans Affairs
RSA Plaza, Suite 530
770 Washington Ave.
Montgomery, AL 36130-2755
Phone 334-242-5077
Web site www.va.state.
al.us

ALASKA
Department of Military &
Veterans Affairs
Office of Veterans Affairs
P.O. Box 5800
Camp Denali
Fort Richardson, AK 99505-
5800
Phone 907-428-6016
Web site www.ak-
prepared.com/
vetaffairs

AMERICAN SAMOA
Office of Veterans Affairs
American Samoa Government
P.O. Box 8586
Pago Pago, AS 96799
Phone 001-684-633-4206

ARIZONA
Arizona Veterans Service Commission
3839 N. Third St., Suite 200
Phoenix, AZ 85012
Phone 602-255-3373
Web site www.azdvs.gov

ARKANSAS
Department of Veterans Affairs
Building 65, Room 119
2200 Fort Roots Dr.
North Little Rock, AK 72114
Phone 501-370-3820
Web site www.veterans.arkansas.gov

CALIFORNIA
Department of Veterans Affairs
1227 O St., Room 200A
Sacramento, CA 95814
Phone 800-952-5626
Web site www.cdva.ca.gov

COLORADO
Division of Veterans Affairs
7465 E. First Ave., Unit C
Denver, CO 80230
Phone 303-343-1268
Web site www.dmva.state.co.us

CONNECTICUT
Department of Veterans Affairs
287 West St.
Rocky Hill, CT 06067
Phone 800-550-0000
or 860-529-2571
Web site www.ct.gov

DELAWARE
Commission of Veterans Affairs
Robbins Building
802 Silver Lake Blvd., Suite 100
Dover, DE 19904
Phone 800-344-9900
or 302-739-2792
Web site veteransaffairs.
delaware.gov

DISTRICT OF COLUMBIA
Office of Veterans Affairs
One Judiciary Square
441 Fourth St. NW, Suite 570S
Washington, DC 20001
Phone 202-724-5454
Web site ova.dc.gov

FLORIDA
Department of Veterans Affairs
4040 Esplanade Way, Suite 152
Tallahassee, FL 32399-0950
Phone 727-319-7421
Web site www.floridavets.org

GEORGIA
Department of Veterans Service
Floyd Veterans Memorial Building,
Suite E-970
Atlanta, GA 30334-4800
Phone 404-656-2300
Web site sdvs.georgia.gov

GUAM
Office of Veterans Affairs
P.O. Box 3279
Agana, Guam 96932
Phone 671-475-4222

HAWAII
Office of Veterans Services
459 Patterson Road
E-Wing, Room 1-A103
Honolulu, HI 96819
Phone 808-433-0420
Web site www.dod.state.hi.us/
doddod/ovs

IDAHO
Idaho State Veterans Services
320 Collins Road
Boise, ID 83702
Phone 208-334-3513
Web site www.veterans.
idaho.gov

ILLINOIS
Department of Veterans Affairs
833 S. Spring St.
P.O. Box 19432
Springfield, IL 62794-9432
Phone 217-782-6641
Web site www.veterans.
illinois.gov

INDIANA
Department of Veterans Affairs
302 W. Washington St., Room E120
Indianapolis, IN 46204-2738
Phone 800-400-4520 or 317-232-3910
Web site www.in.gov/dva

IOWA
Department of Veterans Affairs
7105 NW 70th Ave.
Camp Dodge, Building A6A
Johnston, IA 50131-1824
Phone 800-838-4692 or 515-242-5331
Web site www.iowava.org

KANSAS
Commission on Veterans' Affairs
Jayhawk Tower, Suite 701
700 SW Jackson St.
Topeka, KS 66603-3743
Phone 785-296-3976
Web site www.kcva.org

KENTUCKY
Department of Veterans Affairs
1111 Louisville Road
Frankfort, KY 40601
Phone 502-564-9203
Web site veterans.ky.gov

LOUISIANA
Department of Veterans Affairs
1885 Wooddale Blvd.
P.O. Box 94095, Capitol Station
Baton Rouge, LA 70804-9095
Phone 225-922-0500
Web site www.vetaffairs.com

MAINE
Bureau of Veterans Services
117 State House Station
Augusta, ME 04333-0117
Phone 207-626-4464
Web site www.maine.gov/
dvem/bvs

MARYLAND
Department of Veterans Affairs
Federal Building, Room 1231
31 Hopkins Plaza

Baltimore, MD 21201
Phone 800-446-4926 or 410-230-4444
Web site www.mdva.state.md.us

MASSACHUSETTS
Department of Veterans' Services
600 Washington St., Suite 1100
Boston, MA 02111
Phone 617-210-5480
Web site mass.gov/veterans

MICHIGAN
Department of Military and
Veterans Affairs
3423 N. M.L. King Jr. Blvd.
Lansing, MI 48906
Phone 517-335-6523
Web site www.michigan.gov/dmva

MINNESOTA
Department of Veterans Affairs
State Veterans Service Building
20 W. 12th St., Room 206C
St. Paul, MN 55155-2006
Phone 651-296-2562
Web site www.mdva.state.mn.us

MISSISSIPPI
State Veterans Affairs Board
P.O. Box 5947
Pearl, MS 39288-5947
Phone 601-576-4850
Web site www.vab.state.ms.us

MISSOURI
Missouri Veterans Commission
205 Jefferson St.
12th Floor Jefferson Building
P.O. Drawer 147
Jefferson City, MO 65102
Phone 573-751-3779
Web site www.mvc.dps.mo.gov

MONTANA
Veterans Affairs Division
1900 Williams St.
P.O. Box 5715
Helena, MT 59604-5715
Phone 406-324-3740
Web site dma.mt.gov/mvad

NEBRASKA
Department of Veterans Affairs
P.O. Box 95083
301 Centennial Mall South,
6th Floor
Lincoln, NE 68509-5083
Phone 402-471-2458
Web site www.vets.state.
ne.us

NEVADA
Office of Veterans Services
5460 Reno Corporate Dr.
Reno, NV 89511
Phone 775-688-1653
Web site www.veterans.nv.gov

NEW HAMPSHIRE
State Veterans Council
275 Chestnut St., Room 517
Manchester, NH 03101-2411
Phone 800-622-9230
or 603-624-9230
Web site www.nh.gov/
nhveterans

NEW JERSEY
Department of Military and
Veterans Affairs
P.O. Box 340
Trenton, NJ 08625-0340
Phone 888-865-8387
Web site www.state.nj.us/
military

NEW MEXICO
Department of Veterans Services
P.O. Box 2324
Santa Fe, NM 87504-2324
Phone 505-827-6300
Web site www.dvs.state.nm.us

NEW YORK
Division of Veterans' Affairs
5 Empire State Plaza, Suite 2836
Albany, NY 12223-1551
Phone 888-838-7697
Web site www.veterans.
state.ny.us

NORTH CAROLINA
Division of Veterans Affairs
1315 Mail Service Center
Raleigh, NC 27699-1315
Phone 919-733-3851
Web site www.ncveterans.net

NORTH DAKOTA
Department of Veterans Affairs
4201 38th St. SW, Suite 104
P.O. Box 9003
Fargo, ND 58106-9003
Phone 866-634-8387 or 701-239-7165
Web site www.nd.gov/veterans

OHIO
Department of Veterans Services
77 S. High St., 7th Floor
Columbus, OH 43215
Phone 877-644-6838 or
614-644-0898
Web site dvs.ohio.gov

OKLAHOMA
Department of Veterans Affairs
P.O. Box 53067
Oklahoma City, OK 73152
Phone 405-521-3684
Web site www.ok.gov/ODVA

OREGON
Department of Veterans Affairs
700 Summer St. NE
Salem, OR 97301-1285
Phone 800-828-8801 or 503-373-2000
Web site www.odva.state.or.us

PENNSYLVANIA
Department of Military and
Veterans Affairs
Bldg S-0-47, FTIG
Annville, PA 17003
Phone 800-547-2838
Web site www.milvet.state.pa.us

PUERTO RICO
Apartado 11737
Fernandez Juncos Station
San Juan, PR 00910-1737
Phone 787-758-5760
Web site www.nasdva.com/puertorico.html

RHODE ISLAND
Division of Veterans Affairs
480 Metacom Ave.
Bristol, RI 02809
Phone 401-253-8000, ext. 695
Web site www.dhs.state.ri.us/dhs/dvetaff.htm

SOUTH CAROLINA
Office of Veterans' Affairs
1205 Pendleton St., Suite 369
Columbia, SC 29201
Phone 803-734-0200
Web site www.oepp.sc.gov/va

SOUTH DAKOTA
Department of Military and
Veterans Affairs
Soldiers & Sailors Memorial
Building

425 E. Capitol Ave.
Pierre, SD 57501
Phone 877-579-0015 or 605-773-3269
Web site www.state.sd.us/applications/MV91MVA
InternetRewrite/Default.asp

TENNESSEE
Department of Veterans Affairs
215 Eighth Ave. N.
Nashville, TN 37243
Phone 615-741-2931
Web site www.state.tn.us/veteran

TEXAS
Texas Veterans Commission
State Headquarters Office
P.O. Box 12277
Austin, TX 78711-2277
Phone 800-252-8387 or 512-463-5538
Web site www.tvc.state.tx.us

UTAH
Department of Veterans Affairs
550 Foothill Blvd. #202
Salt Lake City, UT 84108
Phone 800-894-9497 or 801-326-2372
Web site veterans.utah.gov

VERMONT
Office of Veterans Affairs
118 State St.
Montpelier, VT 05620
Phone 802-828-3379
Web site www.va.state.vt.us

VIRGIN ISLANDS
Office of Veterans Affairs
1013 Estate Richmond
Christiansted, St Croix, VI 00820-4349
Phone 340-733-6663
Web site www.nasdva.com/usvirginislands.html

VIRGINIA
Department of Veterans Services
900 E. Main St.
Richmond, VA 23219
Phone 804-786-0286
Web site www.dvs.virginia.
gov

WASHINGTON
Department of Veterans Affairs
1102 Quince St. SE
P.O. Box 41150
Olympia, WA 98504
Phone 800-562-0132
or 360-725-2200
Web site www.dva.wa.gov

WEST VIRGINIA
Division of Veteran's Affairs
1321 Plaza East, Suite 101
Charleston, WV 25301
Phone 888-838-2332
or 304-558-3661
Web site www.wvs.state.
wv.us/va

WISCONSIN
Department of Veterans Affairs
30 W. Mifflin St.
P.O. Box 7843
Madison, WI 53707-7843
Phone 800-947-8387
or 608-266-1311
Web site dva.state.wi.us

WYOMING
Wyoming Veterans Commission
851 Werner Court #120
Casper, WY 82601
Phone 307-265-7372

Appendix B

VA Regional Benefits Offices

*T*he Department of Veterans Affairs operates more than 1,300 major facilities throughout the United States and its territories. In this chapter you can find the addresses and phone numbers of VA Regional Benefits Offices. For information on Medical Centers, Vet Centers, and National Cemeteries, see appendixes C, D, and E.. Information about most of these facilities can also be found at the VA Web site at www.va.gov.

Alabama

Montgomery Regional Office
345 Perry Hill Road
Montgomery, AL 36109
Phone 800-827-1000

Alaska

Anchorage Regional Office
2925 DeBarr Road
Anchorage, AK 99508-2989
Phone 800-827-1000

American Samoa

VA American Samoa CBOC
Fiatele Teo Army Reserve
Building
P.O. Box 1005
Pago Pago, AS 96799
Phone 684-699-3730

Arizona

Western Area Office
3333 N. Central Ave., Suite 3026
Phoenix, AZ 85012-2402
Phone 800-827-1000

Phoenix Regional Office
3333 N. Central Ave.
Phoenix, AZ 85012
Phone 800-827-1000

Arkansas

North Little Rock Regional Office
2200 Fort Roots Drive, Building 65
North Little Rock, AR 72114-1756
Phone 800-827-1000

California

Los Angeles Regional Office
Federal Building, 11000 Wilshire
Blvd.
Los Angeles, CA 90024
Phone 800-827-1000

Oakland Regional Office
1301 Clay St., Room 1300 North
Oakland, CA 94612
Phone 800-827-1000

San Diego Regional Office
8810 Rio San Diego Dr.
San Diego, CA 92108
Phone 800-827-1000

Colorado

Denver Regional Office
155 Van Gordon St.
Lakewood, CO 80228
Phone 800-827-1000

Connecticut

Hartford Regional Office
555 Willard Ave.
Newington, CT 06111
Phone 800-827-1000

Delaware

Wilmington Regional Office
1601 Kirkwood Highway
Wilmington, DE 19805
Phone 800-827-1000

District of Columbia

Washington D.C. Regional Office
1722 I St. N.W.
Washington, DC 20421
Phone 800-827-1000

Florida

St. Petersburg Regional Office
9500 Bay Pines Blvd.
St. Petersburg, FL 33708
Mailing Address:
P.O. Box 1437
St. Petersburg , FL 33731
Phone 800-827-1000

Georgia

Atlanta Regional Office
1700 Clairmont Road
Decatur, GA 30033
Phone 800-827-1000

Hawaii

Honolulu Regional Office
459 Patterson Road, E-Wing
Honolulu, HI 96819-1522
Phone 800-827-1000

Idaho

Boise Regional Office
805 W. Franklin St.
Boise, ID 83702

Illinois

Chicago Regional Office
2122 W. Taylor St.
Chicago, IL 60612
Phone 800-827-1000

Indiana

Indianapolis Regional Office
575 N. Pennsylvania St.
Indianapolis, IN 46204
Phone 800-827-1000

Iowa

Des Moines VA Regional Office
210 Walnut St.
Des Moines, IA 50309
Phone 800-827-1000

Kansas

Wichita Regional Office
5500 E. Kellogg
Wichita, KS 67211
Phone 800-827-1000

Kentucky

Louisville Regional Office
321 W. Main St., Suite 390
Louisville, KY 40202

Louisiana

New Orleans Regional Office
701 Loyola Ave.
New Orleans, LA 70113

Mailing Address:
671 A Whitney Ave.
Gretna, LA 70056
Phone 800-827-1000

Maine

Togus VA Medical/Regional Office Center
1 VA Center
Togus, ME 04330
Phone 800-827-1000

Maryland

Baltimore Regional Office
31 Hopkins Plaza
Baltimore, MD 21201
Phone 800-827-1000

Massachusetts

Boston VA Regional Office
JFK Federal Building
Boston, MA 02203
Phone 800-827-1000

Michigan

Detroit Regional Office
Patrick V. McNamara Federal Building
477 Michigan Ave.
Detroit, MI 48226
Phone 800-827-1000

Minnesota

St. Paul Regional Office
1 Federal Drive, Fort Snelling
St. Paul, MN 55111-4050
Phone 800-827-1000

Mississippi

Jackson Regional Office
1600 E. Woodrow Wilson Ave.
Jackson, MS 39216
Phone 800-827-1000

Missouri

St. Louis Regional Office
400 S. 18th St.
St. Louis, MO 63103
Phone 800-827-1000

Montana

Fort Harrison Medical and
Regional Office
William Street off Highway
Fort Harrison, MT 59636
Mailing Address:
3633 Veterans Dr., P.O. Box 188
Fort Harrison, MT 59636
Phone 800-827-1000

Nebraska

Lincoln Regional Office
5631 S. 48th St.
Lincoln, NE 68516
Phone 800-827-1000

Nevada

Reno Regional Office
5460 Reno Corporate Dr.
Reno, NV 89511
Phone 800-827-1000

New Hampshire

Manchester Regional Office
Norris Cotton Federal Building
275 Chestnut St.
Manchester, NH 03101
Phone 800-827-1000

New Jersey

Newark Regional Office
20 Washington Place
Newark, NJ 07102
Phone 800-827-1000

New Mexico

Albuquerque Regional Office
500 Gold Ave. SW
Albuquerque, NM 87102
Phone 800-827-1000

New York

Buffalo Regional Office
130 S. Elmwood Ave.
Buffalo, NY 14202-2478
Phone 800-827-1000

New York Regional Office
245 W. Houston St.
New York, NY 10014
Phone 800-827-1000

North Carolina

Winston-Salem Regional Office
Federal Building
251 N. Main St.
Winston-Salem, NC 27155
Phone 800-827-1000

North Dakota

Fargo Regional Office
2101 Elm St.
Fargo, ND 58102-2417
Phone 701-451-4600

Ohio

Cleveland Regional Office
A. J. Celebrezze Federal Building
1240 E. 9th St.
Cleveland, OH 44199

Oklahoma

Central Area Office
Federal Building
125 S. Main St.
Muskogee, OK 74401-7025

Oregon

Portland Regional Office
1220 SW 3rd Ave.
Portland, OR 97204
Phone 800-827-1000

Pennsylvania

Philadelphia Regional Office
5000 Wissahickon Ave.
Philadelphia, PA 19101
Phone 800-827-1000

Pittsburgh Regional Office
1000 Liberty Ave.
Pittsburgh, PA 15222
Phone 800-827-1000

Puerto Rico

San Juan Regional Office
150 Carlos Chardon Ave.
Hato Rey, PR 00918
Phone 800-827-1000

Rhode Island

Providence Regional Office
380 Westminster Mall
Providence, RI 02903
Phone 800-827-1000

South Carolina

Columbia Regional Office
1801 Assembly St.
Columbia, SC 29201
Phone 800-827-1000

South Dakota

Sioux Falls Regional Office
2501 W. 22nd St.
Sioux Falls, SD 57117
Phone 800-827-1000

Tennessee

Southern Area Office
3322 West End, Suite 408
Nashville, TN 37203
Phone 800-827-1000

Nashville Regional Office
110 9th Ave. S.
Nashville, TN 37203
Phone 800-827-1000

Texas

Houston Regional Office
6900 Almeda Road
Houston, TX 77030
Phone 800-827-1000

Waco Regional Office
1 Veterans Plaza, 701 Clay Ave.
Waco, TX 76799
Phone 800-827-1000

Utah

Salt Lake City Regional Office
550 Foothill Dr.
Salt Lake City, UT 84158
Phone 800-827-1000

Vermont

White River Junction Regional
Office
215 N. Main St.
White River Junction, VT 05009
Phone 800-827-1000

Virginia

Roanoke Regional Office
210 Franklin Road SW
Roanoke, VA 24011
Phone 800-827-1000

Washington

Seattle Regional Office
Federal Building
915 2nd Ave.
Seattle, WA 98174
Phone 800-827-1000

West Virginia

Huntington Regional Office
640 Fourth Ave.
Huntington, WV 25701
Phone 800-827-1000

Wisconsin

Milwaukee Regional Office
5400 W. National Ave.
Milwaukee, WI 53214
Phone 800-827-1000

Wyoming

Cheyenne VA Medical/Regional Office
Center
2360 E. Pershing Blvd.
Cheyenne, WY 82001
Phone 800-827-1000

Appendix C

VA Medical Centers

• •

*T*his appendix contains the addresses and phone numbers of VA Medical Centers all over the USA. For more information about most of these facilities, please visit the VA Web site at www.va.gov.

Alabama

Birmingham VA Medical
Center
700 S. 19th St.
Birmingham, AL 35233
Phone 866-487-4243 or
205-933-8101

Central Alabama Veterans
Health Care System East
Campus
2400 Hospital Road
Tuskegee, AL 36083-5001
Phone 800-214-8387 or
334-727-0550

Central Alabama Veterans
Health Care System West
Campus
215 Perry Hill Road
Montgomery, AL 36109-
3798
Phone 800-214-8387 or
334-272-4670

Tuscaloosa VA Medical
Center
3701 Loop Road
East Tuscaloosa, AL 35404
Phone 888-269-3045 or
205-554-2000

Alaska

Alaska VA Healthcare System and
Regional Office
2925 DeBarr Road
Anchorage, AK 99508-2989
Phone 888-353-7574 or 907-257-4700

Arizona

Northern Arizona VA Health Care
System
500 N. Highway 89
Prescott, AZ 86313
Phone 800-949-1005 or 928-445-4860

Phoenix VA Health Care System
650 E. Indian School Road
Phoenix, AZ 85012
Phone 800-554-7174 or 602-277-5551

Southern Arizona VA Health Care
System
3601 S. 6th Ave.
Tucson, AZ 85723
Phone 800-470-8262 or 520-792-1450

VA Southwest Health Care Network
6950 E. Williams Field Road
Mesa, AZ 85212-6033
Phone 602-222-2681

Arkansas

Eugene J. Towbin Healthcare Center
2200 Fort Roots Dr.
North Little Rock, AR 72114-1706
Phone 501-257-1000

Fayetteville VA Medical Center
1100 N. College Ave.
Fayetteville, AR 72703
Phone 800-691-8387 or 479-443-4301

John L. McClellan Memorial
Veterans Hospital
4300 W. 7th St.
Little Rock, AR 72205-5484
Phone 501-257-1000

California

Livermore
4951 Arroyo Road
Livermore, CA 94550
Phone 925-373-4700

Menlo Park
795 Willow Road
Menlo Park, CA 94025
Phone 650-614-9997

San Francisco VA Medical Center
4150 Clement St.
San Francisco, CA 94121-1598
Phone 415-221-4810

VA Central California Health Care
System
2615 E. Clinton Ave.
Fresno, CA 93703
Phone 888-826-2838 or 559-225-6100

VA Loma Linda Healthcare System
11201 Benton St.
Loma Linda, CA 92357
Phone 800-741-8387 or 909-825-7084

VA Long Beach Healthcare System
5901 E. 7th St.
Long Beach, CA 90822
Phone 888-769-8387 or 562-826-8000

VA Greater Los Angeles
Healthcare System
11301 Wilshire Blvd.
Los Angeles, CA 90073
Phone 800-952-4852 or
310-478-3711

VA Northern California Health
Care System
10535 Hospital Way
Mather, CA 95655
Phone 800-382-8387 or
916-843-7000

VA Palo Alto Health Care System
3801 Miranda Ave.
Palo Alto, CA 94304-1290
Phone 800-455-0057 or
650-493-5000

VA San Diego Healthcare System
3350 La Jolla Village Dr.
San Diego, CA 92161
Phone 800-331-8387 or
858-552-8585

Colorado

Grand Junction VA Medical Center
2121 North Ave.
Grand Junction, CO 81501
Phone 866-206-6415 or 970-242-0731

Connecticut

Newington Campus
555 Willard Ave.
Newington, CT 06111
Phone 860-666-6951

West Haven Campus
950 Campbell Ave.
West Haven, CT 06516
Phone 203-932-5711

Delaware

Wilmington VA Medical Center
1601 Kirkwood Highway
Wilmington, DE 19805
Phone 800-461-8262 or
302-994-2511

District of Columbia

Washington DC VA Medical Center
50 Irving St., NW
Washington, DC 20422
Phone 888-553-0242
or 202-745-8000

Florida

Bay Pines VA Healthcare System
10000 Bay Pines Blvd.
P.O. Box 5005
Bay Pines, FL 33744
Phone 888-820-0230
or 727-398-6661

James A. Haley Veterans' Hospital
13000 Bruce B. Downs Blvd.
Tampa, FL 33612
Phone 888-716-7787 or 813-972-2000

Lake City VA Medical Center
619 S. Marion Ave.
Lake City, FL 32025-5808
Phone 800-308-8387 or 386-755-3016

Malcom Randall VA Medical Center
1601 S.W. Archer Road
Gainesville, FL 32608-1197
Phone 800-324-8387 or 352-376-1611

Miami VA Healthcare System
1201 N.W. 16th St.
Miami, FL 33125
Phone 888-276-1785 or 305-575-7000

Orlando VA Medical Center
5201 Raymond St.
Orlando, FL 32803
Phone 800-922-7521 or 407-629-1599

West Palm Beach VA Medical Center
7305 N. Military Trail
West Palm Beach, FL 33410-6400
Phone 800-972-8262 or 561-422-8262

Georgia

Atlanta VA Medical Center
1670 Clairmont Road
Decatur, GA 30033
Phone 800-944-9726 or 404-321-6111

Carl Vinson VA Medical Center
1826 Veterans Blvd.
Dublin, GA 31021
Phone 800-595-5229 or 478-272-1210

Charlie Norwood VA Medical Center
1 Freedom Way
Augusta, GA 30904-6285
Phone 800-836-5561 or 706-733-0188

Hawaii

VA Pacific Islands Health Care
System
459 Patterson Road
Honolulu, HI 96819-1522
Phone 800-214-1306 or 808-433-0600

Idaho

Boise VA Medical Center
500 W. Fort St.
Boise, ID 83702
Phone 208-422-1000

Illinois

Edward Hines Jr. VA Hospital
5th & Roosevelt Road
P.O. Box 5000
Hines, IL 60141
Phone 708-202-8387

Jesse Brown VA Medical Center
820 S. Damen Ave.
Chicago, IL 60612
Phone 312-569-8387

Marion VA Medical Center
2401 West Main
Marion, IL 62959
Phone 866-289-3300
or 618-997-5311

North Chicago VA Medical Center
3001 Green Bay Road
North Chicago, IL 60064
Phone 800-393-0865 or 847-688-1900

VA Illiana Health Care System
1900 E. Main St.
Danville, IL 61832-5198
Phone 217-554-3000

Indiana

Fort Wayne Campus
2121 Lake Ave.
Fort Wayne, IN 46805
Phone 800-360-8387 or 260-426-5431

Marion Campus
1700 East 38th St.
Marion, IN 46953-4589
Phone 800-360-8387 or 765-674-3321

Richard L. Roudebush VA Medical
Center
1481 W. 10th St.
Indianapolis, IN 46202
Phone 888-878-6889 or 317-554-0000

Iowa

Des Moines Division
3600 30th St.
Des Moines, IA 50310-5774
Phone 800-294-8387 or 515-699-5999

Iowa City VA Medical Center
601 Highway 6 W.
Iowa City, IA 52246-2208
Phone 800-637-0128 or 319-338-0581

Knoxville Division
1515 W. Pleasant St.
Knoxville, IA 50138
Phone 800-816-8878 or 641-842-3101

Kansas

Colmery-O'Neil VA Medical Center
2200 SW Gage Blvd.
Topeka, KS 66622
Phone 800-574-8387
or 785-350-3111

Dwight D. Eisenhower VA Medical
Center
4101 S. 4th St.
Leavenworth, KS 66048-5055
Phone 800-952-8387
or 913-682-2000

Robert J. Dole VA Medical Center
5500 E. Kellogg
Wichita, KS 67218
Phone 888-878-6881
or 316-685-2221

Kentucky

Leestown Division
2250 Leestown Road
Lexington, KY 40511
Phone 888-824-3577
or 859-233-4511

Lexington VA Medical Center
1101 Veterans Dr.
Lexington, KY 40502-2236
Phone 859-233-4511

Louisville VA Medical Center
800 Zorn Ave.
Louisville, KY 40206
Phone 800-376-8387
or 502-287-4000

Louisiana

Alexandria VA Medical Center
2495 Shreveport Highway 71 N.
Pineville, LA 71360
Mailing Address:
P.O. Box 69004
Alexandria, LA 71306
Phone 318-473-0010 or 800-375-8387

Overton Brooks VA Medical Center
510 E. Stoner Ave.
Shreveport, LA 71101-4295
Phone 800-863-7441 or 318-221-8411

Southeast Louisiana Veterans Health
Care System
1601 Perdido St.
New Orleans, LA 70112
Mailing Address:
P.O. Box 61011
New Orleans, LA 70161-1011
Phone 800-935-8387 or 504-412-3700

Maine

Togus VA Medical Center
1 VA Center
Augusta, ME 04330
Phone 877-421-8263 or 207-623-8411

Maryland

Baltimore VA Medical Center
10 N. Greene St.
Baltimore, MD 21201
Phone 800-463-6295 or 410-605-7000

Baltimore VA Rehabilitation and
Extended Care Center
3900 Loch Raven Blvd.
Baltimore, MD 21218
Phone 410-605-7000

Perry Point VA Medical Center
Perry Point, MD 21902
Phone 800-949-1003
or 410-642-2411

Massachusetts

Brockton Campus
940 Belmont St.
Brockton, MA 02301
Phone 508-583-4500

Edith Nourse Rogers Memorial
Veterans Hospital
200 Springs Road
Bedford, MA 01730
Phone 800-422-1617
or 781-687-2000

Jamaica Plain Campus
150 S. Huntington Ave.
Jamaica Plain, MA 02130
Phone 617-232-9500

Northampton VA Medical Center
421 N. Main St.
Leeds, MA 01053-9764
Phone 800-893-1522
or 413-584-4040

West Roxbury Campus
1400 VFW Parkway
West Roxbury, MA 02132
Phone 617-323-7700

Michigan

Aleda E. Lutz VA Medical Center
1500 Weiss St.
Saginaw, MI 48602
Phone 800-406-5143 or 989-497-2500

Battle Creek VA Medical Center
5500 Armstrong Road
Battle Creek, MI 49037
Phone 888-214-1247 or 269-966-5600

Iron Mountain VA Medical Center
325 E. H St.
Iron Mountain, MI 49801
Phone 906-774-3300

John D. Dingell VA Medical Center
4646 John R
Detroit, MI 48201
Phone 800-511-8056 or 313-576-1000

VA Ann Arbor Healthcare System
2215 Fuller Road
Ann Arbor, MI 48105
Phone 800-361-8387 or 734-769-7100

Minnesota

Minneapolis VA Medical Center
1 Veterans Dr.
Minneapolis, MN 55417
Phone 866-414-5058 or 612-725-2000

St. Cloud VA Medical Center
4801 Veterans Drive
St. Cloud, MN 56303
Phone 800-247-1739 or 320-252-1670

Mississippi

G. V. (Sonny) Montgomery VA
Medical Center
1500 E. Woodrow Wilson Dr.
Jackson, MS 39216
Phone 800-949-1009
or 601-362-4471

VA Gulf Coast Veterans Health
Care System
400 Veterans Ave.
Biloxi, MS 39531
Phone 800-296-8872
or 228-523-5000

Missouri

Harry S. Truman Memorial
800 Hospital Dr.
Columbia, MO 65201-5297
Phone 800-349-8262
or 573-814-6000

Jefferson Barracks Division
1 Jefferson Barracks Dr.
Saint Louis, MO 63125-4101
Phone 800-228-5459
or 314-652-4100

John Cochran Division
915 N. Grand Blvd.
Saint Louis, MO 63106
Phone 800-228-5459
or 314-652-4100

John J. Pershing VA Medical Center
1500 N. Westwood Blvd.
Poplar Bluff, MO 63901
Phone 573-686-4151

Kansas City VA
Medical Center
4801 Linwood Blvd.
Kansas City, MO 64128
Phone 800-525-1483
or 816-861-4700

Montana

VA Montana Health Care System
3687 Veterans Dr.
P.O. Box 1500
Fort Harrison, MT 59636
Phone 406-442-6410

Nebraska

Grand Island Division
2201 N. Broadwell Ave.
Grand Island, NE 68803-2196
Phone 866-580-1810 or 308-382-3660

Lincoln Division
600 S. 70th St.
Lincoln, NE 68510
Phone 866-851-6052 or 402-489-3802

Omaha Division
4101 Woolworth Ave.
Omaha, NE 68105
Phone 800-451-5796 or 402-346-8800

Nevada

Mike O'Callagan Federal Hospital
4700 N. Las Vegas Blvd.
Nellis AFB, NV 89191-6601
Phone 702-653-2260

VA Sierra Nevada Health Care System
1000 Locust St.
Reno, NV 89502
Phone 888-838-6256 or 775-786-7200

VA Southern Nevada Healthcare System
901 Rancho Lane
Las Vegas, NV 89106
Mailing Address:
P.O. Box 360001
North Las Vegas , NV 89036
Phone 888-633-7554 or 702-636-3000

New Hampshire

Manchester VA Medical Center
718 Smyth Road
Manchester, NH 03104
Phone 800-892-8384 or
603-624-4366

New Jersey

East Orange Campus
385 Tremont Ave.
East Orange, NJ 07018
Phone 973-676-1000

Lyons Campus
151 Knollcroft Road
Lyons, NJ 07939
Phone 908-647-0180

New Mexico

New Mexico VA Health Care
System
1501 San Pedro Dr. SE
Albuquerque, NM 87108-5153
Phone 800-465-8262
or 505-265-1711

New York

Albany VA Medical Center Samuel
S. Stratton
113 Holland Ave.
Albany, NY 12208
Phone 518-626-5000

Batavia
222 Richmond Ave.
Batavia, NY 14020
Phone 888-798-2302
or 585-297-1000

Bath VA Medical Center
76 Veterans Ave.
Bath, NY 14810
Phone 877-845-3247 or 607-664-4000

Brooklyn Campus
800 Poly Place
Brooklyn, NY 11209
Phone 718-836-6600

Buffalo
3495 Bailey Ave.
Buffalo, NY 14215
Phone 800-532-8387 or 716-834-9200

Canandaigua VA Medical Center
400 Fort Hill Ave.
Canandaigua, NY 14424
Phone 585-394-2000

Castle Point Campus
Route 9D
Castle Point, NY 12511
Phone 800-269-8749 or 845-831-2000

Franklin Delano Roosevelt Campus
2094 Albany Post Road
Route 9A, P.O. Box 100
Montrose, NY 10548
Phone 800-269-8749 or
914-737-4400, ext. 2400

James J. Peters VA Medical Center
130 W. Kingsbridge Road
Bronx, NY 10468
Phone 800-877-6976 or 718-584-9000

Manhattan Campus
423 East 23rd St.
New York, NY 10010
Phone 212-686-7500

Northport VA Medical Center
79 Middleville Road
Northport, NY 11768
Phone 800-551-3996 or 631-261-4400

Syracuse VA Medical Center
800 Irving Ave.
Syracuse, NY 13210
Phone 800-792-4334
or 315-425-4400

North Carolina

Asheville VA Medical Center
1100 Tunnel Road
Asheville, NC 28805
Phone 800-932-6408
or 828-298-7911

Durham VA Medical Center
508 Fulton St.
Durham, NC 27705
Phone 888-878-6890
or 919-286-0411

Fayetteville VA Medical Center
2300 Ramsey St.
Fayetteville, NC 28301
Phone 800-771-6106
or 910-488-2120

Salisbury – W. G. (Bill) Hefner VA
Medical Center
1601 Brenner Ave.
Salisbury, NC 28144
Phone 800-469-8262
or 704-638-9000

North Dakota

Fargo VA Medical Center
2101 Elm St.
Fargo, ND 58102
Phone 800-410-9723
or 701-232-3241

Ohio

Chalmers P. Wylie Independent
Outpatient Clinic
543 Taylor Ave.
Columbus, OH 43203-1278
Phone 888-615-9448 or 614-257-5200

Chillicothe VA Medical Center
17273 State Route 104
Chillicothe, OH 45601
Phone 800-358-8262 or 740-773-1141

Cincinnati VA Medical Center
3200 Vine St.
Cincinnati, OH 45220
Phone 888-267-7873 or 513-861-3100

Dayton VA Medical Center
4100 W. 3rd St.
Dayton, OH 45428
Phone 800-368-8262 or 937-268-6511

Louis Stokes VA Medical Center
10701 East Blvd.
Cleveland, OH 44106
Phone 216-791-3800

Oklahoma

Jack C. Montgomery VA Medical Center
1011 Honor Heights Dr.
Muskogee, OK 74401
Phone 888-397-8387 or 918-577-3000

Oklahoma City VA Medical Center
921 N.E. 13th St.
Oklahoma City, OK 73104
Phone 866-835-5273 or 405-270-0501

Oregon

Portland VA Medical Center
3710 SW U.S. Veterans
Hospital Road
Portland, OR 97239
Phone 800-949-1004 or 503-220-8262

VA Roseburg Healthcare System
913 NW Garden Valley Blvd.
Roseburg, OR 97470-6513
Phone 800-549-8387
or 541-440-1000

Pennsylvania

Coatesville VA Medical Center
1400 Black Horse Hill Road
Coatesville, PA 19320-2096
Phone 610-384-7711

Erie VA Medical Center
135 E. 38th St.
Erie, PA 16504
Phone 800-274-8387 or 814-868-8661

H. John Heinz III Progressive Care
Center
Delafield Road
Pittsburgh, PA 15260
Phone 866-482-7488
or 412-688-6000

Highland Drive Division
7180 Highland Dr.
Pittsburgh, PA 15206
Phone 866-482-7488
or 412-365-4900

James E. Van Zandt VA
Medical Center
2907 Pleasant Valley Blvd.
Altoona, PA 16602-4377
Phone 814-943-8164

Lebanon VA Medical Center
1700 S. Lincoln Ave.
Lebanon, PA 17042
Phone 800-409-8771 or 717-272-6621

Philadelphia VA Medical Center
University and Woodland Avenues
Philadelphia, PA 19104
Phone 800-949-1001 or 215-823-5800

University Drive Division
University Drive
Pittsburgh, PA 15240
Phone 866-482-7488

VA Butler Healthcare
325 New Castle Road
Butler, PA 16001-2480
Phone 800-362-8262 or 724-287-4781

Wilkes-Barre VA Medical Center
1111 East End Blvd.
Wilkes-Barre, PA 18711
Phone 877-928-2621 or 570-824-3521

Puerto Rico

VA Caribbean Healthcare System
10 Casia St.
San Juan, PR 00921-3201
Phone 800-449-8729 or 787-641-7582

Rhode Island

Providence VA Medical Center
830 Chalkstone Ave.
Providence, RI 02908-4799
Phone 866-590-2976 or 401-273-7100

South Carolina

Ralph H. Johnson VA Medical
Center109 Bee St.

Charleston, SC 29401-5799
Phone 888-878-6884
or 843-577-5011

Wm. Jennings Bryan Dorn VA
Medical Center
6439 Garners Ferry Road
Columbia, SC 29209-1639
Phone 803-776-4000

South Dakota

Fort Meade Campus
113 Comanche Road
Fort Meade, SD 57741
Phone 800-743-1070
or 605-347-2511

Hot Springs Campus
500 N. 5th St.
Hot Springs, SD 57747
Phone 800-764-5370
or 605-745-2000

Sioux Falls VA Medical Center
2501 W. 22nd St.
P.O. Box 5046
Sioux Falls, SD 57117-5046
Phone 800-316-8387
or 605-336-3230

Tennessee

Alvin C. York
(Murfreesboro) Campus
3400 Lebanon Pike
Murfreesboro, TN 37129
Phone 800-876-7093 or 615-867-6000

Memphis VA Medical Center
1030 Jefferson Ave.
Memphis, TN 38104
Phone 800-636-8262
or 901-523-8990

Mountain Home VA Medical Center
Corner of Lamont St. and Veterans Way
P.O. Box 4000
Mountain Home, TN 37684
Phone 877-573-3529 or 423-926-1171

Nashville Campus
1310 24th Ave. S.
Nashville, TN 37212-2637
Phone 800-228-4973 or 615-327-4751

Texas

Amarillo VA Health Care System
6010 Amarillo Blvd. W.
Amarillo, TX 79106
Phone 800-687-8262 or 806-355-9703

Central Texas Veterans Health Care
System
1901 Veterans Memorial Dr.
Temple, TX 76504-7451
Phone 800-423-2111 or 254-778-4811

Dallas VA Medical Center
4500 S. Lancaster Road
Dallas, TX 75216
Phone 800-849-359 or 214-742-8387

El Paso VA Health Care System
5001 No. Piedras St.
El Paso, TX 79930-4211
Phone 800-672-3782 or 915-564-6100

Kerrville VA Medical Center
3600 Memorial Blvd.
Kerrville, TX 78028
Phone 830-896-2020

Michael E. DeBakey VA Medical
Center
2002 Holcombe Blvd.
Houston, TX 77030-4298
Phone 800-553-2278 or 713-791-
1414

Olin E Teague Veterans' Center
1901 Veterans Memorial Dr.

Temple, TX 76504
Phone 800-423 2111
or 254-778-4811

Sam Rayburn Memorial Veterans
Center
1201 E. 9th St.
Bonham, TX 75418
Phone 800-924-8387 or 903-583-
2111

South Texas Veterans Health Care
System
7400 Merton Minter Blvd.
San Antonio, TX 78229

Waco VA Medical Center
4800 Memorial Dr.
Waco, TX 76711
Phone 800-423-2111
or 254-752-6581

West Texas VA Health Care
System
300 Veterans Blvd.
Big Spring, TX 79720
Phone 800-472-1365
or 432-263-7361

Utah

VA Salt Lake City Health Care
System
500 Foothill Dr.
Salt Lake City, UT 84148
Phone 801-582-1565

Vermont

White River Junction VA
Medical Center
215 N. Main St.

White River Junction, VT 05009
Phone 866-687-8387 or 802-295-9363

Virginia

Hampton VA Medical Center
100 Emancipation Dr.
Hampton, VA 23667
Phone 757-722-9961

Hunter Holmes McGuire VA Medical
Center
1201 Broad Rock Blvd.
Richmond, VA 23249
Phone 800-784-8381 or 804-675-5000

Salem VA Medical Center
1970 Roanoke Blvd.
Salem, VA 24153
Phone 888-982-2463 or 540-982-2463

Washington

Jonathan M. Wainwright Memorial VA
Medical Center
77 Wainwright Dr.
Walla Walla, WA 99362
Phone 888-687-8863 or 509-525-5200

Spokane VA Medical Center
4815 N. Assembly St.
Spokane, WA 99205-6197
Phone 800-325-7940 or 509-434-7000

VA Puget Sound Health Care System
1660 S. Columbian Way
Seattle, WA 98108-1597
Phone 800-329-8387 or 206-762-1010

Vancouver Campus
1601 E. 4th Plain Blvd.
Vancouver, WA 98661
Phone 800-949-1004
or 360-696-4061

West Virginia

Beckley VA Medical Center
200 Veterans Ave.
Beckley, WV 25801
Phone 877-902-5142
or 304-255-2121

Clarksburg – Louis A. Johnson VA
Medical Center
1 Medical Center Dr.
Clarksburg, WV 26301
Phone 800-733-0512
or 304-623-3461

Huntington VA Medical Center
1540 Spring Valley Dr.
Huntington, WV 25704
Phone 800-827-8244
or 304-429-6741

Martinsburg VA Medical Center
510 Butler Ave.
Martinsburg, WV 25405
Phone 800-817-3807
or 304-263-0811

Wisconsin

Clement J. Zablocki Veterans
Affairs Medical Center
5000 W. National Ave.
Milwaukee, WI 53295-1000
Phone 888-469-6614
or 414-384-2000

Tomah VA Medical Center
500 E. Veterans St.
Tomah, WI 54660
Phone 800-872-8662 or 608-372-3971

William S. Middleton Memorial Veterans
Hospital
2500 Overlook Terrace
Madison, WI 53705-2286
Phone 608-256-1901

Wyoming

Cheyenne VA Medical Center
2360 E. Pershing Blvd.
Cheyenne, WY 82001
Phone 888-483-9127 or 307-778-7550

Sheridan VA Medical Center
1898 Fort Road
Sheridan, WY 82801
Phone 866-822-6714 or 307-672-3473

Appendix D

Veterans Centers

• •

*1*n this appendix you can find the addresses and phone numbers of the Vet Centers near you. Information about most of these facilities can also be found at the VA Web site at www.va.gov.

Alabama

Birmingham Vet Center
1201 2nd Ave. S.
Birmingham, AL 35233
Phone 205-212-3122

Mobile Vet Center
2577 Government Blvd.
Mobile, AL 36606
Phone 251-478-5906

Montgomery Vet Center
215 Perry Hill Road, Bldg 6,
2nd Floor
Montgomery, AL 36109
Phone 334-272-4670

Alaska

Anchorage Vet Center
4201 Tudor Centre Dr., Suite 115
Anchorage, AK 99508
Phone 907-563-6966

Fairbanks Vet Center
540 4th Ave., Suite 100
Fairbanks, AK 99701
Phone 907-456-4238

Kenai Vet Center Satellite
Bldg. F, Suite 4, Red Diamond Center
43335 Kalifornsky Beach Road
Soldotna, AK 99669
Phone 907-260-7640

Wasilla Vet Center
851 E. West Point Dr., Suite 111
Wasilla, AK 99654
Phone 907-376-4318

Arizona

Chinle Vet Center Outstation
P.O. Box 1934
Chinle, AZ 86503
Phone 928-674-3682

Hopi Vet Center Outstation 2
1 Main St.
P.O. Box 929
Hotevilla, AZ 86030
Phone 928-734-5166

Phoenix East Valley Vet Center
1303 South Longmore, Suite 5
Mesa, AZ 85202
Phone 480-610-6727

Phoenix Vet Center
77 E. Weldon, Suite 100
Phoenix, AZ 85012
Phone 602-640-2981

Prescott Vet Center
161 S. Granite St., Suite B
Prescott, AZ 86303
Phone 928-778-3469

Tucson Vet Center
3055 N. First Ave.
Tucson, AZ 85719
Phone 520-882-0333

Arkansas

Little Rock Vet Center
201 W. Broadway St., Suite A
North Little Rock, AR 72114
Phone 501-324-6395

California

4B Pacific Western Regional Office
420 Executive Court N., Suite G
Fairfield, CA 94534
Phone 707-646-2988

Chico Vet Center
280 Cohasset Road, Suite 100
Chico, CA 95928
Phone 530-899-8549

Concord Vet Center
1899 Clayton Road, Suite 140
Concord, CA 94520
Phone 925-680-4526

Corona Vet Center
800 Magnolia Ave., Suite 110
Corona, CA 82879
Phone 951-734-0525

East Los Angeles Vet Center
5400 E. Olympic Blvd., #140
Commerce, CA 90022
Phone 323-728-9966

Fresno Vet Center
3636 N. 1st St., Suite 112
Fresno, CA 93726
Phone 559-487-5660

Los Angeles Veterans Resource Center
1045 W. Redondo Beach Blvd., Suite 150
Gardena, CA 90247
Phone 310-767-1221

Modesto Vet Center
1219 N. Carpenter Road, Suite 12
Modesto, CA 95351
Phone 209-569-0713

Northbay Vet Center
6225 State Farm Dr., Suite 101
Rohnert Park, CA 94928
Phone 707-586-3295

Oakland Vet Center
1504 Franklin St., Suite 200
Oakland, CA 94612
Phone 510-763-3904

Orange County Vet Center
12453 Lewis St., Suite 101
Garden Grove, CA 92840
Phone 714-776-0161

Peninsula Vet Center
2946 Broadway St.
Redwood City, CA 94062
Phone 650-299-0672

Redwoods Vet Center
2830 G St., Suite A
Eureka, CA 95501
Phone 707-444-8271

Sacramento Vet Center
1111 Howe Ave., Suite #390
Sacramento, CA 95825
Phone 916-566-7430

San Bernardino Vet Center
155 W. Hospitality Lane, Suite 140
San Bernardino, CA 92408
Phone 909-890-0797

San Diego Vet Center
2900 Sixth Ave.
San Diego, CA 92103
Phone 619-294-2040

San Francisco Vet Center
505 Polk St.
San Francisco, CA 94102
Phone 415-441-5051

San Jose Vet Center
278 N. 2nd St.
San Jose, CA 95112
Phone 408-993-0729

San Marcos Vet Center
One Civic Center Dr., Suite 140
San Marcos, CA 92069
Phone 760-744-6914

Santa Cruz County Vet Center
1350 41st Ave., Suite 102
Capitola, CA 95010
Phone 831-464-4575

Sepulveda Vet Center
9737 Haskell Ave.
Sepulveda, CA 91343
Phone 818-892-9227

Ventura Vet Center
790 E. Santa Clara St., Suite 100
Ventura, CA 93001
Phone 805-585-1860

West Los Angeles Vet Center
5730 Uplander Way, Suite 100
Culver City, CA 90230
Phone 310-641-0326

Colorado

Denver Regional Office
4A Western Mountain
789 Sherman St., Suite 570
Denver, CO 80203
Phone 303-393-2897

Boulder Vet Center
2336 Canyon Blvd., Suite 103
Boulder, CO 80302
Phone 303-440-7306

Colorado Springs Vet Center
416 E. Colorado Ave.
Colorado Springs, CO 80903
Phone 719-471-9992

Denver Vet Center
7465 East First Ave., Suite B
Denver, CO 80230
Phone 303-326-0645

Fort Collins Vet Center Outstation
1100 Poudre River Dr. (Lower Level)
Fort Collins, CO 80524
Phone 970-221-5176

Grand Junction Vet Center
2472 F. Road, Unit 16
Grand Junction, CO 81505
Phone 970-245-4156

Pueblo (Colorado Springs Vet Center)
509 E. 13th St., Room 18
Pueblo, CO 81001
Phone 719-546-6666, ext. 133

Connecticut

Norwich Vet Center
2 Cliff St.
Norwich, CT 06360
Phone 860-887-1755

Hartford Vet Center
25 Elm St., Suite A
Rocky Hill, CT 06067
Phone 860-563-8800

New Haven Vet Center
141 Captain Thomas Blvd.
West Haven, CT 06516
Phone 203-932-9899

Delaware

Wilmington Vet Center
VAMC, Bldg 3
1601 Kirkwood Highway
Wilmington, DE 19805
Phone 302-994-1660

District of Columbia

Washington Vet Center
1250 Taylor St., NW
Washington, DC 20011
Phone 202-726-5212

Florida

3A Southeast Regional Office
RCS, 10B/RC3A VA Medical Center,
Bldg. T203
Bay Pines, FL 33744
Phone 727-398-9343

Fort Lauderdale Vet Center
713 NE 3rd Ave.
Fort Lauderdale, FL 33304
Phone 954-356-7926

Fort Myers Vet Center
Lee County Veterans
Service Office
2072 Victoria Ave.

Fort Myers, FL 33901
Phone 239-938-1100

Gainesville Vet Center
105 NW 75th St., Suite 2
Gainesville, FL 32607
Phone 352-331-1408

Jacksonville Vet Center
300 E. State St., Suite J
Jacksonville, FL 32202
Phone 904-232-3621

Key Largo Vet Center Outstation
105662 Overseas Highway
Key Largo, FL 33037
Phone 305-451-0164

Melbourne Vet Center
2098 Sarno Road
Melbourne, FL 32935
Phone 321-254-3410

Miami Vet Center
8280 NW 27th St., Suite 511
Miami, FL 33122
Phone 305-718-3712

Orlando Vet Center
5575 S. Semoran Blvd., #36
Orlando, FL 32822
Phone 407-857-2800

Palm Beach Vet Center
Spectrum Center
2311 10th Ave. N., #13
Lake Worth, FL 33461
Phone 561-585-0441

Pensacola Vet Center
4501 Twin Oaks Dr., Suite 104
Pensacola, FL 32506
Phone 850-456-5886

Sarasota Vet Center
4801 Swift Road, Suite A
Sarasota, FL 34231
Phone 941-927-8285

St. Petersburg Vet Center
2880 1st Ave. N.
St. Petersburg, FL 33713
Phone 727-893-3791

Tallahassee Vet Center
548 Bradford Road
Tallahassee, FL 32303
Phone 850-942-8810

Tampa Vet Center
8900 N. Armenia Ave., #312
Tampa, FL 33604
Phone 813-228-2621

Georgia

Atlanta Vet Center
1440 Dutch Valley Place,
Suite 1100
P.O. Box 55
Atlanta, GA 30324
Phone 404-347-7264

Macon Vet Center
750 Riverside Dr.
Macon, GA 31201
Phone 478-477-3813

North Atlanta Vet Center
930 River Centre Place
Lawrenceville, GA 30043
Phone 770-963-1809

Savannah Vet Center
308 A Commercial Dr.
Savannah, GA 31406
Phone 912-652-4097

Guam

Guam Vet Center
222 Chalan Santo Papa, Reflection
Center Suite 201
Agana Guam, GU 96910
Phone 671-472-7160

Hawaii

Hilo Vet Center
126 Pu'uhonu Way, Suite 2
Hilo, HI 96720
Phone 808-969-3833

Honolulu Vet Center
1680 Kapiolani Blvd., Suite F-3
Honolulu, HI 96814
Phone 808-973-8387

Kailua-Kona Vet Center
73-4976 Kamanu St., Suite 207
Kailua-Kona, HI 96740
Phone 808-329-0574

Kauai Vet Center
3-3367 Kuhio Highway., Ste 101
Lihue, HI 96766
Phone 808-246-1163

Maui Vet Center
35 Lunalilo St., Suite 101
Wailuku, HI 96793
Phone 808-242-8557

Idaho

Boise Vet Center
5440 Franklin Road, Suite 100
Boise, ID 83705
Phone 208-342-3612

Pocatello Vet Center
1800 Garrett Way
Pocatello, ID 83201
Phone 208-232-0316

Illinois

Chicago Veterans Resource Center
7731 S. Halsted St.
Chicago, IL 60620-2412
Phone 773-962-3740

Chicago Heights Vet Center
1600 Halsted St.
Chicago Heights, IL 60411
Phone 708-754-0340

East St. Louis Vet Center
1265 N. 89th St., Suite 5
East St. Louis, IL 62203
Phone 618-397-6602

Evanston Vet Center
565 Howard St.
Evanston, IL 60202
Phone 847-332-1019

Oak Park Vet Center
155 S. Oak Park Ave.
Oak Park, IL 60302
Phone 708-383-3225

Peoria Vet Center
3310 N. Prospect Road
Peoria, IL 61603
Phone 309-688-2170

Quad Cities Vet Center
1529 46th Ave., #6
Moline, IL 61265
Phone 309-762-6954

Rockford Vet Center Outstation
4960 E. State St., #3
Rockford, IL 61108
Phone 815-395-1276

Springfield Vet Center
1227 S. Ninth St.
Springfield, IL 62703
Phone 217-492-4955

Indiana

Evansville Vet Center
311 N. Weinbach Ave.
Evansville, IN 47711
Phone 812-473-5993

Fort Wayne Vet Center
528 W. Berry St.
Fort Wayne, IN 46802
Phone 260-460-1456

Gary Area Vet Center
6505 Broadway Ave.
Merrillville, IN 46410
Phone 219-736-5633

Indianapolis Vet Center
3833 N. Meridian St., Suite 120
Indianapolis, IN 46208
Phone 317-988-1600

Iowa

Cedar Rapids Vet Center Satellite
1642 42nd St. NE
Cedar Rapids, IA 52402
Phone 319-378-0016

Des Moines Vet Center
2600 Martin Luther King Parkway
Des Moines, IA 50310
Phone 515-284-4929

Sioux City Vet Center
1551 Indian Hills Dr., Suite 214
Sioux City, IA 51104
Phone 712-255-3808

Kansas

Manhattan Vet Center
205 S. 4th St., Suite B
Manhattan, KS 66502
Phone 785-587-8257

Wichita Vet Center
251 N. Water St.
Wichita, KS 67202
Phone 316-685-2221

Kentucky

Lexington Vet Center
301 E. Vine St., Suite C
Lexington, KY 40507
Phone 859-253-0717

Louisville Vet Center
1347 S. Third St.
Louisville, KY 40208
Phone 502-634-1916

Louisiana

Baton Rouge Vet Center
5207 Essen Lane, Suite 2
Baton Rouge, LA 70809
Phone 225-757-0042

New Orleans Veterans Resource
Center
2200 Veterans Blvd., Suite 114
Kenner, LA 70062
Phone 504-464-4743

Shreveport Vet Center
2800 Youree Dr.
Bldg. 1, Suite 105
Shreveport, LA 71104
Phone 318-861-1776

Maine

Bangor Vet Center
352 Harlow St., In-Town Plaza
Bangor, ME 04401
Phone 207-947-3391

Caribou Vet Center
York Street Complex
456 York St.
Caribou, ME 04736
Phone 207-496-3900

Lewiston Vet Center
Parkway Complex
29 Westminster St.
Lewiston, ME 04240
Phone 207-783-0068

Portland Vet Center
475 Stevens Ave.
Portland, ME 04103
Phone 207-780-3584

Sanford Vet Center
628 Main St.
Springvale, ME 04083
Phone 207-490-1513

Maryland

1B Mid Atlantic Regional Office
305 W. Chesapeake Ave., Suite 300
Towson, MD 21204
Phone 410-828-6619

Aberdeen Vet Center Outstation 2
223 W. Bel Air Ave.
Aberdeen, MD 21001
Phone 410-272-6771

Baltimore Vet Center
1777 Reisterstown Road, Suite 199
Baltimore, MD 21208
Phone 410-764-9400

Cambridge Vet Center Outstation 1
830 Chesapeake Dr.
Cambridge, MD 21613
Phone 410-228-6305

Elkton Vet Center
103 Chesapeake Blvd., Suite A
Elkton, MD 21921
Phone 410-392-4485

Silver Spring Vet Center
1015 Spring St., Suite 101
Silver Spring, MD 20910
Phone 301-589-1073

Massachusetts

Boston Vet Center
665 Beacon St., Suite 100
Boston, MA 02215
Phone 617-424-0665

Brockton Vet Center
1041L Pearl St.
Brockton, MA 02301
Phone 508-580-2730

Hyannis Vet Center
474 W. Main St.
Hyannis, MA 02601
Phone 508-778-0124

Lowell Vet Center
73 E. Merrimack St.
Lowell, MA 08152
Phone 978-453-1151

New Bedford Vet Center
468 North St.
New Bedford, MA 02740
Phone 508-999-6920

Springfield Vet Center
Northgate Plaza
1985 Main St.
Springfield, MA 01103
Phone 413-737-5167

Worcester Vet Center
691 Grafton St.
Worcester, MA 01604
Phone 508-753-7902

Michigan

Dearborn Vet Center
2881 Monroe St., Suite 100
Dearborn, MI 48124
Phone 313-277-1428

Detroit Vet Center
4161 Cass Ave.
Detroit, MI 48201
Phone 313-831-6509

Escanaba Vet Center
3500 Ludington St., Suite 110
Escanaba , MI 49829
Phone 906-233-0244

Grand Rapids Vet Center
2050 Breton Road SE
Grand Rapids, MI 49546
Phone 616-285-5795

Saginaw Vet Center
4048 Bay Road
Saginaw, MI 48603
Phone 989-321-4650

Minnesota

Duluth Vet Center
405 E. Superior St.
Duluth, MN 55802
Phone 218-722-8654

St. Paul Veterans Resource Center
550 County Road D, Suite 10
New Brighton, MN 55112
Phone 651-644-4022

Mississippi

Biloxi Vet Center
288 Veterans Ave.
Biloxi, MS 39531
Phone 228-388-9938

Jackson Vet Center
1755 Lelia Dr., Suite 104
Jackson, MS 39216
Phone 601-965-5727

Missouri

2 Central Regional Office
2122 Kratky Road
St. Louis, MO 63114
Phone 314-426-5864

Kansas City Vet Center
301 East Armour Blvd., Suite 305
Kansas City, MO 64111
Phone 816-753-1866

St. Louis Vet Center
2901 Olive
St. Louis, MO 63103
Phone 314-531-5355

Montana

Billings Vet Center
1234 Avenue C
Billings, MT 59102
Phone 406-657-6071

Missoula Vet Center
500 N. Iliggins Ave.
Missoula, MT 59802
Phone 406-721-4918

Nebraska

Lincoln Vet Center
920 L St.
Lincoln, NE 68508
Phone 402-476-9736

Omaha Vet Center
2428 Cuming St.
Omaha, NE 68131-1600
Phone 402-346-6735

Nevada

Las Vegas Vet Center
1919 S. Jones Blvd., Suite A
Las Vegas, NV 89146
Phone 702-251-7873

Reno Vet Center
1155 W. 4th St., Suite 101
Reno, NV 89503
Phone 775-323-1294

New Hampshire

1A Northeast Regional Office
15 Dartmouth Dr., Suite 204
Auburn, NH 03032
Phone 603-623-4204

Berlin Vet Center
515 Main St.
Gorham, NH 03581
Phone 603-752-2571

Manchester Vet Center
103 Liberty St.
Manchester, NH 03104
Phone 603-668-7060

New Jersey

Jersey City Vet Center
110A Meadowlands Parkway, Suite 102
Secaucus, NJ 07094
Phone 201-223-7787

Newark Vet Center
2 Broad St., Suite 703
Bloomfield, NJ 07003
Phone 973-748-0980

Trenton Vet Center
934 Parkway Ave., Suite 201
Ewing, NJ 08618
Phone 609-882-5744

Ventnor Vet Center
Ventnor Building
6601 Ventnor Ave., Suite 105
Ventnor, NJ 08406
Phone 609-487-8387

New Mexico

Albuquerque Vet Center
1600 Mountain Road NW
Albuquerque, NM 87104
Phone 505-346-6562

Farmington Vet Center Satellite
4251 E. Main, Suite B
Farmington, NM 87402
Phone 505-327-9684

Las Cruces Vet Center
230 S. Water St.
Las Cruces, NM 88001
Phone 575-523-9826

Santa Fe Vet Center
2209 Brothers Road, Suite 110
Santa Fe, NM 87505
Phone 505-988-6562

New York

Albany Vet Center
17 Computer Dr. W.
Albany, NY 12205
Phone 518-626-5130

Babylon Vet Center
116 W. Main St.
Babylon, NY 11702
Phone 631-661-3930

Bronx Vet Center
130 W. Kingsbridge Road, Suite 7A-13
Bronx, NY 10468
Phone 718-367-3500

Brooklyn Veterans Resource Center
25 Chapel St., Suite 604
Brooklyn, NY 11201
Phone 718-624-2765

Buffalo Vet Center
564 Franklin St., 2nd Floor
Buffalo, NY 14202
Phone 716-882-0505

Harlem Vet Center
55 W. 125th St., 11th Floor
New York, NY 10027
Phone 212-426-2200

Manhattan Vet Center
32 Broadway, 2nd Floor, Suite 200
New York, NY 10004
Phone 212-742-9591

Middletown Vet Center
726 E. Main St., Suite 203
Middletown, NY 10940
Phone 845-342-9917

Queens Vet Center
75-10B 91 Ave.
Woodhaven, NY 11421
Phone 718-296-2871

Rochester Vet Center
1867 Mount Hope Ave.
Rochester, NY 14620
Phone 585-232-5040

Staten Island Vet Center
150 Richmond Terrace
Staten Island, NY 10301
Phone 718-816-4499

Syracuse Vet Center
716 E. Washington St., Suite 101
Syracuse, NY 13210
Phone 315-478-7127

Watertown Vet Center
210 Court St.
Watertown, NY 13601
Phone 866-610-0358

White Plains Vet Center
300 Hamilton Ave., 1st floor
White Plains, NY 10601
Phone 914-682-6250

North Carolina

Charlotte Vet Center
223 S. Brevard St., Suite 103
Charlotte, NC 28202
Phone 704-333-6107

Fayetteville Vet Center
4140 Ramsey St., Suite 110
Fayetteville, NC 28311
Phone 910-488-6252

Greensboro Vet Center
2009 S. Elm-Eugene St.
Greensboro, NC 27406
Phone 336-333-5366

Raleigh Vet Center
1649 Old Louisburg Road
Raleigh, NC 27604
Phone 919-856-4616

North Dakota

Bismarck Vet Center Outstation
1684 Capital Way
Bismarck, ND 58501
Phone 701-224-9751

Fargo Vet Center
3310 Fiechtner Dr., Suite 100
Fargo, ND 58103-8730
Phone 701-237-0942

Minot Vet Center
1400 20th Ave. SW
Minot, ND 58701
Phone 701-852-0177

Ohio

Cincinnati Vet Center
801B W. 8th St., Suite 126
Cincinnati, OH 45203
Phone 513-763-3500

Cleveland Heights Vet Center
2022 Lee Road
Cleveland, OH 44118
Phone 216-932-8471

Columbus Vet Center
30 Spruce St.
Columbus, OH 43215
Phone 614-257-5550

Dayton Vet Center
6th Floor, East Medical Plaza
627 Edwin C. Moses Blvd.
Dayton, OH 45408
Phone 937-461-9150

McCafferty Vet Center Outstation
4242 Lorain Ave., Suite 201
Cleveland, OH 44113
Phone 216-939-0784

Parma Vet Center
5700 Pearl Road, Suite 102
Parma, OH 44129
Phone 440-845-5023

Oklahoma

Oklahoma City Vet Center
1024 NW 47th St., Suite B
Oklahoma City, OK 73118
Phone 405-270-5184

Tulsa Vet Center
1408 S. Harvard Ave.
Tulsa, OK 74112
Phone 918-748-5105

Oregon

Eugene Vet Center
1255 Pearl St., Suite 200
Eugene, OR 97402
Phone 541-465-6918

Grants Pass Vet Center
211 SE 10th St.
Grants Pass, OR 97526
Phone 541-479-6912

Portland Vet Center
8383 NE Sandy Blvd., Suite 110
Portland, OR 97220
Phone 503-273-5370

Salem Vet Center
617 Chemeketa St. NE, Suite 100
Salem, OR 97301
Phone 503-362-9911

Pennsylvania

DuBois Vet Center
100 Meadow Lane, Suite 8
DuBois, PA 15801
Phone 814-372-2095

Erie Vet Center
Renaissance Centre
1001 State St., Suite 102
Erie, PA 16501
Phone 814-453-7955

Harrisburg Vet Center
1500 N. Second St., Suite 2
Harrisburg, PA 17102
Phone 717-782-3954

McKeesport Veterans Resource Center
2001 Lincoln Way
McKeesport, PA 15131
Phone 412-678-7704

Philadelphia Vet Center
801 Arch St., Suite 102
Philadelphia, PA 19107
Phone 215-627-0238

Pittsburgh Vet Center
2500 Baldwick Road
Pittsburgh, PA 15205
Phone 412-920-1765

Scranton Vet Center
1002 Pittston Ave.
Scranton, PA 18505
Phone 570-344-2676

Williamsport Vet Center
49 E. Fourth St., Suite 104
Williamsport, PA 17701
Phone 570-327-5281

Puerto Rico

Arecibo Vet Center
50 Gonzalo Marin St
Arecibo, PR 612
Phone 787-879-4510

Ponce Vet Center
35 Mayor St., Suite 1
Ponce, PR 730
Phone 787-841-3260

San Juan Vet Center
Cond. Medical Center Plaza,
Suite LC 8, 9, & 11
Urb. La Riviera
Rio Piedras, PR 0921
Phone 787-749-4409

Rhode Island

Providence Vet Center
2038 Warwick Ave.
Warwick, RI 02889
Phone 401-739-0167

South Carolina

Charleston Vet Center
5603-A Rivers Ave.
N. Charleston, SC 29406
Phone 843-747-8387

Columbia Vet Center
1513 Pickens St.
Columbia, SC 29201
Phone 803-765-9944

Greenville, SC Vet Center
14 Lavinia Ave.
Greenville, SC 29601
Phone 864-271-2711

South Dakota

Pine Ridge Vet Center Outstation
105 E. Highway 18
P.O. Box 910
Martin, SD 57747
Phone 605-685-1300

Rapid City Vet Center
621 6th St., Suite 101
Rapid City, SD 57701
Phone 605-348-0077

Sioux Falls Vet Center
601 S. Cliff Ave., Suite C
Sioux Falls, SD 57104
Phone 605-330-4552

Tennessee

Chattanooga Vet Center
951 Eastgate Loop Road,
Bldg. 5700, Suite 300
Chattanooga, TN 37411
Phone 423-855-6570

Johnson City Vet Center
1615A Market St.
Johnson City, TN 37604
Phone 423-928-8387

Knoxville Vet Center
2817 E. Magnolia Ave.
Knoxville, TN 37914
Phone 865-545-4680

Memphis Vet Center
1835 Union Suite 100
Memphis, TN 38104
Phone 901-544-0173

Nashville Vet Center
1420 Donelson Pike, Suite A-5
Nashville, TN 37217
Phone 615-366-1220

Texas

3B South Central Regional Office
4500 S. Lancaster Road,
Building 69
Dallas, TX 75216
Phone 214-857-1254

Amarillo Vet Center
3414 Olsen Blvd., Suite E
Amarillo, TX 79109
Phone 806-354-9779

Austin Vet Center
1110 W. William Cannon Dr., Suite 301
Austin, TX 78745
Phone 512-416-1314

Corpus Christi Vet Center
4646 Corona, Suite 250
Corpus Christi, TX 78411
Phone 361-854-9961

Dallas Vet Center
10501 N. Central, Suite 213
Dallas, TX 75231
Phone 214-361-5896

El Paso Vet Center
1155 Westmoreland, Suite 121
El Paso, TX 79925
Phone 915-772-0013

Fort Worth Vet Center
1305 W. Magnolia St., Suite B
Fort Worth, TX 76104
Phone 817-921-9095

Houston Vet Center
2990 Richmond, Suite 325
Houston, TX 77098
Phone 713-523-0884

Killeen Heights Vet Center
302 Millers Crossing, Suite 4
Harker Heights, TX 76548
Phone 254-953-7100

Laredo Vet Center
6020 McPherson Road, Suite 1A
Laredo, TX 78041
Phone 956-723-4680

Lubbock Vet Center
3208 34th St.
Lubbock, TX 79410
Phone 806-792-9782

McAllen Vet Center
801 Nolana Loop, Suite 140
McAllen, TX 78504
Phone 956-631-2147

Midland Vet Center
3404 W. Illinois, Suite 1
Midland, TX 79703
Phone 432-697-8222

San Antonio Vet Center
231 W. Cypress St., Suite 100
San Antonio, TX 78212
Phone 210-472-4025

Utah

Provo Vet Center
1807 North 1120 West
Provo, UT 84604
Phone 801-377-1117

Salt Lake Vet Center
1354 East 3300 South
Salt Lake City, UT 84106
Phone 801-584-1294

Vermont

South Burlington Vet Center
359 Dorset St.
South Burlington, VT 05403
Phone 802-862-1806

White River Junction Vet Center
Gilman Office, Building #2,
222 Holiday Inn Dr.
White River Junction, VT 05001
Phone 802-295-2908

Virginia

Alexandria Vet Center
6940 S. Kings Highway, #208
Alexandria, VA 22310
Phone 703-360-8633

Norfolk Vet Center
1711 Church St., Suites A&B
Norfolk, VA 23504
Phone 757-623-7584

Richmond Vet Center
4902 Fitzhugh Ave.
Richmond, VA 23230
Phone 804-353-8958

Roanoke Vet Center
350 Albemarle Ave. SW
Roanoke, VA 24016
Phone 540-342-9726

Tacoma Vet Center
4916 Center St., Suite E
Tacoma, WA 98409
Phone 253-565-7038

Yakima Valley Vet Center
1111 N. 1st St., Suite 1
Yakima, WA 98901
Phone 509-457-2736

Virgin Islands

St. Croix Vet Center Satellite
The Village Mall, RR 2 Box 10553
Kingshill
St. Croix, VI 00850
Phone 340-778-5553

St. Thomas Vet Center Satellite
Buccaneer Mall, Suite 8
St. Thomas, VI 00802
Phone 340-774-6674

Washington

Bellingham Vet Center
3800 Byron Ave., Suite 124
Bellingham, WA 98229
Phone 360-733-9226

Everett Vet Center
3311 Wetmore Ave.
Everett, WA 98201
Phone 425-252-9701

Seattle Vet Center
2030 9th Ave., Suite 210
Seattle, WA 98121
Phone 206-553-2706

Spokane Vet Center
100 N. Mullan Road, Suite 102
Spokane, WA 99206
Phone 509-444-8387

West Virginia

Beckley Vet Center
1000 Johnstown Road
Beckley, WV 25801
Phone 304-252-8220

Charleston Vet Center
521 Central Ave.
Charleston, WV 25302
Phone 304-343-3825

Huntington Vet Center
3135 16th St. Road, Suite 11
Huntington, WV 25701
Phone 304-523-8387

Logan, West Virginia
Vet Center Outstation
21 Veterans Ave.
Henlawson, WV 25624
Phone 304-752-4453

Martinsburg Vet Center
900 Winchester Ave.
Martinsburg, WV 25401
Phone 304-263-6776

Morgantown Vet Center
1083 Greenbag Road
Morgantown, WV 26508
Phone 304-291-4303

Parkersburg Vet Center Outstation
2311 Ohio Ave., Suite D
Parkersburg, WV 26101
Phone 304-485-1599

Princeton Vet Center
905 Mercer St.
Princeton, WV 24740
Phone 304-425-5653

Wheeling Vet Center
1206 Chapline St.
Wheeling, WV 26003
Phone 304-232-0587

Wisconsin

Madison Vet Center
706 Williamson St.
Madison, WI 53703
Phone 608-264-5342

Milwaukee Vet Center
5401 N. 76th St.
Milwaukee, WI 53218
Phone 414-536-1301

Wyoming

Casper Vet Center (Satellite)
1030 North Poplar, Suite B
Casper, WY 82601
Phone 307-261-5355

Cheyenne Vet Center
3219 E Pershing Blvd.
Cheyenne, WY 82001
Phone 307-778-7370

Appendix E

National Cemeteries

*T*his appendix contains information about the locations, addresses, and phone numbers of the National Cemeteries throughout the country. More information can be found at the VA Web site at www.va.gov.

Alabama

Alabama National Cemetery
3133 Highway 119
Montevallo, AL 35115
Phone 205-933-8101

Fort Mitchell National Cemetery
553 Highway 165
Seale, AL 36856
Phone 334-855-4731

Mobile National Cemetery
1202 Virginia St.
Mobile, AL 36604
Phone 850-453-4846

Alaska

Fort Richardson National
Cemetery
P.O. Box 5-498, Bldg 58-512, Davis
Highway
Fort Richardson, AK 99505
Phone 907-384-7075

Sitka National Cemetery
803 Sawmill Creek Road
Sitka, AK 99835
Phone 907-384-7075

Arizona

National Memorial
Cemetery of Arizona
23029 N. Cave Creek Road
Phoenix, AZ 85024
Phone 480-513-3600

Prescott National Cemetery
500 Highway 89 N.
Prescott, AZ 86313
Phone 520-776-6028

Arkansas

Fayetteville National Cemetery
700 Government Ave.
Fayetteville, AR 72701
Phone 479-444-5051

Fort Smith National Cemetery
522 Garland Ave. and S. 6th St.
Fort Smith, AR 72901
Phone 479-783-5345

Little Rock National Cemetery
2523 Confederate Blvd.
Little Rock, AR 72206
Phone 501-324-6401

California

Bakersfield VA National Cemetery
30338 E. Bear Mountain Road
Arvin, CA 93203
Phone 661-632-1894

Fort Rosecrans National Cemetery
P.O. Box 6237, Point Loma
San Diego, CA 92166
Phone 619-553-2084

Golden Gate National Cemetery
1300 Sneath Lane
San Bruno, CA 94066
Phone 650-589-7737

Los Angeles National Cemetery
950 S. Sepulveda Blvd.
Los Angeles, CA 90049
Phone 310-268-4675

Riverside National Cemetery
22495 Van Buren Blvd.
Riverside, CA 92518
Phone 951-653-8417

Sacramento Valley VA National
Cemetery
5810 Midway Road
Dixon, CA 95620
Phone 707-693-2460

San Francisco National Cemetery
1 Lincoln Boulevard, Presidio of
San Francisco
San Francisco, CA 94129
Phone 650-761-1646

San Joaquin Valley National
Cemetery
32053 W. McCabe Road
Santa Nella, CA 95332
Phone 209-854-1040

Colorado

Fort Logan National Cemetery
4400 W. Kenyon Ave.
Denver, CO 80236
Phone 303-761-0117

Fort Lyon National Cemetery
15700 County Road HH
Las Animas, CO 81054
Phone 303-761-0117

Florida

Barrancas National Cemetery
80 Hovey Road
Pensacola, FL 32508
Phone 850-453-4108

Bay Pines National Cemetery
10000 Bay Pines Blvd. N.
Bay Pines, FL 33708
Phone 727-398-9426

Florida National Cemetery
6502 S.W. 102nd Ave.
Bushnell, FL 33513
Phone 352-793-7740

Jacksonville VA National Cemetery
4083 Lannie Road
Jacksonville, FL 32218
Phone 904-358-3510

Sarasota VA National Cemetery
9810 State Highway 72
Sarasota, FL 34241
Phone 877-861-9840

South Florida VA National Cemetery
6501 S. State Road 7
Lake Worth, FL 33449
Phone 561-649-6489

St. Augustine National Cemetery
104 Marine St.
St. Augustine, FL 32084
Phone 352-793-7740

Georgia

Georgia National Cemetery
2025 Mount Carmel Church Lane
Canton, GA 30114
Phone 866-236-8159

Marietta National Cemetery
500 Washington Ave.
Marietta, GA 30060
Phone 770-428-3258

Hawaii

National Memorial Cemetery of
the Pacific
2177 Puowaina Dr.
Honolulu, HI 96813
Phone 808-532-3720

Illinois

Abraham Lincoln National
Cemetery
20953 W. Hoff Road
Elwood, IL 60421
Phone 815-423-9958

Alton National Cemetery
600 Pearl St.
Alton, IL 62003
Phone 314-845-8320

Camp Butler National Cemetery
5063 Camp Butler Road
Springfield, IL 62707-9722
Phone 217-492-4070

Danville National Cemetery
1900 E. Main St., VA Medical Center
Danville, IL 61832
Phone 217-554-4550

Mound City National Cemetery
Junction Highways 37 & 51
P.O. Box 128
Mound City, IL 62963
Phone 314-845-8320

Quincy National Cemetery
36th & Maine St.
Quincy, IL 62301
Phone 309-782-2094

Rock Island National Cemetery
Bldg, 118, Rock Island Arsenal
Rock Island, IL 61299
Phone 309-782-2094

Indiana

Crown Hill National Cemetery
700 W. 38th St.
Indianapolis, IN 46208
Phone 317-674-0284

Marion National Cemetery
1700 East 38 St.,
VA Medical Center
Marion, IN 46952
Phone 765-674-0284

New Albany National Cemetery
1943 Ekin Ave.
New Albany, IN 47150
Phone 812-948-5234

Iowa

Keokuk National Cemetery
1701 J St.
Keokuk, IA 52632
Phone 319-524-1304

Kansas

Fort Leavenworth National
Cemetery
Hancock or Biddle St.
Fort Leavenworth, KS 66027
Phone 913-758-4105

Fort Scott National Cemetery
900 E. National Ave.
Fort Scott, KS 66701
Phone 620-223-2840

Leavenworth National Cemetery
4101 S. 4th St. Traffic Way
P.O. Box 1694
Leavenworth, KS 66048
Phone 913-758-4105

Kentucky

Camp Nelson National Cemetery
6980 Danville Road
Nicholasville, KY 40356
Phone 859-885-5727

Cave Hill National Cemetery
701 Baxter Ave.
Louisville, KY 40204
Phone 502-893-3852

Danville National Cemetery
277 N. First St.
Danville, KY 40442
Phone 859-885-5727

Lebanon National Cemetery
20 Highway 208
Lebanon, KY 40033
Phone 270-692-3390

Lexington National Cemetery
833 W. Main St.
Lexington, KY 40508
Phone 859-885-5727

Mill Springs National Cemetery
9044 W. Highway 80
Nancy, KY 42544
Phone 859-885-5727

Zachary Taylor National Cemetery
4701 Brownsboro Road
Louisville, KY 40207
Phone 502-893-3852

Louisiana

Alexandria National Cemetery
209 E. Shamrock Ave.
Pineville, LA 71360
Phone 601-445-4981

Baton Rouge National Cemetery
220 N. 19th St.
Baton Rouge, LA 70806
Phone 225-654-3767

Port Hudson National Cemetery
20978 Port Hickey Road
Zachary, LA 70791
Phone 225-654-3767

Maine

Togus National Cemetery
VA Medical & Regional
Office Center
Togus, ME 04330
Phone 508-563-7113

Maryland

Annapolis National Cemetery
800 West St.
Annapolis, MD 21401
Phone 410-644-9696

Baltimore National Cemetery
5501 Frederick Ave.
Baltimore, MD 21228
Phone 410-644-9696

Loudon Park National Cemetery
3445 Frederick Ave.
Baltimore, MD 21228
Phone 410-644-9696

Corinth National Cemetery
1551 Horton St.
Corinth, MS 38834
Phone 901-386-8311

Natchez National Cemetery
41 Cemetery Road
Natchez, MS 39120
Phone 601-445-4981

Massachusetts

Massachusetts National Cemetery
Connery Ave.
Bourne, MA 02532
Phone 508-563-7113

Michigan

Fort Custer National Cemetery
15501 Dickman Road
Augusta, MI 49012
Phone 269-731-4164

Great Lakes National Cemetery
4200 Belford Road
Holly, MI 48442
Phone 866-348-8603

Minnesota

Fort Snelling National Cemetery
7601 34th Ave. S.
Minneapolis, MN 55450
Phone 612-726-1127

Mississippi

Biloxi National Cemetery
400 Veterans Ave.
Biloxi, MS 39535
Phone 228-388-6668

Missouri

Jefferson Barracks
National Cemetery
2900 Sheridan Road
St. Louis, MO 63125
Phone 314-845-8320

Jefferson City
National Cemetery
1024 E. McCarty St.
Jefferson City, MO 65101
Phone 314-845-8320

Springfield National
Cemetery
1702 E. Seminole St.
Springfield, MO 65804
Phone 417-881-9499

Nebraska

Fort McPherson National
Cemetery
12004 South Spur 56A
Maxwell, NE 69151
Phone 308-582-4433

New Jersey

Beverly National Cemetery
R.D. #1, Bridgeboro Road
Beverly, NJ 08010
Phone 609-880-0827

Finn's Point National Cemetery
R.F.D. No. 3, Box 542,
Fort Mott Road
Salem, NJ 08079
Phone 609-880-0827

New Mexico

Fort Bayard National Cemetery
P.O. Box 189
Fort Bayard, NM 88036
Phone 915-564-0201

Santa Fe National Cemetery
501 N. Guadalupe St.
Santa Fe, NM 87501
Phone 505-988-6400

New York

Bath National Cemetery
VA Medical Center, San Juan Ave.
Bath, NY 14810
Phone 607-664-4853

Calverton National Cemetery
210 Princeton Blvd.
Calverton, NY 11933
Phone 631-727-5410

Cypress Hills National Cemetery
625 Jamaica Ave.
Brooklyn, NY 11208
Phone 631-454-4949

Gerald B. H. Solomon Saratoga
National Cemetery
200 Duell Road
Schuylerville, NY 12871-1721
Phone 518-581-9128

Long Island National Cemetery
2040 Wellwood Ave.
Farmingdale, NY 11735-1211
Phone 631-454-4949

Woodlawn National Cemetery
1825 Davis St.
Elmira, NY 14901
Phone 607-664-4853

North Carolina

New Bern National Cemetery
1711 National Ave.
New Bern, NC 28560
Phone 252-637-2912

Raleigh National Cemetery
501 Rock Quarry Road
Raleigh, NC 27610
Phone 252-637-2912

Salisbury National Cemetery
501 Statesville Blvd.
Salisbury, NC 28144
Phone 704-636-2661

Wilmington National Cemetery
2011 Market St.
Wilmington, NC 28403
Phone 910-815-4877

Ohio

Dayton National Cemetery
VA Medical Center
4100 W. Third St.
Dayton, OH 45428
Phone 937-262-2115

Ohio Western Reserve
National Cemetery
P.O. Box 8
10175 Rawiga Road
Rittman, OH 44270
Phone 330-335-3069

Oklahoma

Fort Gibson National Cemetery
1423 Cemetery Road
Fort Gibson, OK 74434
Phone 918-478-2334

Fort Sill National Cemetery
2648 NE Jake Dunn Road
Elgin, OK 73538
Phone 580-492-3200

Oregon

Eagle Point National Cemetery
2763 Riley Road
Eagle Point, OR 97524
Phone 541-826-2511

Roseburg National Cemetery
1770 Harvard Blvd.
Roseburg, OR 97470
Phone 541-826-2511

Willamette National Cemetery
11800 SE Mt. Scott Blvd.
Portland, OR 97086-6937
Phone 503-273-5250

Pennsylvania

Indiantown Gap National
Cemetery
RR2, Box 484, Indiantown Gap
Road
Annville, PA 17003-9618
Phone 717-865-5254

National Cemetery of the
Alleghenies
1158 Morgan Road
Bridgeville, PA 15017
Phone 724-746-4363

Philadelphia National Cemetery
Haines Street and Limekiln Pike
Philadelphia, PA 19138
Phone 609-877-5460

Puerto Rico

Puerto Rico National Cemetery
Avenue Cementerio Nacional #50
Barrio Hato Tejas
Bayamon, PR 00960
Phone 787-798-8400

South Carolina

Beaufort National Cemetery
1601 Boundary St.
Beaufort, SC 29902-3947
Phone 843-524-3925

Columbia/Ft. Jackson Area National Cemetery
4170 Percival Road
Columbia, SC 29229
Phone 866-577-5248

Florence National Cemetery
803 E. National Cemetery Road
Florence, SC 29501
Phone 843-669-8783

South Dakota

Black Hills National Cemetery
20901 Pleasant Valley Dr.
Sturgis, SD 57785
Phone 605-347-3830

Fort Meade National Cemetery
Old Stone Road
Sturgis, SD 57785
Phone 605-347-3830

Hot Springs National Cemetery
VA Medical Center
Hot Springs, SD 57747
Phone 605-347-3830

Tennessee

Chattanooga National Cemetery
1200 Bailey Ave.
Chattanooga, TN 37404
Phone 423-855-6590

Knoxville National Cemetery
939 Tyson St. NW
Knoxville, TN 37917
Phone 423-855-6590

Memphis National Cemetery
3568 Townes Ave.
Memphis, TN 38122
Phone 901-386-8311

Mountain Home National
Cemetery
VA Medical Center Building 117
P.O. Box 8
Mountain Home, TN 37684
Phone 423-461-7935

Nashville National Cemetery
1420 Gallatin Road S
Madison, TN 37115-4619
Phone 615-860-0086

Texas

Dallas-Fort Worth National
Cemetery
2000 Mountain Creek Parkway
Dallas, TX 75211
Phone 214-467-3374

Fort Bliss National Cemetery
5200 Fred Wilson Road
P.O. Box 6342

El Paso, TX 79906
Phone 915-564-0201

Fort Sam Houston National Cemetery
1520 Harry Wurzbach Road
San Antonio, TX 78209
Phone 210-820-3891

Houston National Cemetery
10410 Veterans Memorial Dr.
Houston, TX 77038
Phone 281-447-8686

Kerrville National Cemetery
VA Medical Center
3600 Memorial Blvd.
Kerrville, TX 78028
Phone 210-820-3891

San Antonio National Cemetery
517 Paso Hondo St.
San Antonio , TX 78202
Phone 210-820-3891

Virginia

Alexandria National Cemetery
1450 Wilkes St.
Alexandria, VA 22314

Ball's Bluff National Cemetery
Route 7
Leesburg, VA 22075
Phone 540-825-0027

City Point National Cemetery
10th Avenue and Davis Street
Hopewell, VA 23860
Phone 804-795-2031

Cold Harbor National Cemetery
6038 Cold Harbor Road
Mechanicsville, VA 23111
Phone 804-795-2031

Culpeper National Cemetery
305 US Ave.
Culpeper, VA 22701
Phone 540-825-0027

Danville National Cemetery
721 Lee St.
Danville, VA 24541
Phone 704-636-2661

Fort Harrison National Cemetery
8620 Varina Road
Richmond, VA 23231
Phone 804-795-2031

Glendale National Cemetery
8301 Willis Church Road
Richmond, VA 23231
Phone 804-795-2031

Hampton National Cemetery
Cemetery Road at Marshall
Avenue
Hampton, VA 23667
Phone 757-723-7104

Quantico National Cemetery
18424 Joplin Road
P.O. Box 10
Triangle, VA 22172
Phone 703-221-2183

Richmond National Cemetery
1701 Williamsburg Road
Richmond, VA 23231
Phone 804-795-2031

Seven Pines National Cemetery
400 E. Williamsburg Road
Sandston, VA 23150
Phone 804-795-2031

Staunton National Cemetery
901 Richmond Ave.
Staunton, VA 24401
Phone 540-825-0027

Winchester National Cemetery
401 National Ave.
Winchester, VA 22601
Phone 540-825-0027

Washington

Tahoma National Cemetery
18600 SE 240th St.
Kent, WA 98042-4868
Phone 425-413-9614

West Virginia

Grafton National Cemetery
431 Walnut St.
Grafton, WV 26354
Phone 304-265-2044

West Virginia National
Cemetery
Route 2, Box 127
Grafton, WV 26354
Phone 304-265-2044

Wisconsin

Wood National Cemetery
5000 W National Ave.,
Building 1301
Milwaukee, WI 53295-4000
Phone 414-382-5300

Index

• N •

• O •

• W •

BUSINESS, CAREERS & PERSONAL FINANCE

Accounting For Dummies, 4th Edition* 978-0-470-24600-9	**E-Mail Marketing For Dummies** 978-0-470-19087-6	**Six Sigma For Dummies** 978-0-7645-6798-8
Bookkeeping Workbook For Dummies† 978-0-470-16983-4	**Job Interviews For Dummies, 3rd Edition*†** 978-0-470-17748-8	**Small Business Kit For Dummies, 2nd Edition*†** 978-0-7645-5984-6
Commodities For Dummies 978-0-470-04928-0	**Personal Finance Workbook For Dummies*†** 978-0-470-09933-9	**Telephone Sales For Dummies** 978-0-470-16836-3
Doing Business in China For Dummies 978-0-470-04929-7	**Real Estate License Exams For Dummies** 978-0-7645-7623-2	

BUSINESS PRODUCTIVITY & MICROSOFT OFFICE

Access 2007 For Dummies 978-0-470-03649-5	**PowerPoint 2007 For Dummies** 978-0-470-04059-1	**Quicken 2008 For Dummies** 978-0-470-17473-9
Excel 2007 For Dummies 978-0-470-03737-9	**Project 2007 For Dummies** 978-0-470-03651-8	**Salesforce.com For Dummies, 2nd Edition** 978-0-470-04893-1
Office 2007 For Dummies 978-0-470-00923-9	**QuickBooks 2008 For Dummies** 978-0-470-18470-7	**Word 2007 For Dummies** 978-0-470-03658-7
Outlook 2007 For Dummies 978-0-470-03830-7		

EDUCATION, HISTORY, REFERENCE & TEST PREPARATION

African American History For Dummies 978-0-7645-5469-8	**ASVAB For Dummies, 2nd Edition** 978-0-470-10671-6	**Geometry Workbook For Dummies** 978-0-471-79940-5
Algebra For Dummies 978-0-7645-5325-7	**British Military History For Dummies** 978-0-470-03213-8	**The SAT I For Dummies, 6th Edition** 978-0-7645-7193-0
Algebra Workbook For Dummies 978-0-7645-8467-1	**Calculus For Dummies** 978-0-7645-2498-1	**Series 7 Exam For Dummies** 978-0-470-09932-2
Art History For Dummies 978-0-470-09910-0	**Canadian History For Dummies, 2nd Edition** 978-0-470-83656-9	**World History For Dummies** 978-0-7645-5242-7

FOOD, GARDEN, HOBBIES & HOME

Bridge For Dummies, 2nd Edition 978-0-471-92426-5	**Drawing For Dummies** 978-0-7645-5476-6	**Knitting Patterns For Dummies** 978-0-470-04556-5
Coin Collecting For Dummies, 2nd Edition 978-0-470-22275-1	**Etiquette For Dummies, 2nd Edition** 978-0-470-10672-3	**Living Gluten-Free For Dummies†** 978-0-471-77383-2
Cooking Basics For Dummies, 3rd Edition 978-0-7645-7206-7	**Gardening Basics For Dummies*†** 978-0-470-03749-2	**Painting Do-It-Yourself For Dummies** 978-0-470-17533-0

HEALTH, SELF HELP, PARENTING & PETS

Anger Management For Dummies 978-0-470-03715-7	**Horseback Riding For Dummies** 978-0-470-09719-9	**Puppies For Dummies, 2nd Edition** 978-0-470-03717-1
Anxiety & Depression Workbook For Dummies 978-0-7645-9793-0	**Infertility For Dummies†** 978-0-470-11518-3	**Thyroid For Dummies, 2nd Edition†** 978-0-471-78755-6
Dieting For Dummies, 2nd Edition 978-0-7645-4149-0	**Meditation For Dummies with CD-ROM, 2nd Edition** 978-0-471-77774-8	**Type 1 Diabetes For Dummies*†** 978-0-470-17811-9
Dog Training For Dummies, 2nd Edition 978-0-7645-8418-3	**Post-Traumatic Stress Disorder For Dummies** 978-0-470-04922-8	

* Separate Canadian edition also available
† Separate U.K. edition also available

Available wherever books are sold. For more information or to order direct: U.S. customers visit www.dummies.com or call 1-877-762-2974.
U.K. customers visit www.wileyeurope.com or call (0)1243 843291. Canadian customers visit www.wiley.ca or call 1-800-567-4797.

INTERNET & DIGITAL MEDIA

AdWords For Dummies
978-0-470-15252-2

Blogging For Dummies, 2nd Edition
978-0-470-23017-6

**Digital Photography All-in-One
Desk Reference For Dummies, 3rd Edition**
978-0-470-03743-0

Digital Photography For Dummies, 5th Edition
978-0-7645-9802-9

**Digital SLR Cameras & Photography
For Dummies, 2nd Edition**
978-0-470-14927-0

**eBay Business All-in-One Desk Reference
For Dummies**
978-0-7645-0430 1

eBay For Dummies, 5th Edition*
978-0-470-04529-9

eBay Listings That Sell For Dummies
978-0-471-78912-3

Facebook For Dummies
978-0-470-26273-3

The Internet For Dummies, 11th Edition
978-0-470-12174-0

Investing Online For Dummies, 5th Edition
978-0-7645-8456-5

iPod & iTunes For Dummies, 5th Edition
978-0-470-17474-6

MySpace For Dummies
978-0 470-09529-4

Podcasting For Dummies
978-0-471-74898-4

**Search Engine Optimization
For Dummies, 2nd Edition**
978-0-471-97998-2

Second Life For Dummies
978-0-470-18025-9

**Starting an eBay Business For Dummies,
3rd Edition†**
978-0-470-14924-9

GRAPHICS, DESIGN & WEB DEVELOPMENT

**Adobe Creative Suite 3 Design Premium
All-in-One Desk Reference For Dummies**
978-0-470-11724-8

**Adobe Web Suite CS3 All-in-One Desk
Reference For Dummies**
978-0-470-12099-6

AutoCAD 2008 For Dummies
978-0-470-11650-0

**Building a Web Site For Dummies,
3rd Edition**
978-0-470-14928-7

**Creating Web Pages All-in-One Desk
Reference For Dummies, 3rd Edition**
978-0-470-09629-1

**Creating Web Pages For Dummies,
8th Edition**
978-0-470-08030-6

Dreamweaver CS3 For Dummies
978-0-470-11490-2

Flash CS3 For Dummies
978-0-470-12100-9

Google SketchUp For Dummies
978-0-470-13744-4

InDesign CS3 For Dummies
978-0-470-11865-8

**Photoshop CS3 All-in-One
Desk Reference For Dummies**
978-0-470-11195-6

Photoshop CS3 For Dummies
978-0-470-11193-2

Photoshop Elements 5 For Dummies
978-0-470-09810-3

SolidWorks For Dummies
978-0-7645-9555-4

Visio 2007 For Dummies
978-0-470-08983-5

Web Design For Dummies, 2nd Edition
978-0-471-78117-2

Web Sites Do-It-Yourself For Dummies
978-0-470-16903-2

Web Stores Do-It-Yourself For Dummies
978-0-470-17443-2

LANGUAGES, RELIGION & SPIRITUALITY

Arabic For Dummies
978-0-471-77270-5

Chinese For Dummies, Audio Set
978-0-470-12766-7

French For Dummies
978-0-7645-5193-2

German For Dummies
978-0-7645-5195-6

Hebrew For Dummies
978-0-7645-5489-6

Ingles Para Dummies
978-0-7645-5427-8

Italian For Dummies, Audio Set
978-0-470-09586-7

Italian Verbs For Dummies
978-0-471-77389-4

Japanese For Dummies
978-0-7645-5429-2

Latin For Dummies
978-0-7645-5431-5

Portuguese For Dummies
978-0-471-78738-9

Russian For Dummies
978-0-471-78001-4

Spanish Phrases For Dummies
978-0-7645-7204-3

Spanish For Dummies
978-0-7645-5194-9

Spanish For Dummies, Audio Set
978-0-470-09585-0

The Bible For Dummies
978-0-7645-5296-0

Catholicism For Dummies
978-0-7645-5391-2

The Historical Jesus For Dummies
978-0-470-16785-4

Islam For Dummies
978-0-7645-5503-9

**Spirituality For Dummies,
2nd Edition**
978-0-470-19142-2

NETWORKING AND PROGRAMMING

ASP.NET 3.5 For Dummies
978-0-470-19592-5

C# 2008 For Dummies
978-0-470-19109-5

Hacking For Dummies, 2nd Edition
978-0-470-05235-8

Home Networking For Dummies, 4th Edition
978-0-470-11806-1

Java For Dummies, 4th Edition
978-0-470-08716-9

**Microsoft® SQL Server™ 2008 All-in-One
Desk Reference For Dummies**
978-0-470-17954-3

**Networking All-in-One Desk Reference
For Dummies, 2nd Edition**
978-0-7645-9939-2

**Networking For Dummies,
8th Edition**
978-0-470-05620-2

SharePoint 2007 For Dummies
978-0-470-09941-4

**Wireless Home Networking
For Dummies, 2nd Edition**
978-0-471-74940-0